a cultural history of

the book of mormon

volume one

setting, a foundation,

of stones to stumble over

daymon m smith

a cultural history of the book of mormon

volume one

setting, a foundation,
of stones to stumble over

daymon mickel smith

# STICK OF JOSEPH,

### TAKEN FROM THE

# HAND OF EPHRAIM.

## A CORRECT COPY

OF THE CHARACTERS TAKEN FROM THE PLATES THE

# BOOK OF MORMON!!

Was translated from—the same that was taken to Professor Anthon of New York, by
Martin Harris, in the year 1827, in fulfilment of Isaiah 29; 11, 12.

"The vision of all is become unto you as the words of a book that is sealed, which men deliver to one that is learned, saying,
Read this, I pray thee: and he saith, I cannot for it is sealed: And the Book is delivered to him that is not learned, saying, Read
this, I pray thee: and he saith, I am not learned."

"Truth shall spring out of the earth."—Psalm 85—11.

"I have written to Ephraim the great things of my law."—Hosea 5—12.

"Thus saith the Lord God, Behold I will take the Stick of Joseph, which is in the hand of Ephraim, and the tribes of
Israel his fellows, and will put them with him, even with the stick of Judah, and make them one stick, and they shall be one
in mine hand.—Ezekiel 37; 19

"Our fathers dwelt here—Sacred Book like the white man have—but it was hid in the ground, once they [were] [a] [...] people
proud against his enemies."—An aged Indian of the Stockbridge tribe.

# Preface

THE MATERIALS FOR THIS VOLUME AND SUBSEQUENT ONES WERE GATHERED for classes attended by friends and passing acquaintances generous with their time, and patient with their instructor's often difficult to discern aims and purposes. Once a week, for nearly a year, I presented some collection of texts—an LDS periodical like *Juvenile Instructor*, or a Deacons manual from 1903, anti-Mormon pamphlets circulating in the early 1830s, or curriculum from Brigham Young University's courses on the Book of Mormon. In preparing these lectures and materials for discussion, I learned more than I can present even in the five volumes of this cultural history of the Book of Mormon. What I think is important for the public to know, I have attempted to present in these volumes, beginning with this introductory one.

A trial run, summarized and presented to a Mormon Stories gathering in Phoenix, Arizona, and later to a similarly convened group in Brazil, further refined the work. I also was introduced to Religious Studies approaches to scripture, by virtue of a kind invitation to participate in a working group at the Institute for Scripturalizing Studies, organized by Vincent Wimbush at Claremont Graduate University. Near what I think of as the Promised Land, east of a city of angels that shelters storytellers to, and of, our entire world, the ISS and its fellows and students are doing work that Mormons should know about and read carefully. Rather than reading "scripture," that term is taken as a starting point for reconsidering how texts circulate in a culture, and create powers, principalities, and dominions, as well as liberated slaves and subversives in general; narratives and hierarchies, tourists and castes. While this volume does not present a "theory of scripture," it does rely on writings about scripture authored by fellows in that working group, and by their mentors like Wilfred Smith, Miriam Levering, Barbara Holdrege, and others prominent in Religious Studies. Being a linguistic anthropologist working on historical documents, the treatment of the Book of

Mormon as something generative of culture, and itself bound into existing traditions, was not a difficult one to take up, and find myself fascinated by. William F. Hanks's brilliant, but perhaps too exhaustive *Converting Words: Maya in the Age of the Cross* (2010) has informed my recent thinking about text-metatext relations, and the fracturing and recirculation that results from grammars, dictionaries and other metatext. Other anthropologists have written on scripture and colonialism, many more on colonialism and the writing of history, or examined the "performative" aspects of texts. Though not directly cited here, more detailed review is given in the next volume. Their work has directly shaped my thinking in this project.

Learning that scholars in other fields have done and are doing similar work—albeit in difficult, often dead or ancient tongues, among texts not yet digitized, and scripturalized for millennia, rather than a mere century—this encouraged me to think like a historian, a critic, a native, and an anthropologist, when writing this first volume. Not every voice is found on every page, and other volumes are obviously more anthropological, critical, or native voiced. These voices were fractured over the last few centuries of scholarship, where once they came from a single person, sure of the workings of the universe. They remain fractured, in a sort of intellectual division of labor, and I have no hope of making them at one in this project. Every effort is made to establish which voice I am taking on, however, for it matters whether one is a historian or a native speaking from a position of belief; of belief in something other than the methods of a historian, that is.

As custom demands, the errors in this text are mine to claim, and the conclusions and their effects, I suppose, should be also traced to me. But this work was very much collaborative, the result of many happy meetings with friends and passing acquaintances, and they should know the parts they like, and agree with, are theirs as well as mine to keep. Being merely the mouth, eyes, hands, and mind that channeled a thousand texts, and some of their ideas and doubts and insights, I must put my name on the cover. And be cited by those few who do such things, if only as a courtesy to this author. The fact is, while you read this book, it is also as much yours as it is mine: your interpretations are your own, good or bad. I have given the words, you must supply their meaning. This text is not to be thought of as the same as metatext it generates, and that includes your own notions, summaries, board games, tours and interpretive dances that it may inspire.

*For RP, the first of many*

'I'll tell you what you show me.  You remember
You said you knew the place where once, on Kinsman,
The early Mormons made a settlement
And built a stone baptismal font outdoors—
But Smith, or someone, called them off the mountain
To go West to a worse fight with the desert.
You said you'd seen the stone baptismal font.
Well, take me there.'

                    'Some day I will.'

                              'Today.'

'Huh, that old bathtub, what is that to see?
Let's talk about it.'

                    'Let's go see the place.'

'To shut you up I'll tell you what I'll do:
I'll find that fountain if it takes all summer,
And both of our united strengths, to do it.'

'You've lost it, then?'

'Not so but I can find it.
No doubt it's grown up some to woods around it.
The mountain may have shifted since I saw it
In eighty-five.'

'As long ago as that?'

'If I remember rightly, it had sprung
A leak and emptied then.  And forty years
Can do a good deal to bad masonry.
You won't see any Mormon swimming in it.
But you have said it, and we're off to find it.
Old as I am, I'm going to let myself
Be dragged by you all over everywhere—'

'I thought you were a guide.'

'I am a guide,
And that's why I can't decently refuse you.'

*--Robert Frost*

"A Fountain, A Bottle, A Donkey's Ears and Some Books"

# A Cultural History of the Book of Mormon

## Volume One
## Setting, a Foundation, of Stones to Stumble Over

# Introduction to a Cultural History
## of the Book of Mormon

W HAT SORT OF BOOK IS THIS? IT IS NOT A HISTORY OF THE CHARACTERS, settings, scenes, doctrines, and so forth as presented in the Book of Mormon. It is a history of how the Book of Mormon has been used, interpreted, read, misread, misinterpreted, and misused, starting in 1829 and continuing onward to today. The volume before you comprehends the years before the publication of the book, and focuses its attention most closely on the years 1830 and 1831. Within a year of its publication, the book was regarded by Restorationists in Ohio as corroborative of their reading of the New Testament, it being also a sign of the dispensation of miracles in our day. By "dispensation" they generally meant, "something dispensed," rather than an "age" or "epoch" as the term now is meant to say by Mormons.

This history begins with the Gold Bible, a sort of imagined text that circulated in public as a title only, standing for a book. That title carried and organized various guesses about the book it stood for: its history, authorship, and purposes. The Gold Bible organizes what I call "metatext," like commentaries, gossip, histories, and so on, about the Book of Mormon, their target text. Metatext carry traditions, circulate histories, and explain doctrines and so forth, said to be found inside the text itself. The history before you begins with metatext, and only at important points brings in the text itself; for example, in chapter two, where theories of restoration are reviewed, including what the Book of Mormon claims about its own project of restoration. Most of what is given here concerns metatext, for it is metatext that develop traditions for reading, here social structures emerge, and churches form with institutional roles and mythologies. Metatext obscures text, standing for it.

SACRED LANDSCAPES MAPPED, COMMODITIES,
Linguistic Material of Social Universe: Phonemes, Graphem
DISCUSSIONS APOLOGETICS EXPLANATION OF "TRU
FAN-FICTION, PSEUDEPIGRAPHA, M
INTERTEXTUAL USAGE IN DEFINED S
Sermons, Rituals, Guidance, Apothe
Allegory, Advertisements, Book
COMMENTARIES, TRANSLAT
SUMMARIES SIMPLIFIEDS
Curriculum
AUDIENCE VERSIONS
Children, Teens, Scholar
EDITIONS
Minor Text
Divergences
COPIES

World
Referred to
Fragments

Style Circulates
Into Other Genres

Fracture
Into Genres

Text Fracturing

INDEXES
DICTIONARIES
TOPICAL GUIDES

Versifying, Chapter Breaks
Footnotes, Printing

METATEXT
SCRIPTURE
folds into
TEXT

Any tangible, cohering
arrangement of linguistic signs
projected from "Scripture" imaginary
CRITICAL TEXT
"UR" TEXT
MEANING
REALITY

ME
BECOMES

SCRIPTURALIZING
PROCESS

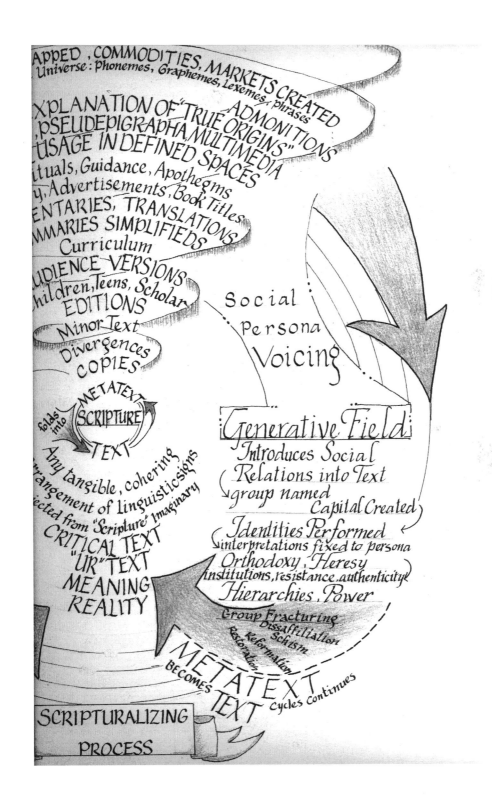

APPED, COMMODITIES, MARKETS CREATED
Universe: Phonemes, Graphemes, Lexemes, Phrases
XPLANATION OF "TRUE ORIGINS"
PSEUDEPIGRAPHA, MULTIMEDIA
ADMONITIONS
USAGE IN DEFINED SPACES
ituals, Guidance, Apothegms
y, Advertisements, Book Titles
ENTARIES, TRANSLATIONS
MMARIES SIMPLIFIEDS
Curriculum
UDIENCE VERSIONS
Children, Teens, Scholar
EDITIONS
Minor Text
Divergences
COPIES

METATEXT
folds into
SCRIPTURE
TEXT

Any tangible, cohering
arrangement of linguistic signs
ected from "Scripture" Imaginary
CRITICAL TEXT
"UR" TEXT
MEANING
REALITY

Social
Persona
Voicing

Generative Field
Introduces Social
Relations into Text
group named
Capital Created
Identities Performed
interpretations fixed to persona
Orthodoxy, Heresy
institutions, resistance, authenticity
Hierarchies, Power
Group Fracturing
Dissaffiliation
Schism
Reformation
Restoration
Cycles Continues

METATEXT
BECOMES
TEXT

SCRIPTURALIZING
PROCESS

As we divide metatext from text, we find that the Book of Mormon becomes unchained from so many traditions, it becomes nearly unintelligible; unreadable as anything other than history and prophecy, a sort of eternal present with memory of the past, and anticipations of the future.

The title "Book of Mormon" names a modern scripture: a relationship between text and metatext. This distinction between text and metatext—the sides of the coin of scripture—is a critical one for readers to grasp. To assist in that effort, I have provided an illustration of the Scripturalizing Process. The illustration can be used as a reference guide for the history before you; a detailed essay in Appendix A also explains the Scripturalizing Process in general.

This is the first in a five volume series. The second and third volumes take up the history of the Book of Mormon as the text was carried about, cut up, interpreted, and otherwise used by Latter Day Saints to make their Mormonism. The second takes the history from the mid-1830s to 1880s, when the book was implicated in a transition from an aspiring state-espousing Mormonism to a church within a state. Three begins in the 1880s amid that transition from state to church, and takes its tale to our present decade, where we find Mormonism as a religion transformed by corporate-oriented practices: market-making, demographic tracking, kitsch creating, fan fictioning, psychologized, mass media culture.

The fourth volume is a history, survey, and rethinking of "the imagination," specifically as it shapes and is shaped by language. Given the prominence of "the tongue of angels," the unconfounded Jaredite speech, translation and its impact on society, and other linguistic matters prominent in the Book of Mormon, this volume's relevance should be obvious. Its place in this series is further clarified by the last volume. Volume Five is a compilation of essays on various subjects—Atonement; the Book of the Lamb and the "Sealed Portion"; the five cycles of Nephi's Vision; Moses and Abraham in the Promised Land; the Remnant; Pleistocene Jaredites; Geography. The subjects are treated imaginatively; that is, they are speculative essays, not conclusive arguments. They take up my own challenge to imagine the Book of Mormon outside the traditions and cultures generated by the Holy Bible.

PART ONE


THE DISCURSIVE LOGIC OF RESTORATION

# ONE  GOLD BIBLE AS METATEXT

FEW BOOKS ENJOY THE SORT OF PRE-RELEASE COVERAGE WE SEE CROWDING around the Book of Mormon in 1829. Little more than a title easily forgotten, a copyright and title page; and a rumor of Indians, pirate ghosts, peepstones, buried treasure, hieroglyphs, some rube farmer gulled by a boy gingerbread seller on the make: "the Book of Mormon," as a phrase, meant any number of things guessed at, puffed up, and floated for brief amusement. Only a small circle convened around Joseph Smith had read or heard from the text itself, and only in doses enough to suggest something more than lazy fakery. There was a void, socially speaking, referred to by "the Book of Mormon." What was Mormon, anyway? Indeed, hardly anyone used its title, insisting instead upon "Gold Bible." That was a title with teeth, gravity, and a figure with familiar history. This chapter traces out the effects of that title: how it created a social map filled with rubes, scoffers, skeptics, religionists and proselytes. These social roles were independent of that text, but also from 1829 onward, added so much embroidery upon it. The map and its roles—more detailed nearer the text's origins, namely, Palmyra, New York, and less so as one moved beyond the publication spheres of local papers—marked out channels to "believers" later run by the actual Book of Mormon.

The map is initially sketched by that false title. It did a lot of work in society, inventing some imaginary—not yet published—book mounting a challenge to all of Christendom and scripture (as a "Bible"), while conveying barely cloaked suspicions of cupidity. Calling it "Gold," moreover, obliged one to explain how such a book was reportedly discovered, of what it was made, and so on. Histories thus travelled alongside these mentions of some supposed new scripture. The de facto title—of a book not yet existing—said a great deal more than the title of the actual book: about one's beliefs regarding some possible Book of Mormon, for example; aligning doubters against the scarce potential reader of the actual text. Radiating outward from Smith's mouth, a new social space organized by that title, and later by the book itself, moved person by person, newspaper to newspaper: threatening, saving and tempting souls along the way. Joseph's uncle Jesse Smith responded to Hyrum's letter in a manner that exemplifies the role alignment accomplished by telling stories about the book. Uncle Jesse replied to Hyrum's description of its discovery and translation by calling him a "Blasphemous wretch," telling tales to "cover your nefarious designs & impose on the credulity of your Grandfather." The uncle quoted the Gospel of Matthew (7:23 and 25:41), warning his nephews that "these are the angels that tell where to find gold books."[1] But there was no book, not yet; not found in public anyway. Public metatext—including one's understanding of the Bible,[2] or of folktales, or the Smith family's neighborliness—these hounded the Book of Mormon even before its publication, and no less doggedly for nearly two centuries, for believers as much as for those set in opposition.

The influence of metatext is easier to discern when a people have not yet encountered the actual anchor text, and so this chapter begins where our history begins: with metatext. You'll find that the first "reports" of the Gold Bible are genre-based satires employing what was in that day a most common style, aping the English of the King James Bible. In July of 1829 "Chronicler" claimed to extract "From the Golden Bible," but merely employed its presumed style to cloak criticisms of ambitious neighbors apparently implicated in long-forgotten drama:

> And it came to pass, in these days the people became sore against Horace, the publican, forasmuch as he had offended them by taking into favor Israel, the darkey paramour, and whom the people had cast off on account of his wickedness. Now this Israel, who is a man of considerable cunning and deceit,

---

[1] Jesse Smith to Hyrum Smith, 17 June 1829. In Dan Vogel, *Early Mormon Documents*, Vol.1 (SLC: Signature Books, 1996), 551. The letter was apparently copied in Joseph Smith Letterbooks (1837-43) in 1839; 2:59-61; original in Joseph Smith Papers, LDS Church Archives, SLC, Utah.

[2] I capitalize *Bible* rather than follow the various prescriptions for capitalizing the first letter when, say, referring to specific editions like "the adultery Bible" or the King James Bible, mainly because I believe that there is no bible that is not also metatext Bible.

had lost the favor of the people, by his abomination; yet nevertheless, he aspired to be one of the counselors and lawgivers of the land.[1]

The style's features are easily described, as found in this writing and other examples. They are also easily reproduced: first names plus occupation (Horace the publican; Chad the money-lender); "internal" monologue phrased as speaking "with himself," rather than described with verbs of thinking; pseudo-archaic vocabulary, like *abomination, beseech, howbeit*; sentence initial *And*, preserving by this form the difficulties of translating from Hebrew, where subordinate clauses are relatively rare; exhortative *O*; apparently difficult to translate passages perhaps being taken from a foreign text, as in, "And Chad extended his jaws, and behold there came forth a noise as the braying of an ass; and he said, Arise, Israel, and relate to me the cause of thy troubles"; obsolete pronouns like *thy* and *thee*. The style juxtaposes an air of ridiculous, pompous hayseedery, wherein high-faluting language is overfilling some tiny rusted tub, as it were, carrying like a raft a gaggle of mud covered jimmy crack corns, all a howdy hee-haw and brim full o' monkey-shine. The style saw renewed vigor after the first pages of the Book of Mormon were published, without the author's consent, by the Palmyra Reflector. Actual names from the text could be tossed out by its editor, Abner Cole (writing under the name "Obadiah Dogberry"), adding color to their putting on of ridiculous airs. The Reflector published a "Chapter of Ontario Chronicles," another Biblese lampoon of hucksters beginning, "It came to pass in the days of J****h the Prophet," there lived a "certain Israelite who dwelt near the temple of Nephi."[2] The prophet, and Nephi's temple were mere appendages, yokel color, as it were, and needed little commentary or overt derision. The style was commentary enough. Indeed, the Reflector reported the most mundane things in Biblese, as though speaking this way immediately cued readers to something laughable. Dogberry printed at least two chapters from its satirical Book of Daniel,[3] followed soon after by the report of "a man whose sir name was John, a descendant of the martyrs, established himself near unto a place called veracity corner," taken from "The First Book of John."[4] Although published bearing these stylistic features—not as satire, of course—the Book of Mormon in 1829 remained little more than

---

[1] Paul Pry's Weekly Bulletin (Rochester, NY) 25 July 1829, 1:12
[2] Palmyra Reflector, 2 Jan 1830, "The Biter bit" no.2:13
[3] Palmyra Reflector, 27 June 1830, 3d series no.10:79; and 4 Aug 1839, 3d series no.11:82
[4] Palmyra Reflector, 14 Aug 1830, 3d series no.12:94

a joke guessed at, encountered mostly in mention. Metatext like these circulated far and wide.

It is never entirely clear what exactly is being poked at, though, in the earliest mentions of the book and its translator: mention is sufficient to position reader and editor, tying markers of genre to social roles ("participant frameworks" is the technical phrase). Rubes and charlatans acted in that world narrated by Biblese, absurd religionists whose phony diction, like their beliefs, deserved exposure on the pages of newspapers. Chronicler continued his social commentary into Chapter III, delivered in August 1829. Only in the concluding sentence do we learn that his tale has Joseph Smith's book as one of its targets: "all these things, yea many more, are graven on the massy leaves of the Golden Book, and are now in the custody of Joseph the prophet."[1] The book itself did not yet exist in printed words, and so as an imagined thing it offered a blank slate for one to write every fancy. The familiar shtick of Bible-satire was thrown at it, often half-heartedly, as an afterthought.

Chronicler inspired writing titled "Chronicles: Chap. I."[2] This little thing says nothing of a Golden Bible, nor Joseph the prophet. Indeed, although it is included in BYU's digital catalogue of early publications on the Book of Mormon, there is nothing that suggests "Chronicles" is doing anything other than lampooning over-sexed religious zealots, the "Westleyets that sojourn in the land of Parma," and their leader, "Roswel":

> Then Roswel the mighty gave judgement against the people, for Roswel was a hardy tool, wherewith the priests might work their will, as his heart was hard and his mind was given unto sin continually. And it came to pass that many of the sisters waxed hot and certain of the brethren went with them, and did shame in the sight of the congregation. But the Westleyets shouted aloud, saying this is the work of the Lord! And all the sisters said amen.

Again, only in the concluding sentence can we even guess Joseph Smith is possibly aimed at by this Rochester writer, who warns that if this people "turn not from the evil of your ways, and do that which is right, ye shall be delivered over to the folly of Smith, and with his exhortations be tormented day and night." Whatever Smith he meant, the author takes no shots at the Book of Mormon. And yet, inclusion of this article in BYU's database reveals something more than

---

[1] Paul Pry's Weekly Bulletin 8 Aug 1829, 1:14
[2] Paul Pry's Weekly Bulletin 29 Aug 1829

oversensitivity by archivists to anti-Mormon sentiment. It shows that the Book of Mormon was not yet a solid thing, but instead could be inferred, perhaps "correctly" or "incorrectly," from any story of a man and a devil's bargain, or a foolish farmer trading his cow for magic beans, or the most mundane gossip cast in Biblese. Indeed, in one Reflector notice, a summary of an otherwise well-known tale is said to be taken as a jab at the Book of Mormon:

> In popping into a corner some few days since, I discovered some four or five respectable (looking) men discussing "the Reflector," when by chance they blundered upon the article headed "John Faust," as copied from the Lutheran Magazine. After pouring over the subject for some time, quite in doubt as to its true import or meaning, never having (before) heard the story of "the Devil and Doctor Faustus," at last came to the sage conclusion that "it must be hit at Jo Smith's gold Bible."[1]

The astonished eavesdropper expresses shock that such men "could not discern a shade of difference between a scrap of grave history, and a burlesque upon one of the most ridiculous attempts at imposture ever witnessed since the days of Sabatai Sevi." Although few had read even a page of it, the Gold Bible was sufficiently named in mockery for any soul with good sense to laugh at its possibility. It was a book finding set for it by newspapermen and the learned rather exceedingly low expectations. The book was a social thing first, then; at least its title was: allowing for folks to position themselves against it, to hoot at its tale, to shoot out their lips at it, and shake their heads; and to spread far and wide the awareness of it, of the spectacle of so benighted a thing coming forth in these enlightened days.

From before its beginning, the Book of Mormon under the guise of Gold Bible made its way in title as one mocked, suffering scorn and derision, judgment even before having its mouth opened by the printing press. The book was encountered first in mention, or satire, representations of it. The Book of Mormon was only by the daring or the gullible truly named, being a byword for imposture, the ridiculous, shameful blasphemy, clownish swindlers and laughable rural scheming. As learned writers often pointed out, only the gullible, the rubes, peepers, religious reformers, vexed of mind, the rural folk and believers in the fantastical could swallow such cure-alls and feel better as well: so let them. Their antics always generated good copy. Wherever one heard of shams, and the diabolical, readers in

---

[1] Palmyra Reflector 1 May 1830, 3d series, no.1:6

the printer's market around Palmyra might guess that the old Gold Bible was hinted at. Not the actual Book of Mormon, but metatext made to stand in for that book. Metatext was bound to the name *Gold Bible*. Its origins were reported under that title, and laughed at, far and wide, as newspapers did the first proselytizing—admittedly by smirking in the background, at the spectacle of such a tale—for Jo Smith's gilded book. There was confusion, however. Just as one might not see that a Bible-based satire poked fun at oneself, or the antics of your neighbors; or even know who this Joseph the prophet, or Smith the exhorter was; readers could easily misconstrue what among the wise needed no saying—being a byword means just this—confusing silence for an editor's cautioned report of something, maybe, possibly even miraculous, already underway. Gold Bible organized all this and tacked it onto the eventual book.

The Book of Mormon was in the beginning merely a title page, a name; a way to position oneself and others vis-à-vis presumed norms of wisdom and prudence, certainties about how the world really worked, and the universe itself was run. Angels? Miracles? Gifts? Bah! The Book of Mormon surely was a vulgar patch of superstition, and would blow away like the color of autumn. As relayed over the last months of 1829, it was a thing begotten by schemes long considered beyond consideration, as its origin story took on canonical print form. Here we move from title to biography as metatext. "The greatest piece of superstition that has ever come within our knowledge, now occupies the attention of a few individuals of this quarter. It is generally known and spoken of as the 'Golden Bible,'" crowed Thurlow Weed's Rochester Advertiser and Daily Telegraph, reprinting a story from the Smith family's local paper, the Palmyra Freeman.[1] The reprint circulated what would become the oft recited, though to most editors ridiculous, origin story of that superstition:

> Its proselytes give the following account of it: In the fall of 1827, a person by the name of Joseph Smith, of Manchester, Ontario county, reported that he had been visited in dream by the spirit of the Almighty and informed that in a certain hill in that town, was deposited this Golden Bible, containing an ancient record of divine nature and origin. After having been thrice thus visited, as he states, he proceeded to the spot, and after penetrating "mother earth" a short distance, the Bible was found, together with a huge pair of spectacles!

---

[1] Rochester Advertiser and Daily Telegraph 31 Aug 1829 "Golden Bible"; reprinting from Palmyra Freeman 11 Aug 1829.

As yet unnamed, not part of any movement nor church, believers in the tale are called by the paper simply "its proselytes." Their voices and minds were metatext that first rendered the Book of Mormon as scripture, rather than satire. Their belief in such a fable was news enough to warrant not only publication, but reprinting by city presses. The above article relates how Smith was, perhaps too conveniently, directed "not to let any mortal being examine them, 'under no less penalty' than instant death! They were therefore nicely wrapped up and excluded from the 'vulgar gaze of poor wicked mortals!'" The quotes seem to embed actual phrases, or reported speech, given by "its proselytes." Preserved by the Freeman and then in the Advertiser—perhaps to provide readers a sense of how dreadfully serious its believers are—their warnings, like speaking of vulgar things in the King's English, further ramped up the hootability of the tale, bouncing it along from town to town. The Advertiser gives its verdict by continuing to reprint the Freeman's commentary upon the tale, clarifying that it does not print contemptible reports because the editors are counted among its proselytes. "An account of this discovery," it claims, "was soon circulated. The subject was almost invariably treated as it should have been—with contempt." Thus readers learned how to position themselves appropriately, should they encounter the tale, enjoying for support the backing of print culture and its imagined masses. Believers were "farmers" and of similar ilk, as the Advertiser related, "A few, however, believed the 'golden' story, among whom was Martin Harris, an honest and industrious farmer of this town (Palmyra)." The book itself is mentioned as an afterthought, and measured by its purported ambition to compare with the Bible: "Its language and doctrine are said to be far superior to those of the book of life!!!" Here we see the Gold Bible generating social roles—farmers, proselytes, and those rightly treating the whole thing with contempt—bearing the "'golden' story," and others comparing the production to "the book of life." Metatext were lining up roles in preparation for the actual book's publication.

Another long-forgotten, pleasant little Rochester rag, claiming to be a "Literary and Miscellaneous Journal," printed an extract from the Advertiser, without acknowledgement. The Gem framed its version this way, having confused the popularly bestowed title with the book's legal name:

> A man by the name of Martin Harris was in this village a few days since endeavoring to make a contract for printing a large quantity of a work called the Golden Bible. He gave something like the following account of it.[1]

---

[1] Rochester Gem, n.d.

The article moves to the familiar, "In autumn of 1827 a man named Joseph Smith…" and slightly rephrases the story given in the Advertiser. The Gem adds its own "literary" comment upon the tale, noting, "The subject attracts a good deal of notice among a certain class." (If you have to ask which class, wink wink, consider yourself in it.) "We shall endeavor to meet it with the comment it may deserve," the editor concludes, as if anything more needed saying. Thus dismissed, the book and its social positioning—class by class, town and gown, literate and ignorant—was conveniently summarized in this article. As with the origin story, so with the de facto title: both make absolutely clear how certain social roles should respond—in fact, are performed in the act of reception, naming and response—when encountering the anchor text. Indeed, Gold Bible was so often taken for the actual title of Harris's printing project, even Joseph Smith seemed somewhat annoyed by all the smirking. In an early letter to scribe Oliver Cowdery, Smith mentions "formadable persacutors" whose intrusions, apparently, were "worse than all the Gold Book business."[1] Here Smith makes clear who uses that title, and who does not, as he voices a persecutor's phrasing.

The Reflector continued to update readers on the Book of Mormon, announcing that when printed, "Great and marvellous things will 'come to pass' about those days," alluding to a phrase that doubly mocked the book: its style, and its impotency.[2] The Reflector's editors shared Grandin's press with that book, yet their declarations show how little they understood its pragmatic potency. Social relations are what they point to: They "understand that the Anti-Masons have declared war against the Gold Bible,"[3] compare "the pretensions of Jo Smith Jr. and his followers" to a "denomination which appeared in Flanders and Brussels, in the year 1511," and regard it smirkingly as akin to "the rapid spread of Islamism."[4] What was this text, and what are we to make of its, um, proselytes-followers? The metatext was silly enough, but now copies of manuscript pages privately circulated were gathering believers?

Near Smith's farm the entire tale was familiar enough that parts of it could be stripped out and introduced in other ridiculous stories. "Jo Smith's magic spectacles" were merely mentioned in articles, sometimes editors wished for their

---

[1] Joseph Smith to Oliver Cowdery, 22 Oct 1829; copied late 1832 into letterbook. In Dan Vogel, *Early Mormon Documents*, Vol.1:7
[2] Palmyra Reflector, 16 Sept 1829, series 1 no.3:10
[3] Palmyra Reflector, 23 Sept 1829, series 1 no.4:14
[4] Palmyra Reflector, 30 Sept 1829, series 1 no.5:18

own "editorial spectacles," presupposing not only reader's familiarity with the phrase, but also their skepticism regarding its referent. Palmyra newspapers added these phrases to otherwise-concerned gossip, merely peppering news with laughable figures: a sort of piling into a "wheel-barrow" all the jugglers, peepers, schemers and rubes in the neighborhood. The Reflector reported that "the building of the TEMPLE OF NEPHI is to be commenced about the beginning of the first year of the Millennium," estimating with a grin that "thousands are already flocking to the standard of Joseph the Prophet."[1] There was no simple descriptor for those folks, even if mostly imaginary flockers: were they believers in the book, or followers of a man? What book, exactly, the Gold Bible or the Book of Mormon? "Gold Bible Apostles" was used by the Reflector, mocking them with an exalted title, but one also belying the uncertainty of the editors with respect to the movement, church, readership thing. Where they deluded? Fools? Blasphemers? Greedy? Pranksters? Apostles? Did the book have doctrines enough even to follow? Was there an actual Book of Mormon, or only the Gold Bible? So long as it remained the Gold Bible—a socially plastic metatext—the book was easily dismissed, its proselytes gulled from a "certain class." And by virtue of that title, whatever text would come forth could be readily assessed and valued, having attempted to join what was, for Christians, a genre with but one volume: The Bible, the Holy Book of Life. Anything similar must be satire, or clumsy blasphemy; its followers, dupes or dupers worthy of the sarcastic honor "apostles." Here religious social roles were generated by the anchor text following on the heels of the Gold Bible's work; honorifics bestowed in mockery, admittedly.

Unsure of what it was, and whether manuscript pages had moved their own readers into proselytes, editors of papers near Palmyra sometimes spoke in terms that veiled their own uncertainty, saying "prophet" when they meant "deceiver," "apostle" for "deluded" and even claiming that "A work bearing this cognomen [Gold Bible, as given in the article's title] is now in the Press," when they knew its legal title.[2] Their situation was precarious, because maybe some readers *did believe*, and they risked losing subscribers. By late 1829, then, there is a notable reluctance to take on Joseph Smith and friends, directly; scorn by association, in excessive deference feigned, satires, or just indifference in mention was sufficient: at least so long as the paper remained locally circulating. Yet, the editors' reliance on readers' ability to see between the lines left them open to the

---

[1] Palmyra Reflector, 7 Oct 1829, series 1 no.6:22
[2] Palmyra Reflector, 9 Dec 1829, series 1, no.15:57

charge of affiliating with the very crowd they thought so contemptible. Even papers positioned one another vis-à-vis the book. The Lyons, New York weekly *Countryman* called the *Reflector* "a sarcastical, obscene little paper," sharing its press with "the infamous, catch-penny work, entitled the 'Book of Mormon,' or as it is generally called, the 'Golden Bible.'" One could not write between the lines, using terms of honor in derision, and also expect non-locals to recover apparently too subtle a mockery. Even the printer, and every other paper he printed, "should be branded with infamy and disgrace . . . . He should be pointed out to the world as an object of scorn and contempt."[1]

When finally published, the Book of Mormon only escaped the notoriety of the Gold Bible where it also passed beyond the networks of Palmyra and Rochester weeklies. As reports move outward from Palmyra, local knowledge presupposed by editors like Obadiah Dogberry—such as required to make sense of and holler about the building of the "TEMPLE OF NEPHI" or "Harris' New Jerusalem"—understanding which Harris (his first name is not given), what "Nephi" means, or which doctrines from "the Gold Bible," exactly, "a man in the town of Mendon had a loud call to go and preach"—such background knowledge remained neighborhood grounded, even as summaries and vague rumor circulated further from Palmyra. Editors more distant filled in by guesswork what all the gossip was about. The Cincinnati Advertiser and Ohio Phoenix, for example, summarized the Wayne County Inquirer's convoluted account of the book's origins in this way, prefacing through the lens of the Bible their reprint of an extract from the Rochester Republican:

> A fellow by the name of Joseph Smith…has been, for the last two years we are told, employed in dictating as he says, by inspiration, a new Bible. He pretended to be entrusted by God with a golden Bible which had been always hidden from the world. Smith would put his face into a hat in which he had a white stone, and pretended to read from it, while his coadjutors transcribed. The book purports to give an account of the "Ten Tribes," and strange as it may seem, there are some who have full faith in his divine commission.[2]

No longer leaving their position implicit, papers further afield than Palmyra stated plainly that Smith pretended by inspiration to dictate "a new Bible," using a "white stone" like that found in the Bible's Revelation, revealing the doings of its

---

[1] The (Lyons, NY) Countryman, 7 Sept 1830
[2] Cincinnati Advertiser and Ohio Phoenix, 2 June 1830

"Ten Tribes." Here the Gold Bible is pushed into the domain of the Bible—its instrumentation and characters—and chided for so blatantly taking from it. Its purported similarity was initially a cause for shock, and the pious taking offense. It also pointed the actual book toward believers in the Bible, but not of any old Bible: of a particular metatext. Which metatext? To readers seeking to live an imagined world it seemingly described, where maybe white stones and the Ten Tribes could be reclaimed.

The book itself, Abner Cole discovered, was far less scandalous than its metatext. As announced the previous week, Dogberry's Reflector pirated and published the first pages of the Book of Mormon on the second day of 1830. Use of pre-release "leaks"—metatext actually derived from anchor text—for building anticipation prior to publication is a practice regularly used by publishers. However, only relations and friends of Joseph Smith, and the straying, curious soul lingering at Grandin had heretofore read passages from the book so easily dismissed with a false title. It is pleasing, I suppose, that a man who sought by ridicule, theft, boycott, satire and intimidation to prevent publication of Jo Smith's imposition was the very first to give it public airing. The desire for readership, perhaps, and increased revenue from advertising and rising subscriptions apparently triumphed over his antagonism toward the book. In the bootlegged first chapter of the First Book of Nephi, unfortunately for readers expecting a good laugh at the Gold Bible, one strains to find anything blasphemous, or patently ridiculous. Content-wise, that is. The suggestion that Jo Smith actually translated gold plates engraved with hieroglyphs was proof enough that it was a fraud, although even Dogberry was forced into a posture not entirely opposed to the book itself, explaining:

> We do not intend at this time, to discuss the merits or demerits of this work, and feel astonished that some of our neighbors, who profess liberal principles, and are probably quite as ignorant on the subject as we are, should give themselves quite so much uneasiness about matters that so little concern them. The Book, when it shall come before the public, must stand or fall according to the whims and fancies of its readers.[1]

The editor admitted he "cannot discover any thing treasonable, or which will have the tendency to subvert our liberties," as though his watchtower was built only to prevent the loss of liberty by so clumsy a thief. Readers not aware that they should

---

[1] Palmyra Reflector, 2 Jan 1830, no.2:1

regard the Book of Nephi as a dirty thing—that is, those few ignorant of the book's reported origins—could be excused from being confused by Dogberry's textual two-step, where he at last makes explicit the function of the "cant cognomen," as if distancing himself from its usage:

> We inadvertently neglected in our remarks last week, respecting this wonderful work, to accompany them with the explanations requisite to, correct understanding of it. The appellation of 'Gold Bible,' is only a cant cognomen that has been given it by the unbelievers—for be it known that this Book, as well as the sacred volume which is held so valuable by all good christians, is not without its revilers and unbelievers—by way of derision.

The Reflector followed this excerpt with more material taken from the First Book of Nephi and the Book of Alma, hardly texts to arouse one's suspicions or irreverent humors. Indeed, those urging "CAUTION AGAINST THE GOLDEN BIBLE" evidenced by their concern for readers that the text itself was not what they imagined, not so gross nor vulgar a superstition as perhaps the Gold Bible should have been.[1] When the Reflector published the first chapter of First Nephi, that is, the guesses and ridicule dissipated. Explaining how and why Joseph Smith—or other conspirators—composed such a thing now became the primary subject for gossip by clergy and newsman. Origin stories abounded, yet nothing conclusive emerged to travel alongside tales of the Gold Bible, to counter the actual book.

Thus the New-York Telescope not only urged caution, but finding his request for proof of actual golden plates plainly rebuffed by Oliver Cowdery, its editor reprinted from the Palmyra Freeman the tale of the book's origins, a story so fantastical it needed no verdict. The writer, C.C. Blatchley, swallowed the bait of Smith's illiteracy, and found himself thereby with puzzle, having read sixteen pages of the illiterate's 600 page translation. The purpose of Blatchley's study is to alert "our missionaries" to an easy path for rejecting the book, yet even he cannot offer a motive for its production. Rather than confront the puzzle directly, he dismisses the text as the work of Smith, "and this declaration is evidenced by its style." In what may be regarded as the first "wordprint" study of authorship, Blatchley proceeds to count the repetitions of "yea," "it came to pass," "now" and "behold," finding them too abundant to be truly scriptural. He reprints the title page, inserting between brackets his own unhumorous, stiffly pedantic rejoinders,

---

[1] New-York Telescope, 20 Feb 1830; 6, no.38:150

like some studious, officious reader red-lining overuse of the colon by Charles Dickens. His supposed stylistic "facts are given to caution people not to spend their money uselessly for a book, that is more probable a hoax—or a money making speculation—or an enthusiastic delusion, than a revelation of facts by the Almighty." What the book was—hoax, delusion, revelation—was less clear after its pages began to circulate; the Gold Bible they'd imagined up, and it was easily dismissed. The Book of Mormon, however, was not so simple a thing. Faced with its complex narrative, varying characters, and simple, if at times redundant prose, one finds few papers inventing satirical imitations of it. The actual book already took over the stylistic features of Biblese satire, and yet it told no silly tale of overheated Westleyets or Luman the Magician. The style commonly used by satirists and cranks in Biblese lampoons—a style obscuring targets and so, often rendering the author safe from rebuttal—was now turned to rather different ends.

It was as if an ambush was set by all the talk of simpleton farmers and peeping plowboys, and now the trap was sprung: the text of the Book of Mormon, readers admitted, had teeth. The longer it was handled, the deeper the bite, perhaps the more potent its toxin. Into that trap strolled editor after editor, decrying the imposition before its pages landed on their desks. The Rochester Daily Advertiser, after the book was published, ran a dismissive review in which the editor scoffs more than he evidences an actual reading. "A viler imposition was never practiced," he echoes popular but by then dated appraisal. "It is an evidence of fraud, blasphemy, and credulity, shocking to the Christian and moralist." Rather than the content, or doctrines, or morality of the book, it was "the style" which was again promoted as the singular evidence of the above crimes. "The style of the work," he concluded, "may be conjectured from the 'preface' and 'testimonials' which we subjoin."[1] With these testimonials and prefaces the book brought along its own metatext, offering them for easy circulation by lazy, over-pious editors.

Notice that these writers cannot decide between fraud or blasphemy (which admittedly are not mutually exclusive), satire and evidence of "credulity." Whatever it was, the book was pushed not only by its de facto title, but also by its stylistic features into the genre of the Bible; that was a genre with a single exemplar and lone member (despite something like 500 different versions produced in

---

[1] Rochester Daily Advertiser, "Blasphemy—'Book of Mormon,' alias The Golden Bible" 2 April 1830

America alone over the previous half century[1]).  Here was an apparently serious text preserving not merely the style but also much of the KJV text.  But it plainly wasn't the Bible.  It relied on what had become—like Latin before it—an obsolete and religious vernacular; but not to poke fun at bumpkins and pious hypocrites. (One can hardly imagine a text appealing to religious folks, in the early 1800s, using a style and vocabulary other than one borrowed from the KJV.)  The Advertiser's assessment of style was summarized (with acknowledgment) in Danville's Village Chronicle.  Its editor less stridently positioned his paper against that book, it being perhaps unnecessary to make their case explicit: "We subjoin, with some hesitancy, one of the certificates [of the witnesses], which smacks pretty strongly of what would once have been called blasphemy." [2]

Reports of the book's origins circulated orally, and then in print and by reprint; and further recited, folks awed, but more often guffawed at the book's purported existence.  They created what is known as "pragmatic" meaning.  It said more about social relations, roles, and power than the book itself.  The false title summarized as much—genre, roles, origins—and created readers and skeptics, roles independently aligned to socioeconomic statuses like farmer or peddler, readers of "a certain class."  The title, satires, and commentary about it, even before publication, moreover, spread seeds of interest many miles wide, in metatext radiating far outward from the Smith farm in New York, and in particular, away from the Palmyra Reflector's pages.  But as we range outward from that center, the pragmatics—the social map—become more vague, as newspapers reprint and summarize more further afield.  As seen above, self-described literary periodicals more distant from Palmyra summarized the more proximal-to-source (i.e., Palmyra) reports of elaborate sequences of he-said-and-it-is-said.  Through these summaries, much confusion came to surround the tales of the book, making it difficult to decide whether all the hubbub was a scheme, a tall tale, or reported something really happening, maybe even a miracle!  Hence, the clear roles presupposed in Palmyra and Rochester were left vague to readers hearing only about some gold book or something, which editors merely mocked. Readers in eastern Ohio, for example, were positioned to have heard about, but not know the details of the Gold Bible.

---

[1] Richard Van Wagoner, *Sidney Rigdon: A Portrait of Religious Excess* (SLC: Signature Books 1994), 72

[2] Village Chronicle, "The Book of Mormon, or Golden Bible." 27 April 1830

In reprints more widely circulated, what we see erased are the social origins—neighbors taking sides, bemused or shocked—of the metatext: where amused and maybe increasingly weary Palmyra townspeople had long rendered a verdict on Jo Smith and his Gold Bible. Verdict is explicit in the distantly circulating reports, even as details became general, to the point of omitting names of persons, towns, and of the book itself. The Buffalo Journal & General Advertiser reported on "The New Bible," caring little for details,

> Some year or two since the credulous were amused with the tale that, guided by inspiration, some one had found many golden plates buried in the earth near Palmyra, Wayne county, in this state, upon which were revealed, in an unknown tongue, (an odd sort of revelation one would think) the whole duty of man.[1]

The clarity of judgment attending reportorial vagueness, however, also rendered many of the reports of the Book of Mormon somewhat doubtful, sketchy even for frontier readers. Reports increasingly contradicted other printed and orally circulating accounts. Under an article titled "Imposition and Blasphemy!!—Moneydiggers, Etc." the Rochester Gem called out "the credulous of the earth," and the "wonderful production" palmed upon them by "an ignoramus near Palmyra, Wayne county." The report, coming months after the Book of Mormon was published, named the production's books as "Nephi, Nimshi, Pukei, and Buckeye," supported by the testimony of three and six witnesses. The work of their ignoramus is compared to "Salem Witch-craft-ism and Jemima Wilkinson-ism, and is in point of blasphemy and imposition, the very summit."[2] With reports like this, overfull of piety and clapping with Puritan thunder, it is a wonder that any soul wasn't talking about Jo Smith and his Golden Bible! Yet a year into the Book of Mormon's life, the Gem's editors would dismiss reports of converts, for "We do not anticipate a very great turning to this heresy. The public are too much enlightened."[3]

So generative was the Book of Mormon, that the Reflector capitalized on the Gem's confusions, and expanded its effort to link moneydiggers to the Smiths, publishing extracts of "the Book of Pukei."[4] Another tiresome Biblese lampoon, "Pukei" aligned the style with story, a sort of early exposé claiming to give the real

---

[1] Buffalo Journal & General Advertiser, "The New Bible" 8 Dec 1830
[2] Rochester Gem, 15 May 1830, p.15
[3] Rochester Gem, "Book of Mormon" 25 Dec 1830
[4] Palmyra Reflector, 12 June 1830, 3d series, no.5:36-37

history of the Smiths. (Because these stories seldom circulated beyond the neighborhood of the Smiths, one still reads today announcements from crestfallen Mormons, having newly discovered Smith's career as a crystal gazer, or peeper.) It describes how "Walters the magician" was summoned by "the idle and slothful," to "inform us where the Nephites hid their treasure." Walters (alluding to an actual person, Luman Walters, called by Brigham Young the most wicked man he ever met) reads from Cicero's *Orations*, drawing in the night with a rusted sword a "magic circle," wherein he sacrificed a cock to propitiate guardian spirits. Such details were later reported by others who claimed to dig for treasure with Joseph Smith (Jr. and Sr.), confirming their involvement in drawing out spirits in exactly this manner. "Now the rest of the acts of the magician," the first chapter of Pukei concludes, "how his mantle fell upon the prophet Jo. Smith Jun. and how Jo. made a league with the spirit, who afterwards turned out to be an angel, and how he obtained the 'Gold Bible,' Spectacles, and breast plate—will they not be faithfully recorded in the book of Pukei?" The second chapter of Pukei came in July, and mostly reported the direction given to "Joseph, surnamed the ignoramus," by a spirit sent from "MORMON, the great apostle to the Nephites."[1] These reports attempt to tell straight history, in order to expose what is regarded as an imposition, and yet themselves seem so fantastical that one may easily dismiss them. Yet, their value is in the telling and its effects: close enough to true to generate conversation with folks familiar with Joseph Smith, but off just enough, and recognized by readers as such, to introduce doubt about which version was, as it were, canonical. Interest in the Gold Bible—its content, history, purposes—was spreading.

So much scandalizing and obvious confusion only increased the desire in hearing the true tale told by an actual believer. The in-town presence of believers in the Book of Mormon, or even letters from folks claiming encounters with them, would become news itself. In other words, even as they mocked and opposed the "superstition," editors like Abner Cole (because of the Book of Mormon, known to history as Dogberry) weekly harrowed, plowed, and planted the seeds of interest in fields of readers spreading from Ohio to Massachusetts. The Brattleboro Messenger, for example, published a letter to the editor from "Clericus," itself extracting news from a letter written "from a town in the State of New-York, where, as I had been previously told, this Jos. Smith has resided from some years."[2] The extracted letter begins, "You have probably heard of the Gold

---

[1] Palmyra Reflector, 3d series, no.8:60
[2] Brattleboro Messenger (Vermont), 20 Nov 1830, 9:43

Bible taken from the earth by Joseph Smith, the money digger." Unsure of what to call believers, he recounts that "The society are increasing. Eighteen have been baptized in a day. H.P. and wife have been baptized, & are very strong in the faith. The girls are under conviction." Clericus adds his own tale, that a woman "immersed formerly by an Elder in this county, has been immersed or baptized again into this new system." What the system was, and what society they were being baptized into, was not explained in this or in other accounts. But the book was gathering Christians to something, and that was news.

That no one had, as yet, coined a socially useful term for these believers made it all the more difficult to learn that one of them was in town, without also being obliged to hear one version or another of what they bothered to come preaching about. Thus the teller of rumor, perhaps laughing to a neighbor, had to explain just what the believers believed in, what the "gold" in the de facto title came from, and the "Bible" part too. Lacking a name to characterize and, so, dismiss them, believers peddling the book benefited from bearers of tales about it who personally thought little of the text. So by the sometimes malicious, understandably prejudiced, at times nonplussed and even bemused labors of non-believers, the Book of Mormon carved out paths to the scarce believer. Believer in what? At first, in some metatext which regarded other metatext—origin stories, genres, and so on—as "true." Hardly anyone was reading any actual Book of Mormon.

The traditional version of the translation of the Book of Mormon looks something like this. Joseph Smith peered into his hat, and recited in English a line of text. Perhaps he looked at plates having the appearance of gold, or saw these in the mind's eye. That oral text, whatever its origin, was transcribed by Oliver Cowdery, its pages passed around, and read by trusted friends and family. These pages were copied and arranged into a "Printer's Manuscript," from which Egbert Grandin and associates arranged the type and published several thousand bound Book of Mormons. But the translation does not stop there, for the books were circulated, and commented upon, read within cultural traditions tied to the Bible, and as we've seen, often dismissed with scorn.

Harris's farm was mortgaged to pay for the initial print run of several thousand, and these books were distributed person by person, preacher by preacher, curious by curious reader. There was no wholesale distribution network, and so the book was always accompanied by commentary, discussion, explanation. Each reading was, let us imagine, a new translation of the text: or what do we mean when we ask, and answer, "what does it mean?" We distinguish "translation" from "interpretation," in popular usage; although often without any good reason, except that we believe English to be one language, and thus "translation" is not applicable to English language texts, read by literate English-speakers. But the distinction blinds us from seeing the reality: Every reading of the Book of Mormon is a translation, and so the process started by a young man talking into his hat continues, for better or worse a million times a day. It is a living thing, although "thing" does not adequately describe the book's processual, imaginative and relational ontology. The tangibility of the page, the fidelity between every printed volume, and their origin in some imagined "critical text," the sameness of each FIRST NEPHI: these features confuse readers into believing their reading *is* the text's meaning. In reality, the book is but a guide, and does not interpret itself. Readers can take its guidance, or unwittingly ignore what is on the page, at every turn. Learning how to read, then, only begins by learning how to translate characters into sounds, words, and phrases.

Just as with translations circulating alongside a text, once sold, an individual book in 1830 might be resold many times, each buyer inscribing his or her name on the inside flap, giving a sort of genealogy of consumers and sellers; a brief history of translators. Thus translations continue through time, finding in space crowds of antagonists or believers who shape their texts in a way fitted to their sense of what makes them a group. But antagonists to what, believers in what? The Book of Mormon, while the title of a book, is understood, when we examine what happens "on the ground," among readers and apologists and preachers—that book is a thing imagined by them, but confused for some singular, ideal and unchanged Book of Mormon. As we've seen in the easier to understand formulation of a metatext called the Gold Bible, texts are imagined things, drawing only part of their existence from the words on the page. As you read this page, in fact, you can imagine other readers interpreting ("translating") its meaning different from yourself, and feeling perfectly justified in their own translation. Find other readers who seem to find in the text the same things you find, and one is well on the way to a society, a cult, a coven, scholarly community or religion. Never mind what the author "intends" or "means": what we can track, empirically and historically in reconstructions like the one before you, what can be studied is what these interpretations bring about.

What they bring about are more or less cohering and durable metatext which *create* readers: and in readers, a sense of belonging by way of reading, to some group. It is as if by magic an entire span of black walnut was set with china, dinner, and guests as well. Much can be added to that dinner party—priesthoods, invented traditions, dress codes, totems, myths, dietary laws—to shore up one's sense of belonging. But it is the text which allows one to "see" on the page one's translation, beguiled thereby as if a mind has been transported onto paper. Marx called this process, in capitalism, commodity fetishism: when social relations are represented in a commodity, and all the value of those relations is confused for the monetary value of a thing. Similar magic is at play in a "scriptural" text: the more readers one finds to translate text in a way deemed like one's own, the more that metatext converges with, and replaces, the actual text. No matter how "far off" their reading may seem to some other group (likewise insisting their translation gives the true interpretation). A strange sort of magic, not easily explained to readers who perform it all day long.

But, you may say, what the book means is what the author meant. Who is the author of the Book of Mormon? Do not be confused into thinking that book on your desk is *The Book of Mormon*, so much as a representation of it. So it depends on which Book of Mormon you mean: the engraved writings on plates having the appearance of gold, apparently compiled from other writers, who described other speakers and lives long passed? The English translation written by hand, or printed in 1830? Joseph Smith's oral recitation? The 1981 text, with footnotes, interpretive cues, dictionary and index? The one presented in manuals, and discussed in a Sunday School class in Argentina? The Reader's version, or the children's version, an anti-Mormon's version, or the version made for the market of *Idiots*? The one read by you? It is a collective work, not unlike the Nation-State, or Christianity, or the Red Sox or Sioux Nation. An imagined thing: we fool ourselves into believing it a factual thing, like a table or a cat. And though a single title and text is legally copyrighted as The Book of Mormon, that is mere placeholding, legal burdens related to the marketplace.

So, a text is a tangible thing, but it is metatext which tell one how to read that thing, how to generate meaning from it. Without metatext, a thingy-text is a mere stack of paper, not even a collectable. Dead. Put a mind before it, and it lives. The Book of Mormon in object form became an attractor for socially circulating metatext framed by the Gold Bible. If one is careful and obsessive enough, metatext can be deconstructed and pulled away from the Book of Mormon, showing it as it *might* be read. (Later essays in another volume show how it might be read, after one has stopped looking for "the meaning," and begun consciously using it as, in fact, it always has been used: to generate imagination.) Many translations of the Book of Mormon (metatext) exist—as many as there are readers, or even folks who've heard of a book by this title—each one pretending to be, and not merely to stand in for, The Book of Mormon. This history attempts to show how a religion, cast in the mold of Religion, emerged imaginatively, and tangibly, as it simultaneously translated the Book of Mormon: creating itself as it created a book for believers to believe in, and be baptized thereafter.

When one is "inside" a group enough to react against its assault, then we are well on our way to a culture, a society, a religion. The few believers in the book-metatext were not silently abiding the less savory assessments of the Gold Bible and the book it represented. Again showing us its embeddedness in local social relations, only the paper most near to the Smith clan bothered to engage them. Dogberry replied to a request from one Luther Howard that he "please erase my name from your list of subscribers," with this bite of nineteenth century venom:

> We have only to regret that this 'little lump of anguish,' who measures something
> more than four feet in his shoes, had not requested an immediate discontinuance,
> as he is the only person of the same description our list contains. It is from the
> enlightened, independent, and liberal minded, that we receive and expect
> support—not from meddlesome, canting, or whining hypocrites—it is not from
> a man who professes, ostentatiously, to belong to a Calvinistic church—where
> himself and his family display a profusion of fine clothing—while he privately
> advocates the "Gold Bible." This man has an itching to appear in print—he shall
> be gratified.[1]

The Reflector later showed its fangs to believers, advising "such ignorant wretches," namely Joseph's brother Hyrum, "and some of his ill-bred associates, not to be quite so impertinent, when decent folks denounce the imposition of the 'Gold Bible'." "Apostles," Dogberry added without concern for self-application, "should keep cool."[2] Now the book was generating copy by way of generating believers, something altogether unexpected, we can suppose, and so all the more worthy of print. Always on the alert for news, Cole's paper announced a most significant event in what became Mormonism: the departure of men to preach "the truth":

---

[1] Palmyra Reflector, 16 March 1830 new series, no.11:89
[2] Palmyra Reflector, 19 April 1830 new series, no.16:130

> The apostle to the Nephites (Cowdery) has started for the East, on board a boat, with a load of 'gOld Bibles,' under a command, (as he says) to declare the truth (according to Jo Smith,) 'in all the principal cities in the Union.'[1]

Oliver Cowdery did not "find his way to the Simsbury mines," as Dogberry suggested, but instead travelled with three others westward, in search of Lamanites. Characters of a book began to take on flesh here, clothed by the imaginations of its readers. The book was reaching beyond its pages, and mapping entire peoples and lands. Native Americans were sought out, as the book was thought to tell them good tidings of great joy. They were to join the Mormons, and build a new Zion. By finding Lamanites among Native Americans—just as many Christians had thought them Hebrews, or primitives in need of salvation—the book was put into what we'd now call a hypothesis. There were promises and prophecies to Lamanites which might fail, when real Indians were encountered. There was risk. What if Lamanite-Indians did not do as the book was held to prophesy? As a "sign," by contrast, there was room to reinterpret, to reconsider plans in the face of apparent failure. Maybe the book itself could just mean something to someone? The text itself would not be risking a prophecy that failed. Rather than prove the content of the new book they carried—some prediction that actual readers (Indians, no less!) would join the Mormonites and bring about the Millennium—instead, what it signaled—whatever some reader thought it meant, as metatext—that would hail Christians along the way. Less problematic, then, was a framing of the Book of Mormon as not only like the Bible, but indeed found inside its imaginary realm, where gifts of the Spirit were dispensed. Any reader could take up this framing, and accept or reject the framing without even reading the text. Following these metatext will take us into European history and forward to Ohio. As Cole presciently, mockingly, announced:

> The age of miracles has again arrived, and if the least reliance can be placed upon the assertions, daily made by the "Gold Bible" apostles, (which is somewhat doubtful,) no prophet since the destruction of Jerusalem by Titus, has performed half so many wonders as have been attributed to that spindle shanked ignoramus Jo Smith.[2]

---

[1] Palmyra Reflector, 1 June 1830 3d series, no.4:28
[2] Palmyra Reflector, 30 June 1830, "A hungry lean-faced villain." 3d series no.7:53-54

The miracle in question was not only the book, but also the exorcism of a demon from the body of Smith's friend, Newel Knight. The Reflector claimed to give its report "as narrated by St. Martin," previously condemned in the paper for "the habit of whipping and otherwise mal-treating his wife for the sole purpose of making her a proselyte to the faith according to Joe Smith."[1] Whatever this new book was, and its proselytes amounted to, it was becoming something more than an imposition, gross superstition, worthy of derision and hardly a second glance; the expansive work of a bumbling ignoramus: credulous, blasphemous, fraudulent.

Outside New York, where the Gold Bible continued to thrive, metatext gathered around the Bible for centuries also had gathered families anxious to restore their New Testament stories, to conjure them into the realm of flesh and blood. Restoration was the thing, and Restorationists had a book describing exactly what ancient things ought to be restored: miracles, churches, rituals, powers. It may still signal a fraud to most Americans; but the Book of Mormon, landing in Ohio among what others might call "the credulous," might among them be a sign of miracles being once again restored to our world. Another scripture? Why not, so long as it corroborated the Holy Word?

---

[1] Palmyra Reflector, 22 June 1830, 3d series no.6:45-46

# Two  Restoration of Something Somehow

STORIES ORGANIZED AROUND THE METATEXT GOLD BIBLE TOLD ABOUT ITS origins, even as its title and parodies of its style framed the book as a challenge to the Bible: specifically, it being granted exclusive residency in the genre of Christian scripture. This metatext was as good an advertisement for the actual book as any author could invent, as we've seen. But it came at a cost: the Book of Mormon was from before its publication compared to the Bible, thinkable only as a religious text, as scripture with all the trappings and social effects diagrammed in Illustration 1. To many observers, a book highly blasphemous; or to the enlightened, patently absurd; when it made believers of doubters, they were often dyed in the wool Bible readers. Ironically, the Book of Mormon was regarded by believers as an unshakable advocate for the historical reliability and divine authority of their Holy Bible. Hence, the text summoned social roles not really of its own making, but firmed up ones tied to a long and established tradition. Rather than some sense of the expansiveness of God's mercy spreading over human history, most believers seemed to have thought it justified their obsession with restoring primitive Christianity.

Christians had been preaching "restoration" for nearly three centuries, and implicit in that attempt was a way of reading the now widely published Bible. Published in vernaculars, it invited readers to never doubt the correctness of their own doctrine and history, for they could be found right there, on its pages. Moreover, the Bible seemed to be the compass to return Man from the waywardness of the Church, undo its flight from the straight and narrow. The Bible, rather than the pope's keys, was after the Reformation the resource for building a kingdom which would endure; and forever, it was said. Restoration of "Biblical Christianity" was thus a political, theological, and every-ogical passion.

Sectarian strife and national wars were inevitable; but that history is told in another chapter. Here we work through two distinct problems: what is restoration, practically and socially speaking; and what does the Book of Mormon say about its own project of restoration?

## THE DISCURSIVE LOGIC OF RESTORATION

Writers on Restorationism in Christianity have done very little theorizing or analysis, but plenty of classifying. Continuing sectarian identity politics across the academic realm, they create taxonomies to refine, expand, or ground this tradition and exclude that one, ever set on argument.[1] Dan Vogel, a historian and skeptic, once claimed that "Mormonism was never simply 'primitivism,' as other studies asserted," and proceeded to define early Mormons as driven by "Seekerism," set apart from ordinary Primitivists on account of their "restoration of charismatic apostleship."[2] When dealing with isms, such reifying, and perpetual work of splitting from and lumping with other isms, can be expected. All isms partake of vagueness, of course, and thus are not good starting points for classifying anything; although as shorthand for complex processes constructed and surveyed by scholars, these isms do have their limited uses. Explaining, historicizing, or classifying human activity are not among them.

The basic problem with beginning one's history with isms is plainly manifest, and even discussed, over the course of numerous essays published in *The Primitive Church in the Modern World*.[3] The volume begins with obligatory navel-gazing, found in an introductory essay by Richard T. Hughes. A Disciples of Christ historian, Hughes's career began with a thesis inspired by Franklin Littell's *The Origins of Sectarian Protestantism*, a foundational history of Protestant primitivism. Titled, "The Meaning of the Restoration Vision," here Hughes tells

---

[1] See, for example, Richard T. Hughes and C. Leonard Allen, *Illusions of Innocence: Protestant Primitivism in America, 1630-1875* (Chicago: U Chicago Press, 1988). More general discussion in the style of the "history of ideas" school, Arthur O. Lovejoy and George Boas, *Primitivism and Related Ideas in Antiquity* (Baltimore: Johns Hopkins U Press, 1935).

[2] Dan Vogel, *Religious Seekers and the Advent of Mormonism* (SLC: Signature Books 1988), 217

[3] Richard T. Hughes, ed. *The Primitive Church in the Modern World* (Urbana, IL: U Illinois Press 1995). Because I often quote from the same resource over the course a single paragraph, I have decided to combine in-text citation with footnotes. The in-text, parenthetical citation refers to the most recently footnoted resource. Thus, page x from Hughes is cited next, as given in parenthesis on the opposite page. Hopefully it makes sense.

us that "Restorationism involves the attempt to recover some important belief or practice from the time of pure beginnings that believers are convinced has been lost, defiled, or corrupted. Restorationism further assumes that at some point in Christian history a fall or apostasy occurred" (x). We've run into the first obstacle to understanding Restorationism outside the folk traditions that generated it, and which advocate its undertaking. The problem with speaking of "belief or practice" is that one is thus moving already from words that represent some belief or practice, into the realm of the Restorationists. They see through words into the ostensible beliefs and practices they imagine are real, and really there in the Bible, and in their heads, and sometimes even found among their own peoples. Words may look the same, and yet mean very different things, of course, when one bothers to pay attention. The materiality of words is the source of a group's seeming unity, as well as of the Restorationists' constant schism and strife. So Hughes seems to inkle at this problem: some movements, he adds, "focus on theology and doctrine, some focus on issues of lifestyle and ethics, some focus on early Christian experience," he continues, "while still others seek to recover the forms and structures they think characterized the ancient church" (xi).

Listing the varieties of what some group wants to restore, however, does little to help us understand how Restorationism works. These lists do work for those interested in multiplying levels for academic taxonomies, sending forth calls for conferences, another journal article and more disputation. Indeed, the father of academic talk about Protestant primitivism, Franklin Littell, contributed an ever growing list of "Primitivists, restitutionist, Restorationist" movements, adding to his domain the "Mennonists, Brethren, Quakers, Baptists, Congregationalists," alongside Methodists and Anglicans, whose prayer book was said to be rooted in the purity of original faith.[1] His addition of Anglicans may seem forced. One Anglican minister did write a theological treatise called *Primitive Worship & The Prayer Book*, however, presenting to Christians every evidence for how the Book of Common Prayer restores and preserves ancient practices, doctrines, and truths. And I mean ancient: "Our first appeal is to the Old Testament with its history of God's ancient Church of Israel."[2] Ancient things restored can be found nearly anywhere, if one merely knows how to look: not too closely. Look to words, names, titles: these are easy to restore, as well.

---

[1]  Franklin Littell, "The Power of the Restoration Vision and its Decline in Modern America" (in Hughes, ed., *The Primitive Church in the Modern World*), 54
[2] Rev. Walker Gwynne, *Primitive Worship & The Prayer Book* (NY: Longmans, Green and Co. 1917), 13

Anyone can possibly be lumped into the category of Primitivist. Other than some unfortunate amnesiac from an Oliver Sacks story, who, we might ask, is not vaguely primitivist, not somewhat nostalgic for a better time, back when things were good and pure? But which sort are you? Richard Hughes once called Alexander Campbell a "rational progressive primitivist," adding thereby at least three other possible primitivist categories.[1] Are Mormons post-Protestant Primitivists, Dispensational Primitivists, Millenarian Dispensational Primitivists, anti-Modernist One-Cuppers, Postmodern Corporate Subjects, or Seekers? What about Mormon-ism? In Mormon historian Thomas Alexander's contribution to the Hughes-edited volume, he dismisses the matter with, "it helps little in our analysis to say that Mormons were Primitivists." Instead he presupposes the term's legitimacy, telling how Mormonism "adapted to modernization," as though that new label does indeed aid our analysis.[2] Such ideal types are, when asked to historical materials, quickly shown to be worse than meaningless, and very often misleading.

This realization seems to have spurred the question from another prominent historian of American religion, George Marsden, whose essay is the very question, "How useful is the concept 'Primitivism' for understanding American Fundamentalism?" Not very, as one ism can be bent or folded into any other, and with equal ease. (He does not, of course, turn the same critical reading on his own bailiwick: Fundamentalism.) In fact, the problem with these terms is not only that they are isms, and poorly suited for analysis. It is also that they were designed by those who use them: by believers, as it were, not by analysts nor historians. They come with concealed compartments, hidden histories, empty calories, very often a trail of blood and pain, and much not favorable to our using them. That is, when one hopes to understand how they came to be, and how they work after they are enunciated and declared by their spokespersons. Anthropologists are familiar with this stumbling block. One must learn the natives' tongue, surely, before attempting to understand their culture. But taking up the natives' terms for the purpose of doing one's analysis with them? This is not often a mistake made by anthropologists, who realize that those terms need explaining, not elaboration and academic advocates or disputants. *Restoration* is such a term. Historians of religion straddle the discursive realm of theologians and

---

[1] Richard T. Hughes, *Reviving the Ancient Faith: The Story of the Churches of Christ in America* (Grand Rapids MI: William B. Eerdmans Publishing Co. 1996), 30
[2] Thomas Alexander, "Mormon Primitivism and Modernization" (in Hughes, ed., *The Primitive Church in the Modern World*), 168

believers when they use the term in what is otherwise historical analysis or reconstruction. So much writing on primitivism, and its variants is a blending of folk tradition with the historian's authority to tell us what really happened. (Later chapters, should I keep on writing, will explore how Mormon historians, by using native terms concoct a similar witches' brew, mingling powers of tradition with those of a historian.) So the *Primitivism* volume includes theologians. Rather than add to the pile of isms for others to reject or refine, theologian John Howard Yoder's contribution, "Primitivism in the Radical Reformation," ironically hits on a rather important insight. Not that "everybody in the sixteenth century wanted to renew original Christianity" (76), which could not possibly be true, nor uttered by any historian. Rather, that "The Churches of Christ, with their British and Puritan backgrounds, and the Churches of God, more Germanic and Pietist," he notes, "used the same words and themes in nineteenth-century Indiana, but they were not quite doing the same thing" (75). Ah, words, confounding our world since Babel.

Restoration is indeed first of all a way of picking up parts of speech—terms ("lexemes"), phrases, archaic morphemes (e.g., the *–th* ending, as in *endeth*), syntactical inversions; all that was mocked in satires of the Book of Mormon; and more—as a way of performing social roles similarly lifted from the pages of the Holy Bible. It is a matter of some importance (though not yet the page for its explanation) that the earliest advocates of the Book of Mormon were not called "Nephites" nor "Lamanites," but Gold Bible Apostles, disciples, and often in derision. The Bible was the reference point—the "matrix text" we'd call it in my field—for translating, as it were, the new book. With respect to the Bible, the "same words and themes" could be taken from the same translations of the various texts in circulation: words like disciple, covenant, grace and faith. Formed into a register, their usage points to one's belonging to some tradition, movement, or group; by speaking thusly, one performs social roles that say a great deal about oneself, but only to similarly initiated players. The millions of Bibles in circulation were the priests, as it were, initiating readers into recognizing and performing such roles. Some seeming unity could emerge among such speakers, or not; they used the same words, but did they mean the same things? That was Restorationism at work for three centuries, prior to the Book of Mormon's publication.

Linguistic forms may seem identical across many King James Versions of the Old and New Testaments. These "same" words may be interpreted by readers as bearing altogether different senses or meanings. Unity can come irrespective of "meaning," that is. For a time, anyway, until someone asks what atonement or sin "really" means. Restorationists used phrases found in the Bible to describe their own lives, moreover, and the lives of others. So a sense of unity becomes, upon further inspection, grounds for often bitter schism. Mormonites were such a schism, as we'll see.

*Restoration* was one word they all knew the meaning of; one still repeated by historians of religion today, although mostly in essays asking whether the term is really very useful. It is, but not for analysis. The term obscures social processes we need to reveal in order to understand how the Book of Mormon was picked up by Restorationists, and with what effects. Believers in restoration of some kind added to the familiar, generically Christian vocabulary of sinner, charity, love, and so on, a variety of social roles like "disciple" for readers to take up. That title carried a heavy burden. As a role it consisted of—was enacted when attended by—other terms taken from the New Testament; terms describing correct or authentic Christianity, supposed to exist among early Christians. Thus, disciple as a role also organized much else taken from the New Testament, and gave doctrines, metaphysics, hierarchies, disputes and dogmas new life in the bodies of new disciples. An enterprising Restorationist minister actually published a book in 1917 which defined social roles carried by names lifted from the New Testament, explaining, "Names stand for things. There is in the name all that there is in the thing designated. A great thing makes a name great. By this test, New Testament names are the greatest."[1] These names are powerful things, he warns, for "The life of Christ is variously set forth in them," and moreover, "The different names are terms by which the Holy Spirit sets forth the richness of our relationship with Christ" (7). In his study you will find essays on the duties, powers, and promises of those called Christians, Saints, Servants, Friends, Brethren, and Disciples: "to be a disciple of Jesus meets the need of the soul for adequate and ultimate instruction in the things of God" (18). "The disciple of Jesus is a channel," he adds, "Through him, and on account of him, the blessing of Jesus is to pass on to others" (21). Ryan's book, in fact, is really a long complaint about misuse of the names, and attempts to prescribe correct use among Christians. Its existence tells us that Bible names were—much to the author's frustration—social things whose meaning was decided by convention and also subject to contention.

Bible names were a big deal in the 1800s; Bible names for Bible things, was the phrase so often repeated. One was said to be a disciple or a "true"

---

[1] M.B. Ryan, *New Testament Names: A study of various scriptural appelations used to designate the followers of Christ* (Cinninati: The Standard Publishing Co., 1917), 5

Christian, however, according to no single measure or definition: disciples were found where also "faith" was correctly understood (in the "biblical" sense, of course), baptism correctly practiced, penance regularly undertaken. Structures and strife and unity come, of course, when we inquire: what sort of faith, how is it obtained, what does it entail? Or about baptism, or about communion (one cup, or many?), or how is one released from, remitted of, cleansed from, forgiven of sin, or of sins? Every role generated by the Bible came with many ever-growing shoots—metaphysics, powers, traditions, stereotypes—that some reading communities duly cultivated, while others pruned away. Rather than unity, it was unity in relation to difference: we are right, they are not. Thus, Protestant Primitivism became the mother of Sectarianism, ironically by way of a Bible which seemed to say the same things in every version, or at least seemed to speak rather clearly to every reader, who could be sure his or her own reading was obviously the correct one. It was right there on the page. Even educated preachers like Thomas and Alexander Campbell trotted out Restoration as the very means to bring about Christian unity: Bible terms for Bible things were their prescriptions for the world's troubles. If one assembled the words of the Bible among this generation, scripted their voices and called them disciples, could not one call that the Kingdom of God? These discursive practices set upon Christians many flaxen cords, and only subtle analysis will untangle their effects.

"Restoration" is, as I've said, not really a description of a kind of religious orientation, movement, or desire; except as used by speakers who consider themselves so oriented, moving, or desiring. It is, practically speaking, much more a way of, almost a binding rule for, building social roles from a text—disciple, apostle, sinner, heathen, saint, priest. It also secures those roles in a metatext Bible that comes to be understood as "true": a circular assessment proclaimed by text-generated social roles. This is why, after Gutenberg, Protestantism is more often than not "primitivist," seeking to take the righteous back to the Golden Days of Yore, when miracles were common, some goods perhaps were common, sometimes wives, too; but, verily, sin was uncommon among the Saints. By taking up Bible roles, then, Restoration readings brought the Bible into everyday life. I speak of roles, rather than persons, because to doubt the Bible as constructed by Restorationists is to no longer be (or, perform the role of) a traditional Restorationist. Roles are scripted across interactions, as it were, by metatext. They have histories which can be told, and functions which social theorists like Max Weber long ago outlined. Roles can be further given durability and consistency across persons (who come and go) by bringing them into an "institution," perhaps formalized in "offices" or "positions"; in fact, the institution is generated last of all, even though it seems to stand independent of what it relies upon. In metatext, then—confessions of faith, testimonies of belief in the truth of a book, sermons, commentaries, pamphlets, scripture itself—one finds the scripts for performing social roles taken from that seemingly singular book. Moreover, they lay the groundwork for a non-human agent, a corporation, nation-state, economy, any sort of ism. Given the text generating the roles of interest here, the institutions we are concerned with were not surprisingly considered religious: churches. These durable and dispersed social roles were encountered by the Book of Mormon before it was even published. It was chained to the Bible, as it was stylistically reduced to imitating its forms, making belivers in it converts to some new movement.

I give this formal analysis of Restoration before the history of it, so that we can see what it does, and not be lost in the narrative.[1] What matters to the history of the Book of Mormon, then, is how the book was fitted into a project of restoration, knitted to the words and roles generated by the Bible. That project is, in fact, a method of reading: of pulling words from passages, and applying those words to actually living bodies, ritual practices, and institutions. Lo here an apostle, lo there a gift of the Spirit, we are church, and so on. We find that *restoration* names a socio-linguistic practice, rather than a doctrine or belief. It is metadiscursive. Once we've reframed the matter as implicated in language, in prescribing spoken and written language in social context—as discourse, that is— our material, Restoration, is removed from the realm of Christian tradition, folk notions and the like, and rendered a subject for analysis. (Over the next few chapters we shall mobilize, more often than not in the background, social theories of discourse in order to reconstruct how the Book of Mormon was taken up by a Restorationist community in Ohio, and with what effects.) So, rather than dispense with the Holy Word of Life, some readers of their Restorationist Bibles found a place for the Book of Mormon in the genre of scripture. That new book spoke of disciples, restoration, baptism, and the like. Surely it meant the same thing as what the Bible meant, when it said those words, right? But which Book

---

[1] Brief mention of H. Michael Marquardt's *Inventing Mormonism: Tradition and the Historical Record* (San Francisco: Smith Research Associates, 1994) should be made. This work concerns traditions around the Smith family, and the apparent "invention" of them by Mormons decades later, as compared to the (apparent non-) invention of them by neighbors some years later. As it is concerned with Smith biographic metatext, and with choosing one tale over another, this work does not inform the Book of Mormon history given here.

of Mormon? And which Bible? Which metatext, I mean? There are historical processes for us to track down, and if I continue with this history, the following chapters and volumes will do just that.

The actual Book of Mormon followed metatext—newspapers, gossip, believers—out from Palmyra in 1830, and received at least cursory readings by readers of the Bible. By its own admission a weak little thing, the Book of Mormon was subordinated to the interpretations and ambitions of its creations—those not yet named Mormons. The core was soon to be discovered by Oliver Cowdery and his companion Parley Pratt, as they camped among Pratt's spiritual family, regarded by outsiders as Restorationists (calling themselves disciples, of course) living communally on Isaac Morley's eastern Ohio farm. Why they found the book moving is not unrelated to what book—that is, metatext—they compared it to: their Bible. Its believers predictably made that unassailable, inerrant and irreproachable wholly Holy Bible colonize its pages. The history of Mormonism in Ohio given over the following chapters is burdened with demonstrating exactly how this process flows—texts, roles, institutions. And also, with explaining how traditions have been revised into orthodox histories, projecting backward the ism of institutional identity to a time in their respective traditions when that identity demonstrably did not exist. Before I explain how the Book of Mormon was rendered corroborative of the Bible, and chopped into fuel for Restorationist engines, we survey two matters. First, what the Book of Mormon says about restoration. Second, what Christian traditions of restoration were originally designed for, and what they became in the American frontier, on the presses of preacher-writers like Alexander Campbell. That second matter is taken up over the next few chapters. The first is attended to here.

Let me not mislead readers into believing that what I give here as "what the Book of Mormon says about Restoration" is anything other than what I think it says. Few Mormons would abide my interpretations given below, and many would object (and have objected) to their being trotted out in spaces like Sunday School or LDS Church-controlled publications. Mine is not an orthodox reading. I could not even get a proposal discussing how the Book of Mormon would look without a Bible framework accepted for a recent conference; one sponsored by a closet orthodoxy of academic sectarians formed into their own Society for Mormon Philosophy and Theology. So, what I give is a mere possibility. It is provided below for the sake of demonstrating an alternate course its 1830s readers could have taken, and to show how odd it was that they took the path they did.

Thus, the reading I give is certainly not one found among 1830s Mormons. I suspect that what was true of them is also true of most Latter-day Saints today. They did not often sit down and read the Book of Mormon; but instead scrounged around in it for parts to plug or jam into whatever system, theology, tradition, institutional program, or personal agenda they were running across its pages.

Few readers come to it having great misgivings about the Bible's authenticity or reliability. Most, I suppose, come already believing in the Bible (and like most believers today, having seldom read it). The earliest Mormons, one Mormon historian claims, "out-Bibled the biblicists."[1] Not the most helpful comparison, but you get the idea. The Bible was the world, and whatever this Book of Mormon was, it would be such by virtue of the Bible's forbearance. This was true of readers in the 1830s, who drew from its deep wells during sermons some estimated 20 to 40 times as often as they turned to the Book of Mormon.[2] It was true over the following century, and for longer. "Except for its abiding centrality in the conversion experience of proselytes," Terryl Givens writes, "the Book of Mormon has been virtually invisible throughout most of the [LDS] church's history" (240). Givens discusses in this context a well known warning to Joseph Smith (D&C 84:54-57) , voiced only two years after the Book of Mormon was published, warning that, "vanity and unbelief have brought the whole church under condemnation. And this condemnation resteth upon the children of Zion, even all. And they shall remain under this condemnation until they repent and remember the new covenant, even the Book of Mormon." "Historically," Givens concludes, "there seems little doubt the censure was deserved. Doctrinally, as we have seen, the Book of Mormon exerted little influence" (241).

The same reliance on the Bible, when taking up the Book of Mormon, is found among Mormon historians today. "The Book of Mormon is a thousand year history of the rise and fall of a religious civilization in the Western Hemisphere beginning about 600 BCE," writes Richard Bushman, a most respected and gentlemanly Mormon historian. He continues somewhat less cautiously, adding it also contains "A briefer history of a second civilization, beginning at the time of the Tower of Babel and extending till a few hundred years

---

[1] Grant Underwood, *Millennial World of Early Mormonism* (Urbana: U Illinois Press 1993), 58

[2] Terryl Givens, *By the Hand of Mormon: The American Scripture that Launched a New World Religion* (Oxford U Press 2002), 191; citing Grant Underwood, Dialogue 17 (Autumn 1984), 53

before Christ."[1]  Although he would a second time identify (on page 102) that second civilization, commonly called "the Jaredites" as fleeing from the Tower of Babel, the Book of Mormon itself makes no such claim.  Or, more correctly, it did not mention "Babel" in the 1830 edition.  That term was obviously taken from GENESIS, and was later added to a chapter introduction given in the (Book of Mormon's) Book of Ether (its namesake was the author of writings edited and added to the history composed by Mormon).  ETHER tells us only that the people of Jared fled from a great tower, "at the time the Lord confounded the language of the people" (ETHER 1:33).  A minor distinction perhaps, but by identifying that tower with Babel, one locates the people of Jared inside the matrix of the Bible: anchoring them to a time (traditionally in the third millennium BCE), and a place (Mesopotamia), as well as binding the entire record in old questions of the Bible's reliability, as a historical record or God's Word.  None of this Babel talk is so clearly set forth in the Book of Mormon.

I mention this matter of Babel not only because the confounding of language seems to have upshifted lately into the outright deception of humanity by way of language, and so as a starting point for talking about *restoration*, the poetry and irony of inserting Babel into the Book of Mormon should be appreciated; but also because eminent historians of Mormonism (and no doubt of other isms as well) give folk traditions for interpretations, when they should know better.  Is that Richard Bushman's interpretation of ETHER, or is he giving a generic Mormon one?  Reading his Bible into the Book of Mormon, Professor Bushman has no difficulty concluding that, "Altogether, the Book of Mormon can be thought of as an extension of the Old and New Testaments to the Western Hemisphere" (86).  Certainly one can think of it as such, or as a meditation on the unwisdom of a barley standard, or as a treatise on the natural history of cement.  His "can be thought of" posture, an open handed gesture of survey, rather than a presenting of dogmatic interpretation, is at times quietly set aside.  The historian loses his posture of surveying merely what has been thought of the book, becoming briefly its missionary, when he summarizes, "The manifest message of the Book of Mormon is Christ's atonement for the world's sins" (108).  What sort of thing he means by *atonement*, however, or by *Christ*, or by *sins*, is not explained.  Here we find that words can bring a sense of unity, of shared understanding, no matter the distance between interpretations of atonement, Christ, or sin.  Historians know better than to write sentences like that; but tradition-tellers do

---

[1] Richard Bushman, *Joseph Smith, Rough Stone Rolling: A cultural biography of Mormonism's founder* (NY: Alfred A. Knopf 2005), 84

not. Having some years ago found myself seated next to Dr. Bushman during Sunday worship at an LDS chapel in Provo, Utah (we resided blocks from one another, briefly), I cannot doubt his faith, nor his intellect. Nor his insistence that one informs and sharpens the other: though I believe the truth may be otherwise. Bushman reveals his history writing is slyly sipping and passing off folk tradition, and not giving some broad survey of opinion, nor an open minded, anything goes interpretation of that book, when he writes that, "The book presents itself as offspring of the Bible. If you believe one, the *Book of Mormon* says, you will believe the other. 'These last records . . . shall establish the truth of the first'" (99). Here he conflates what tradition has taught him, as a Mormon, into what the book itself proclaims. That passage he quotes can be read in a very different way, one not at all affirming a happy relationship between the Bible and the Book of Mormon.

Bushman is not alone in his reading: "In fact, the Book of Mormon presents its own relationship to the Bible as one of corroboration, not supplement or replacement," interprets Professor Terryl Givens. A man of Letters rather than of History, Givens freely interprets the text's meaning, found in its brief account of a vision of Nephi's (discussed in a later essay), that, for the Book of Mormon,

> to 'establish' the truth of the Bible meant to restore its original message and intent. In the process, the Bible's deficiencies, as well as core value, would be emphasized: 'and [these records] shall make known the plain and precious things which have been taken away from them.' The process by which those elements were 'taken away' to begin with, in a historical process called by Mormons the Great Apostasy, was described as well.[1]

Having decided the matter of its relation to the Bible, Givens later admits there is something of a ". . . paradox of the Book of Mormon as both confirming and impugning the status of the Bible as scripture," one which also "finds formal expression in a document presented to the church at the time of incorporation" (189). His paradox, as we'll see, comes from quoting text, and plugging in metatext referents. This desire to have the Bible as a frame for the Book of Mormon, and the Book of Mormon as a corrective for that frame—as though a lens might undistort the frame that carries it—runs back to 1829, at least. So Givens gives us tradition, in this paradox; and not something indisputably attributable to the book itself, as Givens surely knows. "It has often been pointed

---

[1] Givens, *By the Hand of Mormon,* 188

out," he admits, "that those beliefs most commonly associated with Mormonism are nowhere to be found in that text" (186). Continuing this posture of academic objectivity, he conceals his own reliance on Mormon traditions, being a believer in such, by remounting his own beliefs in the traditions of the past: "In fact, the accounts of early converts to Mormonism confirm that it was the *congruence* of Book of Mormon teachings with the New Testament that dampened their objections to a new scripture and allowed it to affect their conversion for reasons other than doctrinal novelty or innovation" (186). He takes for granted what "teachings" the book held forth to converts—faith, repentance, and so on—as confirming some reading of the New Testament.

These are the confusions of tradition-tellers, and not the careful reconstructions of historians. The transition is subtle in Mormon histories, and comes from a failure to distinguish between the text and metatext. That failure is a symptom of reading the book as scripture, a relationship of text and metatext, and reveals Mormons cloaking their traditions under the posture of writing history. When one claims that so-and-so in 1830 said this about the Book of Mormon, that is plain history; when one says such-and-such is said in the Book of Mormon, and yet finds the text paradoxical and contradictory to one's report, one is giving metatext for text, and has turned from historian to tradition-teller.

One can find any number of teachings, traditions, or isms in the Book of Mormon. Indeed, another prominent historian who caught the earliest wagon of Primitivism then passing through departments of History, Marvin Hill found that the Book of Mormon had as its primary theme the Christian desire for restoration of primitive faith.[1] Rather than summarize what the book's message really is, or how it confirms some "core values" in some other metatext, let's actually read words taken from its pages. We have seen what I think about the Christian project of Restoration: it is a social and discursive practice, a way to build the appearance of communities from shared use of a religious register (or vocabulary) by role enactors. What does the Book of Mormon I read say about restoration: who, what, how?[2]

---

[1] Marvin S. Hill, *The Role of Christian Primitivism in the Origin and Development of the Mormon Kingdom, 1830-1844* (PhD Diss. U Chicago, 1968).

[2] Subsequent references from the Book of Mormon are taken from the LDS 1981 edition. Some terms, like House or Brass, have been capitalized in quoted text.

Being themselves exiles, Book of Mormon characters show more than a little concern over the matter of their people's restoration. But restoration to what? Where? The patriarch of the family around which the history is told was given a dream after his company departed Jerusalem. In the dream he sees a tree, a river bordered by a rod of iron and a narrow path, and a great tower that draws souls to its scoffing horde, pointing fingers at those approaching the tree. Commenting on his father's dream, Nephi (for whom all Nephites were named) explains to his brother Laman (for whom all Lamanites were named),

> our father hath not spoken of our seed alone, but also of all the house of Israel, pointing to the covenant which should be fulfilled in the latter days; which covenant the Lord made to our father Abraham, saying: In thy seed shall all the kindreds of the earth be blessed. And it came to pass that I, Nephi, spake much unto them concerning these things; yea, I spake unto them concerning the restoration of the Jews in the latter days (1 NEPHI 15:18-19).

What he means by "restoration," however, is not here clarified. Restored to lands? Restored to health? By what means? Tied to a promise given to some Abraham character, Nephi's summary leaves much open to speculation, and for filling in by metatext, bible names creating bible things. Nephi's source text for this sermon on Lehi's dream draws from "the words of Isaiah," found in "recovered" Plates of Brass:

> And I did rehearse unto them the words of Isaiah, who spake concerning the restoration of the Jews, or of the House of Israel; and after they were restored they should no more be confounded, neither should they be scattered again. And it came to pass that I did speak many words unto my brethren, that they were pacified and did humble themselves before the Lord (1 NEPHI 15:20).

We have here a statement of effect, that after restoration the people "should no more be confounded" nor "scattered again." These are reportedly the words of Isaiah. This imagined author—I say "imagined" because he exists only in the text, and must be imagined up as existing outside it—is extensively quoted in the Book of Mormon, with little variation from a translation in contemporaneous King James Versions of the Old Testament. Why? It would seem unnecessary for

Moroni to preserve such writings for almost a thousand years, only to find them in the most widely published book in history. Most Mormon readers seem to take it as proof of the correctness of the Bible. Others now doubt the Book of Mormon because it contains parts of ISAIAH they think ought not be there. Plagiarism is as easily charged to Smith as is the supposed Book of Mormon's corroborating—as a "second witness"—by infallible revelation the entirety of the Bible. The congruence between the Book of Mormon's Isaiah and modern Old Testament translations has thus given Mormons scriptural reading traditions that range from outpacing Evangelical Christians in their literalism, to denying the authenticity of the entire work, doubting the writings of Isaiah (and Deutero-Isaiah) given in the Hebrew Bible. Isaiah in the Book of Mormon creates divisions among readers, then. Neither reading, however, takes into account what else the Book of Mormon has to say about the writings compiled into the Christian Bible, nor figures in its promises of books (like so many!) yet forthcoming. Shaping the trajectories of these readings are interpretations of the noun *restoration*—used in the Book of Mormon variously, as this chapter will show. One trajectory brought the Book of Mormon into alignment with Christian movements long concerned with their own ideas of restoration. Another trajectory relies on the book's own definition of "restoration," as we'll see, which cannot be enjoyed by Israel without these promised books. That is to say, it matters whether the Bible and the Book of Mormon as "one record" fulfill prophecy, or whether the Book of Mormon urges readers to look for books other than the Bible, in order to restore the House of Israel.

The Book of Mormon builds over the course of six hundred pages a theory of restoration which may altogether differ from any known traditions predating the nineteenth century. Whatever restoration is found here, of a people no longer confounded, it cannot happen without another book or two, as explained in the Second Book of Nephi. Just before his death in the Promised Land some forty years later, Lehi gathered these same sons, and pronounced blessings upon them. His youngest son, Joseph, was tied not only by name but also by blessing and prophecy to another Joseph who figures prominently in the Plates of Brass:

> And now, behold, my son Joseph, after this manner did my father of old prophesy. Wherefore, because of this covenant thou art blessed; for thy seed shall not be destroyed, for they shall hearken unto the words of the book. And there shall rise up one mighty among them, who shall do much good, both in word

and in deed, being an instrument in the hands of God, with exceeding faith, to work mighty wonders, and do that thing which is great in the sight of God, unto the bringing to pass much restoration unto the house of Israel, and unto the seed of thy brethren (2 NEPHI 3:22-24).

Here we learn that after hearing the words of "the book," presumably the same one mentioned in earlier verses, "one mighty" will rise up to work wonders and bring restoration, whatever that may be. Mormons did and continue to regard that book as the Book of Mormon, the very book which came about bearing this translation of Lehi's blessing. The evidence is not conclusive, however, for identifying the Book of Mormon as the book that so interests the seed of Joseph, nor for Joseph Smith being the mighty seer who brings it out of darkness. Lehi claims that a Joseph carried captive into Egypt obtained a promise from the Lord (a garbled version seems to have made its way into GENESIS), that his descendants would see the Messiah, "in the spirit of power, unto the bringing them out of darkness into light," and turn from "captivity unto freedom" (2 NEPHI 3:5). The prophecy reportedly taken from the Brass Plates is not, let's say, entirely clear about who and what brings about their liberation. Nor precise about how the seed of Joseph, son of Lehi, descendant of Egypt's Joseph fits into our ethnic, racial, geographic, or genetic classifications. Lehi mentions a seer "out of the fruit of thy loins," who brings Lehi's surviving descendants "to the knowledge of the covenants which I [God] have made with thy [Joseph's] fathers" (2 Ne.3:7). He has no other work to do—not the founding of a church, nor the restoration of earlier churches, neither running for president. His work is, Lehi recites the promise of the Lord, to "bring forth my word unto the seed of thy [Joseph's] loins," and not only this, but "to the convincing them of my word which shall have already gone forth among them" (2 Ne.3:11). So we find that restoration of the House of Israel requires two divine books, described in verse twelve as one written by the "fruit of thy [Joseph's] loins," and another, preceding this Josephite text, "written by the fruit of the loins of Judah." Tradition names these two the Book of Mormon and the Holy Bible.

But. There is a stated effect we can use to test this identification, fortunately. After they "shall grow together," then is the "confounding of false doctrines and laying down of contentions, and establishing peace among the fruit of thy loins, and bringing them to the knowledge of their fathers in the latter days, and also to the knowledge of my covenants, saith the Lord." While no deadlines are set for when this blessed day should dawn, it seems rather certain that no such event has occurred, wherever the Bible and the Book of Mormon have been stitched into a single volume. If the effect is not observed, we have a duty to doubt the accuracy of the traditional identification of these two books. Moreover, the description of the seer seems doubtfully to depict Joseph Smith: "out of weakness he shall be made strong, in that day when my work shall commence among all my people, unto the restoring thee, O house of Israel," (v.13), for "they that seek to destroy him shall be confounded" (v.14). Given that Smith was murdered in 1844, I think it is safe to doubt he is that seer, thereby throwing further into question the received tradition that names the Bible the writings of Judah, and the Book of Mormon as the writings of Joseph. Indeed, it seems a little boastful, and something of a dead end, to have a prophecy about a book in the very book prophesied about: but that is circular self-satisfaction of tradition for you. When concocted by the earliest readers, however, we can see that such an interpretation made a bit more sense: Joseph was alive, he was the only seer around, and the Bible was still highly regarded as history and prophecy. Today, well, things have changed. That the reading continues today is merely our recitation of tradition, and less deserving of forbearance.

This seer is seemingly named in verse fifteen as Lehi quotes Joseph of Egypt: "his name shall be called after me; and it shall be after the name of his father." Here is the only reason—note, the single, perhaps too definite, reason—for naming Joseph Smith, Jr., as this seer. Nothing else seems to fit, given the benefit of historical perspective. One can see, however, how Mormon tradition began in 1829 by naming Smith as that seer, after doing some genetic gymnastics awarding him descent from Joseph of Egypt (through Lehi, no less, in 1830 regarded as father of American Indians). Yet nothing else in the prophecy conforms to his biography—he being dead some fifteen decades, and the remnant of Joseph being a title applied wherever one finds converts: neither peace nor purity has blossomed among its readers (in any manner differing from their non-believing neighbors, I mean). That fifteenth verse, moreover, continues, "he shall be like me [Joseph]: for the thing which the Lord shall bring forth by his hand, by the power of the Lord, shall bring my people unto salvation" (v.15). Given we have no proven, stable definition of "my people," nor even of "salvation"—which are not also definitions reworked whenever situations demand—it may be wisdom to put off slotting this one and that one into Lehi's prophecy. What we can say is that some books bring about restoration of Israel, and that one can doubt Israel has been restored by the Book of Mormon being stitched to the Bible. Only when we rename Israel as "Church," and call "peace" among the fruit of the loins of

Joseph (let's say, Native Americans) something like rampant diabetes, depression, alcoholism, poverty, and reservation living, can we seriously say the traditional reading of Lehi's promise to his son Joseph has been fulfilled. I mention this promise because it concerns restoration, and is the first opening to an alternative reading of the Book of Mormon. The traditional reading also shows itself to be riding on the proof of durability, that it can be found being taught by Mormons today is its only proof.

We are given somewhat more understanding about how the book of Joseph comes to be: "It will be given unto him, that he shall write the writing of the fruit of thy loins, unto the fruit of thy loins; and the spokesman of thy loins shall declare it" (v.18). Mormons identified this seer-writer as Joseph Smith, Jr., and the spokesman variously as Oliver Cowdery or Sidney Rigdon. But these roles were reversed in history: Smith was the voice, while Cowdery and Rigdon, among others, were scribes writing his words. Cowdery and Rigdon, moreover, also prophesied and had visions. This misplacement of Cowdery as spokesman had real consequences. It was the identification of Cowdery, initially, which directed him to the mission to the "Lamanites" in fall of 1830. Taken up in later chapters more fully, that mission resulted in Smith moving to Kirtland among Campbellites-Mormonites, and side-by-side Sidney Rigdon. Much of what I describe over the next chapters I give as evidence, moreover, against the traditional reading naming Cowdery the seer's scribe, and the Book of Mormon the instrument for making delightsome those Lamanites.

As I said, my version is not orthodox, but I believe it has the support of both history and text. There are problems with the received tradition, obviously, and the stability of the tradition must be accounted for in my history. One must first realize that the Book of Mormon's earliest readers, few and far between even among "converts," located themselves on a map brought over from Christian tradition. They were to restore primitive Christianity. Fitted to this map were a few terms and phrases from the Book of Mormon: restoration, Israel, Abraham, baptism. Nothing is found in the 1830s that looks like a careful exposition of that book's purpose, message, and promises. Hardly any Mormons read it through, before finding in it their New Testament metatext confirmed. To wait for future books, other seers, and build a readership able to endure the long haul of centuries was not, apparently, a notion widely espoused by Mormons. They found their own people in the prophecies—Lo, the Indians are Lamanites, and Smith this seer—and looking to a near future apocalypse or millennium, they figured two decades would round out the world's history. And so readings which began by looking forward are now all looking backward, guesses turned into traditions. Yet none of the promised events have occurred. Their absence is reason enough to reconsider the traditional readings of these prophecies. A question is all I can seriously hope to raise, at this point, before returning to the matter of Restoration.

Near the end of his life, Lehi's son Nephi would further sketch the social environment that marks the beginning of the restoration of the House of Israel. Prior to the emergence of a seer of the line of Joseph of Egypt, we find that "it must needs be that the Gentiles be convinced also that Jesus is the Christ, the Eternal God" (2 NEPHI 26:12). Their convincing comes "by the power of the Holy Ghost," and only "according to their faith" (v.13). So Nephi begins a final prophecy by again expanding on Isaiah, "concerning the days when the Lord God shall bring these things forth unto the children of men" (v.14). Identifying antecedents is a problem on nearly every page, and here one is at a loss to find which "things," so long as one looks backwards at preceding passages. Rather, "these things" refers to events Nephi describes thereafter, when "the seed of my brethren shall have dwindled in unbelief, and shall have been smitten by the Gentiles," yet "all those who have dwindled in unbelief shall not be forgotten" (v.15). Their restoration comes by a rather circuitous path. Nephi claims, "those who shall be destroyed shall speak unto them out of the ground" (v.16). But "them out of the ground" cannot refer to those dwindling in unbelief, for "They [the destroyed] shall write the things which shall be done among them, and they shall be written and sealed up in a book, and those who have dwindled in unbelief shall not have them, for they seek to destroy the things of God" (v.17). This prohibition is a critical part of the argument that the Book of Mormon was not supposed to go to "the Lamanites," however defined. It would seem instead that they were forbidden to have "them," that is, the writings (and not merely "the book" or the metal plates, at least not before they receive other writings, that is). So it makes sense that Mormons do not have very clear ideas about exactly who are those having "dwindled in unbelief." Some other book is given for their restoration, but that book does not yet exist. Restoration remains rather distant, it would seem.

At this point the prophecy seems to take a detour through the foolishness of the Gentiles, "lifted up in the pride of their eyes," they have "stumbled because of the greatness of their stumbling block" (v.20). It is the removal of that block which anticipates the release of other books. So what is that block? Here we encounter a tragic irony. The very thing which frames the Book of Mormon for its earliest and most recent readers, is the same thing they stumble over. In an early vision, Nephi charged a particular text with being that stumbling block: one which "hath gone forth through the hands of the great and abominable church," immediately following the Crucifixion, and which institution removed "plain and precious things" and took away "many covenants of the Lord" from "the book of the Lamb of God" (1 NEPHI 13:26-28). What happens after this editing is unclear, but it is said to have been undertaken in order to "pervert the right ways of the Lord, that they might blind the eyes and harden the hearts of the children of men" (v.27). Another book, apparently imitating the Book of the Lamb, instead "goeth forth unto all nations of the Gentiles," with the effect that "an exceedingly many to stumble, yea, insomuch that Satan hath great power over them" (v.29). Here is Terryl Givens's supposed paradox, although I cannot see the Book of Mormon seeking to redeem the book of the Great and Abominable Church, so much as eliminate its evils. How?

Nephi later learns that the stumbling block of the Bible is diminished only after "much of my gospel" is given to the Gentiles, out of mercy (1 Ne.13:34). That "much" is to be identified, presumably, with content in the Book of Mormon, as Mormon tradition generally asserts. With "much of my gospel," the Gentiles may begin to show faith in its depicted god, working wonders for their delight and joy, showing mercy to the softening of their hearts. Not all the stumbling blocks are removed with the Book of Mormon's publication: "it shall come to pass, that if the Gentiles shall hearken unto the Lamb of God in that day, that he shall manifest himself unto them in word, and also in power, in very deed, unto the taking away of their stumbling blocks—and harden not their hearts against the Lamb of God, they shall be numbered among the seed of thy [Nephi's] father [i.e., Lehi]" (1 Ne.14:1-2). The Book of Mormon is merely the beginning. Here we find three distinct manifestations: word, power, deed. Let us identify the "much" of the Book of Mormon as the word; the "power" with something not yet known, though I offer a guess later in this chapter; and "deed" with a "marvelous work" not yet begun.

The Book of Mormon is, in this reading, the first of three great wonders concluding with the restoration of the House of Israel. Its namesake, Mormon, claims the book contains "the gospel of Christ, which shall be set before you; not only in this record but also in the record which shall come unto the Gentiles from the Jews, which record shall come from the Gentiles unto you." Here we have another passage that seems to invite readers to cling to their Bibles. Writing in the fourth century of the Common Era, Mormon probably does not mean the Holy

Bible, however; which book Nephi calls a stumbling block designed to captivate and bring humanity under Satan's rule, and which was, in any case, already among those regarded as Gentiles. Some other book will go from the Jews to the Gentiles: a restoration of what Nephi names the Book of the Lamb of God, long ago corrupted into the Gentile Bible for the purpose of hardening hearts and blinding the eyes.

"Because of the greatness of their stumbling blocks," Nephi continues, "they have built up churches," and "put down the power and miracles of God," preaching their "own wisdom and learning," expressly for the purpose that "they may get gain and grind upon the face of the poor" (2 NEPHI 26:20). These churches predate and also coincide with the gift of "much" of the gospel given in the Book of Mormon, a first attempt to pick the Bible's lock on Christianity. These churches cause strife and seem to work alongside "secret combinations," by which the Devil "leadeth them by the neck with a flaxen cord, until he bindeth them with his strong cords forever" (v.22). In a remarkable linguistic twist, most philologists find the word *religion* coming from Latin *re-ligare*, to tie and tie again, like a ligature; and what finer cord to tie souls with, than words bearing thoughts, and imaginations constructed from subtle texts?

His mention of the dark ways of the Devil seems to invite a contrast, so Nephi explains how the Lord God "worketh": first, "not in darkness"; second, he "loveth the world, even that he layeth down his own life,"; third, his economy differs from ours, for he says, "Come unto me, all ye ends of the Earth, buy milk and honey, without money and without price"; fourth, salvation is given "free for all men," and "all men are privileged the one like to other, and none are forbidden," neither Jew nor Gentile or heathen; fifth, furthering the contrast with Satanic churches and combinations, is that God "commandeth that there shall be no priestcrafts," men who set themselves as a "light unto the world, that they may get gain and praise of the world" (2 Ne.26:23-33). Having condemned, it would seem, religion itself as we understand it, Nephi foresees "all the nations of the Gentiles and also the Jews . . . upon all the lands of the earth, they will be drunken with iniquity and all manner of abominations" (2 Ne.27:1). It is to these besotted souls that the Book of Mormon is prescribed, though its medicine comes in a child's dose.

So Nephi again draws from Isaiah, noting that the "Lord hath poured out upon you the spirit of deep sleep. For behold, ye have closed your eyes, and ye have rejected the prophets, and your rulers; and the seers hath he covered because of your iniquity" (v.5). In their coma, and finally addressed as "you," the "Lord

God shall bring forth unto you the words of a book, and they shall be the words of them which slumbered" (v.6). Having already explained the role of the Book of Mormon, this later book expands from much to very much indeed: for "in the book shall be a revelation from God from the beginning of the World to the ending thereof" (v.7). Despite this description not matching at all the content of the Book of Mormon, tradition nonetheless identifies the Book of Mormon again as this book, and Joseph Smith as the man to whom "the book shall be delivered" (v.9). But, Nephi notes, "because of the things which are sealed up, the things which are sealed shall not be delivered in the day of the wickedness and abominations of the people. Wherefore the book shall be kept from them" (v.8). So, rather than face the possible problem of being in wickedness and full of abomination, early Mormons instead put on a smile, preached and baptized, regarding some others as wicked, and themselves the righteous, blessed with the unsealed Book of Mormon. Having seldom read that book, one can see how they might overlook the absence of a revelation of God from the beginning of the world to the ending of it. This marvelous book, however, would seem to be the one mentioned by Lehi in his promise to Joseph, which has a seer (defined in the Book of Mormon as one who uses "the interpreters," seeing stones designed for translating languages) and a spokesman. Nephi concludes with a passage mirroring ISAIAH 29. He foretells, "the book shall be delivered to a man, and he shall deliver the words of the book, which are words of those who have slumbered in the dust, and he shall deliver these words unto another" (v.9). What follows this passage in Nephi's prophecy is a series of exchanges of words and books: to one man, one learned, then another, unlearned, three witnesses and others witnesses, which tale I will not discuss here (although, I expect to take up the matter in a later essay). It is merely to be noted that Mormons have identified all the characters in this prophecy, as, yes, Joseph Smith (and his companions) and the Book of Mormon. That tradition may well be correct. Or not. When in doubt, fill in the line with Smith's name, and that book, and carry on. What can be stated is that Nephi's prophecy concludes with a cause and effect statement: the sealed book comes forth, "written unto the Gentiles," is sealed up again, and its unsealed words are carried "unto the remnant of our seed" (2 Ne.30:3). The effect of this book—that "the gospel of Jesus Christ shall be declared among them"— restores them also to "the knowledge of their fathers," for which they rejoice (v.5). They become "pure and delightsome"; the Jews "shall begin to believe in Christ," being convinced, apparently, by the two books running as one (v.6-7). No such transformations, I can safely assert, have been seen by me in my lifetime. The "restoration of his people," that is, of the Lord's people, commences only after these books come forth, although to what they are restored is no more clear now, than it was several pages ago. Presumably that matter is at last answered in these other books: the last ones which establish the truth of the first.

As our concern here is with the term *Restoration*, and not necessarily with sealed books and prophets, except as they restore knowledge to readers, let us move on from Nephi to later prophets who explain what restoration is, and how knowledge brings it about. Other Book of Mormon prophets do confirm this interpretation: that it is by books filled with good words that restoration will come to the House of Israel. Himself regarded as a "Lamanite" by Book of Mormon authors, Samuel was told by an angel, apparently, to warn the inhabitants of the city of Zarahemla that if they failed to repent, they would be destroyed during the tumults of the Crucifixion. Not all would be destroyed; their "brethren, the Lamanites" would remain on the land, long after the Nephites were exterminated. "Yea, even if they should dwindle in unbelief the Lord shall prolong their days," Samuel taught what must have seemed absurd fancies to the Nephites. Their enemy the Lamanites would live, "until the time shall come which hath been spoken of by our fathers, and also by the prophet Zenos, and many other prophets, concerning the restoration of our brethren, the Lamanites, again to the knowledge of the truth" (HELAMAN 15:11). Although "driven to and fro upon the face of the earth," and hunted, smitten, "scattered abroad, having no place for refuge, the Lord shall be merciful to them" (v.12). How is this mercy dispensed? In words: for "they shall again be brought to the true knowledge, which is knowledge of their Redeemer, and their great and true shepherd, and be numbered among his sheep" (v.13). There is a logic to all this restoration by words. Recall that Gentiles were brought into captivity by a corrupted book, and will be made free by its restoration? The reverse, but not the opposite, is true of Lamanites. These not-yet enlightened souls descend from Lamanites long ago brought to a knowledge of the true god through the preaching of the gospel drawn from the Plates of Brass. Their story is given in the Book of Mormon, which also recounts their fall away from that truth into their current benighted state, awaiting their people's restoration.

First among these preachers was Abinadi, made a martyr several generations before Samuel. In MOSIAH we find the words of Abinadi, which declare in contradiction with Mormon theology, apparently, that "God himself shall come down among the children of men, and shall redeem his people," being called "the Son of God" as well as "the Father": "one God," not two, "yea, the very

Eternal Father of Heaven and Earth" (MOSIAH 15:1-4). As Givens noted above, the Book of Mormon seems to teach a different theology than one propounded by Mormon theologians and professors of religion.[1] (Let us move on with the text and its theory of restoration, and leave theology for another essay.) Humans become the children of God (and of the Son of God, perhaps) not by some ritual, Abinadi explains, but in the same manner by which one becomes a son of perdition: by believing specific statements (MOSIAH 15:11). In this case, Abinadi speaks of the words of the prophets who reveal the word of God, received directly; as well as those read from the Plates of Brass (from which text he preaches). Among his audience is one Alma, a priest of wicked King Noah (not the ark builder) who eventually puts Abinadi to the flame. Moved by Abinadi's teachings, Alma forsook wickedness and the lucre and fame obtained by priestcraft. His own son will later teach from the Plates of Brass, bringing many Lamanites— presumably, Samuel among them—into kinship with God. This relation brings paternal mercy to them, leading at last to their resurrection (v.21-22). "And these are they," Abinadi concludes, "who have part in the first resurrection; and these are they that have died before Christ came, in their ignorance, not having salvation declared unto them. And thus the Lord bringeth about the restoration of these; and they have a part in the first resurrection, or have eternal life, being redeemed by the Lord" (v.24).

Alma son of Alma the priest later taught about the power of words to graft one into the line of God. He used the image of a tree growing, from a seed of faith planted in the soul, into a fruitful tree of life (ALMA 32). His words took root in one Amulek, who instructed a sophist named Zeezrom on the nature of God. "Is the Son of God the very eternal father?" Zeezrom inquired (ALMA 11:38).

---

[1] Some of its more problematic declarations were resolved, however, by adding "clarifying" insertions. One such fix in 1837 revised Nephi's vision of the condescension, crucifixion and resurrection of God, adding "son of" multiple times before the phrase "everlasting God." These alterations do not trouble Terryl Givens, who somehow finds the text in conformity with some vague "first principles from the New Testament." Of course, the revisions were made precisely to make the book fit a certain reading of the New Testament, as we'll see. If one's text does not conform to metatext, I suppose one can always revise the original, add a chapter introduction, or maybe another god where two are better than one. More often than not, one can count on metatext to conceal passages not altogether in conformity with one's doctrinal, and redundantly titled, "first principles." Givens did admit in that same passage, while "The Book of Mormon has had a tremendous role to play in the establishment of the Latter-day Saint church . . . . This role appears to have little or nothing to do with particular doctrines that are explicitly taught in the revealed record" (*By the Hand of Mormon,* 196).

"Yea, he is the very eternal father of Heaven and of Earth," echoing Abinadi's theology in reply, "and all things which in them are; he is the beginning and the end, the first and the last" (v.39). This god redeems his people, "those who believe on his name: and these are they that shall have eternal life, and salvation cometh to none else" (v.40). Blessed to be judged by a merciful judge, these believers are resurrected, and "the spirit and the body shall be reunited again in its perfect form," as though in the beginning we *were* made perfect (v.43). "Now this restoration," he explains, "shall come to all, both old and young, both bond and free, both male and female, both the wicked and the righteous" (v.44). Restoration seems rather greater than the lifting of words from an old book, and making one's biograpy and body its metatext. Rather, body is restored to perfection when biography shows the fruits of hearing and believing the many words attributed to God. Books like the Brass Plates carry those words, and their restoration begins this full restoration.

We have in the Book of Mormon absolutely clear definitions, and not merely mention or usage, of *restoration*. Alma's son, also called Alma, explained that his own preaching was accomplished among the Lamanites, "even to the restoration of many thousands of the Lamanites to the knowledge of the truth," and that God "hath shown forth his power in them, and he will also still show forth his power in them unto future generations: therefore, they shall be preserved" (ALMA 37:19). It would seem this is the "power" that follows the "word" identified with the Book of Mormon, as discussed above. In agreement with his earlier teaching, this same Alma explains to his own son Corianton that the reuniting of the "soul and body," brought "to stand before God, and be judged according to their works," that "this bringeth about the restoration of those things which has been spoken by the mouths of the prophets" (ALMA 40:21-22). In case his son missed the definition, Alma reiterates the definition: "The soul shall be restored to the body, and the body to the soul . . . And now, my son, this is the restoration, of which has been spoken by the mouths of the prophets" (v.23-24). After this restoration, "then shall the righteous shine forth in the Kingdom of God" (v.25). In case his son missed the definition, Alma again returns to the matter of restoration: "for behold, some have wrested the scriptures, and have gone far astray because of this thing" (ALMA 41:1). He explains that "the plan of restoration is requisite with the justice of God: for it is requisite that all things should be restored to their proper order" (v.2). As if his son has been put under the spirit of deep sleep, Alma states it as plainly as can be: "the meaning of the word *restoration* is *to bring back again*: evil

- 53 -

for evil, or carnal for carnal, or devilish for devilish; good for that which is good, righteous for that which is righteous, just for that which is just, merciful for that which is merciful" (ALMA 41:13). The father generalizes the effects of restoration in a way not unfamiliar to professors of karma: "that which ye do send out shall return unto you again, and be restored; therefore, the word *restoration* more fully condemneth the sinner, and justifieth him not at all" (v.15). Thus, good books are brought back, and good souls long ago made perfect are again restored to that state. Workers of evil have their bitter fruits returned, and the pits they dig for their neighbors will they fall into.

Finally, the book's editor and compiler, Mormon himself, addressed the Gentiles directly, commanding them to repent of wickedness and abominations, envy and strife, all the evils listed by Nephi some thousand years previous and discussed above (2 NEPHI 30:1-2). Mormon addresses them in the voice of Jesus, in the very book which was to come to them, presumably because as readers they suffer from these ills (and not because they have overcome them, and don't mind hearing how evil *other* Gentiles are, who aren't reading the book). Gentile readers are invited to "come unto me," that is, Jesus, "and be baptized in my name, that ye may receive a remission of your sins, and be filled with the Holy Ghost, that ye may be numbered with my people who are of the House of Israel" (v.2). What is it to be baptized "in my name"? Who is Israel? If we leave behind our Bible metatext, the Book of Mormon becomes very much suggestive, merely "much." Perhaps just enough to shake Gentile readers as gently as possible, to their awakening. Its concluding author, Moroni son of Mormon, addresses "ye unbelieving" readers (MORMON 9:6). In this address he ties together the book's theory of restoration, at last. Unbelievers are asked to turn to the Lord, "that perhaps ye may be found spotless, pure, fair and white," just as was prophesied for those who accept the not-yet-released words from the writings of Judah and of Joseph (v.6). This Lord is not like the god of Gentiles, full of sound and fury, but is a "god of miracles," of healings and tongues and prophecies, "that same god who created the Heavens and the Earth, and all things that in them are. Behold, he created Adam, and by Adam came the Fall of Man. And because the Fall of Man came Jesus Christ, even the Father and the Son; and because of Jesus Christ came the redemption of Man" (v.11-12). If miracles are no longer seen, if "he ceaseth to do miracles among the children of men," the reason is not that he has changed, but "because they dwindle in unbelief" (v.20).

The primary cause of their unbelief is not hard to guess: it is because "they know not the God in whom they should trust" (v.20). Their god is derived from a book designed to captivate their minds, and lead them by subtle chains down to Hell. If its readers knew this true God, and believed in what they learned, they could "ask the Father in the name of Christ," and "it shall be granted him; and this promise is unto all, even to unto the ends of the earth" (v.21). Moroni explains that "these things," namely, what is translated and published in 1830 as the Book of Mormon, "are written that we may rid our garments of the blood of our brethren who have dwindled in unbelief" (v.35). He and his father, among others, have desired "their restoration to the knowledge of Christ" (v.36), a return to wholeness made possible only by those two books—of Joseph and Judah—books currently regarded as the Book of Mormon itself, and the Holy Bible: that great stumbling block to the Gentiles, and cord of their nursing by the Devil.

Not only is the Book of Mormon absent from much of Mormonism, but so is, surprisingly, Joseph Smith himself. Before he ever knew Sidney Rigdon and his Restorationists, Smith apparently told his father that "our Bible is much abridged and deficient," who reportedly said as much to his jailhouse companion, Eli Bruce.[1] The senior Smith was locked up for not paying a debt of exactly four dollars, while Bruce was being held for conspiracy in the abduction of William Morgan, whose disappearance flared up anti-Masonic sentiment. Morgan had written an exposé of Masonry in New York, and Bruce was believed to be involved in his disappearance. To add to the irony, after his induction into Nauvoo's Masonic Order, Joseph Smith, Jr., would later marry Morgan's widow, although she had by that time already been wed to another. Very little about Mormon history is simple, clean, and straight forward, nor without irony.

What further evidence of captivity could you ask for, than the book which explains how the Bible captivates readers would be hailed as a champion of that Bible? Surely the word "stumbling block" does not mean a thing skipped over, with ease, when one is really sincerely trying to be good? We stumble over what we do not see. The translator of that vision of Nephi's, too, was not without a sense of irony. When Joseph Smith preached to believers gathered in June 1830 for the first conference of their Church of Christ (formed in April), his text came not from the Book of Mormon, but from EZEKIEL in the Old Testament. Smith apparently read from chapter fourteen. While the thirty-seventh chapter of EZEKIEL would eventually become a favorite of Mormon preachers, the fourteenth

---

[1] Eli Bruce Diary, 5 Nov 1830. In Dan Vogel, *Early Mormon Documents*, vol.3 (SLC: Signature Books 2000), 4

seems like an odd choice. But maybe not . . . Smith was something of a clever man, and found himself preaching to captives. The text reads, in part:

> Then came certain of the elders of Israel unto me, and sat before me. And the word of the LORD came unto me, saying, Son of man, these men have set up their idols in their heart, and put the stumblingblock of their iniquity before their face: should I be enquired of at all by them? Therefore speak unto them, and say unto them, Thus saith the Lord GOD; Every man of the house of Israel that setteth up his idols in his heart, and putteth the stumblingblock of his iniquity before his face, and cometh to the prophet; I the LORD will answer him that cometh according to the multitude of his idols; That I may take the house of Israel in their own heart, because they are all estranged from me through their idols.
>
> Therefore say unto the house of Israel, Thus saith the Lord GOD; Repent, and turn yourselves from your idols; and turn away your faces from all your abominations. For every one of the house of Israel, or of the stranger that sojourneth in Israel, which separateth himself from me, and setteth up his idols in his heart, and putteth the stumblingblock of his iniquity before his face, and cometh to a prophet to enquire of him concerning me; I the LORD will answer him by myself: And I will set my face against that man, and will make him a sign and a proverb, and I will cut him off from the midst of my people; and ye shall know that I am the LORD. And if the prophet be deceived when he hath spoken a thing, I the LORD have deceived that prophet, and I will stretch out my hand upon him, and will destroy him from the midst of my people Israel (v.1-11).

Twelve years later Smith would read the same passage from EZEKIEL to a gathering of women, this time commenting on its meaning. As reported in the Nauvoo Relief Society Minutes, Joseph "Said the Lord had declared by the prophet that the people should each one stand for himself and depend on no man or men in that state of corruption of the Jewish Church." Rather than a historical exposition, Smith "applied it to the present state of the church of Latter Day Saints—Said if the people departed from the Lord, they must fall." And where had they failed? Smith told them "that they were depending on the prophet hence were darkened in their minds from neglect of themselves."[1]

---

[1] Relief Society Meeting Minutes, 26 May 1842. In Ehat and Cook, ed., *The Words of Joseph Smith* (Deseret Book Company, First Computer Edition 1996), 120.

Restoration is tricky business: evil for evil, good for good. Early readers of the Book of Mormon surely read all the same passages given above, but came to different conclusions. By the end of the first decade of Mormonism, one hears it regularly propounded that Mormons are the House of Israel restored, and that their task is the conversion of Gentiles in Europe, India, and Asia to the "fullness of the gospel." Gentiles became identified with those not reading the book. Mormons apparently regarded passages addressing Gentiles as not really speaking to them, but to imagined, potential converts among Gentiles nations. Sort of like gossiping about them, I guess. When one converted, the book no longer concerned that reader, except as he or she hoped to bring other Gentiles to be numbered among the House of Israel. As we'll see in a later volume, Brigham Young eventually worked out a queer theory of eugenics that rendered every Mormon convert a covert Israelite, and every soul who does not believe the Book of Mormon as being a Gentile. A convenient theory, no doubt, but one impossible to disprove or falsify. It also confounds the Book of Mormon, giving its stated audience as the Gentiles.

Mormon historians also claim that early Mormonism is distinct from other Restoration movements because it had an "Old Testament orientation," namely this concern with the House of Israel. But what did they mean by "House of Israel"? Grant Underwood (professor of history at BYU) includes in his work on early Mormon millennialism a series of tables that display his assessments of the "Principal Themes" of sermons and writings, "Based on Classification of Book of Mormon Passages Cited."[1] Not surprisingly, "Restoration of Israel" tops the chart. "Prophecies relating to the restoration of Israel," Underwood summarizes, "and the fate of the Gentiles were by far the principal interests of the early Saints" (96). The tables Underwood gives rely on criteria he does not state; and so we are left wondering how he decided such and such a sermon was indeed related to prophecies concerning the House of Israel. That is, his classifications are based on his own sense of what the texts mean—derived from Mormon tradition, no less— and not really about how the sermons were interpreted by their hearers in the 1830s. To give you a sense of how convoluted the terminology of their day was, consider this quote from Richard Bushman: "Joseph [Smith] characterized [Joseph] Knight as a Universalist; Knight spoke of himself as a 'Restorationar,' one

---

[1] Underwood, *Millennial World,* 79

who believed all would be saved after a period of punishment."[1]   Knight apparently advocates principles Smith considered "Universalist," which our historian has defined as comprehensive salvation.    But he has defined "Universalist," not "restorationar"; presumably one who attempts to restore the primitive Christian church.  So terms self-applied or for classifying others are not always transparently meaningful; apparently one could be both, or not know the "correct" meaning.  Indeed, adding to our confusion, Bushman explains in a note, "For other Christians, the word 'restoration' meant the restoration of the New Testament church.  For early Mormons, restoration first meant restoring Israel. This gave Mormonism a strong Old Testament cast from the beginning" (585, n.75). He directs us to seek for answers in Jan Shipps's *Sojourner*.  The same story is told by Grant Underwood, who claims that various ceremonies conducted at the Kirtland, Ohio temple (completed in 1836) "reinforced in LDS minds the reality of their identity as modern Israel" (71).

These sorts of claims made by historians of Mormonism make too much of the whole "we are Israel restored" gasconade of early Mormons.  They learned to speak of being Israel from other Christians, primarily from Restorationists. Most Christian Restorationists, Primitivists, and other –ists related to some project of restoration, considered themselves a new Israel, under a new covenant.  When they turned to the Old Testament, they did so as Christians: using Israel as a biblical name for their church.  Puritans apparently believed they were the newest Israel, setting forth on this continent under a covenant with God (so witches were put on notice), because the old Israel, England, had failed to keep its covenant with God.  At the same time we find the Covenanters of Scotland signing the National Covenant, called the Confession of Faith of the Kirk of Scotland, in 1639.  It begins by quoting not from the New Testament, but from JOSHUA 24:25, "So Joshua made a covenant with the people that day, and set them a statue and an ordinance in Shechem."  Added to this apparently unique orientation to the Old Testament, and to being a people of the true covenant religion—"this only is the true Christian faith and religion, pleasing God, and bringing salvation to man, which is now, by the mercy of God, revealed to the world by the preaching of the blessed evangel"—was a passage describing the covenant made by Jehoiada "between the Lord and the king and the people, that they should be the Lord's people" (2 KINGS 11:17).   Finally, the Covenant quotes from what Mormon historians would have you believe is something of a uniquely Mormon concern, the words of Isaiah prophesying about how "another shall subscribe with

---

[1] Bushman, *Rough Stone Rolling*, 114

his hand unto the Lord, and surname himself by the name of Israel" (ISAIAH 44:5).

This National Covenant was merely the latest such covenant passed around Scotland, where calling yourselves a new Israel hardly showed original thinking. The Dutch did it, so did Anabaptists. It is hard to find a movement which didn't talk of some covenant, and of being Israel restored. But among the Scots so many of these movements converged and collided. Their latest national covenant was signed by half a million Scots in rebellion to Acts of Uniformity passed by King Charles I, who was eventually sent on the path to execution after the Covenanters defeated his armies in the Bishops Wars of 1639 and 1640. These wars had their origins in the performance of Mass at St. Giles in Edinburgh, during which an old woman tossed a stool at the bishop (throwing things at Catholics was by then something of a national pastime) and a riot swept through the city. They were certain that Catholicism was not the pure, restored Christianity, and so it must go. Riot turned to war, and outright civil war swept across three kingdoms. These wars would eventually send Alexander Campbell across the waters of the Atlantic, speaking of restoration of ancient things, of Bible words for Bible things, of three orders of priesthoods and new dispensations. So much gravity came of his teachings, so binding were they on body and book, that the Gold Bible itself was turned from its (perhaps confusing) course of restoring the Lamanites to a knowledge of their fathers, and was reset upon the old project of the church's restoration.

To understand Mormonism, Mormon historians who recite tradition; and how the term *restoration* was carried from Christian traditions grounded in the King James Bible, and painted across the Book of Mormon, we must descend among these Scottish Covenanters: from them Alexander Campbell learned about his Bible. From Campbell, Sidney Rigdon received much that would become Mormonism, contriving restoration as he sat scribbling during Joseph Smith's "translation" of the Holy Bible; like some counselor covertly running a kingdom, whispering, seated upon the right hand of the king.

The start — riots set off by Jenny Geddes.

**"A**T THE BEGINNING OF THE NINETEENTH CENTURY," SO ONE WRITER
paints an underdog, log-cabin setting, "a young man without
reputation, living in a remote district, far from the centers of the world's thought,
made an attempt, in many respects not unlike those which had preceded, to bring
about the union of Christians."[1]  This young man preached that union would
proceed from the "Restoration of Ancient Things," a return of the primitive
church of the early Christians.  His mother, we learn from one biographer
enamored of such details, "was tall, but well proportioned, exceeding erect and
dignified in carriage, but, at the same time, modest and remarkably retiring in her
manners and disposition."  Her child was possessed of her "Roman nose, the
expression and color of the eyes, surmounted by prominent frontal developments,
the outline of the mouth, and the general form and character of the face."  His
father, Thomas, was "of medium stature, compactly built, in form and feature
eminently handsome," for his "forehead was somewhat square, and massive, his
complexion fair and ruddy."  Once while at prayer for a stretch longer than his
own father would bear, "on account of his rheumatism," Thomas's father "was so
soon upon his feet that, in a sudden gust of passion, he began greatly to the
surprise and scandal of all present, to belabor poor Thomas with his cane."[2] The
Campbell family was divided over the matter of secession from the Church, it
being held by the cane-wielding father that Parliament and God demanded and

---

[1] W.E. Garrison, *Alexander Campbell's Theology: Its Sources and Historical Setting* (St. Louis:
Christian Publishing Co. 1900), 24

[2] Robert Richardson, *Memoirs of Alexander Campbell, embracing a view of the origin, progress
and principles of the religious reformation which he advocated.* 2 vols. (Cincinnati: Standard
Publishing Co., 1897), 1:20, 21, 24

deserved allegiance. But Thomas Campbell persisted, and entered an Anti-Burgher school of theology in Scotland, where the Bible was again made to speak of reformation. Of Thomas it was said no feature, not even his forehead, marked him more prominently than his reverence for the Holy Word. If asked, Campbell would inform you that he was, therefore, an Old Light Anti-Burgher.

Mormons would come almost a century later, and yet it is from the now obscure history of Scottish religious and political strife that they would inherit much, nearly all, of their tartan-like warp of theology crossed by ritual "primitivism." Uniquely American Religion? How about, Scottish anti-Establishment Dutch – Covenanter, Radical – Reformation – Restorationism, decontextualized upon the American Frontier, added to the portent of the Book of Mormon? But then, what is more American than forgetting one's past, pretending to start over, and taking credit for the whole lot? As Richard T. Hughes, historian of the Disciples of Christ noted in a manual for use in Disciples' Sunday School, "Rather than escaping tradition, we who are heirs of Barton Stone, Alexander Campbell, and David Lipscombe simply have failed to recognize the traditions at work in our midst." Much of what he and C. Leonard Allen write about the Churches of Christ is all too applicable to Mormons: "While imagining that they stood alone, they actually stood shoulder to shoulder with Zwinglians, Puritans, Baptists, and others who also imagined they stood alone."[1]

It remains one the ironies of American religion that movements professing to restore ancient history also show the least interest in learning history. As Hughes lamented in another book, "Often, these people have argued that they have restored the primitive church of the apostolic age and are therefore nothing more or less than the true, original church described in the New Testament." Enacting rather than understanding, Restorationists, he notes, "have expressed little or no interest in their particular history" and, like Mormons, "remain to this day virtually ignorant of Alexander Campbell." He finds the cause of their ignorance in a "fear that to acknowledge dependence on any human leader would make them a denomination with a human founder rather than the true, primitive church founded by Christ."[2] For Mormons, of course, a human leader like Joseph Smith is central to the ostensible restoration; what are we to make of a Mormonism which, as we'll see, scarcely differs from Campbell's own religion,

---

[1] Richard T. Hughes and C. Leonard Allen, *Discovering Our Roots: The Ancestry of the Churches of Christ* (Abilene TX: ACU Press, 1988), 3

[2] Richard T. Hughes, *Reviving the Ancient Faith: The Story of the Churches of Christ in America* (Grand Rapids MI: William B. Eerdmans Publishing Co., 1996), 2

when Campbell was supposed to be getting it all from the New Testament, but really was not? Here folk notions of revelation, prophets, seers, and the like seem to induce the same ignorance which Hughes finds appallingly common inside his own faith. So like Mormons, members of the Churches of Christ are "susceptible to the illusion that they have escaped the influence of history and culture altogether."[1]

We begin this chapter near Campbell and work backwards. Hughes and Allen would take us back to the Christian humanism of Erasmus, during the late Renaissance; overcompensating for readers' small knowledge of their own faith's origins, in a sort of apology to the muse of history. We need not go back to the first man who pined for a return to the first golden age, in order to understand Christian primitivism, however. Let us begin in eighteenth century Scotland.

Anti-Burghers formed in response to the royal decree that Scottish burgesses could nominate parsons for churches under their domain, and bind them with an oath of faith. It was a revisiting of the Patronage Act of 1711, a ploy to place pro-English or Presbyterian ministers into parish vacancies throughout the kingdom.[2] The bloody covenants that so often rallied Scottish parishes were renewed, vigorously. It is no surprise that the religious revolt followed in step with a peasant uprising against the *Lairds,* who attempted to abolish clans and force shepherding on the Highlands. Here also was Bonny Prince Charlie Stuart, "the Pretender," raising belatedly the Jacobite flag in challenge to the newly ruling House of Hanover, leading an army into England against King George. It seems, however, that Scotland was too fractious, and after disguising the prince as Betty Burke, maid to young Flora MacDonald, the young man ended up in France by 1746. The tartan was then banned for nearly forty years, and the clans failed to be other than so many stripes and shades hatching at cross purposes. Similarly, rather than a unified opposition being its fruit, the question of whether burgesses could nominate parsons split the young Secession Church in 1747, with Anti-Burghers dividing into "Old Light" or "Originals," opposed to the "New Light Burghers"; each insisting on its right to interpret the Bible.[3] These sects were all considered "Scotch Independents," a term uniting three distinct strains opposed to

---

[1] Hughes, *Reviving the Ancient Faith,* 2
[2] Hiram Van Kirk, *A History of the Theology of the Disciples of Christ* (PhD dissertation U Chicago; St. Louis: Christian Publishing Co. 1907), 74
[3] Richardson, *Memoirs,* 1:54-56; Van Kirk, *A History,* 75

Presbyterians and Episcopalians. These Independents are a dominant father of Mormonism.

First of the three strains were the "Old Independents" formed by John Glas (1685-1773), whose primary concern was securing firm division between church and state, so that they might be free to worship. In what manner? "The aim of this body," writes one historian, "was to 'restore the primitive New Testament practices.'"[1] Reformation and restoration were so indistinct before the seventeenth century, that Hughes and Allen actually explain the difference this way:

> The Lutheran approach we will call 'reformation.' It sought to reform and purify the historic, institutional church while at the same time preserving as much of the tradition as possible. The Reformed approach we will call 'restoration.' It sought to restore the essence and form of the primitive church on biblical precedent and example; tradition received scant respect.[2]

The distinction is shown to be ahistorical, a contrivance based on tradition, as soon as one realizes that "to reform and purify the historic" very often means "restore the essence and form of the primitive church." It seems that *reformation* at first meant what was later designated by *restoration*, although the distinction only became one marking different approaches and institutions after Primitivists like the Anabaptists started what others would call the Radical Reformation. Scottish Independents could be considered lesser inheritors of a radical approach, which Paul Tillich explained, came from reformers proclaiming that God spoke through the Holy Spirit directly into their hearts. One very radical reformer-restorer "said it was always possible for the Spirit to speak through individuals,"[3] a notion not entirely in conflict with the teachings of Martin Luther; teachings Tillich summarizes thus: "that anyone today who had the Spirit as powerfully as the prophets and apostles could create new Decalogues and another Testament. We must drink from their fountain only because we do not have the fullness of the Spirit" (243). The important difference, apparently, was not found in the words they used to describe how they hoped to accomplish a break from Rome; but rather in how explicit they were in breaking from their Bibles. For Luther, as

---

[1] Hiram Van Kirk, *A History*, 76

[2] Hughes and Allen, *Discovering Our Roots*, 23

[3] Paul Tillich, *A History of Christian Thought: From its Judaic and Hellenistic Origins to Existentialism.* Carl E. Braaten, ed. (NY: Simon and Schuster 1968), 239

Tillich explains, "the revelation is always connected with the objectivity of the historical revelation of the Scriptures, and not the innermost center of the human soul" (241). Radicals got their name by setting aside their Bibles, when it conflicted with the Spirit, and with the interpretations of scripture sent from the newly powerful state churches of the Reformation. So *Restoration* as a Christian designation came to be divided from *Reformation*, although it is hardly as great as the difference between dogs and wolves. Scottish Independents insisted on being both radical, and firmly grounded *sola scriptura*. Theirs was, as is said of so many, a middle way: the Holy Spirit would inspire readers of the Bible to seek out the correct doctrines and practices in need of restoration. *Restoration* was a popular term at least since the 1660 return of the English monarchy under Charles II; and in its usage we see how religion, book and body, and, of course, politics intertwined. Even restaurants began their reign over dinnertime by speaking of restoration: once a Frenchman named Boulanger advertised his mutton soup as "restorante." Restoration of good health by soup was a claim not without dispute, even, as the *traiteurs*, a catering guild, sued to block his retailing of cooked meat, finally taking the matter in 1765 before the French Parliament.[1] Restoration was first a political doctrine, of course; and like the king, a full-bodied religious matter as well. But it was an aim, a process, a plan; not a thing in itself. The puzzle confronting Scottish Independents concerned what to restore—what names and nouns to take from the Bible. As a minister of the Kirk of Scotland in Tealing, Glas offered his answer, and was suspended in 1728 for it. The matter concerned, again, the separation of church and state.[2] Glas also argued the "rite of communion . . . was not strictly in accordance with the pattern of apostolical churches," and, turning religion into politics, refused admission to the Lord's Supper any supplicant who hankered for one hand to hold both crook and scepter.[3] Glas published a "Letter" quoting many Old Testament scriptures that seemed to argue for a "perpetual obligation" of the Scottish to keep their covenant with God, or suffer as Israel long ago suffered. A state church for Glas would break that everlasting covenant. Although himself said to be very much influenced

---

[1] James Trager, *The People's Chronology*, 311. Historical dates were cross-checked with Trager's volume, itself a gift to the curious reader, although his dates are not always reliable.

[2] Richardson, *Memoirs*, 70

[3] Whitsitt, William, *Origin of Disciples of Christ (Campbellites): A contribution to the centennial anniversary of the birth of Alexander Campbell* (NY: A.C. Armstrong and Son, 1888), 2

by Puritans,[1] Glas thought the Protector Oliver Cromwell "had liv'd a compleat Example of Prudence in Counsel, Valour in the Field, Hypocrisie in the Church, and Wickedness in his Usurpation" (31). So every religious dispute was a political one, during these centuries. So the aim of restoration had sound political motives, namely: unity against the established church, whether the Church of England or the Presbyterian Kirk of Scotland. What was identified as essential to restore was also good for bringing together otherwise fractious clans.

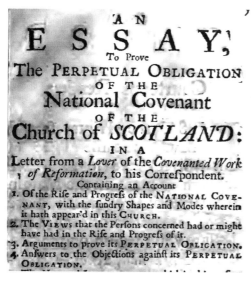

John Glas (1727)

As we'll see, abstract nouns—faith, repentance, revelation, authority, restoration, even experience—these terms brought Christians together, no matter their unique definitions or actual usage. These forms of things were grounded in the Bible, and continued their work wherever readers of it were found. Glas's parishioners practiced much that remained, if only briefly, in Mormonism: the weekly "Lord's Supper," as opposed to the more common quarterly feast; the "kiss of charity" before and after meetings; they practiced "feet washing," collected a "fellowship" for the poor, were administered to by a plurality of "elders" who oversaw a limited "community of goods," and, perhaps less biblically, enjoyed guiltless public amusements like balls and plays. Methodists also carried similar practices into Mormonism, and not coincidentally, Independents and Methodists share common origins. Glas's son-in-law was the notable Robert Sandeman, whose learning laced a Dutch-acquired metaphysic into the restored practices of these independents. His response to James Hervey of Oxford first moved him into public prominence. Hervey deserves brief mention, I suppose.

---

[1] George Richard Phillips, *Differences in the Theological and Philosophical Backgrounds of Alexander Campbell and Barton W. Stone and Resulting Differences of Thrust in Their Theological Formulations.* (PhD Diss Vanderbilt U 1968), 134

With the Wesley brothers, he started a society deemed "Methodists" in the 1730s, so called by schoolboys deriding their too-strict discipline, regular fasting and reading of the New Testament. Scripture would be revived in their own disciplined bodies, and upon their tongues. Charles Wesley even devoted poems and hymns to "Primitive Christianity."[1] Its restoration from text to flesh was the heavy muse feeding his imagination. Hervey's "Dialogues between Theron and Aspasio" argued for experience: a feeling or something tangible: embodiment of one's "adoption" being the path to "saving faith."[2] The body of Christ, then, demanded the body of Bible readers, making of them its metatext. This "sense of adoption" became the foundation of a Methodist's "experimental" conversion. Experiments were all the rage, Oxford and elsewhere. Popularly understood, experiment was not part of a "scientific method," bound up with empiricism and sense impressions, John Locke and Newton as well. Among this new society, *experiment* was the fruit of *experience*. Rather than the effect of experience, Sandeman countered that faith is of the intellect, and comes when truth is apprehended by the mind hearing the Word. Rather than empiricism, he drew from the seventeenth century's reservoir of rationalism (and so deep was it that Campbell also drew many a bucket on the American frontier). The change of heart so eagerly sought by Christian Protestants, having no priesthood to assure their redemption from sin, was, according to Sandeman, an effect of faith; not its cause.[3]

When Joseph Smith walked into the woods for his own spiritual experiment, as many a biographer has noted, he was following good Wesleyan protocol, having admitted a fondness for Methodism. When his walk was said to be inspired by hearing the Word (from JAMES), he was drawing faith from Sandeman, by way of Scots-Irish preachers. That he returned with a tale indicating something beyond a "sense of adoption" was, perhaps, one of those instances were we see how gods delight in answering quaintly innocent questions with definite and yet, for many Mormons, apparently ambiguous answers: They are all wrong, and their creeds an abomination. *Ahem,* yes, *all of them.*

"Sandemanianism" became a by-word among Methodists and Baptists, useful for ignoring anyone advocating that faith came from believing some

---

[1] John H. Yoder, "Primitivism in the Radical Reformation" (in Richard T. Hughes, *The Primitive Church in the Modern World*0), 96 n.37

[2] Winfred Earnest Garrison, *The Sources of Alexander Campbell's Theology* (St. Louis Christian Publishing Co. 1900), 213

[3] Garrison, *Sources of Alexander Campbell's Theology*, 214

testimony.[1]  Sectarian jealousy apparently informed this debate over faith.  The definition offered by Sandeman—both functional and an outcome of hearing the Word preached—made for more converts than did the sometimes too officious "sense" sought by Methodists.  Are you really converted?  I mean, is your heart really changed?  *Fully?*  Not unlike Linus of *Peanuts* awaiting the Great Pumpkin, unsure whether his patch is indeed the most sincerely believing, *really* believing.  One's performance before a board of examiners itself became the sign of faith in Methodism.  Again ritualism—patterned forms representing the validity of content—rescued supplicants flailing under the surveillance of committees and self-induced examination.  That, and, as we'll see, merely fabricating an experience.  How one told it, I mean, was as important to Methodists as the experience one confessed.

By contrast, faith under Scottish Independents could be generated by one doing the examining, namely, the preacher.  These same preachers would baptize, too, providing a one-stop-saving experience.  Engineered for moving quickly through society, Sandeman's evangelism—as church building, and, possibly, nation making—spread among Independents; and also saturated the seminaries its faithful had sponsored across Scotland.  Campbell studied Sandeman's writings in these seminaries, concluding that indeed "faith is the belief of testimony.  Where testimony begins, faith begins."[2]  Through Campbell this definition came to Sidney Rigdon, and it was formalized and elaborated in the Mormon *Lectures on Faith*.  A series of essays not entirely consistent in their definition and theory of faith, composed, some say, by Joseph Smith, others by Sidney Rigdon, the uneven text enjoys quasi-canonical status in Mormonism.  Given the grand autopoetic status allotted faith in the first lecture, and its diminishing potency over the course of five others, it seems reasonable that both Smith and Rigdon contributed.  The third lecture begins,

> Let us here observe, that three things are necessary in order that any rational and intelligent being may exercise faith in God, unto life and salvation.  First, the idea that he actually exists.  Second, a correct idea of his character, perfections, and attributes.  Thirdly, an actual knowledge that the course of life which he is pursuing is according to his will.  For without an acquaintance with these three important facts, the faith of every rational being must be imperfect and unproductive.

---

[1] Phillips, *Differences*, 134
[2] Garrison, *Sources of Alexander Campbell's Theology*, 217

Idea, correct idea, actual knowledge: three conditions of faith, and nowhere is experience, sense of adoption, or anything not attributed to the mind. Where to get these ideas? Rigdon regarded the scriptures as providing reliable testimony regarding the only suitable object of one's faith: thus "we have been indebted to a revelation which God made of himself to his creatures," citing JOB and CORINTHIANS as giving examples of revelation.[1] Hence Mormons adopted Sandeman's definition, conveniently severed of its dialogue with Methodism. (Though it continued to irritate Methodists' ears out on the frontier.) While lost on a few Mormon historians too eagerly embracing the demonstrably false notion that their religion somehow drew from untapped wells, pure and refreshing in 1830, many inheritances were by one Campbell biographer noticed, even the "sentiment of the Sandemanians in the matter of theatres, dancing, and other diversions, appears to have survived in the Mormon community."[2] These are mere forms, however—words, shapes, gestures, rules—and scarcely were the exclusive practices of Sandemanians. Rather than match up this and that, and speak of "influence," we want to see what these things do: how movements are made as they make metatext.

The second branch of Independents came under the leadership of Archibald McLean, who brought a following from the established Presbyterian Church in 1767. They differed from Glas's group by immersing their bodies when enacting the biblical rite called baptism. Campbell would eventually adopt immersion, as well, but only after he sailed to Pennsylvania. Third in our ancestry are the New Independents: evangelists, formed in rebellion by Robert Haldane after lay preaching was condemned by General Assembly of the Presbyterian Church. Haldane participated with the East India Company, sought and was denied the Church's support of his plan to carry the gospel alongside the faith of quasi-state run corporate capitalism.[3]

Whatever their idiosyncrasies of doctrine, the Bible, obviously, was to be the organizing element among these believers. The Bible metatext, I mean: A structure to train missionaries grew into a seminary system, which was organized

---

[1] Lecture 3: 2-7. Notice the use of "revelation" here to mean, "God revealing himself, as recorded in the scriptures," and not, "a revelation," as in "authoritative declarations about reality."

[2] Whitsitt, *Origins*, 13.

[3] Phillips, *Differences*, 139

in Glasgow around Greville Ewing, a charismatic teacher who guided Alexander Campbell's education.[1] When the younger Campbell crossed the Atlantic and set up pew in Pennsylvania, the political environment which drove his theology was left behind, far across the sea. Hughes and Allen, in that Disciples' Sunday School manual, dismiss the influence of Glas, Sandeman, and Haldane on their faith's founders, finding these men "simply conduits for a perspective rooted deeply in the Puritan past."[2] Alexander Campbell, however, once wrote in a letter (1815) explaining, tongue-in-cheek, "In the first place I became a Scotch Independent, next a Sandemanian, then a Separatist with John Walker, then a Baptist, and am now an Independent, a Sandemanian in faith . . . and a Baptist insofar as respects Baptism."[3]

These terms quickly lost their significance—once rooted in political disputes and bearing theological subtleties—when planted in the frontier. What were religious movements organized for political purposes, with terms backed by long debates and often excruciatingly dull Latin treatises, would become on the frontier strange notions, gilded Pharaoh's barks freighted with Mystery. Where once Restoration was regarded as the only path to unify the Body of Christ politically and religiously (ironically, as noted above, a variant term described the virtues of a gruel made from lamb's meat), it landed in the land of expanding optimism, where unity was more of a burden than an ideal. A frontier between reality and dream, even if only so many Disneylands, here nothing was not achievable, even by the lone mythical individual. Here Restoration became a thing to make for its own sake. Mormons encountered Restoration on the frontier, where politics and religion were less intertwined, and they like others would explain, eventually, that Restoration was necessary because of wholesale Christian "Apostasy." A new dispensation was required, but what "dispensation" meant was a not altogether simple and timeless, either.

## SUGAR AND SLAVES AND NOTHING VERY NICE

Though convenient to ignore the political origins of what would become Mormon theology, one thereby fails to appreciate how completely the Campbell-Rigdon-Restorationists shaped, even overcame, Joseph Smith's then small—and

---

[1] Amos S. Hayden, *Early History of the Disciples of Christ in the Western Reserve, Ohio* (Cincinnati: Chase & Hall, Publishers 1875), 75-77
[2] Hughes and Allen, *Discovering*, 47
[3] 1815. Quoted in Phillips, *Differences*, 132

when it came to theology, mostly unconcerned—loosely knit following. They *were* Mormonism by 1831, and their translation of the Book of Mormon (into metatext) cannot be understood without a brief, bloody tour of Europe. The Scottish Independents that gave us Alexander Campbell, and through him, Sidney Rigdon and the majority of early Mormon leaders, had seceded from John Knox's Established Church, the Kirk of Scotland. Working backward from Thomas Campbell's tutelage under Independents, in 1732 the Erskine brothers orchestrated the "first great schism of the Church of Scotland," and formed a presbytery that became the Independent's Secession Church.[1] Let us jump back two centuries more, to see what was seceded from: for these are the looms that wove theology into politics, biblical phrases into relations of authority; so many blood spattered robes worn by ancient altar-attending priesthoods, forms for the later covering of our early Mormons, dispensing restoration from their new book.

Once a radical reformer, Knox instituted the Calvin-inspired "Covenants" in Scotland by 1557. Covenants were hardly the concern of the English alone, although their version of the Bible—translated by Tyndale and published in the Netherlands—put that theme front and center, suggesting "England was a new Israel."[2] As Tyndale reportedly explained, "if we meek ourselves to God, to keep all his laws after the example of Christ, then hath God bound himself to us, to keep and make good all the mercies promised in Christ throughout the scriptures."[3] Monarchs were put on notice, alongside witches. "The movement was really a rebellion against the regime of the Queen-regent," one historian said, and even Bloody Mary "was compelled to make concessions to it."[4] Mary's position was precarious, following the death of her half-brother Edward VI, under whose reign Tyndale's teachings became popular. Victim of the regular tuberculosis epidemics, in death Edward showed peasants that God no longer discriminates between the royals and everyone else, although a slightly puritanical lifestyle might obtain his favor (or at least limit the spread of germs). Not even the burning of astrology texts, magic treatises, and books on geography averted the contagion. So Catholic Mary was crowned amid another plague, leading radical reformers to suppose, "They had failed to recover the primitive church and now, as a result, God was afflicting them with divine wrath."[5] Many fled to the

---

[1] Hayden, *Early History*, 44; quote taken from Richardson, *Memoirs*, 54
[2] In Allen and Hughes, *Discovering*, 38
[3] Ibid.
[4] Van Kirk, *A History of Theology*, 71
[5] Allen and Hughes, *Discovering*, 44

Netherlands and Holland, or hid among the Swiss reformers' newly unornamented churches, Zwingli setting himself the task of restoring spartan, early Christian interior design.

Mary was wed to Spain's Philip "the inept." Inexplicably the son of a most remarkable, brilliant, but now former Holy Roman Emperor, Philip took over for his father, Charles V, who had the year before resigned, and mostly concerned himself with meditating at a monastery in Estremadura. Mary tied England to Philip's concerns in Spain, the Netherlands, Milan, Naples, and the vast and too bountiful colonies of New Spain. Her reign imposed Roman Catholicism across a landscape only recently, often forcibly, converted to an Anglicanism contrived for Henry VIII. Only a decade before her rule, Anglicanism had gathered political opposition into a religious body, newly quickened by the Act of Uniformity issued in 1549. That Act forbade the use of prayer books other than the Book of Common Prayer composed by Thomas Cranmer, Archbishop of Canterbury. Before the Church of England could be officially established under Elizabeth I, Cranmer would succumb to the flames set by Bloody Mary's religious fervor, faith in one's god being again confused with lacking fealty to a crown. Indeed, the Inquisition had also begun lighting its many pyres, as Pope Paul IV set to build a wall around the Jews of Rome, in that ghetto made to ponder their chosen status.

Under the slightly less bloody reign of Elizabeth I, John Knox drew up a confession of faith denying Roman Catholicism. By such denials he drew confessors to her side, and into political strife with young Mary Queen of Scots. Wed to Francois II (age 14), Mary relied on French, rather than Scottish, troops to press her claim against Elizabeth. In the reddened soil of France the English found plenty of reasons to deny Mary her Catholic reign. Under orders issued by Francois II's brother, French Huguenots were massacred; and they having learned evil, returned it by raping nuns and murdering priests. Brief civil war followed, to the delight of Mary—for it weakened the English Crown's financial standing, as credit across Europe became scarce. Mary's husband was murdered several years later, and after she was captured and forcibly wed in a Protestant church, the Scottish nobles deserted her, as would her head from her own body, by order of Elizabeth. Scotsmen proclaimed her infant son James VI of Scotland.

Ten years after Calvin's Geneva Bible was published in 1560, complete with footnotes and commentary, some disputing the divine right of kings, Huguenots by the tens of thousands were again slaughtered in what is known as the Massacre of St. Bartholomew. The Pope praised Catherine de Medici for her handling of the Calvinist traitors, whose ransacking of monasteries and churches in the Netherlands—war yet again brought famine to already lean peasants—earned them no mercy from the Empire. Forced, rather than incidental, starvation was imposed on Irish rebels in 1580 by the English, opposing by these means the interference of Spanish cross-bearers on their own emerald isle. As below, so above. Mary like so many would lose her too contrary head seven years later, drawing by its rolling the invincible Spanish Armada into sea-battle against the mostly piratical English fleet. It was said that John Dee, magician-mathematician to the Crown, wizard extraordinaire and a friend to peepers and scryers, conjured up a storm to decide the battle. By that wind he set up the English sail for three centuries, another Colossus bestride the world. Their rule finally ran out fittingly, signaled in omen, S by O by S, as the unsinkable Titanic slipped into darkness.

With England gaining power as the 1500s ended, wars spread like locusts across Europe. Slaves and sugar and silver threw economies into tailspins, and tropical diseases made their way through ports and markets, from pews to brothels and high courts. Lucrative Antwerp sugar refineries distributed product from Portuguese slave plantations, one of many fruits of war between Dutch, French, English, Spanish and "the Indians." The "Dutch Golden Age" thus began in war, amid a thirty years war, among other wars. Theories and institutions gilded here would fascinate Mormons, and the modern world itself, centuries later. Rome itself, I suppose, was being restored. Called by one historian Europe's first central bank,[1] the Bank of Amsterdam, for instance, was founded on silver ingots mined by South American slaves (in Latin the term that gave us *Argentina* refers to "glory," as in the glory of the church, its silver). The public regulation of money was revived, even as a plague of madness spread by guessing the value of tulips ran through Holland.

Much else was sprouting, though only later spreading like some mustard seed, thriving in the vast lands of the New World. The Union of Arras (1579) joined Catholic Walloons with Dutch in Hainaut and Artois, and the Dutch Republic was born, first of many. Newspapers, too, began in Antwerp. The dodo was exterminated by Dutch colonists in Madagascar, as slavers spread out from the Gold Coast in search of human capital. Perhaps the scene of Dutch slavers purchasing from the Canarsie Indians the island of Manhattan—for a few trinkets, hair pins and wimples, crimping irons and sixty guilders—represents the spirit of the age: No fools, the Canarsie merely sold lands controlled by the Manados. This

---

[1] Edward Chancellor, *Devil Take the Hindmost: A History of Financial Speculation* (NY: Farrar, Strauss and Giroux, 1999), 9

gilded seventeenth century began with the United East India Company, "the first joint-stock company to receive an official government charter, was established with a monopoly on Eastern trade."[1] Another historian described "the Verenigde Oostindische Companie, known as VOC," as "The most obvious instrument for their ability to create states and wage war in the interest of grasping as much commerce as possible." VOC was essentially a sovereign power free from loyalty to citizen or subject, so all things might bend the knee before its profit.[2] While they cannot claim to have invented the corporation (monasteries were the first), free markets—mostly free from local competition, that is—were one among their many contributions to modern life. The occupation *Capitalist* finally appeared on Dutch tax registers.

With the creation of a money exchange, supported by the state and commercial finance, the Dutch also restored the ancient Roman religion of Speculative Investment, and set their Semper Augustus upon its altar. A tulip, that is; at one time selling for more than a country estate. Beware the fruits of its restoration: "most transactions," writes one historian, "were for tulip bulbs that could never be delivered because they didn't exist and were paid for with credit notes that could never be honoured because the money wasn't there."[3] While one may laugh at their folly today, it was mostly the rising and working classes who were left holding meaningless notes for worthless bulbs.[4] VOC directors and Calvinist merchants took advantage of easy credit and insider knowledge to extract more than florins from the workers; something not less painful and undignifying in 1637 than it was in 2008. Nor many centuries before, even, as when this religion was young. In the Roman Republic the priesthood of the *Quaestor* ("seeker") and his companion *Speculare* arrived. Petronius Arbiter lamented,

---

[1] Chancellor, *Devil Take the Hindmost*, 9

[2] Harold J Cook, *Matters of Exchange: Commerce, Medicine, and Science in the Dutch Golden Age* (New Haven: Yale U Press, 2007), 60

[3] Chancellor, *Devil Take*, 18

[4] *Tulip*, in a strange twist of linguistic fate, was taken from the Turkish *tulipan*, the turban decorated with that flower. Known more for poppy cultivation, and for crashing not merely a market, but the World Trade Center itself—built like a fortress to embody the principles found all along the Dutch's old Wall Street, marking what was once New Amsterdam—the later Taliban seem less likely to spread a madness quite so curable as the one carried along by flower bulbs. Perhaps more bitter is the irony that their name derives from the Pashto word for students, taken from the Arabic *talib*, one who studies the Quran, perhaps seeking to restore Islam to its original, fundamental purity, like a tulip in the early spring. Two things so similar in form, and almost indistinguishable in sound—tulipan and Taliban—could not be more different in their meaning; yet sometimes almost indistinct in their ruinous effects.

"filthy usury and the handling of money had caught the common people in a double whirlpool, and destroyed them . . . the madness spread through their limbs, and trouble bayed and hounded them down like some disease sown in the dumb flesh."[1]

Yet again, but surely not for the last time, professors and politicians in the Netherlands convinced their fellows through print, pulpit, and appeals to "common sense," that self-interest, being "natural law" and newly fancied up by the French as *amour-propre*—really just naked greed—that vice itself was converted by the market into so many public virtues. Not even churchmen blanched at the laurels again set upon greed. The wars with Catholic Spain led to loosened restrictions on usury, which if otherwise engaged in prevented one from receiving communion. Preacher and pew-sitter alike succumbed to what an exiled Spanish Jew called "an affair of fools," bent to this "enchanting witchery" whose believers showed all the works of a spirit. Effects later pointed to by early Mormons (and Methodists, and Baptists, and so on) as proof of their own calling: itching, relentless itching; endless, mindless laughter; "paralytic distemper"; the various exercises (shouting, falling, barking); even, Joseph Penso de la Vega said, acting as if possessed by two spirits in a single body.[2] Bankers and money changers nodded with pastors, then, that "The general good," morally and for the state, "could result from the acquisitive spirit or even from immoral promptings like greed."[3] Such teaching was an example, apparently, of their much ballyhooed "plain speaking," promoted by merchants and middle-class folk philologists as also morally right. Agreeing across the Channel were Puritans, prescribing the same cure for discursive inefficiencies in England. Thus, our "first modern economy"[4] bearing a culture severed of place—reducing religion to dress codes and spurs to greed; unaesthetic, realist and sentimental in its poetry; regularly trotting out in sermons enticements to shop, shop, shop—would unwittingly colonize the world, having sailed from Amsterdam. Thus was Mammonism restored, unbelievably, among Christians. Like the United States, its supposed most American religion would inherit many of these Dutch restorations.

The Dutch republic became a fruitful field for new theologies taking a second growth from Calvinism, and fed from legal theories that shaped the modern world. Hugo Grotius would publish the *Mare Liberum*, and following his

---

[1] In Chancellor, *Devil Take*, 5

[2] In Chancellor, *Devil Take*, 11

[3] Cook, *Matters*, 70

[4] Cook, *Matters*, 57

argument for free seas, and free markets, his *De Jure Belli et Pacis* formed the groundwork for international law. The work was timely, for shipping brought wealth and conflict; and also solutions to Europe. Flemish cartographer Gerhardus Mercator's projection method only exacerbated the trends, however, as shipping—of slaves, sugar and silver—became vastly more efficient and profitable (although minor merchants ignored his maps for a century). Born Gerhard Kramer, the great map-maker was himself imprisoned briefly on suspicion of heresy.[1] The world he imagined was not like anything we'd seen before. In his vast, open America, Mormons eventually sketched the Garden of Eden, and there placed a religion he might not find altogether disagreeable. Neither would its garments be clean of that age's gilding of conquest, greed, violence and vanity. An ocean, after all, does not divide what is carried in words, on ships and in hearts set on reading particular books.

Scottish ministers over the seventeenth century also were trained by the Dutch, and they in turn trained others who "converted" to, in fact themselves became, Mormonism. Theirs is the earliest American religion: liberty not free from greed; subjugation in the service of freedom; too realist for idealism, confusing utilitarianism with pragmatism; having creeds deploring creeds themselves; paradoxically self-sacrificing, and like some god finding that self at the center of all things; refusing to admit to professing any single -ism. As described later, their teachings were carried by Alexander Campbell and Sidney Rigdon to Parley Pratt.

We should not release ourselves from the matrix of these doctrines, given in mere historical outline, just yet. Back to 1600, then. Exhausted not only by rumors of wars, but also by actual wars, France's Henri IV issued the Edict of Nantes in 1598, granting Huguenots in some regions rights equal to those enjoyed by Catholics. As Protestant stars rose, however, so the fortunes of Catholics fell. Scotland's James VI, son of Mary Stuart, issued an Act of Uniformity in 1603. Supported by Puritans and Anglicans, the Act banished Jesuits and other Catholic leaders from Scotland. The Kirk's record of the "Articles Aganis Papists, &c." issued in 1600, gives us a sense of what the Bible's restored Christianity had wrought. The Kirk declared, first, "That all Jesuits, and excommunicated Papists, be apprehended and kept in ward ay and whill they be converted or punished, according to the Acts of Parliament, or be banished the countrey." Second, "That

---

[1] John Noble Wilford, *The Mapmakers: The Story of the Great Pioneers in Cartography—From Antiquity to the Space Age* (NY: Alfred A Knopf, 1981), 74-77

their resetters and friends finde caution, under a pecuniall mulct, according to their abilitie, never to reset them againe."[1] These prescriptions for renewing their covenant with God—forsaking them by virtue of their kindness toward Catholics—not only advocated torture, imprisonment or banishment, and the fining of "their resetters and friends," but also punitive measures for the Scottish. In 1601 they sought "Remedies of the Former Evils," such as "unreverent estimation of the gospel"; "negligence of ministers in not discovering of apostates"; "Division and distraction of mynds"; "The impunitie of skippers transporting hither Jesuits, priests, &c., under the name of passengers." By disciplines of the body they thought to bring again the favor of Heaven, declaring "A general humiliation over the wholl land, and fast for the sins of the land and contempt of the gospel, to be keeped the two last Sabbaths of June." Not only for their own Covenanters, plans were also decreed, "That the names of all non-communicants through the wholl land be taken up in a roll, subscryvit by the minister respective of each pariosh where they are, . . . that ordour may be taken with such enemies of religion."[2]

The infamous Guy Fawkes responded with his failed Gunpowder Plot in 1605, as the Spanish sympathizer brought modern physics into what were surely no mere theological disputes. The Kirk responded in a panic foreshadowing our own attempts to "root out terrorists": "Some of thir were putt in Blacknes, some in the castell of Stirlin, some in the castell of Doun; but the Councill spared some of the ministers who excused their doing, and said, that they were sorie for their doeing."[3] It was in this, obviously explosive, environment that James I commissioned the new translation of the Bible: one with decidedly little to say concerning Tyndale's covenants, or how they might supplant the divine right of kings. The brief lull in everyday famine, pox and war concluded in 1625, as James's son Charles I was crowned, and married by proxy the sister of France's Louis XIII. An Anglo-Dutch alliance was also formed against Spain, the Crown Jewels being offered as security for Dutch loans. Such capital was thought to provide the king some independence from the always bothersome English Parliament.

Opposed to the turn taken by Charles I, and his imposition of Anglican liturgy across their lands, Scottish ministers soon revolted, as did Cromwell and

---

[1] John Row, *The History of the Kirk of Scotland, From the year 1558 to August 1637.* (Edinburgh: Printed for the Woodrow Society, 1842), 199

[2] Row, *The History of the Kirk*, 206-7

[3] Row, *The History of the Kirk*, 229

the Puritans. The new act of uniformity angered Calvinists and Covenanters alike, prompting a now famous old granny to toss a stool at the head of the Dean of Edinburgh, as he conducted service in the Cathedral of St. Giles. A riot followed, Knox's Covenant was revived, renamed the famous National Covenant, or Confession of Faith. It was signed by half a million: many swearing in blood, deeply accented, "till death." Scottish Covenanters eventually seized Edinburgh Castle, as two Bishops' Wars followed, and episcopacy was replaced by presbytery. Scotland was finally restoring a more obviously true Christian administrative model, renewing covenants with God as his new Israel. Out of their new union would come the Westminster Confession of Faith: by one Disciple looking for the respect begotten by deeper tradition, the Confession is said to have "grandly framed the most basic beliefs of American Disciples long before the birth of Alexander Campbell or Barton Stone."[1] After war, the Scottish forced Charles into a disadvantageous treaty.

Weakened publicly and not a little humiliated, Charles sent loyalists to challenge the still troublesome, and now Puritan, merchant and middle class friendly Parliament. The ensuing civil wars ground upon the face of England, as Cromwell's Ironsides and Roundheads defeated Charles's Cavaliers. The king eventually surrendered to Scottish armies, but rejected their Covenant; counting on yet another schism between the Presbyterians in power and the army's Covenanters and Independents. He was no fool, and though sold by the Scottish to Parliament for £400,000, Charles fled to the Isle of Wight as Parliament drove out Cromwell's army. A second civil war wrecked the kingdoms, as Royalist killed Roundhead, and Presbyterian slaughtered Independent. While exiled in Wight, Charles signed a secret treaty with Scotland, promising to abolish episcopacy and (against rising Independents) restore Presbyterianism to their land. Following Cromwell's second great victory, however, Parliament discovered the Scottish bargain, and brought Charles to trial. On the king's neck was set the iron blade of the common executioner. Once again kings were sacrificed so that the land would be no longer barren. With Cromwell's victory secure, in 1646 the Westminster Confession of Faith was accepted by the General Assembly of Scotland.

Among Cromwell's soldiers was one Edward Fisher, who wrote *Marrow of Modern Divinity* in 1644. The book was a Puritan popularization of the *Marrow*

---

[1] David Edwin Harrell, Jr., "Christian Primitivism and Modernization in the Stone-Campbell Movement" (in Hughes, *The Primitive Church in the Modern World*), 109

*of Theology*, published by the learned William Ames in Amsterdam.[1]   In the church's Latin, Ames's text was to be given in lecture form to wealthy merchants' sons in Leyden.  Fisher's popularized version posed a theological dialogue between Evangelista the minister and Nomista, the legalist counter to the minister's argument for absolute reliance on grace.  His aim was to promote that old middle way, and his book sat mostly unread until the reign of a restored Charles II. Crowned at Edinburgh's Stone of Scone (said to have been planted by Jeremiah, of biblical fame, even while grafting the line of Judah onto the royal oaks kept by Celtic druids), Charles II would be like so many before him, easily dispatched by Cromwell's forces.  As many had before him, and the Rolling Stones long afterward, he then fled to France.  Opposition demolished, Cromwell proceeded to forbid Anglican preaching, censored the press, and ordered Catholic priests to follow Charles across the Channel, or his father's head to the hole.  The new Israel must be purged of sin, its covenant renewed.  But fortune turns her wheel, even at times favoring the decidedly non-brave.  Thus, following Cromwell's death in 1658, Charles II was crowned king, and Restoration at last had its banner moment.

It flew over another Act of Uniformity, this time requiring university fellows like Isaac Newton to accept the Book of Common Prayer.  Goods and prisoners, and the predictable declarations of war, arrived from the once-accursed Holland (Elizabeth pronounced a curse upon all nations engaging in slavery, then proceeded to finance slavers herself).  Another Black Death came and terrorized London.  Only the Great Fire of 1666—the miraculous year of Isaac Newton, enjoyed among apple trees and rainbows, spanning the countryside and the walls of his darkened study—could purge the city of these sins.  To give you some measure of the stature of human dignity in these years, some enterprising pimp spread rumors that syphilis cured the plague, and brothels were overwhelmed by men seeking its healing virtues.  Wars and rumors of wars?  That and more, as the Dutch again came home to roost, spreading slaves and sugar like a pox, and their glorious silver like so much sugar.

They invaded long before William of Orange, whose Glorious Revolution of 1688 solved a problem for the English.  They also put fire under a financial revolution that spread like so much syphilis through their realm.  The National Debt was created, a bank chartered to minister it; Exchequer bills appeared, and

---

[1] William Ames, *The Marrow of Theology*.  Translated from the Latin edition, 1629, and edited by John D. Eusden (Durham, NC: The Labyrinth Press 1983)

promissory notes made debts transferrable, thereby opening a market for them.[1] All was well in England. In Scotland, however, the Anglo-Dutch pillow talk ran into a deep brogue. Even a single man, William Paterson, for example, could do no wrong when founding the Bank of England; but when starting the Scottish Darien Company in order to control that isthmus—where later Mormons would place their Nephites—things turned weird. Weird, as in religious: described by Sir John Dalrymple, then Secretary of State, "the frenzy of Scots to sign the Solemn League and Covenant never exceeded the rapidity with which they ran to subscribe to the Darien Company."[2] Just as it was for the later Mississippi Company founded by Scotsman John Law (fresh from destroying the French economy with a weapon forged of greed, unalloyed ignorance, and the South Seas Company), Paterson's company was another Semper Augustus: a promise not kept, and a fancy; puffed up with ease, its bloom just as soon blown away.

While everyone, apparently, could agree on the goodness brought to them by greed, political matters remained contentious, and yet again became religious. The Glorious Revolution of 1688—and the rise of Hanover—opened a cold war in Scotland between Presbyters and Independents. In an environment made tenser following the Patronage Act's passing six years earlier, we find Thomas Boston in 1717 reading from that soldier of Cromwell's book, Fisher's *Marrow*, before the Scottish General Assembly (Scottish Parliament being dissolved in 1707). The book was "received as though it were apostolic," wrote one Lutheran minister with the delightful name of Holmes Rolston III, who confessed, "It was Calvin who rescued me from the Calvinists."[3] Calvin's name like a later Smith was called on by the movement; his own system being simplified into a two covenant scheme, supposedly grounded in the Bible. The result of Boston's performance was the portentously named "Marrow Movement," leading Independents into that utopian middle way. It was a prelude to the Erskine-led Great Secession of 1732. Into that divide, divided from divisions upon divisions of a middle way, steps, at last, our patriarch: old Thomas Campbell. Restoration of Primitive Christianity was the only way to bring unity to so much variation, he was taught; ending strife and brothers fighting brothers. The Campbells carried their learning and ambitions to the U.S., even if they left behind the Houses of Hanover and Stewart, and so many Rob Roys. Though an ocean separated them,

---

[1] Chancellor, *Devil Take*, 32
[2] Chancellor, *Devil Take*, 51
[3] Holmes Rolston III, *John Calvin Versus the Westminster Confession* (Richmond VA: John Knox Press), 12, 6

seemingly, their understanding of God, method of reading the New Testament, and positions on baptism, union, and restoration cannot be severed from European sectarian contentions, and attempts to calm her tumults. That history is knit into their theology, into the language, into restoration: from that we do not sail away so uncaptivated.

Alexander Campbell, for instance, understood the condescension, incarnation and death of God within the widely accepted, hardly doubted Satisfaction Theory of St. Anselm. His own periodical published in 1840 a long dialogue with W. Barton Stone exploring everything biblical about their traditions regarding the sacrifice of God.[1] Each preacher stood atop a tower of prooftext, from which high seat he ascribed to the other the holding of some "relic of unauthorized tradition." While surely able to split the finest angel's hair atop the tiniest pin—if disputation was on order—Campbell espoused a common Christian doctrine of reconciliation of Man to God by Jesus' sacrifice for sin. Few Christians doubted its scripturality, although Stone was among them. Atonement in this tradition can be given brief attention here (a later volume does take up the subject of Atonement with greater detail). Anselm proposed that the death of Christ satisfies the demands of justice: infinite in detail and demand, really beyond counting. No mortified flesh could mollify the honor of our God, bruised purple from that forbidden fruit's eating. So God's own perfect son suffered, that we might be reconciled to his father. Satisfaction Theory was The Theory for medieval Christians, even if not enunciating it quite so confidently as Anselm. It presumed two gods: Father and Son, one pleasing the other; although a few sophisticates continued to insist they were one in being and substance. This "atonement" became almost intuitive for landed nobles and peasantry alike, whose own sons so regularly fell upon the altars of Moloch and of Mammon. Their intuitions were not, moreover, unrelated to the dominance maintained by the Holy Roman Empire. Its church, as later theologians like Aquinas would argue, mediated that gift of grace by offering "works": the sacraments (e.g., baptism, christening, confession, etc.). Duns Scotus extended Aquinas's justification of Church rule, claiming that the will of God itself was manifest through the power of the Church. One can see how inquisitorial boards might be set up under that sort of manifest destiny, and why reformation was inevitable.

When came later so many capitalisms and Protestants, Divine Satisfaction would be got inside the columns of debt and credit, not feudal honor and

---

[1] "Atonement: An exchange between Barton W. Stone and Alexander Campbell" in the Millennial Harbinger, 1840-1841.

appeasement. This monetized, as it were, Catholic theology; returning to Latin roots for economic words like *grace/gratis, mercy/merchandise,* and *dispensation.* Taking no more direction home from Anselm than they did the British tax code, the Rolling Stones—our modern rejoinder to Anselm—proposed that perhaps satisfaction cannot be had in so calculating a manner. Keith Richards tells how Satisfaction—its opening chords are among the most well-known of any song—came by a sort of inspiration, while living in St. John's Wood:

> I wrote "Satisfaction" in my sleep. I had no idea I'd written it, it's only thank God for the little Philips cassette player. The miracle being that I looked at the cassette player that morning and I knew I'd put a brand-new tape in the previous night, and I saw it was at the end. Then I pushed rewind and there was "Satisfaction."[1]

Indeed. Refusing guidance from some street-fighting man sympathetic to the Devil, Mormons instead take Anselm's theory for granted, even today (few know the theological history of their notion of Atonement). And like Duns Scotus's Church, the Church in Mormonism has taken up mediating God's work on Earth, restoring—even grimthorping—a pillar long ago knocked out, blood a-spilling, by the Protestant Reformation and its Catholic Counter. In Mormonism the priesthood was said to be restored. In bloodier days, when priesthood became a doubtful profession, however, a whole new theory of how one accessed grace was sought: it was found in the Bible, in the very names of its grand division. By now, however, you may be asking, which Bible, and whose reading of it?

Some historians look to grimier, fringier, and sexier groups like grifters, peepers, counterfeiters, alchemists, scryers, magicians, slaves, masons, water-witches, hermeticists and Gnostics, Alfred North Whitehead, imaginary ancient Hebrews, Methodists, maybe Gothic Chick-Lit, and, why not, cunning men bearing stones (but not the Stones themselves), to find the "origins" of Mormon theology. Indeed anything so obscure, scarcely preserved in the historical record, worthy of bizarre illustrations, and full of isms able to bear the weight of vast generalizations without enduring the scrutiny of knowing readers. The truth about Mormon theology, when put into interpreting the Book of Mormon, is more mundane: look to the Netherlands. Here in the seventeen century—among preachers of greed-is-goodism—you'll find Johannes Kock (John Cock; or as he

---

[1] Keith Richards with James Fox, *Life* (Little, Brown, and Company. NY 2010), 176

understandably preferred, Coccejus) meeting Hugo Grotius at school, and finding a shared love of contracts. "Contracts," one historian states flatly, "became the bedrock of society in the low countries." The Dutch Revolt was justified because a king was in breach of contract, "Even divine relationships could be viewed similarly."[1] Whereas the Roman Catholic Church once positioned itself between God and Man, and was said to manifest His will, these Dutch thinkers dropped the pretense of priesthood. Self-interest manifested His will, conveniently enough; though also requiring notaries and lawyers to ensure compliance. "God was therefore like a merchant," summarized a historian mentioning a pamphlet that called God, "the great Factor (meaning the head of a trading station)."[2]

Contract, Covenant, Man and God: this was the Dutch minister's education, learned for reasons surely having little to do with justifying one of the world's most disciplined (and perhaps among the briefest) slave-finance-states. Their contract disease was, indeed, "around long before receiving its clearest definition from the Leiden professor of theology."[3] He, Coccejus that is, taught Theology and Bible Philology for nearly forty years, being the principal intercessor for Scottish ministers seeking to learn "Covenant Theology."[4] In Dutch schools the trend in commerce and self-love, in tulip speculation, and in converting slaves into sugar molded into artful tulips—in short, of monetizing all the world, ridding it of bitterness for some, and of sweetness for others—here the merchant's contract theory was gilded with theology. Calvin was called up, and being dead, offered little resistance to their interpretations.

Contract theory was like fighting the Spanish, selling slaves, illustrating striped tulips or tasting refined sugar: all the rage among the petit bourgeois. Coccejus's brand of contract theory *qua* covenant or federal (*fœdus*) theology resolved two serious drawbacks of Calvinism: namely, the matter of "Election," and our state of "Reprobation." "Election" held that according to God's will some souls were predestined for damnation, others for salvation. A much loathed notion in Mormonism, predestination (apparently derived from Calvin's writings, and according to some readers, not expressly attributable to him) itself had some justification: if one's works could not redeem one's soul, because one was an absolute reprobate incapable of changing one's own heart, then how could any soul be saved? If you think about, it does not seem unreasonable: lucky for us, *we*

---

[1] Cook, *Matters of Exchange*, 55
[2] Cook, *Matters of Exchange*, 71
[3] Cook, *Matters of Exchange*, 55
[4] Van Kirk, *A History of Theology*, 32

are among the elect, though. *Right?* Reprobation bound one to Election, for without grace simply being bestowed, no matter the works (i.e., sacraments), all souls would be condemned to eternal damnation. Justice could not be robbed, nor God's anger left unmollified; and Man (slaves and scholars alike) could only receive mercy, not earn it. What runs the machine of this universe is bloody sacrifice, an infinite pain secures the eternal workings of Law: through the payment of blood, even life, by one without blemish, Law might be perfected. It all made so much sense: to slaves and slave masters, bankers and borrowers. The obvious question, though, is, Why not simply elect *everyone?* A possible answer: then what are we to do with all our religions, sacrifice, slaves, peasantry, and Puritanical codes?

Was any of this in the Bible? Calvin apparently held that, "All that we have attempted to do is to restore the native purity from which the Christian ordinances have degenerated."[1] Others like Holmes Rolston release Calvin from the burden of Calvinism. He probably provided the language for Restorationists. From his Bible, apparently, he learned that the elect had been placed under an eternal covenant, "foederatus," and when that failed most recently under the stewardship of the Patriarchs, the eternal covenant fell "under shadows," pointing Man to hope in Christ, and a new dispensation of the everlasting covenant.[2] *Foederaltheologie* like some afternoon talk show toddler has been traced to a hundred different fathers—Ursinus, Musculus, Calvin, Zwingli, Robert Rollock, Tyndale, Irenaeus, Jesus—and in nearly every case it proposes two covenants: one of grace, and one of works. It's right there in the titles of the two big books in your Bible, so it must be right, right? Some have the dispensation of the covenant of grace as continual, others locate it with the Resurrection; works may or may not still be operative in the covenant. It depends on who you ask. What matters is that talk of dispensation of covenants was widespread, and seemingly grounded in the Bible, and would eventually inform Mormon explanations of their new book.

Grace was essential, this theology concluded, but it was not dispensed willy-nilly as Calvinism had propounded; nor universally. Covenant theology in the hands of Coccejus—his *Summa doctrinae de foedere et testamento dei* was published in 1648—had other uses, too. He sliced the holy book into historical segments. He argued that the well developed and widely discussed "dispensation of the Covenant of Grace" most recently came with the condescension of Our

---

[1] Allen and Hughes, *Discovering*, 32
[2] Rolston, *John Calvin Versus*, 59

Lord.[1]  Grace could come from—be dispensed in—a sort of social contract: God and Man filling in as Party A and Party B.  Grace could be achieved, warranted, or perhaps at least implied and hinted at, as something you'd not mind receiving; merely by meeting the terms of the contract.  Now the question was, where was the contract?  Where would you look?  Yes, I thought so: the Bible.  But which part?  The chapter on stoning harlots?  Here again we find ourselves dealing with metatext, "the Bible," encountered through translation-interpretation, offered by one minister or another, lo here and lo there, one church before another.  Coccejus and his Scottish students argued for development of the "plan of salvation" (the phrase is not original to Mormonism), evolving from the Old Testament to the New.  He proceeded to focus their scriptural studies on the dispensation of the Covenant of Grace.  By "dispensation" he meant something was being dispensed; the something was the Covenant of Grace, which had occurred at a definite time.  The time of its dispensing, as developed by Coccejus, distinguished it from the dispensation of the Covenant at Sinai, one of "works," or the previous one concerning strict obedience in Eden.  "Dispensation" was linked not only to covenants, but also to biblical-historical ages, misleading many listeners, and later preachers, into forgetting their English.  They read or heard that term as referring to an "age" or historical segmentation.  (Mormons followed this confusion, and concocted many dispensations.)  The confusion grew from the phrase being built in conversation with Calvinism; but once Calvinism faded, as it did on the frontier, Dispensation like Restoration took on entirely new meanings.  Now one can join a hundred-fold varieties of dispensationalists, a field of fruit fertilized by careless misunderstanding of a single word commonly tossed around by preachers of the Bible.

Having conveniently severed most of the Bible from the realm of what was relevant for one's salvation—that is, the entirety of the Hebrew Bible, with the exception of passages on covenants—covenant theology came with a method for reading and also for preaching.  It invented another Bible by this method, effectively: one separated into dispensations selected according to which parts pertained to salvation; that is, what ministers should read and build movements upon.  This metatext Bible allowed Covenanters to boast like many Protestants to rely entirely upon the Bible: that one, right in front of you, which I will proceed to interpret.  Put into heads crasser than Coccejus, covenant theology became utilitarian, making the way straight for Prosperity Gospels sold weekly in our own times.  Man could contract with God and negotiate very favorable terms;

[1] Van Kirk, *A History of Theology*, 34

particularly if one needed only pronounce belief in "Jesus" or whatever, donate cash to a mega-church, or protest "social justice," in order to grease open the benevolent, at times buggy, and often inscrutably managed Windows of Heaven. Perhaps the only thing reliably selling on Sundays in Utah and across the Bible Belt is this gospel. Embedded in contexts of dispensation of grace, covenant theology put the matter of salvation—how to act to be in the covenant as was ancient Israel, for one could no more merit Grace than they—as a question for metatext Bible.

Restoration was only one such solution to sectarianism offered by covenant theology. The Dutch looked after many a Scottish minister, providing safe haven for Descartes as well as John Locke. No stranger to blood, Locke's own boyhood school was only blocks from Whitehall, where the head of King Charles fell from the body politic. The historian-philosopher's *Letters on Toleration* provided a sociological rationale for again attempting the unification of all Christians; something like putting the king's head back on, humpty-dumpty like. Rather than fight over doctrines which change from place to place, and time to time, Christians should tolerate individual differences, Locke noted; and so seek to unify the Body of Christ, perhaps, to make way for the godhead. Toleration was practical, given so many Bibles and schools for learning that one's reading was, fortunately, the correct one. It is the original "whatever" meta-dogma, and needed no posture of Restoration; although Locke did believe the Bible worth preserving (which one?). Alongside his toleration, popularized by Cambridge Platonists under the wonderful term, "Latitudinarianism," strode Locke's theory of knowledge. In a nasty, brutish, short definition: the mind is a blank slate written upon by the senses. This pair—social policy of tolerance, and epistemology grounded in observable nature—provided two legs for building a movement without Bible creeds, relying upon "natural light" for one's wisdom.[1] Some were serious about it. Forget the Bible was admonition of writers like Lord Herbert of Cherbury, whose *De Veritate* suggested that the Bible was not the solution, but the problem. Man should look to the Second Book of God: Nature. So would conclude the Deists of the Scottish Enlightenment, whose blend of federal and natural theology would inspire Thomas Jefferson as well. Being a generation before Thomas Campbell, and led by Adam Smith, the Encyclopaedia Britannica,

---

[1] Garrison, *Sources of Alexander Campbell's Theology*, 85-90; 108-109. *Toleration* has since fallen on hard times among Christian fundamentalists, who treat it as pulled from the Devil's bottomless bag of tricks: sounding Christian, in practice allowing for gays to marry and destroy The Family.

and David Hume, these Scotsmen offered an alternative to Restoration for souls seeking the path to unity. Here in Locke, Newton, Smith, Herbert and Hume was material for unity long sought by Scottish reformers, and the Bible and its restoration did not figure so very prominently. But huge efforts to educate the populace would be required, and most preferred to read or hear the Bible, rather than some Cambridge or Edinburgh scholar's theories. So after Protestants discovered their Reformation yet another Paradise Lost, it was obvious to some Scottish and English ministers in the seventeenth century that a total restoration of Primitive Christianity would be needed. Covenant theology had a method for finding in the Bible exactly which practices and doctrines could be restorative, imaginatively drawing up a replica play thing from the past: a whole church readymade for post-Reformation political environments dominated by the nation-state, and maybe making the way straight for capitalism, too.[1]

Unlike Deists, Independents refused to carry out Locke's reduction of religion as the mere teaching of ethics and morality. Church and Bible mattered, if only because the former was political in Scotland, and the latter their lingua franca. And morality never won no battle. Keep the Bible, then, and find in it the vocabulary for unity. Thus "restoration of Primitive Christianity" became a catchphrase for many seeking political liberation from England, including Alexander Campbell.[2] Although he rejected much of the Scottish Enlightenment, he like other Scots-Irish ministers remained a naturalist theologian throughout his life, proclaiming upon authority that spiritual experiences were a delusion of the mind. What, then, could take one's knowledge beyond this sinful realm? The Bible, in a name, was Campbell's prescription for both fallen individuals and ailing societies. Which Bible? The one he translated-interpreted. Campbell, then,

---

[1] I can already hear some second-year graduate student tsk-tsking my use of isms. In some chapters I speak of various "isms" which are not, admittedly, subjected to the same critique I take to "Mormonism" and "restorationism." Given that this history is not a history of capitalism, nor mercantilism, or Republicanism, and yet such terms are useful, if only approximately accurate; inevitably vague notions, their usefulness in telling a brief history justifies their lack of "critical engagement." Were I, of course, to allow the same easy entrance into the argument of this book for words like "Mormonism," readers would be justified in holding the argument itself in doubt, because of my reliance on that particular unexamined ism. That I do not discriminate between the imagined varieties of Protestantism, capitalism, and so on, I mean to suggest, this should not mean I do not doubt their complexity, historical development, or ignore the scholarly debates. At least, I do not, *outside* this book. This book concerns Mormonism, and shows how that ism came to be: vague, and yet real.

[2] Garrison, *Sources of Alexander Campbell's Theology*, 72-73

leaned upon one leg of Locke's (admittedly, presented here as a straw) man: naturalism. The unity some philosophers hoped to find in tolerance and rational argument was replaced by insistence that a book could bring together Christians, at last. Into Locke's theory of knowledge, where the natural world writes its laws upon the minds of the inquiring, Campbell inserted his reading of the Bible. To the Second Book of Nature Campbell would stitch the Bible.

He and others could find there vague terms to define, practices to quibble over, rituals to divide one man from his brother. It alone gave mortals divine knowledge, he was taught; dictated by the Holy Spirit, naturally through senses like vision and hearing. All had ears to hear, and eyes to see what was preached from and written upon a page. That was not supernaturalism, but a spiritualization of the philosopher-theologian's practice of being "inspired" by a text. Later writers would speak of him as a Baconian inductive rationalist, meaning he thought inspired readers (like Alexander Campbell) could jump from biblical facts into general laws of the divine economy. It was just like science. Campbell was scarcely original in these thoughts, although on the frontier he was seldom inclined to acknowledge their origins. "His confidence in his own reason," wrote one historian, "was so complete that he believed he possessed no theories."[1] Like so many Restorationists he enjoyed a view of himself that, by virtue of the Bible—and no little inspired reading of it—he had at last escaped tradition, history, culture, and arrived at the Truth. At one point, one scholar noted, "The agreement of Mr. Campbell's 'Ancient Order of Things' with the tenets and practices of these Independents was so marked that the charge of identity was often laid at his door," but out on the frontier he was free to claim his debt was "mainly a negative one."[2] Campbell carried covenant theology and talk of restoration across the sea, and proceeded to localize his traditions in a widely circulated newspaper. But you will not find me claiming that Campbell alone created Mormonism. Only that he brought the vocabulary and call for Restoration to a region where the Book of Mormon landed: the Western Reserve. What Campbell and those who became Mormons brought to their reading of that book was mostly extracted from a matrix of war, greed, and covenants I am sketching in this chapter. Added to this extraction was the ridiculous notion that history had been left behind and traditions no longer called upon them. Such was their tradition, in fact. The land and politics they'd left, but not so their words and the imaginings these invoked.

---

[1] Phillips, *Differences*, 49

[2] Van Kirk, *A History of Theology*, 78

Returning to once Calvinist Scotland with their revised covenant theology, ministers like Greville Ewing set up seminaries, sending out elders to preach their Bible. "As a true theological system," federal theology "was born and reared on Scots and English soil."[1] A theology conservatively tailored for political submission (one could renegotiate the covenant, and the King's divine authority, even, could be summoned to draw up terms), Covenant was instead ordered to get kilted up for battle. You want Restoration of a King, *we'll give you Restoration*. The Primitive Church was to be invented anew, pulled from the pages of the King James Bible, so that no other King James would dictate their readings of their Bibles. By the time the Campbell's carried their covenant theology, doctrine of dispensations (as a reading method, and not simply a historical sequence), and erudition into the frontier of Ohio, the tartans were framed behind show-glass, as it were; being mere objects of veneration, relics of lineage, and of dubious historicity. On the frontier, covenant theology revived; answered many a folk-theologian's practical inquiry: How can we satisfy God, and merit grace? How can we live Bible religion (was there any other religion)? Must I read the Old Testament for any reason other than for confirming the New Testament? Dispensations and covenants were ready made for non-university, non-Trinitarian, non-Scholastic non-high church, make-do-or-do-without, terrifically superstitious frontiersmen. The Catholic sacraments were thus pared down to one or two; the Bible inversely generated another thousand personal religions born of ten thousand readings, as Joseph Smith realized.

Everything Christian could be doubted, or not: that was one fruit of Restorationism. John Cotton, an early Puritan figure in New England, purified the Psalms ostensibly used by the early church, restoring a psalmody which "fetcheth antiquity from the ancient of days."[2] Exiled from those Puritans, Roger Williams doubted that baptism could be performed, unless God dispensed new authority. One could not discover in the New Testament the correct form, as Williams, having faced many a Restorationist's scheme, thought only the apostolic order was there preserved. But Baptists heeded not his concern, and set off to restore the Kingdom of Heaven in America. William Penn wrote on restoration. Joseph Priestly wrote three volumes called *History of the Corruptions of Christianity*, required reading for learned Restorationists at the close of the eighteenth century. His ideas would circulate far and wide, even among the illiterate. Less

---

[1] Rolston, *John Calvin Versus*, 12
[2] In Allen and Hughes, *Discovering*, 58

pessimistically, Morgan Edwards wrote a long book in 1768 called *The Customs of Primitive Churches* that described exactly what the Bible failed to make quite clear enough: structure, officers, ordinances, and proper titles of the restored church. Others would add volume upon volume, describing what was to them so clearly sketched on the pages of the Old and New Testaments, and which words and things were not, not yet, anyway, truly restored among Christian people.

Baptism, for example, was perhaps not a substitute for circumcision, so Alexander Campbell supposed after applying to it the dispensations theory. He wondered about it again after the birth of his son. Eventually, in America, the preacher tossed out the water of infant baptism while saving the baby of covenants.[1] Mormons tossed that water too, and inherited his equivocations on baptism: both an ineffectual "symbol" of an inner state of faith, and a quasi-magical rite with spiritual powers to remit one's sins, whether God consented or not . . . *almost*. Such was the power of the covenant. At least, sins might be remitted when performed correctly; that is, by immersion. Why make immersion necessary for the covenant? It couldn't be sprinkling, as that was the Papists' way, obviously. Campbell insisted also that faith (such a convenient term) was the necessary condition for felicitous baptism.[2] But how did baptism work, really? "The efficacy of his blood," Campbell opined, "springs from his own dignity and from the appointment of his Father. The blood of Christ, then, really cleanses us who believe from all sin." Belief cleanses? Well, Campbell mumbling somewhat, continued, "Behold the goodness of God in giving us a formal token of it, by ordaining a baptism expressly 'for the remission of sins.' The water of baptism, then, formally washes away our sins. The blood of Christ really washes away our sins."[3] So, the preacher explained, the physical effect of water has metaphorical impact, being but a token; an imagined and, in any case, long ago flowing fluid literally washes away certain spiritual things? On the frontier, apparently, understanding the metaphysics of baptism mattered somewhat less than the frequent practice of it.

Rather than resolve the metaphysical conundrum that Campbell similarly swam around, Mormons simply clarified and clearly simplified, during the early 1830s, the matter of whose baptism: ours, not theirs. By this argument, the everyday social function of baptism—making evident by ritual initiation one's membership to a group—was geared up into a machine for producing hierarchies

---

[1] Garrison, *Sources of Alexander Campbell's Theology*, 237
[2] Garrison, *Sources of Alexander Campbell's Theology*, 241
[3] Richardson, *Memoirs*, vol.2:82

(e.g., priesthoods) within that group. By contrast, Campbell argued that the Christian ministry was not a substitute for the Levitical priesthood, for now Christ alone was the great high priest, dispensing a new covenant. One's faith was one's calling, he argued, and there was no greater authority.[1] So, do not mistake my argument as something like, "everything Campbell preached was carried into Mormonism." Covenanter theology of dispensations, for instance, was refracted by Mormons in the 1830s through a (re- or mis-)understanding of the "Restored Church" and its claim to priesthood. Something seeming religious, devoid of the despair or inexplicable pride attending Calvinism, but also politically feasible: that was the goal of Covenanters. It makes sense, given the context of being too often faced with Huguenots, French and Spanish Catholics, and wily English armies lurking outside the gates. Mormons would reduce Campbell's already simplified model of dispensations into an explanation of their Church's supposed restoration, a cyclical opening of the Heavens in every dispensation; this "last dispensation" (that is, age) commencing with one or another events in the life of Joseph Smith. They preserved the break between the Old and New Testaments introduced by covenant theology, but did not preserve the logic of dispensations as a way to use the Bible and not also obligate Levitical diets for Christians, Levirate marriage for Onanists, neither the stoning of harlots, nor the offering of sacrifices.

Rather than a political movement, Restoration was regarded by Mormons as necessary because, it was realized, well, um, because of the Great Apostasy: a sort of convenient filling in of the back story heard by them, explaining why Restoration was essential (now that unity against a church had become politically irrelevant). Restoration explained their new Book of Mormon: a sign of restored miracles, and little else. In time it also moved from Campbell's ecclesiastical concern, being lensed through the newly claimed authority ostensibly bound up with "the priesthood." In Mormonism, as we'll see, priesthood was introduced publicly by the mid 1830s and effectively obscured the Scottish and Campbellite roots of Mormonism's claim to being a restored church. Even Rigdon's followers would forget that as recently as 1827 they were already a restored church; and the authority to baptize and be baptized was the faith one gained by hearing the Word (i.e., the Bible); that and, if we are officious, having been commissioned by the preacher from one's congregation.

---

[1] Terryl L. Givens and Matthew J. Grow, *Parley P. Pratt: The apostle Paul of Mormonism* (Oxford University Press 2011), 26. Emerson's formulation, that one's *talent* is the calling, makes more sense; practically speaking, to me, anyway; faith being too abstract a noun to hammer *every* nail with.

Mormons would literally write priesthood back into their earlier records, and even prominent historians continue to swallow or propound the tale that "priesthood authority" was presented by Mormon missionaries to Restorationists in Ohio. It was this power, we are to believe, they were waiting to see restored, and seeing it, jumped right into the waters of baptism. But if Mormon elders indeed marched into Kirtland and flashed their priestly credentials, waving them like some brass serpent, they would've been surprised to learn that Alexander Campbell had outfoxed them, having preached about their Melchizedek and Aaronic priesthoods a few years earlier. And in true Campbell form, he basically plagiarized writings about three dispensations of priesthood from another Irishman named Alexander Crawford. A brief review is upon us: of Campbell's work in the decade before a junior partner named Sidney Rigdon would shape his own movement among the Mormonites, dispensing to Smith and others the wisdom of Campbell and company—priesthoods, restorations, offices, dispensations and powers—all found right there, in the Holy Bible.

## Four   Campbell's Restorative Soup

Taking to heart the popular but ironically mistaken reading of John 5:37, to search the scriptures, "for in them ye think ye have eternal life," Campbell found in them "the only rule to direct how we may glorify and enjoy God here and hereafter."[1]   The Bible was sufficient to save society, too. Alexander Campbell declared, "On the subject of religion, I am fully persuaded that nothing but the scriptures ought to have been published."[2]   Graced with an abundant absence of self-reflection, Campbell would add some sixty volumes to what he thought should not have been published.   His influence across American religion can never be doubted nor added up.   Perhaps one obstacle to summing it is found in the term "influence"?   Let us instead speak of words: used here, and then there, and with what effects.   In this chapter, we consider how Mormon historians wrestle with evidence that their restored gospel was preached by Campbellite elders and bishops at least three years before their own church was "restored."   Then I turn to the biography of Alexander Campbell, preparing the way for our reconstruction of how his followers and subjects would become Mormonites, carrying his doctrines into the text which he later showed in a twelve-page critique to be highly unbiblical.

Was there something about Campbell himself, or was it the project of restoration—its peculiar way of binding readers into social roles seemingly revealed in their Bibles, and then into churches said to restore, purify, or otherwise revive a dead thing from its pages—a project pronounced for centuries, but on the frontier having its greatest success?   Most Mormons have never heard the name *Alexander Campbell*; most Mormons have never not heard the phrase *Restored Church*, on any given Sunday.   Its very structure came from Campbell, although just as soon it

---

[1] Richardson, *Memoirs*, 1:145
[2] Campbell in Garrison, *Sources of Alexander Campbell's Theology*, 206

lost its pedigree, and seemingly appeared on the pages of the Book of Mormon. In number 30 of his series in the Christian Baptist on the "Ancient Order of Things," the Irishman listed all the names in the "religious theatre of public actors."[1]  Ministers, Divines, Clergymen, Elders, Bishops, Preachers, Teachers, Priests, Deacons; and less familiar to Mormons, Deans, Prebendaries, Cardinals, Popes, Friars, Abbots, Priors, and Licentiates populate his long list.  Only a precious few deserved the status of "scriptural names": deacon, bishop, elder and evangelist. All others, he writes, come under the word "antichrist" (44). Not-Yet-Mormons would take up these offices under the ostensible bishopric of Sidney Rigdon, in the late 1820s—their congregation being designated derisively (and incorrectly, except in the most vague sense) as Campbellite.  By the time they were renamed Mormonites in 1831 they had forgotten the various rules Campbell gave for designating a man an elder (only elderly men), a bishop (requiring a congregation he oversees), deacon (for male public servants), and evangelist (for what was popularly called a missionary).  The terms created the structural durability of the new movement, regardless of Campbell's definitions.  They collectively expanded Joseph Smith's church from a flat body bearing a single title of *elder*, given indiscriminately to all men (Smith being later designated "first," with Cowdery the "second," although it is not clear that the enumeration continued to mark every ordained man).  Everyone else was called a disciple or saint, just as they were among the Campbellites, other Restorationists, and many non-high churches.

So, I cast my vote for the project of restoration—engineered by radical reformers to create unity out of the most widely published and obsessively read book in known history—as our maker of Mormonism.  It was made from a religious register, a vocabulary that organized social roles with not altogether clear expectations, derived at times willy-nilly from the pages of the Bible.  From the Bible it was carried into metatext Book of Mormon.  It was from Campbell, though, that Mormons learned, and then forgot his voice gave them, the language and uses of restoration.  His biography matters to the Book of Mormon because Sidney Rigdon took from Campbell so many parts, and not everything; nor very systematically.  He carried bits and pieces of the man's work into Smith's little Church of Christ, believers in (something about) his recent translation.  These parts came along not only with Rigdon, but as we'll see in following chapters, with a community twice the size of Smith's existing church.  Carried upon their tongues and bodies, these Restorationists reorganized the church as Christians

---

[1] Christian Baptist, vol.7, 43

practiced it: this time, however, drawing their restoration inside the pages of the Book of Mormon, and forming it outside in congregations of a new readership. The astonishing durability of their effort is evident today, among professional historians and other scholars who pronounce tradition as though it was history.

Metatext created by Rigdon and his loose flock—distributed across social roles, institutional structure, and the pages of the actual book—has given us historians who read the Book of Mormon as corroborative of the Bible, although careful professors of English do find that conclusion somewhat "paradoxical," as we've seen. Terryl Givens would also claim—whatever he said about the absence of Book of Mormon doctrines in Mormonism itself—that "Doctrinally, then, the Book of Mormon was conservative rather than radical," and it (rather than how it was read) "fulfilled Restorationist [*sic*] hopes by reverting to simple truths seen by converts as at the heart of biblical religion."[1] What were these truths? Richard Bushman would say of Rigdon's preaching companion Walter Scott that he "reduced the Gospel to five simple points: faith, repentance, baptism by immersion, remission of sins, and the gift of the Holy Spirit."[2] Acknowledging that Rigdon "taught doctrines close to Campbell's," the dean of Mormon history later admits that Mormon missionaries also "taught a gospel almost exactly like Walter Scott's Campbellite doctrine that had converted hundreds in northeast Ohio." Bushman continues, without acknowledging a single primary document in support,

> Although Mormonism appeared to be a bizarre offshoot of mainline Christianity, the revelations and the *Book of Mormon* actually stressed a basic Christian message of faith in Christ, repentance, and baptism with promises of spiritual blessings (153).

There is more going on here, under the shadow of restoration, than Mormon traditions masquerading as histories have yet revealed. Scott was said to be one of "three witnesses" to the "the Restoration" of the "Ancient order of things," alongside W. Barton Stone and Alexander Campbell.[3] (Rigdon has been all but erased from Disciples of Christ histories, just as Campbell has disappeared from most Mormon histories.) The words of Scott moved through the frontier, and

---

[1] Givens, *By the Hand of Mormon*, 197

[2] Bushman, *Rough Stone*, 149

[3] Mark Lyman Staker, *Hearken, O Ye People: The Historical Setting for Joseph Smith's Ohio Revelations* (SLC: Greg Kofford Books 2009), 19

were said to be found in the Bible itself. After the Book of Mormon appeared, the same scheme—from Walter Scott, ultimately—would be used to reframe the Book of Mormon. By the late 1800s even the text itself was cut up and re-arranged to fit Scott's "plan of salvation." Here is a social process which must be reconstructed.

Rather than begin with Mormonism as some sort of autopoetic social movement that hopped into our World free of tradition, we must look to Campbell and his elders, evangelists, and bishops. They preached these "Restorationists' hopes" around the frontier. Their gospel was simplified into a five-finger scheme given by Walter Scott, sponsored by Campbell as a full-time preacher in the Ohio region. This "restored gospel" is given differently in every text; meaning, it circulated in various forms, and was never trademarked, I suppose. Generally it consisted of faith (from hearing the Word); repentance (upon recognition of one's place in the Word, as a "sinner" vis-à-vis Christ); baptism (a tacit admission of the social role of elder, and his power to perform in some way effective biblical ritual); and the reception of the Holy Spirit (somewhat less tangibly defined, although surely related to one's newfound ability to read the Bible correctly; that is, as others in the movement also interpret it). Early versions would also tack on "eternal life" or some such Christian riding-off-into-the-Heavenly-sunset. His five-finger scheme was no mere list, but a program for engineering an embodied movement out of a single text: social roles, script from and creative of metatext, hierarchical relations of authority and submission. It was all right there, in the Bible, right? Thus regrounded, Scott's sequence could be broken from his preaching, and recirculated among Bible readers and preachers. This was Scott's "plan of salvation," the same title given it in official LDS curriculum today. Mormons would claim, and continue to claim, that this five-sequence gospel is the restored Gospel, unwittingly reciting Scott's claim while seldom acknowledging his preaching as their source.

Finding the "same" words in their Book of Mormon—faith, repentance, and so on—they are astonished to hear Scott preaching the very same sequence they now see (without evidence) in that book. Consider this historian's attempt to preserve his tradition—that Joseph Smith revealed the "plan of salvation" and it is still to be found in the pages of the Book of Mormon—when faced with the obvious fact of Scott's preaching it as early as 1827. "But when Scott asserted that, 'in 1827 the True Gospel was restored,' what he meant," Mark Staker clarifies, "was his understanding and articulation that year of God's 'plan of salvation,' a term he used to describe his 'restoration' of the essential elements of the gospel."

Employed by the LDS Church to rebuild and restore log homes and old stores as part of the church's sacred tourism initiative, Staker continues, "These elements were 'faith, repentance, baptism, remission of sins, the Holy Spirit, and eternal life."[1] Staker's ridiculous but quaint explanation? That Smith's "plan of salvation" taught, unlike Scott's version, that it was not "faith per se but faith in Jesus Christ that needed to precede baptism. Furthermore, the gift of the Holy Ghost could be received only through proper authority." That is, the priesthood, which would not be publicly spoken of by Mormons until several years after Scott, as we'll see. "However, the main outline of the 'plan'," he admits, "remained intact with one significant adjustment." What was the adjustment apparently rendering Scott's plan unusable, and Smith's purported one a revelation from Heaven?

> [T]he "Plan of Salvation" for Latter-day Saints became progression of faith, repentance, baptism for the remission of sins, and receipt of the Holy Spirit followed by "Enduring in righteousness to the end of the mortal probation" and the receipt of the Holy Spirit of promise. "Eternal life," revelation confirmed, was indeed at the end of this progression of events (325-6).

Staker honestly wrestled with the problem of his tradition conflicting with historical evidence. Professor Terryl Givens does not so much wrestle as slice and dice. I give his account as found on page 70 of his widely read and lauded, *By The Hand Of Mormon*. "One of Campbell's associates," Givens explains,

> Walter Scott, had inadvertently paved the way for Mormon missionaries when he 'contended ably for the restoration of the true, original apostolic order which would restore to the church the ancient gospel as preached by the apostles. The interest became an excitement. All tongues were set loose in investigation, in defense, or in opposition. . . . The air was thick with rumors of a 'new religion,' a 'new Bible.'

Givens quotes from Disciples historian Amos S. Hayden, who witnessed the Mormonite schism and took up his own ministry after Rigdon departed. By omitting some passages from Hayden, Givens makes him hint of the Book of Mormon's emergence, a new Bible with a new religion. By turning to Hayden's text, however, we see how Givens leads Mormon readers into that interpretation

---

[1] Staker, *Hearken*, 321

somewhat more than Hayden would have. Here is the quoted text, with Givens's ellipses restored:

> The interest became an excitement. All tongues were set loose in investigation, in defense, or in opposition ; which foreshadowed good results. Nothing so disastrous to the sailor as a dead calm. Let the vessel heave under a tempest, rather. The Bibles were looked up, the dust brushed off, and the people began to read. "I do n't believe the preacher read that Scripture right." "My Bible does not read that way," says another. The book is opened, and lo! there stand the very words! In the first gospel sermon, too—the model sermon—as what "began at Jerusalem" was to be "preached to the ends of the earth." The air was thick with rumors of a "new religion," a "new Bible," and all sorts of injurious, and

Hayden, Early History, 121

It is obvious that the "new Bible" was the same old one, reinterpreted. This new metatext moved Scott's words independent of his voice, fragmenting on the frontier alongside covenant theology and dispensations, and popular aspirations to supplant the House of Israel by restoring ancient Christianity. His words were indeed taken from their Bibles, although "discovering" their true sequence required his helping hand. The language of early Mormon-Campbellite-Restorationers was built up with terms and puffery taken from the New Testament. In the Gold Bible the same words would congregate, be reordered by Scott's listeners, and re-organize into Mormon doctrines. A vocabulary and, thereafter, a people were long and well nursed to spiritual health by the canned soup of Alexander Campbell. Condensed with pride for over a century in the highlands of Scotland, its reconstituting cups of water being left over from the reclaimed soil taken from the sea, long ago by those enterprising Dutch who added sugar to slavery. The metaphor is not only contrived, admittedly, but also not far from correct in its proportions: by adding fire and a little water—hardly new wine—to his soup, they appeared to some as a new movement; most importantly, to Campbell and his preachers, who wanted nothing to do with the Gold Bible business. And so the talk of influence began very early; and continues without end: did X idea come from Y, or Z?

In a biography of Parley Pratt scrutinized in a later chapter, Givens (and co-author Matthew Grow) evidences a reading of Disciples' traditions regarding Scott, Smith, Rigdon and Campbell. Citing for his authority a wonderful blend of tradition and facts composed by a Disciples historian, Givens explains:

> Campbell's followers had in many cases found the Mormon message amenable to their version of the gospel, the ones who were not drawn in by that message could be especially resentful of Mormons, whom they considered religious plagiarists and poachers. Campbell himself accused Smith of simply stealing, with Rigdon's complicity, elements of his own theology. Many parallels clearly existed. For instance, Campbellite Walter Scott emphasized the five cardinal doctrines of the 'Gospel Restored': faith, repentance, and baptism for the remission of sins. To these Scott added the gift of the Holy Spirit and eternal life. [1]

Smith dropped from Scott's sequence, Givens explains, I suppose with a straight face, "the fifth as a first principle and preferred to call the fourth the gift of the Holy Ghost." Another historian sees Seekerism in Mormonism, even while quoting from a letter, written by "a Campbellite who observed the growth of Mormonism in Ohio," claiming that Joseph Smith "stole (not all but the best part) of his thunder from the Disciples by taking their plea for the restoration of primitive Christianity."[2] That curious phrase—stolen thunder—is attributed to playwright John Dennis (1657-1734), who invented the sound effect of thunder for his own play. Quickly cancelled, his play and its simulation of God's wrath so pleased the stage owner that Dennis's thunder maker was employed for a later production of Macbeth, which he attended, and then realized, that indeed his was the first of many stolen thunders. It is easy to trace the theft of a mustard bowl and a gong; more difficult is discovering how much of Campbellism "influenced" Smith, and whether Smith is even to be regarded as metonymous with Mormonism itself. Whose Mormonism? And can there be (anything but) simulations of such an ism, so much thunder rolling around a bowl, imitating the Heavens?

---

[1] Givens and Grow, *Parley Pratt,* 74. Citing Garrison and DeGroot, *The Disciples of Christ: A History* (St. Louis, MO: Bethany, 1958, 188). James Garrison was yet another historian-minister writing in the age of Church History. He previously published the *Story of a Century: A Brief Historical Sketch and Exposition of the Religious Movement Inaugurationed by Thomas and Alexander Campbell, 1809-1908*; he also was editor of The Christian Evangelist, published out of St. Louis, Missouri.

[2] Vogel, *Religious Seekers,* ix

Claims of influence, of founding, and of cultural theft are more often tossed at men and movements one wishes to diminish; or, be separated from in the minds of readers. One Disciple, both a minister and a historian, published a book titled, *Sidney Rigdon, The Real Founder of Mormonism* (William H. Whitsitt, 1885). Hughes and Allen, more recent historians among the Disciples of Christ, also diminish the role of Campbell in making Mormonism. They reply to claims that Sidney Rigdon, "an apostate preacher in the Campbell movement" supposedly "taught Smith restoration philosophy" with the vague supposition that "given the pervasive appeal of the restoration idea in the early nineteenth century, it is likely that Mormonism would have adopted restoration principles regardless."[1] To give some sense of how carefully considered their supposition is, you may turn to their definition of *restoration*, as reportedly found among Mormons:

> Restoration meant, above all, recovering direct communion and conversation with God himself as in biblical days. Since the apostasy had closed the Heavens and stilled direct communion with God and humankind, so the first objective of the Mormon restoration was to revive direct communion with the Spirit of God (96).

They trot out this definition in their own manual addressed to students in Churches of Christ Sunday Schools, and so they can be forgiven, perhaps, their total fabrication of it. Mormon historians have their traditions, Disciples their own; and often they agree that neither the teachings of Campbell nor of Joseph Smith (coinciding with "their" churches) were in any way related, neither were their followers at all connected in anything more than the most general of ways. In a special address to the Mormon History Association, Richard T. Hughes would say that two "great restoration movements—movements that sought to restore the purity of the Christian faith—emerged on the American frontier in the early nineteenth century."[2] He finds Joseph Smith guilty of being a "product of powerful forces in American life," without bothering to name or explain these forces, and contrasts him with Campbell, "a child of the eighteenth-century Enlightenment," who had "no use for the romantic notion that God might speak to men and women through dreams and revelations" (34). Hughes concludes this vacuous comparative study with, "What I am saying is simply this, that in the early nineteenth century, popular American culture thrived on the cosmic rhythm of

---

[1] Hughes and Allen, *Discovering*, 95
[2] Hughes, "Joseph Smith as American Restorationist" BYU Studies Vol.44, no.4:31

restoration and millennium. And these are the very themes that informed not only Joseph Smith and his Latter-day Saints but a host of other new religions as well," among them he lists "Campbell's Churches of Christ, Ann Lee's Shakers, and John Humphrey Noyes's Oneida Community" (38). One might notice that he never cites a text attributed to Joseph Smith, but instead relies on summaries of Smith composed by Bushman, Vogel and Jan Shipps. Tradition has been laundered, and certified as History; and both Disciple and Mormon practitioners of this laundering are pleased that the stains of human effort came out, leaving garments clean of specifics: Smith and Campbell were influenced by cosmic rhythms, cultural forces, and restoration ideas.

Brigham Young University professors long ago figured out how to explain the presence of restored Mormon doctrines and practices among Campbellites. In an early study (1959) of Restorationism in America published in BYU Studies, Hyrum Andrus begins with what would become received tradition by the next decade. He notes that "analysis of the origin of Mormonism in its historical setting reveals several interesting relationships," and proceeds to solve the riddle of how so many "principles and objectives and the trends of society of the day" found their way into his Mormonism, in this way:

> Although these relationships do not warrant the conclusion that Joseph Smith borrowed his major ideas from his historical setting, they do show that the claims he made and the principles he set forth were compatible with the spirit and aspirations of the age, and were accepted by many as the means of attaining the goals they urgently sought.[1]

Andrus proceeds to discuss Alexander Campbell, and "The state of expectancy in the religious world," where all awaited the restoration of "divine authority" and the true gospel. When he reaches Walter Scott, he draws on Amos S. Hayden's history. His quote from Hayden, describing how thick the air was with talk of a "new Bible" and a "new religion" was actually the source for Terryl Givens's explanation presented above; a use of secondary materials in place of primary ones which unluckily passed the editor's pen at Oxford University Press.[2] Andrus was writing for Mormons, and telling history in a way to preserve tradition, when he

---

[1] Hyrum Andrus, BYU Studies Vol.1, no.2:71

[2] Givens, *By the Hand*, does cite Andrus (BYU Studies 1.2 (Autumn 1959), 80), on his page 262, footnote 26, in reference to Andrus's reading of Campbell's pamphlet, "The Christian System." Givens relies on Andrus to voice the tradition of "waiting for restoration," unfortunately incurring a giving of tradition weight equal to that of actual history.

concluded that "Campbell could not better have prepared the people for the message of Mormonism had he planned his work toward that end from the beginning" (81).

One tradition calls the others *seekers*, waiting for the restoration of authority to perform early Christian rites; the other says they are beguiled by a leader shaped by forces, carrying his silly book. Mormons ignore Campbell, and his historians are happy for it. Smith is just another Restorationist to them, his Mormons part of a general primitivist trend. History tells a different story, as we'll see. Mormonites did not exist until Restorationists admitting belief in the Book of Mormon (something about it, for very few read it) were intentionally marginalized by their new name, a name popularized by (now "Campbellite") Restorationists. Neither wants to hear that one church not only came from the other, but was indeed the other before being renamed by those it spurned. Where Smith fits in remains a matter for serious investigation.

Joseph Smith, it turns out, was indeed concerned with "the restoration idea," if we leave it at the use of the term; and long before he ever met Sidney Rigdon. So perhaps the appeal was pervasive. Perhaps the term was more widely known than some single idea it designated, however. We have seen what Smith's translated text said about restoration. In a copy of an early letter addressed to "Colesville Saints," in New York, Smith advised them to "pray earnestly for the best gifts." He speaks not of his own calling and power, nor comments upon dispensations of authority; rather of "the restoration of all things," promising that such restoration "shall be fulfilled which all the Holy Prophets have prophesied of even unto the gathering in of the House of Israel."[1] We have seen what Christians thought of that House's restoration—they being self-nominated to its usufruct by right of covenants newly made. What Smith meant when he spoke of the House of Israel is not entirely clear; nor what Holy Prophets he had in mind, although it is an easy solution to insert what we think he meant by these phrases: Bible words for Bible things. All we know, however, is that he often used Bible passages to pronounce what were to Christians decidedly non-biblical things, more like a wresting oration: pre-existence of spirits, the divinity of Man, Eden in America, plurality of gods, prophets deceived and followers' minds darkened, and so on. Surely Smith is more complicated than our historians have ambition or courage to see. Calling him a genius or puzzler or charlatan only shows the truth of that sentence. Why should Smith translate (or even author) a book which even some Mormons read as describing the Bible as a work of Satan, designed to bring them

---

[1] Smith to Colesville Saints, 28 Aug 1830. In Dan Vogel, *Early Mormon Documents* vol.1:14

into captivity; and then proceed to do what every other Christian was doing at the time? Something does not fit in these histories, and tradition has concealed how poorly our explanations account for Joseph Smith and what becomes Mormonism.

It is a complicated task to identify "influence" upon Smith. Less difficult, however, is tracking the movement of terms—often bearing simplified notions—from Campbell into Rigdon, and serving as the discursive script of what would become Mormonism. Many historians inside that movement, however, deny the effort of tracing cultural sources is even possible, a sort of hand-wringing that conceals a foolish ambition to make Smith the origin of all things they consider Mormon. Rather than Campbell, LDS historians have looked to Methodism. From the Methodists early Mormons apparently borrowed (even copied) their hymnody, administrative calendar, and, depending on how general one's history shall be, and to whom it shall be written, many "doctrines" or "practices" or "theology" and whatnot. One BYU masters thesis, insightful when read as a review of Mormon historians stumbling over themselves to link Mormonism—not to Campbellism—with Methodism, shows just how many cultural forms were carried by Methodist converts into the movement. Yet, even after presenting many cases of obvious borrowing, the student-author parrots the party line:

> Attempting to trace provenance of one group's theology and religious practices is difficult because of the lack of primary sources that actually document such transmissions . . . . Despite the high numbers of Mormon converts who came from Methodist backgrounds, and the generally positive appraisal of Methodist religion by those individuals, there are no sources suggesting a direct borrowing of Methodist beliefs and practices by early Mormons. Few serious scholars of Mormonism would doubt that Joseph Smith did, in fact, draw from his cultural surroundings. And by paying close attention to the language used by Smith and early Mormons to describe their religious experience, one can draw parallels that *suggest* a direct influence. The trouble, though, is attempting to *demonstrate* the impact of those influences.[1]

The first problem comes from starting with the folk notion of "influence" as a way of describing how culture works. This is not only this student's problem. I say "folk notion" because a century of writing on culture by anthropologists has been

---

[1] Christopher C. Jones *"We Latter-day Saints are Methodists": The influence of Methodism on Early Mormon Religiosity* (MA Thesis Brigham Young U, 2009), 74

only in a cursory way treated by most historians, who seem content to think they know what they mean when speaking of culture, because they mostly speak to their peers.   (No doubt historians also sigh when anthropologists write of "histories.")  Rather than some well or reservoir of ideas, abstract nouns, and so on, capable of effluxing influences occult, like some distant malicious star, *culture* is a term that describes a process.  What is that process?  Inside our community we sometimes call it "semiosis," interaction that generates signs with observable effects (i.e., "meaning").  As a process by which observable things carry meaning into effects, to its flow we sometimes add heuristically isolatable "contexts" (crudely put: economic, historical, religious, etc.).  These constrain or push, figuratively, that process to take particular trajectories.  It's all very metaphorical seeming, but useful analytics— beyond introducing into the range of this text—have been developed in linguistic anthropology, discourse analysis, and semiotics.  Let us jettison this notion of "cultural influence," or of "cultural contexts," for it smells of apologetics: having an indefinite standard drawn from metaphors, and yet no clear measures for deciding where one thing becomes another thing.  Realize instead that culture is the context, and the influence, and not something one draws from, when doing such and such a thing.  There is no "impact" to demonstrate.  Culture is carried along and instructs by forms, like words which stand for ideas that cannot exist but in tangible form.

What distinguishes history from tradition, then, can be stated here: histories attempt to recover what a term meant among some community at some time, and have specific ways of finding out its meaning.  Tradition-tellers project back their sense of what a term means and find that their own definitions are indeed those meant by the very communities they claim descent from. Restorationists practice similar discursive sleights of hand.  To lament that one cannot show influence, but only the carry-over of Methodist terms and practices or Campbell's teachings is to miss the obvious fact: terms, practices, and teachings are carried along as forms which stand for other things.  These are exactly what must be tracked, moving from, say, the Netherlands to Scotland to Pennsylvania into the mouth of Sidney Rigdon as he sidled up to Joseph Smith in early 1831. Recovering what they meant is not so easy a task.

We've solved our difficulty of not being able to show direct or indirect influence, because we are not concerned with how Methodism as a "culture" bumps into "Mormonism" as a culture, like two balls on green felt.  Is it enough to show that the same phrases were taken by the same people, who in 1830 were called "Restorationists" (or "Campbellites") but by 1831 were (by Campbellites) christened "Mormonites"? Surely that is not a matter of influence but of folks taking what they knew about the Bible and God and history, and not forgetting it when they were called something else by new found enemies and scoffers. I do not speak of "influence"; but of circulation and uptake of terms and social roles, and of relations built out of text.

It is one thing to speak in generalities of influence—so many isms. New isms can be invented, others discarded, and all of it leading to little more than academic priests dancing and prattling to preserve their (concealed) folk traditions. Very different it is to say that such a term came from such a place, and does not merely resemble an early Mormon teaching or practice, but actually was it. So it is time to show how the man himself, Alexander Campbell, spoke, taught, and walked with Sidney Rigdon; how "Faith, Repentance, Baptism for the remission of sins, and the Gift of Holy Ghost," as a catchphrase was preached to Sidney by a minister in the service of Alexander Campbell; and how Parley Pratt and other early Mormon leaders got all those Scottish Independent readings adapted for frontier life well knotted into what Joseph Smith would later call, in exhaustion, so much unsplittable hemlock. Or, as one Latter-day Saint (whose esteem seems based on how often he uses the term "prophet") declared in a book published by the LDS Church's commercial arm, "Joseph Smith, prophet of the Restoration, cannot be separated from Kirtland, Ohio, the town that became the headquarters for The Church," for "Before summoning Joseph, his twenty-five-year-old prophet, to Kirtland, however, the Lord prepared the area for his coming."[1]

Restoration as a metadiscursive term has made the historian's task a difficult one. Traditions given as histories were preserved for later investigators to stumble over, and call in their confusion something close to facts: being hard, long-lived, and like Lincoln's description of 1860s Mormonism, too tall to climb and too rooted to dig up. Others have gone around, or pretended to write "faithful histories" or cultural histories. I am not inclined to walk further afield than necessary, and so will keep on chopping. Traditions have been built into histories by the earliest believers, confirmed by later minister-historians, and more recently carried into scholarly histories offered by (sometimes careless, and secondary literature-reliant) professors. So much hemlock can only be split after we understand restoration as: a prescription for engineering Bible-folk, biographies and bodies as metatext. Restoration not only offers a scheme for engineering, but as this first volume has come to realize, it also cultivates a hemlock of tradition

---

[1] Karl Ricks Anderson, *Joseph Smith's Kirtland: Eyewtnss accounts* (SLC: Deseret Book, 1989), 1

feeding on the detritus—forms—found in historical text. The Book of Mormon has almost been lost in so much growth, I admit; but only when we've cleared the ground can we hope to drag it away from soporifics, poison and crowding, glowering shades.

ALEXANDER CAMPBELL AS A DAEMON OF RESTORATION

As early as 1810 the Campbells sought for membership with the Pittsburgh Presbyterian synod, it being more liberal in its profession than those in Scotland. Their application, as Alexander foresaw, was returned with a summary *no thanks*. Their views, it was decided, "were so baleful in their tendency and so destructive."[1] The Brush Run Church was thus formed in Pennsylvania upon no explicit creed, although application to the local Baptist Society, creed in hand, was a foregone conclusion. Campbell's real work came later, when he like Emerson moved from the pulpit to the printing press. He published his claims about Bibles and non-creeds in his exceedingly influential Christian Baptist, a monthly magazine whose total print run over seven years, from 1823 to 1830, came to an estimated 46,000 copies. His writings reached many more readers than that, instructing many more besides (perhaps including yourself, if you regard yourself as an orthodox Latter-day Saint). Of particular interest to me is his stance on language: that every word carried a single meaning, or idea. The Bible, of course, when translated correctly could convey the very ideas of Heaven to its readers. (But first a people must be prepared by living its doctrines and restoring its church, having learned correct definitions from inspired preachers, and so on.)

Rather than strictly quoting from the Bible and letting its words be the yea and nay of his conversation, Campbell allowed for decontextualization of words and phrases, asking readers,

> Suppose that all these would abandon every word and sentence not found in the Bible and, without explanation, limitation or enlargement, quote with equal pleasure and readiness and apply on every suitable occasion every word and sentence found in the volume; how long would divisions exist?[2]

A prescription for scripts taken from scripture, Restoration was set to its old task, and the Bible again was brought to life in the bodies and tongues of readers. Less

---

[1] Richardson, *Memoirs*, 1:83

[2] In Garrison, *Sources of Alexander Campbell's Theology*, 205

emphatically, Campbell also published lists of words proscribed for the true Restorationist: experimental religion, total depravity, sovereign grace, the Eucharist, Testament, Trinity, the power of keys, three persons of one substance.[1] What he meant was, Catholicism and Anglicanism and Methodism and Presbyterianism; and he turned the Bible into an oracle useful for finding true Christians among so many tares planted by the spittably named, much hated Papists and Prelates. Its words could bring factions together, although on the frontier the motive was no longer unification against some greater power. It was Restoration for its own sake, a turn which gave the movement far greater flexibility, for one did not seriously need to keep readers unified in the face of actual soldiers or lighted pyres. On the frontier very little blood was shed over religion, and though restoration was taken very seriously by many Bible readers, it was also more like a hobby than a plan for revolution, or for survival. Unity could be metaphorized, loosely or shabbily imagined more than actually experienced; and so restoration as a term of high approval could be slapped onto many practices bringing nothing like unity nor ancient things, but only increased sectarianism.

Restoration on the frontier became something like a language game, where in Europe it was a war game. When doctrines of restoration encountered the frontier—riding high on the backs of newspapers circulating far and wide, with great ease; severed from the hard realities of Europe (which held preachers to some standards, like what notions one was willing to die for)—the social dynamic I have outlined at last became, as was said of a similar machine, a long time ago in a galaxy far, far away: *fully operational*. On the frontier, restoration did its real work of creating Bible-folk: people certain some part of themselves was found in their Bibles. Words mediated this transfer from page into bodies and then histories; metatext secured the words across societies. Thus Campbell like others did not seriously advocate nor practice limiting his vocabulary to the printed Word, although he often wrote about those words. Posturing in this manner— repeating the paternal dictum, "where the Bible speaks, we speak; where the Bible is silent, we are silent"—while dressing in the habiliments of university education, moreover, that did win him thousands of subscribers. Here was print culture reaching a mass of readers, gaining faith by the Word; lo there, a small dilapidated Brush Run church on occasion filled with dozens of congregants. Print culture, then, it was for Campbell: that decision to metatext his way into American history makes tracking his creation of Mormonism both very difficult, for his words

---

[1] Robert Frederick West, *Alexander Campbell and Natural Religion* (New Haven: Yale U Press, 1948), 32

dispersed so broadly; and also possible because he left a trail thick with textual breadcrumbs. His metadiscourse concerned the Bible: language should be such and such, words ought to come from it. His actual discourse, however, only occasionally followed these rules. He put its words into relationship with social dynamics, and the project of church restoration took off.

Campbell's own biography is not entirely clear: like, for example, when he was born. Tradition dates his birth year to 1788, having observed a proper delay following the 1787 marriage of paterfamilias Thomas to bride Jane. Thomas, however, perhaps addled into honesty by old age, or into a simpleton's carelessness, recalled that Alexander was born in County Antrim, Ireland, in the year of Our Lord, 1786. Whatever scandal might have brought historians together in conference to decide the matter has since dissipated, as the records of his birth were most inconveniently lost at sea, having followed Campbell's ship, *Hibernia*, full fathom five to the roots of the Hebrides. Set on following his father to America, Alexander Campbell found himself shipwrecked in Scotland in 1808. Like a less adventurous Crusoe (from Rousseau's favorite book, reportedly), Campbell spent his days at Glasgow University in study of Greek, French, Logic, Experimental Philosophy, Advanced Greek, and Latin; every day but Sunday. Sundays he attended Greville Ewing's Seceder Church, convened, perhaps poetically appropriate, at an abandoned circus hall.[1] The ties between Independents and their brother Methodists are more than theological: Wesley once took over a gun factory to teach his ways of sensing God's grace being given.

One might imagine a flowering of the poetic element, in the train of a recently passed Scottish Enlightenment, with talk of James Macpherson's Ossian cycle on every scholar's mind. "Campbell combined a Romantic infatuation with nature," one historian explains not at all clearly, "and the deistic emphasis on natural theology, with the typically Calvinist attitude that man's sin prevented him from seeing God through nature until special revelation disclosed God."[2] However disposed to nemophilism—like some druid searching out "divine acceptance" among stands of oak and mistletoe—concerning his poetic spirit, another biographer generously found Campbell "more disposed to exercise it upon the sentiment . . . than upon the expression   . . . and much more sensible of defective imagery than of defective rhythm."[3] Words in his world should have but one meaning: the true one. Sometimes it came from Greek etymologies, or Latin

---

[1] Richardson, *Memoirs*, 1:187
[2] Phillips, *Differences*, 33
[3] Richardson, *Memoirs*, 1:117

commentary, or just what Campbell himself divined. But always in fear and trembling. Alexander would write of the tongue, and its muse of fire: "it defies the whole body and setteth on fire the course of nature, and is set on fire of hell," tracing the tongue's iniquity to the "heart so deceitful," "so depraved, so awfully depraved, as to be the habitation of every unclean thought, the spring of all filthy communication, the source of every sinful action."[1] Rather than raising Celtic bards and English poets, his early Calvinism indeed instilled sentiment; specifically, as Alexander recalled, the conviction of being a sinner, a social role that bore the burden of an entire metaphysics of justice, sacrifice, and guilt:

> This caused me much distress of soul, and I had much exercise of mind under the awakenings of a guilty conscience. Finally, after many strugglings, I was enabled to put my trust in the Savior, and to feel my reliance on him as the only Savior of sinners. From the moment I was able to feel this reliance on the Lord Jesus Christ, I obtained and enjoyed peace of mind.[2]

What he meant in this, his younger years, by "peace of mind" is unclear. He concludes that one returns to Jesus only after confession, "sincerely supplicating mercy through the priesthood of Jesus, heartily adopting his word [New Testament] as the rule of our practice," and, don't stop there, for one must be "constantly calling upon him, by prayer." After this daily labor, Jesus will, Campbell taught, "give us his Holy Spirit, and graciously forgive our daily shortcomings," but only if we are "constantly looking for pardon and acceptance only through his blood." It does not take much imagination to picture a stern, unsmiling unsatisfied and cane-wielding patriarch standing in for this youthful Campbell's deity; such was his view of "true religion, this is true Christianity."[3] Where is the Mormonism in all this dreadful, proudly humiliating manic self-loathing, you ask? The cheery spirit of Joseph Smith did much to alleviate the despairing faith of Campbell. The frontier's endless space, improving fortune, and possibility for realizing hopes also turned the heart of Campbell away from its youthful iniquity. More recent and ill-advised turns in Mormonism, however—increasingly less optimistic or happy about "the World"—have moved Smith's work not so far from Campbell's early unpoetic, let us say, shipwrecked sentiments. Such courses may be expected when one speaks fondly, and

---

[1] Richardson, *Memoirs*, 1:142-3
[2] Richardson, *Memoirs*, 1:49
[3] Richardson, *Memoirs*, 1:145

uncritically, of restoring ancient things. So the gloom of Calvinism has spread among his distant progeny, although the Irishman himself slowly bled out by the leech of American frontier what despair his education had not dissolved.

Landed and united with his father in 1809, the boy was now a man. Soon the son became the leader, the father one of many followers. He had a sense for how to run in America which his father, too old for adapting, never acquired. The Campbells' first American publication, "A Declaration and Address of the Christian Association of Washington, Pa" (1809), advocated the sort of machine that might fly through the frontier: "Bible religion," opposed to groupie-gathering Sectarianism; associations formed to promote "simple, evangelical Christianity"; and, be sure to read to the end, that "each member, according to ability, cheerfully and liberally subscribe a specified sum, to be paid half yearly, for the purpose of raising of funds to support a pure Gospel ministry."[1] Funded by the masses' scarce but in volume, reliable excess capital, his religion would seemingly be grounded in each donor's Bible; but in fact "a pure Gospel" was spread through the ministerial labors of trained preachers advocating Campbell's metatext of the Bible.

What Scottish Independents used to build opposition to established churches, and even kings and parliaments, would do well enough amid sparse populations and eager-to-be-saved readers spread over the frontier. The way? Speak from the Bible seemingly read by every would-be congregant, and claim that one's interpretations are taken directly from the page; and, most importantly, train enough capable preachers to do this, consistently from village to village, so that Americans begin to hear, from town to town, Campbell metatext uttered by babes, even from the mouths of non-preachers. Advertisers dealing in viral media and social networks would sharpen the tools of their often clumsy craft by looking to preaching networks of the sort established by Campbell. His influence was the greater, you see, when it ran backwards, as it were; when one heard his interpretations before actually hearing him, or his preachers.

Thus, as in the recollections of Parley Pratt discussed later, one might hear from where one knows not of some "ancient church" and its offering of baptism upon confession of faith; and *then* encounter a Campbellite preacher who taught of the by-all-appearances same church, drawing out in detail from the New Testament, offering quick baptism in the bargain. The key to the entire movement was the tangible thing called the Bible, but which needed interpretation-translation in order to be a socially existing force. The thing-metatext relation—the Bible as a book; and a mess, often convoluted, of

---

[1] Richardson, *Memoirs*, 1:243

translations, interpretations, dogma and tradition, as metatext—this relationship is what is meant when some convert speaks of "the Bible" or "the scriptures." Where Restoration was positioned—Bible words for Bible things—was at the fruitful meeting point of this relation: it allowed everything one wrote or even did to be commentary or exposition on the Bible. A reader's inability to see how the real thing organizes and anchors the socially moving forces? This occlusion generated what we call Mormonism, when the Book of Mormon was drawn into the gravity of the Bible. Much was captive to its magnetism, to the lure that a perfect society could be engineered upon the compass of its pure words.

Campbell's position on the Bible as the preacher's text was regularly stated, emphatically, if not always consistently. As his biographer summarized, "God himself should speak to them, and they should receive and repeat his words alone. No remote influences, no fanciful interpretations, no religious theories of any kind, were to be allowed or to alter or pervert its obvious meaning."[1] Campbell's insistence that the Bible (as God) speak for itself (his Bible, that is, his interpretation, or metatext); while practical and making for easy converts, this insistence also left a void threatening with schism any growing movement. Surely the same contradictory argument about the Bible being the only rule (such a rule is not in the Bible, but is of its metatext), would not have more salubrious effects than it did during, say, the Hundred Years War, the Peasants' or Bishops' Wars, or one or another civil war. So unstable was his material that Campbell only secured brief, seeming unity; and that came with the monthly installment of his Christian Baptist, and a stable of well fed, hand-picked, and at times well-heeled preachers. Without an actual center, as Yeats and then Achebe noticed, things do tend to fall apart. The Bible was more useful as a thing to stand on, you see; to shoe hobby horses with, than an ark for all to inhabit. Free of traditions grounded in cathedral and Prayer Book and lineage and vengeance, Campbell could hope in the frontier to delay schisms that came when readers realized their Bible was not everyone's Bible. With a more plain translation, perhaps, a Bible-based Restoration could hope for persisting unity and growing numbers: exactly what Campbell had long sought. In the terms of this chapter, unity could come from Bible metatext—bound up with ministers, congregants, translations and interpretations, spread hither and thither without suffering resistance from competing metatext. Unity in the face of, well, not armies, but other sects—that is not as difficult to secure.

Thus he "translated" the New Testament in 1827. Metatext was realized, that is, literally, into an actual text. Although Campbell translated the New

---

[1] Richardson, *Memoirs*, 1:237

Testament in 1827, another bible that wasn't the Bible? That is one too many for Alexander Campbell, as we'll see later. The Bible was sufficiently self-explanatory—when one knew Greek, Ancient Greek, Latin, French, and a smattering of Hebrew, alongside Christian theology, Covenanters, and modern philosophy—that a Golden Bible could not be anything but superfluous. God not only hated vacuums, but also like a good Puritan, despised superfluity (and fancy words, too). "The silence of the Bible," his position was summarized in his memoirs, "is to be reverenced equally with its teachings."[1] (To his credit, Campbell abandoned "paedobaptism" after a Dickensian-named Doctor Riddle challenged his father to find it practiced in the New Testament.[2]) Concerning Campbell's one-word-one-idea theory of language, it has been noted that "his practice was perhaps better than his theory, and the two were sometimes distinctly opposed," for the man's mind had fused uncritically "Renaissance principles of literary interpretation" to a "rationalist theory of language," one better suited for algebra than the translation of Plato.[3] Campbell's work-around for the contradictory claim that the Bible was the purest book, but also required extensive commentary and his own re-translation, is the meta-linguistic notion of *revelation.*

For the preacher, revelation made the text plain; "among intelligent Christians," he found its correct definition: "a Divine communication concerning spiritual and eternal things, a knowledge of which man could never have attained by the exercise of reason upon material and sensible objects."[4] His doctrine of revelation was creative; creative of his own authority. There was some truth in his claim that, "the word of God is a means of regeneration," its fruit faith, "the full and firm persuasion, or hearty belief of the divine testimony concerning Jesus."[5] Should you accept his translation as your faith, you also realize his reception of "a Divine communication." Power, that is to say, travelled alongside translation. Campbell had some inkling that such was the nature of his work, arguing that a preacher's calling was not found in "certificates nor the clergyman's swearing that he is called by the Holy Spirit," but "Only the evidence of a miracle could prove that he possessed such a call and that he cannot produce." One could not call upon miracles for evidence, for "Spiritual gifts were only temporary to place the

---

[1] Richardson, *Memoirs*, 1:351
[2] Richardson, *Memoirs*, 1:250-251; 401
[3] Phillips, *Differences*, 51-52
[4] In West, *Alexander Campbell and Natural Religion*, 95
[5] Richardson, *Memoirs*, 1:99

infant church upon its feet."[1]  The only rational basis for a minister's call, then, "is a social contract and the minister need not fool others and himself."[2]  Thus Campbell was charged by Baptists generally, and among those he first joined in the Redstone Association, with denying the Holy Spirit.  For him, however, the Bible could be carved up just right, to ensure the correct reading and translation, precisely because he enjoyed the Spirit's everyday guidance.

"Campbell asserted that the books of the Bible are the only ones of divine authority in the world," but not all of the Word carried the same revelatory punch: "the historical and non-revelatory parts contain facts," he divined, facts, "necessary because of their intimate connection with the people to whom Divine Revelations were made."[3]  That is a round-about way of saying this: Alexander Campbell could discern what was revelatory—what some passage really meant, and its significance to your own personal salvation—and which parts were mere historical and of temporary duration.  If a reader accepted his reading—often involving discussions of language, interpretation, and the other metadiscursive matters—that was in effect accepting a social contract that called him to the minister's role.  By that social contract's sealing, one granted him—and any other preacher similarly inclined—interpretative rights over the entire Word.  From the Bible he might sketch out one's biography, and point to correct uses of one's body.  He was bound to texts regarded as sacred but somehow always in need of someone's commentary and interpretation.  The real power came, you can understand, when Campbell stepped away from the pulpit and took up the translator's desk.

The Redstone Baptist Association to which he joined the Brush Run Church eventually charged him with heresy, having taken his interpretation of scripture into the elimination of too much scripture, and arguing that Christians were no longer under the old law.  A "New Covenant of the Gospel of Christ" had transcended the old.  It was the Baptists who were wrong, then, about spiritual gifts and whatever else Campbell sensed might constrain his powers of interpretation; and his rejection of their dogma did not stop him from naming his paper *The Christian Baptist*, nor himself from claiming to receive continual inspiration or revelation while reading the Holy Word.  "At times Campbell was vague if not inconsistent in his tendencies toward interpreting the authority and inspiration of the Scriptures," one generous historian said, "To say the least, he was

---

[1] In West, *Alexander Campbell and Natural Religion*, 137

[2] In West, *Alexander Campbell and Natural Religion*, 10

[3] West, *Alexander Campbell and Natural Religion*, 145

unsystematic."[1] When Campbell and other primitivists sourced their claims to the Bible, they often offered descriptions of how language was used in the Bible: one word had a single true meaning, and they could give it. They also offered categories for distinguishing between kinds of usage: e.g., revelatory versus historical. One might find in its passages general laws, like the nature of covenants. Use of covenant theology, thus, was four-fold: first, it broke the Bible into two parts, as we've seen. More importantly, by summoning our place in the second part, it offered social roles for readers to take up, and so to translate terms into their very own flesh and daily interactions. Feeling oneself a sinner is the embodiment of metaphysics taken from the pages of metatext. It is not a natural state, apparently. Third, being put into social roles like saint and sinner and disciple also moved the reader into relations with deity described in the pages of the New Testament: specifically, the Holy Spirit. As a saint or disciple or Christian or one saved, a reader might claim to enjoy revelation regarding some passage of scripture, to assert that such-and-such is what it *really* means, and to feel the truth of that reading. Spoken metatext and phenomenological metatext would be knit with unwavering certitude. Now the fourth effect: metatext could be generated which not only offered to translate or comment upon some passage of slippery scripture, but also to declare principles of interpretation; for discerning true from false revelation, for deciding who was right, wrong, and confused. Unity and schism abound. These were and are the fruits of covenant theology, and they are scattered across the entirety of the Book of Mormon, by Mormons after 1830. Mormonism, of course, left behind the discussions of covenants that aroused men like Grotius and Knox and Tyndale, far in the background. Effects of their reading, terminology, and of organizing around the term *Restoration*, however, remain bound up in the bodies and minds of readers of the Bible, and of their metatext Book of Mormon. Terms like *dispensation, revelation* and *priest* ordered a readership who found restoration upon its pages.

Let's return to Campbell's Brush Run Church, organized in 1811; two years later affiliated with the Redstone Baptist Association. Brush Run members are described in official histories like so many other religionists of the day: devoted and poor, meeting at homes to pray and read, often carrying on throughout the night.[2] He was not to be confined to their meetings, however. By virtue of affiliation with

---

[1] West, *Alexander Campbell and Natural Religion*, 146
[2] In I. Daniel Rupp, *An Original History of the Religious Denominations at presently existing in the United States* (Phila, PA: J.Y. Humphrey, 1844), 253

a Baptist society, "then the numerically strongest denomination in America," Campbell "at one stroke secured a great audience of friendly listeners."[1] That audience would not hear him for another decade. Meanwhile, he wrote somewhat, studied ancient languages and theology as piously as ever; farmed, started a family, requested an impolitic re-baptism from a minister, and thus made enemies in Redstone; and in good Independent fashion, formed Buffalo Seminary in Bethany, (West) Virginia.[2] When his status as a good Baptist came under scrutiny, Campbell deflected and dissembled. He turned to the Bible, imagining that a church could "come firmly and fairly to original ground, and take up things just as the apostles left them," that is, in "pristine purity and perfection."[3] The Western Reserve was the right place for colonizing that imagined ground.

It was born amid (lucrative) confusion among Europeans about American geography, with many land patents in Connecticut extending to the "South Sea," and not all running along lines parallel one with another. Thus in 1786 Connecticut ceded charter-lands west of the western limits of the Reserve, finally fixing the confusion by conceding in 1801 that entire Reserve as well.[4] The open lands seemed to expand Campbell's mind and soften his heart, so that of the sermons from his early American days, "none are to be found of a partisan or disputatious character, and none of them are directed at any existing denomination."[5] He marked out only two offices appropriate (that is, biblical) to the church: bishop and deacon, in plurality, ordained by "imposition of hands."[6] Outside the church would roam preachers, elders, and "evangelists," but "every church was independent," selecting its leaders and upon approval from the broader Society, "set apart by formal ordination."[7] Dogma and creed were forbidden, and tolerance the stated rule for adherents. The goal was to grow. According to his *Memoirs*, admission to the church required mere consent to the claim that "Jesus is the Son of God," (being different from God the Father); although the deciding question was more opaquely, and more respectably given by later Church of Christ historians as, "What is the meritorious cause of the sinner's acceptance with God?"[8]

---

[1] Richardson, *Memoirs*, 1:100

[2] Richardson, *Memoirs*, 1:105

[3] Richardson, *Memoirs*, 1:257

[4] Hayden, *Early History*, 14

[5] Richardson, *Memoirs*, 1:355

[6] Richardson, *Memoirs*, 1:384-5

[7] Richardson, *Memoirs*, 1:386

[8] Richardson, *Memoirs*, 1:408; *in* Rupp, *An Original History*, 253

As it did for another religious seeker, the year 1820 marked a turning point in the career of Campbell. That year he read a pamphlet published by the "Scotch Baptist" church of New York City, and after meeting Walter Scott in Pittsburgh, he was convinced that baptism was conducted for the remission of sins.[1] That conclusion led him to ask about preconditions, hows and whys and what nows. Educated in Edinburgh, Scott flirted with Baptists, though too sought restoration.[2] Two had come together using that word. Scott would, several years later, provide the sequence which Mormons would take on as the "first principles of the gospel," being surprised that it took him, a simple preacher, to discover what had been hidden for eighteen centuries. Campbell never really worked out solutions to his questions about baptism for remission of sins, however.

June 1820, at Mt. Pleasant, Ohio, Campbell put his new understanding of baptism to the test, debating in public John Walker, minister among Seceders, and thus, a man to measure how far the student had moved over the decades. Though transcribed, the debate is not to be consumed by modern readers; it having an expiration date long ago passed. The transcript was published in a run of 4000 and was studied by Adamson Bentley who had met the elder Campbell a decade earlier.[3] His own sister recently married a rising star among ministers, the naturally gifted and hard-working Sidney Rigdon. The pair travelled to Campbell's Brush Run Church, and after talking through the night, hearing that Redstone was maneuvering to disfellowship his church, they offered Campbell a place in the more tolerant Mahoning Baptist Association, named for a river in Ohio, and recently divided from the more officious Beaver Association.[4] The association had been formed in August 1820 with this creed: "Three persons in Godhead: Father, The Word, and the Holy Ghost; and these three are one."[5] But creeds mattered little. Common for Campbell, he underplayed the political strategy, and recollected in his Millennial Harbinger that their conversation was strictly biblical:

> Beginning with the baptism that John preached, we went back to Adam and forward to the final judgment. The dispensations—Adamic, Abrahamic, Jewish and Christian—passed and repassed before us. Mount Sinai in Arabia, Mount

---

[1] Whitsitt, *Origin*, 92

[2] Van Kirk, *A History of Theology*, 90

[3] Richardson, *Memoirs*, 2:43

[4] Hayden, *Early History*, 19; Richardson, *Memoirs*, 2:44

[5] Mary Agnes Monroe Smith *A History of the Mahoning Baptist Association* (MA Thesis West Virginia U, 1943)

Zion, Mount Tabor, the Red Sea and the Jordan, the Passovers and the Pentecosts, the Law and the Gospel, but especially the ancient order of things and the modern, occasionally engaged our attention.[1]

Campbell consoled, as he tells it, a fawning Rigdon, who confessed, "if he had within the last year taught and promulgated from the pulpit one error, he had a thousand."[2] The visit came at a good time, and their offer made sense. The ambitious and crafty Irishman proceeded to secure letters of dismissal from a relieved Redstone, happy to show him the door, declaring him in good standing. He began moving members from Brush Run into the new Wellsburg church. Careful to observe the niceties of church etiquette, however, Campbell waited until 1825 before attending the Mahoning Association's annual conference.[3] Its conferences showed, even prior to his attendance, that "the Association was more 'Campbellite' than 'Regular Baptist.'"[4] Neither Baptist nor Presbyterian, the learned writer often printed the meeting's minutes, gave its sermons, and soon turned it into a mouthpiece for Restoration.

Campbell stopped often in Pittsburgh to visit Bentley and his right hand man, now laboring less glamorously as a tanner, taking dead things and preparing them for craftier hands to make of his skins something fashionable. This labor of Rigdon's is often over-emphasized, in part to show the man as a friend of the common worker, but also to diminish his role in declaring Campbell's goal to restore the "Ancient order of things." Bushman would state that Rigdon "discussed religion with Alexander Campbell and Walter Scott, two independent and vigorous young preachers who wished to restore the Christian church to its original purity."[5] An earlier biographer found him tanning as little as possible, however; and otherwise proclaiming Campbell's texts on Sundays at the Allegheny County courthouse.[6] Rigdon had joined Walter Scott's "Kissing Baptists" in 1824; a New Light Presbyterian congregation.[7] He was no mere pew-sitter nor hymnal passer-outer.

---

[1] Millennial Harbinger 1848:532, in Richardson, *Memoirs*, 2:45

[2] Richardson, *Memoirs*, 2:45

[3] Hayden, *Early History*, 24

[4] Smith, *A History of the Mahoning*, 63

[5] Bushman, *Rough Stone*, 123

[6] Mark McKiernan, *The Voice of One Crying in the Wilderness: Sidney Rigdon, Religious Reformer 1793-1876* (Lawrence KS: Coronado Press 1971), 23

[7] Richard S. Van Wagoner *Sidney Rigdon: A Portrait of Religious Excess* (SLC: Signature Books, 1994), 35. Scott also educated young men in the minister's craft, and among his

Like Campbell he had his run-ins with Baptist ministers. Rigdon had joined Peters Creek Baptist Church some years before, and was licensed to preach in 1819, certified by ordination the next year. No reports of grave failings in the man can be found from his days as its preacher, and he attended the Mahoning Association's annual conference every year after it was formed in 1820. His fellow men of the cloth, however, later spread no few tares in the field of Rigdon's reputation; and a great many after he took up Joseph Smith's heresy. Mormons followed in kind, after Rigdon failed to consent to Brigham Young's rule. He died with few friends, a pauper, mostly mad, a reputation for playing false being too easy for former friends to recite. One man reported Rigdon some years later confessed of his Baptist initiation, that "When I joined the church I knew I could not be admitted without an experience; so I made up one to suit the purpose, but it was all made up, and was of no use." Pastor Philips of Peters Creek oversaw his baptism, and like others who beheld no flaws in the man before he became a Mormon, Philips later recalled that Rigdon was "not possessed of the spirit of Christ, notwithstanding his miraculous conversion," and that Rigdon would be "a curse to the church of Christ."[1]

His fall into the muck of tanning, suffering its stain of poverty, was the result of what some call a "resignation," and more recent biographers find a dishonorable "release" from his position as a minister with the Pittsburgh Regular Baptist congregation. The distinction is important, for it suggests he suffered for his beliefs, rather than briefly tired of preaching. The future visionary Mormon leader was charged in October 1823 with heresy, for teaching what we now recognize were the doctrines of Alexander Campbell. Among them, that Christians are not under Mosaic law, which dispensation of priesthood made its adherents "children of Hell"; and that the change of heart was really a mere change in views coming after hearing the testimony of the evangelists, being followed by baptism. He also held like his mentor that "religious experience" was not biblical; that use of the Lord's Prayer (prominently endorsed in the Book of Mormon, although entirely absent from Mormonism) was likewise non-biblical.[2] What is not given among his crimes is belief in the restoration of priesthood authority, nor dispute over spiritual gifts.

---

better pupils was Robert Richardson, later composer of the confusingly titled *Memoirs of Alexander Campbell*, taking credit only for his role in their editing. The writing is actually biography.

[1] Samuel Williams, *Mormonism Exposed* (1842); in Van Wagoner, *Sidney Rigdon*, 8
[2] Van Wagoner, *Sidney Rigdon*, 31

Rigdon was self-taught and graduated cum laude bearing his school's brand of ambition, slight vanity and lack of confidence. As a youth he gathered hickory bark to light as a candle to read by, giving enough glow to turn a page to, but not enough to wake his father and earn himself a beating. His brother Laommi was declared the brains of the Rigdon clan, however. Laommi later returned Sidney's unwanted toil for his brother's education by diagnosing the old man as some sort of crazy, feverish of nervous distemper or otherwise disordered, having fallen as a youth from a horse while working on the farm.[1] Referring to himself in the third person for most of his autobiography did not dispel the charge of periodic lunacy, but it likely derives more from Rigdon's self-education, and desire to appear learned, than from any schizoid break. Being forced into the tannery, and having, as his biographer Van Wagoner said, "no talent for poverty," Sidney can be forgiven his many sins of overreaching and ambitious seeking. No worse judge of character than Joseph Smith called him, in late 1833, "a man whom I love but is not capable of that pure and steadfast love for those who are his benefactors," an advantage-taking that had exhausted Smith's patience by 1842; guilty of "little things such as a selfish and independence of mind which too often manifest destroys the confidence of those who would lay down their lives for him." In a conclusion which reveals as much about Smith as it does about Rigdon, the figurehead would say, "notwithstanding these things he is very great and good man." That generous assessment, however, was responding to a higher authority, calling him "high and lifted up, yet he shall bow down under the yoke like unto an ass that c[r]oucheth beneath his burthen; that learnesth his master's will by the stroke of the rode: thus saith the Lord."[2]

For most of the decade before he met Joe Smith, Rigdon would be as dedicated a preacher of Campbell's texts as the man himself was. (Campbell, however, maintained no direct line through the 1820s, changing doctrines and orthodoxies as often as circumstances or new translations demanded.) Invited to deliver a funeral oration in eastern Ohio, Rigdon preached so thorough a sermon on restoration—one can hear his fear of returning to the tannery overwhelming any other—that the congregation invited him to replace the man he eulogized.[3] The man proclaimed by his peers the "walking Bible" was free of the tanner's stain, and had at last set himself a-restoring ancient things. Disciples of Christ historians would later claim that it was "Through Mr. Campbell's influence," and

---

[1] McKiernan, *The Voice of One*, 14-15

[2] Nov 1833. *The Joseph Smith Papers: Journals* vol.1 (Church Historian's Press 2008), 17-18

[3] Van Wagoner, *Sidney Rigdon*, 40; 63

not by his own talents, that "Sidney Rigdon was induced to accept a call from this [Mentor] church to be its pastor."[1] Also guiding the Mentor church and now free to pass "like a meteor through the Western Reserve" was elder Walter Scott.[2]

Now there were three Restorationists. Finding himself free to invent or reject the ancient things, Campbell rejected the Holy Kiss (practiced by Scott's Baptists) as "oriental custom"; wrote against forbearance and toleration, finding them unnecessary because no injury could come from believed doctrines, anyway; and realized his youthful "pharisaic plan and the monastic" would leave him alone, and far from his goal of a unified, non-partisan community of Christians.[3] Yet he was not interested in coming together, right now, merely for the sake of unity. Since 1823 his heart was set on the restoration of the ancient order of things, and any unity must come through that corridor, as built to specifications given in his Christian Baptist. He thus made himself a by-word for sectarianism, among good Baptists and the like. Like Joseph Smith, Campbell was called every evil thing then known: Socinian, Antinomian (!), Pelagian (!!), Deist, and, gasp, Unitarian; a drunk, a horse thief; his own books would kindle flames, not of the Spirit nor the iniquitous tongue, but literally.[4] The years of 1820s were increasingly unkind to him. Preachers sought him out, and turned against him; others criticized his wealth, and perhaps jealously held him high in the honors of a cardinal hypocrite. Campbell grew less tolerant, more insistent. God seemed not entirely interested in his career.

―――― ● :―: ● ――――

## ANECDOTE.

DURING a late revival at Camillus, New York, a man who had been sprinkled in his infancy wished to be baptized and join the Presbyterian church. The Presbyterian divines would not baptize him because he had been sprinkled. The Baptists would not immerse him because he wanted to join the Presbyterians. At length a new sort of Christians, called 'Smithites,' immersed him. He then joined the Presbyterians. The church was satisfied with his sprinkling, and he with his dipping.

*Christian Baptist* vol.3:102

---

[1] Richardson, *Memoirs*, 2:47

[2] Van Kirk, *History of Theology*, 139; Richardson, *Memoirs*, 2:99

[3] Richardson, *Memoirs*, 2:129; 133; 137

[4] Errett Gates *The Disciples of Christ* (NY: The Baker & Taylor Co. 1905), 122

One year Campbell was sure of the Restoration's achievement, only to find himself not yet living in its promised Millennium. And so it went, year by year. These were days to try the faith of a preacher-writer, having buried three children over a decade; his wife in 1827; his standing with Baptist Associations often in doubt. One historian wrote he was increasingly "moved with the spirit of the most furious iconoclasm. Nothing escaped his invective, in the use of which he was an adept."[1] Among his favored targets were the Presbyterians, although his bridge-building with the Baptists would too become consumed in his burning for restoration, a sort of foolish and vain grasping at time's arrow.

It was during debates, first in 1820, and then one in 1823, where he acquired and perfected that black art of invective. With Sidney Rigdon as his travelling companion, Campbell set out for Kentucky in October 1823 to debate the Presbyterian minister, Mr. W. L. M'Calla, over the course of a week, on much that apparently captivated the mind back then: infant baptism, circumcision, dispensation, and so on. M'Calla called Campbell his "adversary" and "accuser," terms so well-known as nick-names for Old Scratch that the debate judge called him to order, and to apologize.[2] It was a rousing six days, for sure. That the audience remained, despite Mr. M'Calla reading prepared remarks, and from a stack of books specially selected, rather than responding extemporaneously to the arguments of Campbell; and that the resulting 400 page publication, from the transcript made by "bishop Sidney Rigdon," was by contemporary standards a best-seller: Collectively these facts tell us we cannot underestimate how thoroughly besotted by the (metatext) Bible were these Christians. While M'Calla years later published his own version (one of those "I wish I had said . . ." revisions) to counter Campbell's "spurious publication of that debate,"[3] Campbell's erudition seemed otherworldly to listeners. One man reported, "That speech on Hebrews lifted me into world of thought of which I had previously known nothing."[4] Favoring the trumpet over the flute, his memoirist-biographer blasted this description, presumably drawn from some report or another:

> The freshness of his thoughts, the extent and accuracy of his biblical knowledge, and his grand generalizations of the wonderful facts of redemption opened up

---

[1] Gates, *The Disciples of Christ*, 120

[2] Richardson, *Memoirs*, 2:77

[3] M'Calla, W.L. *A Discussion of Christian Baptism, as to its subject, its mode, its history, and its effects upon . . . in Two Volumes* (Phila, PA: George M'Laughlin 1828)

[4] Richardson, *Memoirs*, 2:93

trains of reflection wholly new, and presented the subject of Christianity in a form so simple and yet so comprehensive as to fill every one with admiration. Nor were they less struck with the perfect ease with which he developed and illustrated the most profound and enlarged conceptions, seemingly by an inexhaustible interior power, unaided by the slightest gesture or any of the arts of elocution.[1]

Striking while the iron was hot, Campbell toured with Rigdon. His Christian Baptist added subscribers and gained influence. Rigdon "circulated the paper, and brought out its views in his sermons. Whatever," wrote one Disciple, "may be justly said of him after he had surrendered himself a victim and a leader of the Mormon delusion, it would scarcely be just to deny sincerity and candor to him."[2]

# CHRISTIAN BAPTIST.

*No. 6—Vol. V]*   BETHANY, B. C. VA. Jan. 7, 1828.   [*Whole No. 54*

*Style no man on earth your Father; for he alone is your father who is in heaven; and all ye are brethren. Assume not the title of Rabbi; for ye have only one teacher:—Neither assume the title of Leader; for ye have only one leader—the MESSIAH.*

[Mat. xxiii. 8—10.]

*Prove all things: hold fast that which is good.*

[Paul the Apostle.]

### ANCIENT GOSPEL.—*No. I.*

#### BAPTISM.

IMMERSION in water into the name of the Father, Son, and Holy Spirit, the fruit of faith in the subject, is the most singular institution that ever appeared in the world. Although very common in practice, and trite in theory, although the subject of a good many volumes, and of many a conversation, it appears to me that this institution of divine origin, so singular in its nature, and so grand and significant in its design, is understood by comparatively very few. In my debate with Mr. Maccalla in Kentucky, 1823, on this topic, I contended that it was a divine institution designed for putting the legitimate subject of it in actual possession of the remission of his sins—That to every believing subject it did *formally*, and *in fact*, convey to him the forgiveness of sins. It was with much hesitation I presented this view of the subject at that time, because of its perfect novelty. I was then assured of its truth, and, I think, presented sufficient evidence of its certainty. But having

---

[1] Ibid.

[2] Hayden, *Early History*, 192

It was the year 1825, after attending Mahoning's meeting, when Campbell began at last to publish on his long considered Restored Gospel. The series covering purity of speech, the office of bishop, baptism, breaking bread, fellowship, and so on, continued through 1828. He outlined his church, as it ought to be, and increasingly, was. "The idea of remuneration from his services," it was said, being "attached to the office [of bishop] from the beginning," Campbell did not refuse compensation; although he was careful "not to take the oversight of the flock 'for the sake of sordid gain.'"[1] It is clear that Campbell was not motivated by love of money in his labors, and seems sincerely devoted to establishing a Christian Church which would please God, being constructed exactly as outlined in his Word.

Where the New Testament was not entirely clear in this regard, Campbell found a way to allow himself invention and rejection, at will. As part of this series, and indeed realized as its very justification in 1826, he asserted that wholesale apostasy was evident in Christianity.

convince or to persuade by such means.

────

### THE POINTS AT ISSUE.

WE contend that all christian sects are more or less apostatized from the institutions of the Saviour, and that by all the obligations of the christian religion they that fear and love the Lord are bound to return to the ancient order of things in spirit and in truth. Our opponents either contend that they are not apostatized, but are just what they ought to be; or if they admit of any defection, they contend that the time is not yet come—they must await the Millennium; and that it is better to keep up the present systems than to attempt any thing else. This is just the naked question, detached from all superfluity, and it would be well for both the friends and opponents of this work frequently to reflect upon it. Ed.

AS it is expected that I will arrive in Mason county, Ky. as soon as this number, no appointments can be intimated for that vicinity; nor can I, owing to various causes, as yet lay down my own route. I intend, if the Lord permit, to make an extensive tour and an expeditious one, through that state and places bordering on it. It is hoped, and I suppose reasonably expected, that those in arrears to this establishment, and the subscribers to the current volume, will pay over to our agents, immediately, that they may be in readiness for a call from us. We are constrained at this time to be somewhat urgent, as justice requires us to liquidate the debts of the establishment as soon as possible.

────

*Christian Baptist* vol.4:96

────

[1] Richardson, *Memoirs*, 2:128

He offered no solution other than reviving practices, with sufficient faith to make them potent. That same year, in April, Campbell completed his rewrite of parts of the New Testament, rendering a plainer translation that benefited from his doctrinal sounding out, and made more clear in what constituted the Ancient Order. He announced "the new version of the New Testament" was finally available for purchase.[1] A new religion, after all, requires a new Bible; here his metatext at last descended into the body of the original Word.

In his translation, Campbell drew from Old World scholarship, adding to this authority his own sense of what was really going on, eighteen centuries previous. The translation was called "Living Oracles," which would seem to support the argument that Campbellites were not opposed to "oracles" being given, so long as they stood atop the New Testament. The work took liberally from a Scottish scholar named George Campbell, and others named MacKnight and Doddridge. It provided "general and special references, hints to reader, and notes," indeed, carried more introduction and "prefatory hints" than actual content. Thereby the work was, he proclaimed, "constituting the most important aid to the study of the New Testament ever published in so compact and cheap a form."[2] It was finally offered for sale in March 1827, and would be the text—a translation as commentary, the most tangible of any metatext—that Rigdon and Parley Pratt presumably preached from. "In those days appeared John the Immerser," Section II of MATTHEW begins, "Who proclaimed in the wilderness of Judea, saying Reform, for the Reign of Heaven approaches." Campbell's Immerser demands of inquiring Pharisees and Sadducees, "Produce, then, the proper fruit of reformation." He proclaims that "I, indeed, immerse you in water, unto reformation."[3] His text (metatext realized into actual text, and itself bearing additional commentary) was not uncontroversial. It seemed like a sectarian attempt to rewrite the gospels (see next page).

[1] Christian Baptist, vol.3:224
[2] Richardson, Memoirs, 2:145
[3] Campbell, Alexander. The Sacred Writings of the Apostles and Evangelists of Jesus Christ, Commonly Style The New Testament (St. Louis MO: Christian Board of Publication, 16th ed., 1914), 59-60.

The Chinese, it is said, who cannot read, when they discover a piece of writing on the ground, will neither tread upon it nor burn it, lest the name of their god be upon it; but here a regenerated christian with a clear conscience designedly commits to the flames the whole testimony of God concerning his favor in the gift of his only begotten Son, and boasts of it as the Catholics in former times boasted of doing God service when they burned the heretics. And why did he burn it? To immortalize his name; yes, to immortalize his piety. I am authorized in concluding this to have been his motive from the fact that he has published in his brother's paper an account of the matter, as follows:—

*"For the Recorder.*

*"Dear Brethren—*I subscribed for Mr. Campbell's Testament, and received it, paid $l 75 for it, kept it five or six months and compared it carefully with one I have loved ever since I was 13 years old. On the first reading I condemned it, but let it remain in my house some two or three months; then tried it again, condemned and burnt it.　　　　　EDMUND WALLER.

*"Jessamine county, January 29, 1827."*

Can the present century equal this? I want a parallel case to put on file with it for the benefit of posterity. He compared it carefully with the common version!! yet it is believed he could not tell the nominative case to a verb, nor the antecedent to a relative, to save himself from the Spanish inquisition. But he is regenerated, and prayed *"ten days"* for light on this subject!!! His one dollar and seventy-five cents cost him ten days praying!!——Criticism, avaunt! This defies you!　　　　　EDITOR.

---

## THE NEW TRANSLATION.

THE first edition of this work is, with the exception of a very few copies, disposed of. It has been well received and highly approved of by many competent judges, alike distinguished for their piety and erudition. The objections made to this translation are not in the proportion of ten per cent. to those made to former translations; and I presume were it generally received, or rather circulated, the objections from all parts of the union would not proportionally amount to more than they now do. Many objections and petitions against the common version, it is said, were presented on its first appearance. The king's decree silenced them at first, or until use had rendered it familiar, and the youth accustomed to read it at school when they arrived to manhood thought well of it, and esteemed all the points and letters in it of divine authority. It is to be hoped that no such means will ever again be resorted to, to give currency to any translation. That only should obtain general reading whose merit deserves it. We have been often requested, (and it is probable at some future day it may be undertaken) to publish a pocket edition of this version. But before a second edition, either of a larger or smaller size, will be proposed or attempted, we wish to receive all the criticisms and emendations which can be proposed by the learned and pious of all denominations. We therefore humbly solicit from all concerned

An all-star preaching event marked the release of the Living Oracles, with Walter Scott laying down the newly discovered ancient sequence of Faith, Repentance, Baptism for the remission of sins, and the Gift of the Holy Ghost. Rigdon's performance was so luminous that many confused him for the great Alexander Campbell, who later in the day developed his theory of dispensations through the metaphor of celestial lights (starlight, moonlight, twilight, and sunlight).[1] Added to this roster was an old veteran of the circuit, Barton Warren Stone, who began his career as a Presbyterian seminarian. Convinced of a single truth, "God is Love," he "yielded and sunk at his feet a willing subject."[2] Stone was a truly gifted preacher, and devoted himself to that message, before taking up with Campbell and company. He rejected the "commercial idea" of Atonement and Reconciliation offered by Anselm and others, seeing that Jesus came to men who were sinners, delivering pardons merely for believing his word.[3]

Stone was there—as some might say about Woodstock, or the 2004 American League Championship Series—and gathered with 35,000 at Cane Ridge, Kentucky in 1801. He preached this "distinguishing doctrine . . . that God loved the whole—the whole world, and sent his Son to save them—that the gospel was the means of salvation—but that this means would never be effectual to this end, until believed and obeyed by us."[4] That famous revival seemed to precipitate a new age, and now Stone had joined with Campbell, Rigdon, and Scott. His followers would join with Campbell's in 1832, forming a seldom unified Disciples of Christ. They would break somewhat by 1906, forming the Churches of Christ.

What Walter Scott lacked for eloquence or erudition, or mere charisma, he made up for in originality. Called "the bright jewel of the 'Ancient Gospel'," his Faith-Repentance-Baptism-Holy Ghost sequence was "so simple, so novel, no convincingly clear, and so evidently supported by the reading of Acts, it won friends and wrought victories where it was proclaimed."[5] By virtue of his discovery of the correct sequence of conversion—called by one writer "his much boasted *ordo salutis*"[6]—Scott was granted a special dispensation, as it were, to preach his

---

[1] Hayden, *Early History*, 35
[2] Gates, *The Disciples of Christ*, 68
[3] Richardson, *Memoirs*, 2:195; see also "Atonement . . . Stone-Campbell Dialogue"
[4] Gates, *The Disciples of Christ*, 73
[5] Hayden, *Early History*, 87
[6] Whitsitt, *Origin of the Disciples*, 107

"plan of salvation."[1] It was that important to the Mahoning Association. His sermons added hundreds of disciples counted on the rolls of Mahoning churches.

In March 1828 Rigdon toured with Scott, and "the missing link between Christ and convicted sinners seemed now happily supplied by the restoration of the way of bringing converts to the knowledge of pardon, which was established by Christ himself in the commission." Rigdon, we learn from writers disposed to make him an insufferable lick-spittle, "was transported with the discovery."[2] Even the Warren church led by Adamson Bentley (often moderating Mahoning conferences), and itself holding association with Scott's sponsor, was "besieged" for eight days, until all gave in and accepted rebaptism. During 1828 he joined with Bentley and Rigdon and baptized and rebaptized another 800 souls.[3] (It is not certain how many were already adherents of Campbell's restoration were rebaptized, and how many were "new" converts.) Scott added to his "plan of salvation" many new elucidations of "the prophecies of Jeremiah and Ezekiel, relating to the return of the Jews," and one historian claims that Sidney Rigdon "seized these views, and with the wildness of his extravagant nature, heralded them every-where."[4] Among the heralded views was Scott's teaching that Adam and Eve lived in a "first estate" deemed "terrestrial," a sort of lesser paradise generally applicable to the entire earth, under their stewardship.[5] This same year Alexander Campbell published an essay on "Three Kingdoms" developing of his theory of dispensations and priesthoods.[6] A vision recorded by Rigdon in 1832, seated next to the guiding, confident and reassuring Joseph Smith, would describe three kingdoms of glory: the Celestial, Terrestrial, and Telestial realms.

Drawn to the excitement of restoration, hearing Scott's plan of salvation, finding it right there in his Bible, and submitting to another baptism, was a young, sturdy, mostly unsuccessful but hopeful farmer named Parley Pratt. "Inspired by his newfound faith," Givens and Grow add what will be a tradition tackled next chapter, "Pratt became a freelance minister during the chaotic years of the Second Great Awakening, but an encounter with the Book of Mormon in the fall of 1830 changed his trajectory." How did it change? "By converting to Mormonism, Pratt added doctrines of priesthood authority to the primitivism and millennialism

---

[1] Gates, *The Disciples of Christ*, 151

[2] Hayden, *Early History*, 192

[3] Van Wagoner, *Sidney Rigdon*, 46

[4] Hayden, *Early History*, 186

[5] Staker, *Hearken O Ye People*, 321

[6] Christian Baptist, Aug 1828:97-99

of the Campbellites."[1]  What he means is that Pratt converted to Mormonism and got priesthood in the bargain.  History concludes otherwise, and so now again we return to Mormon traditions, and set about the stumbling block's splitting.

In what is for my money the best history of early Mormonism in Ohio, written by Mormon historical archaeologist Mark Staker (the restorer of sacred tourist sites), we encounter some curious confusions.  Staker correctly tracks the origins of Campbell's notions about priesthood to Alexander Crawford, who "outlined three priesthoods: 'the patriarchal,' 'the Aaronic,' and a priesthood of Jesus Christ." "Sometimes he referred to these priesthoods in his writing as the 'order of Melchizedec,' the 'order of Aaron,' and the 'office as priest' of Jesus Christ," all of which would become Mormon phrases by 1834.[2]  Rather than leave us to consider Crawford's orders and priesthoods, Staker interprets what he had dug up.  He inadvertently shows how Mormons broke covenant theology in a way that disguises the origins (in retrospection, as we'll see) of their contemporary doctrine of priesthood authority.  "The end of the Abrahamic covenant marked a change in dispensations," Staker explains, "Crawford viewed each of three changes in dispensations as also warranting a change in priesthood.  'For the priesthood being changed, there is made of necessity a change also of the law" (149).

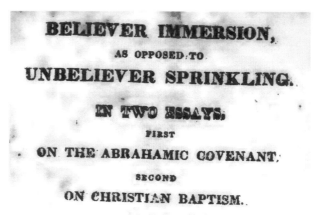

Alexander Crawford (1827)

---

[1] Givens and Grow, *Parley Pratt,* 4
[2] Staker, *Hearken O Ye People*, 149

What must be noticed is Staker's misunderstanding of how Crawford's and Campbell's use of the term *dispensation*. Rather than referring to an age, as it would later for less theologically trained Bible readers, dispensation meant "something dispensed." What was dispensed? The covenant to be administered by a priesthood.

Staker quotes for us (on page 150) Campbell's plagiarism from Crawford, found in his 1835 *Christianity Restored*, and we can be sure he reads these words from Campbell: "The whole Bible comprehends *three* distinct dispensations of religion, or three different administrations of mercy to the human race. These are the Patriarchal, Jewish, and Christian ages of the world." Having defined dispensations as "administrations of mercy," Campbell is using what would become an obsolete definition, one tied to a history of Catholic indulgences. The trading in such finally provoked Martin Luther to publish his Ninety-Five Theses. The Latin form of the term (*dispensatio*) was used to translate the Greek *oikonomos*, which also gave us our *economy*. So, in a little learned pun, Campbell concludes (and is quoted by Staker), "There are three high-priesthoods, viz., that of Melchizedek, that of Aaron, and that of Jesus the Messiah; and under each of these there will be found a different economy of things" (150). A dispensation of a new covenant—for Campbell the governing covenant was of Grace—required a new priest to administer it to humanity. Seeing a new dispensation, we find him reasoning that a new priesthood was also formed, this time with Christ as high priest. Displaying his Mormon tradition, Staker curiously summarizes Campbell's differences from Mormonism thusly:

> There was no need to maintain priesthood ties with previous dispensations and no need to pass authority from one generation to the next as part of an attempt to restore "the ancient order of things" (150).

To Campbell the notion that "priesthood ties" could be maintained with "previous dispensations" would make very little sense. Priesthood was the thing administering the dispensation, not an authority found inside it. So indeed the matter of authority was of little interest to Campbell and his convinced readership, for Jesus having administered a dispensation of Grace to all believers, humanity required no further authority than a moral one derived from a social contract accepted by one's congregation. Staker's confusion is a common one found among Mormons, for whom "dispensation" has become an age, and priesthood the authority/group/power acting in the age with full rights to administer the

Gospel anew. So they speak of the "dispensation of the fullness of times," as might other Christians, understanding that a new "dispensation" was not given to Joseph Smith, but was instead opened as one might a jar or a door. Such a definition obviously cannot be carried to the end of the phrase without introducing considerable confusion: the age of the fullness of times? It has become a slogan, a sort of trademark. Using Mormon-speak, the slogan points to the time of restoration, when the true (LDS) church was restored and the House of Israel also, having all the authority—Aaronic and Melchizedek orders—necessary for the Lord's priesthood to administer the plan of salvation. Confused by sly terms extracted from European conflicts, Mormons found an opening to introduce traditions regarding priesthood authority and explain that its restoration was the real draw for Campbellites gathered in Kirtland, Ohio. This particular knot we untie in a later chapter.

The doctrines of the four housekeepers of the Restoration—Scott, Stone, Rigdon and Campbell—were not so transporting to Baptists in the Redstone and Washington Associations. They failed to invite adherents of "Campbellism" to their annual conference by 1829, withdrawing the hand of fellowship once given Mahoning, for "disbelieving and denying many of the doctrines of the Holy Scriptures."[1] Among their doubtful doctrines, in addition to Scott's efficient conversion sequence, was the claim "that the scriptures are the only evidence of interest in Christ," that there is "no direct operation of the Holy Spirit on the mind prior to baptism"; but that confession of belief was sufficient for baptism administered unto salvation, for it "procures the remission of sins and the gift of the Holy Ghost." Finally, they held that "all baptized persons have the right to administer the ordinance of baptism."[2] These same doctrines must be recalled when we read about Parley Pratt's preaching in Kirtland and his mass rebaptism of Restorationists.

Severed of their ties to Baptists and newly christened Campbellites or Restorationers by their detractors, the loose network of an estimated 30,000 believers anticipated marvelous things,[3] even prompting Campbell to discontinue the Christian Baptist in early 1830. Readership was sufficient to strike out on his own, under a new, non-sectarian banner. The Mahoning Association was also dissolved that summer. Before it died a quiet and quick death, Rigdon had asked about restoring community of goods. His reading of the Bible seemed to include

---

[1] Gates, *Disciples of Christ*, 160-161
[2] Gates, *Disciples of Christ*, 162
[3] Gates, *Disciples of Christ*, 183

it among the things practiced by Christians. The same subject had been taken up by Campbell in debate the year before with the secular communalist Robert Owen. Considered "the richest, most prosperous farmer in what eventually became West Virginia,"[1] Campbell denied that community of goods was essential to the restored gospel. Rigdon was asking permission, not for an exposition, and that too late.

He had some obligation toward a small group calling itself "the Family," gathered on a farm south of his Mentor congregation. A man named Isaac Morley and his friend Lyman Wight started the family in February 1830, outside Kirtland; and converted another fifty souls to its practice in nearby Mayfield. While he did not join the Family, neither did Rigdon advise them to discontinue their communal living. "His reason for not joining," a recent biographer adds, "is not known."[2] Perhaps he hoped to join them to his congregation. The Mentor congregation overseen by Campbell was investing in Rigdon's long term security, building a fine home for their worthy, devoted minister. Whether they knew of Rigdon's visits to the Family is not known, but it is unlikely he informed them of the communal family. Newspapers continued to announce their minister's preaching itinerary by calling him a "Campbellite,"[3] suggesting that Rigdon's second family remained his little secret. We approach a critical season in the history of the Book of Mormon. Recently published metatext representing the actual book had widely circulated, even reaching Ohio. There is no evidence, however, that Rigdon or any Restorationist attended to such rumors. They were busy preparing for the Millennium, having restored the Ancient Order as fully as may be. They had in preparation dissolved their formal associations with the Baptists. They were disciples and their churches the restored body of the Church of Christ.

---

[1] Van Wagoner, *Sidney Rigdon,* 21
[2] Van Wagoner, *Sidney Rigdon,* 51; also, McKiernan, *The Voice of One,* 29: "The reason he never joined Morley's 'family' has not been recorded."
[3] Van Wagoner, *Sidney Rigdon,* 55

PART TWO

CIRCLING TRADITIONS

# Shakespeare's *Twelfth Night*

**Act II, scene iii.**

*Maria.* The devil a Puritan that he is, or anything constantly but a time-pleaser; an affectioned ass, that cons state without book and utters it by great swarths; the best persuaded of himself; so crammed, as he thinks, with excellencies that it is his grounds of faith that all that look on him love him; and on that vice in him will my revenge find notable cause to work.

*Toby.* What wilt thou do?

*Maria.* I will drop in his way some obscure epistles of love . . .

**Act II, scene iv.**

*Enter Malvolio, reviewing a letter he found on a path he walked.*

*Malvolio.* M, O, A, I. This simulation is not as the former; and yet, to crush this a little, it would bow to me, for every one of these letters are in my name. Soft, here follows prose. *[Reads]* 'If this fall into thy hand, revolve. In my stars I am above thee, but be not afraid of greatness. Some are born great, some achieve greatness, and some have greatness thrust upon 'em. Thy Fates open their hands; let thy blood and spirit embrace them; and to inure thyself to what thou art like to be, cast thy humble slough and appear fresh. Be opposite with a kinsman, surly with servants. Let thy tongue tang arguments of state; put thyself into the trick of singularity. She thus advises thee that sighs for thee. Remember who commended thy yellow stockings and wished to see thee ever cross-gartered. I say, remember. Go to, thou art made, if thou desir'st to be so.'

. . .

*Malvolio.* I thank my stars, I am happy. I will be strange, stout, in yellow stockings, and cross-gartered, even with the swiftness of putting on. Jove and my stars be praised. Here is yet postscript.

# FIVE  AIN'T GONNA WORK ON MORLEY'S FARM NO MORE

NOBODY SHOULD KNOW THE NAME PARLEY PRATT SOME TWO CENTURIES after he came into the world: a nobody in a nowhere town, his name about the only thing he inherited. Another hard luck frontiersman, a leaf on some genealogical tree full of nobodies but grandfathers, fathers, sons, grandsons. Had he not wandered off into the wilderness for God knows what reason, nobody would know his name belonged to him and my neighbor's son would surely not be named in his honor. A man of the dirt, little educated but concerned with readying his soul for its maker, Pratt instead contributed to an autobiography still in publication (edited by his son, Parley). His own writings have been granted "collected" status by more than one press and a recent biography bears his name for its title. The work is published by no less a name than Oxford University Press. He did wander off from Ohio, where Rigdon and Scott were mentors and spiritual fathers, carrying a bible given by the hand of Campbell.

Little is known of Parley's early life—before he became an apostle in Joseph Smith's Gold Bible movement—which is not learned from Pratt himself. Written in the 1850s, his autobiography would be edited by his son and first published in 1874. As a text it preserves some fascinating things found in early Mormonism; and also writes Mormon traditions back onto its earliest days. And like so much of Mormon history, it was edited by a son, but we cannot know for sure where the *Autobiography* shows the son's silent editorial work and which passages were authored by the father, nor the year of their composition. This chapter will attempt to unravel traditions explaining what Parley Pratt found when he arrived in Joseph Smith's hometown; and what he did when he returned to Sidney Rigdon's second family. After his tale, we consider versions told by historians of Mormonism, and ask about the evidence for them. Contrasting these histories mingled with tradition are versions told by historians from the Disciples of Christ. Their own inheritances are considered, and tell us much about the versions declared by Mormons regarding disputes between Rigdon, Campbell, and Pratt. Finally, we read contemporary newspaper reports in light of a new understanding of Mormon history, released from its long sustaining of knotty contradictions of tradition.

## PRATT'S BIOGRAPHY AS METATEXT

Pratt reports first attending Baptist services like so many lost to history, as a youth in the wilderness. Following his examination, being found fully converted, Pratt was scheduled for baptism.[1] He reports bristling at the delay, which seemed unbiblical; or maybe he suspected they doubted his experience. "Perhaps he fudged the evidence to gain baptism," a biography suggests, "but if so it was with persistent misgivings."[2] Eventually, by Mr. Scranton, Pratt was, as he tells it, "duly initiated into the Baptist society."[3] By "initiated" Parley means baptized, the result of his telling a suitably faith-evidencing "experience." "Pratt had not had any such experience," his biographers later explain, "and he sought baptism rather as a means to a more spiritual life. Even so, and lacking an identifiable moment of rebirth, he petitioned for and was accepted into fellowship with the Baptist flock; Scranton baptized him that summer [1825]."[4] How they discerned his lack of "experience" cannot be known. Its purported absence, however, fits into a narrative Pratt himself encouraged, regarding his search for divine truth and the power of Heaven. Relying on Pratt's *Autobiography*, biographers find themselves telling tradition as history.

Following some misfortunes, marriage, and setting up house in Ohio, Pratt went to hear the famous Sidney Rigdon, Walter Scott, and Alexander Campbell: "and what was my astonishment when I found he preached faith in Jesus Christ, repentance toward God, and baptism for the remission of sins, with the promise of the gift of the Holy Ghost to all who would come forward . . . ." He recollected, "Here was the ancient gospel in due form. Here were the very principles which I had discovered years before; but," he added, "could find no one

---

[1] Pratt, Parley P. *Autobiography of Parley Pratt* (SLC:Deseret Book 1938/1975), 26
[2] Givens and Grow, *Parley Pratt*, 28
[3] Pratt, *Autobiography*, 26
[4] Givens and Grow, *Parley Pratt*, 17

to minister in."[1]  That discovery of "principles" is only vaguely alluded to in his preceding story—Pratt is never dishonest—and seems to have been acquired second-hand from Campbell's widely circulating series on Restoration.  The immediately following sentence in his tale details, for the first time in the narrative, a concern over "the authority to minister in holy things—the apostleship, the power which should accompany the form.  This thought," he writes, "occurred to me as soon as I heard Mr. Rigdon make proclamation of the gospel."[2]  As if to convince us, the next paragraph cultivates this thought into many questions concerning chains of ordination, from Peter to such and such.  Pratt concludes certain that both "old Baptists and these Reformers" (he refuses to call them Restorationists) cannot claim succession from Peter.[3]  Despite these recollected concerns over authority, Pratt was again baptized; an event described rather curiously: "After hearing Mr. Rigdon several times, I came out, with a number of others, and embraced the truths which he taught."[4]  "Clearly the deficiency" in authority, his biographers note, "did not loom large enough in Pratt's mind at the time to dissuade him from switching allegiances from the former [Baptists] to the latter [Reformers].  That summer of 1829, Pratt joined Rigdon's flock."[5]  They mean he was baptized and attended the Mentor congregation, apparently; he was not of the Family.

Parley likewise downplays his own voluntary preaching following ordination by Rigdon, writing, "I took it upon me to impart to my neighbors, from time to time, both in public and in private, the light I had received from the Scriptures concerning the gospel, and," even more vaguely presupposing, "also concerning the fulfillment of the things spoken by the holy prophets."[6]  The next paragraph has him, not preaching, mind you, but "constrained to devote my time in enlightening my fellow men on these important truths, and in warning them to prepare for the coming of the Lord."[7]  After some disputable dealings with property, he left his wife (amiably) on a canal boat, and wandered through Joseph Smith's territory, at last encountering from an old Baptist deacon the story of a "VERY STRANGE BOOK!"[8]  Gold plates, hieroglyphs, visions of angels: we've

---

[1] Pratt, *Autobiography*, 31

[2] Pratt, *Autobiography*, 31-32

[3] Pratt, *Autobiography*, 32

[4] Pratt, *Autobiography*, 32

[5] Givens and Grow, *Parley Pratt*, 26

[6] Pratt, *Autobiography*, 32

[7] Pratt, *Autobiography*, 33

[8] Pratt, *Autobiography*, 36

read this metatext before. Convinced of its claims after a night's reading, Pratt searches out "the translator" of the book. Finding him absent, he unfolds to Smith's brother Hyrum his experiences in search after truth. This was their night's discussion, and, "together with that which I felt was lacking, viz: a commissioned priesthood, or apostleship to minister in the ordinances of God."[1] Mormons who read this description after two centuries of tradition have shaped the definition of terms like "apostle" and "priesthood" and "dispensation"; after a corporation owning the trademark *Church of Jesus Christ of Latter-day Saints* modeled after General Motors redefined them inside its own administrative structure. In Pratt's account, however, we discern no clear signs showing what he meant by these words.

We can doubt his recollections were so clearly worked out in 1830, and need only consider: If such skepticism about authority indeed haunted a youthful Parley, why be baptized twice? And ordained to preach, before even learning of the Book of Mormon? Moreover, why dust over the tracks of baptism and ordination in one's autobiography, except maybe you did not so clearly in thy youth formulate these notions of restoration of authority, so much as sort of wish you had, years later? There is no shame in being fooled once, even twice; hiding it, however, makes it seem somehow worse. The context of his conversion can be reconstructed, and they cast doubt on his recollections. Campbell was preaching about priesthood by 1828, relying on the Crawford pamphlet *Believer Immersion* to distinguish three dispensations of covenants to man: Patriarchal, Levitical, and Christian. With each dispensation a priesthood was called to administer its laws and ensure obedience to the terms of the contract. Such was Campbell's doctrine of priesthood, one making his own concerns about whether God recognized his performance of baptisms decidedly low on the list of things keeping him up at night. Campbell's authority like Rigdon's was found in accepting a call and finding a congregation to ratify it. So it was with Pratt, we can assume, having no evidence in primary materials from 1830 saying anything contrary.

What he seems to have sought for was "the apostleship," a social role having nothing necessarily to do with authority. Instead the role evidences a ramped up desire to do the works of apostles: speak in tongues, heal the sick, raise the dead, and so on. Most Restorationists noticed their absence among Christians. Campbell answered them that the gifts dispensed to early Christians were merely to raise the infant to its feet upon a faith confirmed by miracles. No longer, he taught, would such gifts be dispensed: now Christ the High Priest would mediate

---

[1] Pratt, *Autobiography*, 38

for Man, and the New Testament would stand in as a crutch where miracles once helped the unbelieving to rise. The church was restored to the degree there were Christians, and to that degree he'd say humanity was residing under millennial glory. There was one glaring omission that exposed Campbell's movement to schism: the New Testament describes characters not only bearing a name, disciple or apostle, but also some of their deeds. Apostle as a role was tied to miracles, and it seems that Pratt desired miracles. Campbell's complicated rationalization for the apparent absence of miracles was not carried along in his Bible, but required extended interaction with other metatext. Pratt's lack of experience with Campbell's metatext, and sincere hope to live in a world of restored Christianity brought him to Joseph Smith's home. That Gold Bible seemed near enough to the New Testament, but was also a new miracle, it seemed. The later Parley, the voice of the autobiography (reported through his son's institutionalized mediation), apparently bootstrapped desire to see the restoration of miracles into a return of the "apostleship," a "commissioned priesthood," which like apostles of old would administer baptism to every believer. Himself called an apostle when *Autobiography* was composed, it makes sense that this term would combine so much Restorationism, allowing it to project a later Mormon concern over authority to perform "ordinances." That term itself sometimes means "rites" in early Mormon writings, other times "rules" or "laws," adding to the confusion.

The authority bound up with "the priesthood" (defined by the mid 1830s as a power and a collective body) has been inserted into his own history, either by Parley, his son, or by the reader. On Parley's side, the insertion has been not well considered. Pratt reports that Hyrum Smith, and not himself nor Rigdon, convinced him that "the whole world were without baptism, and without the ministry and ordinances of God."[1] Later—to the frustration of Mormon historians looking for a linear tale of restoration—he would speak of a "dispensation or commission" of the "high priesthood," first given to him in June 1831. We should take up that June dispensation in a later chapter, I suppose. For now let us note its place in this revision and conflation of restoration of gifts into authority to perform baptism, and move forward with his tale. Following his third baptism, and being "ordained to the office of an Elder in the Church, which included authority to preach, baptize, administer the sacrament, administer the Holy Spirit, by the laying on of hands in the name of Jesus Christ," Pratt now felt "that I had authority in the ministry."[2] He and three other men—among them,

---

[1] Pratt, *Autobiography*, 38

[2] Pratt, *Autobiography*, 42.

Oliver Cowdery, scribe of the Book of Mormon, identified as the seer's spokesman directed to reveal the word to Lamanites—set off to preach the gospel and redeem the Book of Mormon's remnant of Joseph. Stopping in Buffalo, New York, they preached to the Tuscarora and Seneca (or "Cattaragus" Indians), who politely invited the men to tea some afternoon, when the preachers were more appropriately dressed to receive the Indians' cultivated hospitality. Surely the filthy Lamanites were more westward sheltered, and lacked fine linens and affected no British mannerisms. So they trekked through the muck and humanless spaces, forest realms free of the lines of plow and of ax cuttings. When Pratt arrived in Chardon, Ohio to minister to his old mentor, Sidney Rigdon, the trajectory of the Book of Mormon had escaped from Abner Cole's Gold Bible satires and scoffing. Pratt had steered it into the orbit of another metatext with far greater potency, reaching Alexander Campbell and his restored Bible. Sharing a vocabulary with most Christians, Smith's Gold Bible was thereafter made to mean the same things as the metatext Bible: when it says *Israel*, it means what we mean by Israel. And so on, through dispensation, restoration, priesthood, baptism, and authority. That brings us to what actually happened when Pratt arrived in Ohio. What Pratt found Rigdon and Campbell up to? There is a tale told so many times it seems true mostly for the frequency of its telling.

We can pick up Pratt's tale in the voices of those he partially created: Mormon historians. Pratt found Rigdon divided from Campbell. Why? Some division apparently left Rigdon less than enthusiastic about Campbell's project of restoration. Here are three versions from Mormon writers, the first from a skeptical Mormon historian attempting to trace Mormonism to "Seekerism." The second comes from a thesis turned biography. The third is taken from a biography by another Mormon, a self-described "rock-ribbed skeptic" not fooled by Joe Smith and his little book. First, the tale of Rigdon's dispute with Campbell:

> Rigdon had separated from Alexander Campbell over what Campbell described as Rigdon's belief that 'supernatural gifts and miracles ought to be restored' along with the primitive gospel. Rigdon believed the restoration of the 'ancient order of things' should include such spiritual gifts as tongues, prophecy, visions, dreams, and discernment of spirits. . . . Campbell also opposed Rigdon's plan to establish a communal society in Kirtland.[1]

---

[1] Dan Vogel, *Religious Seekers*, 37

The author (Dan Vogel) takes Campbell's quote from Richardson's *Memoirs*; adds to this source a reference to Amos S. Hayden's *Early History* (itself drawing on the *Memoirs*); and another from a biography of Rigdon written by Mark McKiernan. McKiernan's thesis tells the same story—Rigdon seeking restoration of "supernatural gifts and miracles" along with primitive communism; Campbell opposing his desires with a more rational Restoration. Not surprisingly, McKiernan's source is Richardson's *Memoirs* (2:346; see page 27). So we come to the single source positioning Rigdon with a desire for gifts against Campbell's rational approach: namely, Alexander Campbell, writing decades later, for others in his movement sharing similar reservations about gifts and miracles.

To Campbell's attempt to disparage Rigdon—he also mentions the preacher's "inconstant" character, fantastic tendencies, and possible lunacy—we find historians adding evidence from "the Family" he consulted with, sharing their goods on Isaac Morley's farm. Our final version of the disputation that Pratt encountered when he returned to Ohio claims that "Theological dissension between Rigdon and Campbell had been simmering for some time. Their points of disagreement focused on the gifts of the Holy Spirit, authority to perform ordinances, and communitarianism."[1] This biographer of Rigdon does not cite a single source, but follows with recollections attributed to Eliza Snow (living just outside Kirtland at the time, and recollecting over a decade later); Edward Partridge (his "journal" was written almost a decade later); and, of course, Parley Pratt. When we look at primary materials dated prior to 1831, however, we find the only dispute between Rigdon and Campbell concerned the restoration—not of gifts, nor authorities—of primitive communism. The Irishman was among the wealthiest farmers in the region. Morley's farm family survived by cutting and pressing peppermint; growing enough vegetables and fruit to qualify as "subsistence farmers" (i.e. peasants); hunting forest game; milking cows and gathering eggs of hens; and by the tedious processing of flax into linen thread.[2] Whatever Rigdon's Mentor congregation knew of his dalliance with Morley's family, we cannot doubt that Campbell was well aware of his break from orthodoxy: his wife's kin—Julia and John Murdock—had taken up the restoration of communism on Morley's farm. Surely this was the source of the preaching duo's personal and theological fracture, along with the dissolution of Mahoning bringing an end to Campbell's posture as a Baptist (as well as a

---

[1] Van Wagoner, *Sidney Rigdon*, 52
[2] Staker, *Hearken O Ye People*, 46

"Reformed Baptist"). Rigdon had been a Baptist for over a decade—and a Restorationist, not instead, but in conformity with his congregational identity. In a long tradition of Baptists, he could trace restoration back to the seventeenth century and their ostensible founder, Roger Williams.

No longer bound to Mahoning, once useful for linking Campbell with other Baptist associations in the east, Campbell was not identified with any sect. Outsiders called his readers and followers *Campbellites*. Campbell insisted on "Christians" or "disciples" (just as Joseph Smith's followers in New York had named themselves). Sidney Rigdon's two congregations referred to themselves with these same biblical names. How divided were Rigdon and Campbell over communism? Having no clear notion of how "close" Rigdon was to Campbell, we cannot measure their separation. Was Sidney reliant on Campbell for wages? Probably not. What about his status as a reformer? Doubtful it changed, as the Mentor church ratified his authority regardless of Campbell's approval, continuing to build him a home as fall set in. Was he no longer a Restorationist? Not at all. Walter Scott and Barton Stone did not cease calling on Rigdon during the summer and early fall of 1830, nor did he stop preaching restoration. We see none of the bitter name-calling, acrimonious gossip and spite that spewed forth in 1831, after Smith appeared in Kirtland. The supposed division of 1830, then, was made all the greater, sharper, and clearer after Rigdon "joined" the Mormons, and as Rigdon and other Mormons told their histories over the next decade. Both Campbell and Rigdon, like historians a century later, could agree that their relationship was hardly more than a passing fancy, and that in no sense did they join one mind to another, nor produce any offspring.

What we know is that Rigdon taught Campbell's texts, and his Mentor congregation attended conferences with a church led by Campbell, and they shared preaching duties with other churches as well. Did any of this change over the summer of 1830? I don't know, but I suspect Campbell was practical and crafty enough to realize that it was better for his project to keep Rigdon as a colleague, than it was to purge "Campbellites" of his heresy (which many others may likewise have aspired to). It will be evident, too, that Rigdon continued to preach Campbell's texts deep into the 1830s, and that Joseph Smith himself would take his words and shape them into Mormon doctrines. What came to light that season the Book of Mormon was published was this: Rigdon's desire to restore community of goods, having found a "family" already practicing it as part of a general restoration. Sidney never joined, suggesting he too was unwilling to separate from Campbell nor from his Mentor church over the matter of restoring communism. The reasons are obvious, in retrospect: Rigdon could not support himself if he joined Morley's farm, and having "no talent for poverty," bringing neither flax nor peppermint, he surely saw little reason to cast his scanty bread upon their scarcely flowing waters; only if Campbell agreed could the "common-stock scheme" be sustained. So long as Rigdon held out hope that Campbell might be convinced, there was no cause for outright opposition. Campbell's own kin, moreover, manifest the rising influence of Rigdon, and rather than directly challenging it, Campbell did nothing. That is, until the opportunity for separation presented itself in the person of Parley Pratt and his talk of a what others called the Gold Bible. This is my version, and it pleases me, not only because it does not embroider with any known traditions this fabric of history.

## THE POWER

Having surveyed how a story told by Alexander Campbell and reiterated by Rigdon was worked up into a citation chain suitable for biographers and historians, we can now turn to similar tradition-to-history conversions found in tales of the mass conversions witnessed by Pratt and his fellow preachers among disciples on Morley's farm. Here we unravel where the tales about "authority" originated, and, as might be expected, they grew from a misunderstanding of the meaning of words. First on our stage is Mark Staker, given the honor because his work is insightful, careful, and honest; and also honestly attempts—like looking at his own eyes to find their blindness—to solve riddles without realizing their source in his own religious traditions. Staker's first error is to project back the title *Disciples of Christ*, thus making them seem like a distinct sect, when in reality it was a common name: no caps. "As a Disciple of Christ," he explains, "Rigdon and a few select leaders sometimes called themselves bishops in an attempt to reflect the pattern of Church administration they saw in the New Testament."[1] The official Disciples of Christ were not formed until 1832, and yet by two capital letters he has made for Rigdon a sect from which he might defect, and convert to another movement. Among the disciples of Christ we find the biological family of Isaac Morley, whose daughter was employed as a maid in a wealthier home in Kirtland. When Pratt found her answering his knock, he proceeded to tell his tale of Gold Bibles and begged food. The teen directed him away from her skeptical employer to the farm of her father, said never to have neglected the needs of any stranger wanting nourishment and rest. Staker guesses,

---

[1] Staker, *Hearken O Ye People*, 31; 33

Oliver [Cowdery] may have shared some of his understanding of priesthood with his companions as they traveled west, but it is not clear what they actually understood of the experience during their brief stay in Ohio or if Oliver's mission companions even knew of multiple angelic messengers before they arrived in Ohio. However, having god-given authority was important to the first members in Kirtland (155).

In support of that conclusion, Staker mentions Campbell's relation, John Murdock, who "stayed up all night at the Morley farm discussing the 'power of godliness' and 'power from on high' with these young elders. The next morning, 'being convinsed that they not only had the truth but also the authority to administer the ordinances of the gospel,' John Murdock was baptized" (155). Mormons would come to speak of priesthood authority as "power from on high," and indeed the "power of godliness" which validated one's baptism in Heaven; but it is not clear that such was the case in 1830. Murdock's account was told many years later, after "priesthood" had been introduced (some say by Rigdon himself). "Others recalled that an emphasis on authority was part of these first sermons as well" (55), Staker adds without giving us the benefit of actual sources said to emphasize "authority." Here is one exception, given three pages later:

> The importance of proper authority that the missionaries emphasized when first arriving in Ohio became a key conversion point. One of the missionaries recalled: "at length Mr. Rigdon and many others became convinced that they had no authority to minister in the ordinances of God; and that they had not been legally baptized and ordained" (58).

Of course, who else but Parley Pratt would recall so clearly a legal matter resolved only by the apostleship? It may be true that indeed "authority" or "the power of godliness" or "power from on high" or just "power" was a concern voiced by various skeptics and believers alike. What these phrases meant at the time, however, is not so easily guessed at. Surely they did not mean all the same thing, and precisely what Latter-day Saints imagine they mean today. We can approach this difficulty from our own reasoning, however. If indeed "authority" or "power" evidencing one's Heavenly commission was found convincing to folks on Morley's farm, we can imagine that it was not the claim itself that convinced them. While it is commonly passed around LDS chapels that its leaders are authorized by

Heaven to hold the keys of salvation, not a soul over eleven years old, I suspect, is convinced by these claims alone. Some other experience must attend the claims, what Mormons call "obtaining a witness"; something like a spiritual experience which seems to assure the inquiring mind that indeed God does "sustain" those men Mormons call "prophets, seers, and revelators" and "apostles" and so on. It is the experience which ratifies the claims, embodied metatext locating its recipient in the imaginary of the Bible and its restoration.

So, if we hear historians saying that Cowdery and Pratt and companions simply showed up and "bore testimony" of their having priesthood authority, we can be assured this version is coming from a committed Latter-day Saint who has put the cart before the evidential horse. We find Staker explaining, "From the very beginning, the missionaries emphasized the Holy Ghost and the intense feelings of confirmation that listeners would experience as they heard the message" (57). He quotes from converts who speak of heart-warmings and so on, precious feelings and the like; these he has classified under "intense feelings of confirmation," elicited by "the Holy Ghost," just as one might expect of a modern Latter-day Saint. From here, he and others leap to "authority" rather than gifts of the Spirit as the take-home message of the Kirtland conversions to the restored church. To give you a sense of how significant all these converts held their rebaptisms at the time (late 1830, that is), we can conclude with Staker's note that, "Believers called themselves 'disciples' in the 'Church of Christ,' but outsiders called the movement 'Mormonism' and its believers 'Mormonites'" (74). What they called themselves in 1829 they also called themselves in late 1830, after a fellow disciple rebaptized them. They remained disciples in the Church of Christ, as they would for several more years, until the name "Latter-day Saints" (akin with former-day saints) came to be.

We now pass quickly through Richard Bushman's less detailed account in his biography of Joseph Smith. He mentions,

> In October, Pratt presented his old teacher with a copy of the *Book of Mormon*. Rigdon was impressed. He did not believe that a twenty-four-year-old could have written the book. After two weeks close study, he accepted baptism at Pratt's hand. His Mentor congregation was furious, refusing him the house, but Rigdon moved to Hiram and formed a little church of Mormon converts.[1]

---

[1] Bushman, *Rough Stone*, 124

"Sidney Rigdon," he writes, was "a luminary in Campbell's reformed Baptist movement" (89). The historian describes Rigdon's conversion with somewhat more detail, drawing on published biographies to explain that Rigdon's was "a search for something more. In late October 1830, on the eve of the Mormons' arrival, Rigdon 'had often been unable to sleep, walking and praying for more light and comfort in his religion." His quote comes from Van Wagoner's biography of Rigdon (p.44, 62; see Bushman's *Rough Stone*, n.21, p.593), itself embellishing Rigdon's recollections given many years later. No Mormons then existed, of course, to arrive at his home. "The next month," Bushman continues, Rigdon "led a parade of believers into Joseph Smith's fold. Campbellites were appalled that people would blindly accept revelations on so little evidence" (149). His presumed source for the principle cause of the Campbellites' blanching at the "parade of believers" is Alexander Campbell, described as "Founder of the Disciples of Christ and one the country's most notable theologians and preachers" (89). Like Staker, Bushman projects back *Disciples of Christ* and makes Campbell seem like the head of an 1830 church known by this name, as it is known today. The truth is that many Christians used the phrase, and that Campbell did not became a "founder" of any church for another two years, and even then the U.S. Patent and Trademark Office did not stop other Christians from calling one another "disciples of Christ." Now the founder of a named church, Campbell can be cast by Bushman as a dead religionist: "Campbell condemned visionary religion," he explains, "but shared the desire for a more pure and powerful religion based on the New Testament. Visionaries sought spiritual gifts; Campbell sought exact conformity to New Testament organization and doctrine" (148). As no sources are cited for this claim about Campbell, I cannot verify their accuracy. Given what I've read about the man, and read by him, it is not unreasonable to summarize his desires thusly. Bushman offers an easy contrast—bureaucracy versus charismatic gifts—which does not, however, fit with the teachings of Campbell regarding the inspiration of the Holy Spirit given to readers of the Word.

Reading by the light of the Spirit, Campbell would say, opens the mind to "continuous revelation"; a gift essential to the disciple. The New Testament, his "Living Oracles," was the site and engine of divine revelation, for there was no other way for sinful Man to augur the economy of Heaven, and to acquire the faith necessary for true repentance, before being immersed in the waters of baptism. So much as the organization—elders, deacons, bishops—was restored according to biblical use, so also, he would find, we approached the Millennium.

But the organization followed from his "inspired" reading of the Word. Organizational features urged by Campbell would be taken up by Mormons, ironically, who scaffolded his two-tiered hierarchy into a corporate entity beyond the reckoning of many a journalist and corporate consultant. Campbell's use and talk of the Bible as a tool for restoration reveals any easy contrast to be little more than tradition-telling. Yet Bushman makes Rigdon out to be a seeker of gifts, his followers parading from the cold structuralism of Campbell's Disciples of Christ into the open-ended charismaticity offered by Joseph Smith's Mormonism. His anachronistic version is a bush of light showing many fruits of truth, when we come under the shadows cast by Terryl Givens's tale.

With the help of Dr. Matthew Grow (employed in the Church History Department of the LDS Church), the professor of English so often found taking traditions as givens also adds many guesses to his biography of Parley Pratt. He suggests that when Pratt conversed with Hyrum Smith, the origin story now told by Latter-day Saints was possibly, even then maybe recited:

> Hyrum likely recounted his brother's early visions—probably not his first 1820 vision of God and Christ . . . but almost certainly the visits from 1823 to 1827 of the angel Moroni who had led him to the gold plates, which Joseph then claimed to translate from an ancient language into English. Pratt raised his perennial preoccupation with the matter of authority. Hyrum detailed "the commissioning of his brother Joseph, and others, by revelation and the ministering of angels, by which the apostleship and authority had been again restored to earth."[1]

Givens cites Pratt's *Autobiography* for the quoted text, and continues by swapping the robes of a raconteur of his own religion's tradition for the cold habits of the objective historian, explaining,

> Later, the church's narrative would represent priesthood authority as descending by literal laying on of hands following an unbroken line from Christ to his apostles, and from resurrected apostles to Joseph Smith. Like Smith's first vision, such accounts took time to become a seamless part of Mormonism's public self-presentation (32).

Citing Gregory Prince's *Power from on High: The development of Mormon Priesthood* (1995), Givens and Grow probe no further the implications that "such

---

[1] Givens and Grow, *Parley Pratt*, 32

accounts took time" to become part of the presentation of Mormonism. Pleased to tell tradition as history, the aptly paired Grow and Givens suggest that "Rigdon was increasingly looking for a broader restoration, including 'supernatural gifts and miracles," and that Owen's debate with Campbell in 1830 had provided Rigdon reasons to ask why not restore New Testament communalism as well (24). The cited passage, of course, comes from the *Memoirs* (vol.2:346), which Givens admits (on page 407) to lifting from Dan Vogel's *Religious Seekers and the Advent of Mormonism*. Richardson's *Memoirs* are seldom objective in their portrayal of "the apostate preacher" Sidney Rigdon. They give Campbell's explanations about gifts, simply to depict his old friend Sidney as a fantasist frenzied into fits by a bump to the head that never really healed. In fact, if one turns to the *Memoirs*, one finds Richardson adding vinegar to Campbell's mockery. The "editor" of the *Memoirs* suggests that Rigdon was behind the conspiracy of the Gold Bible, seeking,

> by obscure hints and glowing millennial theories, to excite the imaginations of his hearers, and in seeking by fanciful interpretations of Scripture to prepare the minds of the churches of Northern Ohio for something extraordinary in the near future. He sought especially in private to convince certain influential persons that, along with the primitive gospel, supernatural gifts and miracles ought to be restored, and that, as at the beginning, all things should be held in common. From his want of personal influence, however, he failed in disseminating his views, except to a very limited extent.[1]

Below I present another of Givens's selective use of Disciples' histories. This time he suggests the spiritual environment anticipated the Mormon restoration. Recall his earlier use of "new Bible" to hint at the Book of Mormon, unfortunately taken from Hyrum Andrus's 1959 BYU Studies essay? The embedded quote below attributed to "A contemporary historian of Western Reserve religion" is actually from Amos Hayden's *Early History* (page 183):

> [T]wo doctrinal seeds in the Book of Mormon struck especially fertile ground in his heart and mind. First, Pratt's millennialist expectations were nourished and heightened by the connections that the Book of Mormon explicitly made—and embodied—to latter-day events. A contemporary historian of Western Reserve religion noted that "the ardor of religious awakenings . . . was very much increased about the year 1830, by the hope that the millennium had now

---

[1] Richardson, *Memoirs*, 2:346

dawned, and that the long expected day of gospel glory would soon be ushered in." Pratt was caught up in those exuberant expectations . . . (29).

So, the Book of Mormon aroused in Parley Pratt a sense of the end of the world, just as "the ardor of religious awakenings" mysteriously spread over the same area? Let me present the restored passage from Hayden:

### EXPECTATION OF THE MILLENNIUM.

The ardor of religious awakening resulting from the new discoveries in the gospel was very much increased about the year 1830, by the hope that the millennium had now dawned, and that the long expected day of gospel glory would very soon be ushered in. The restoration of the ancient gospel was looked upon as the initiatory movement, which, it was thought, would spread so rapidly that existing denominations would almost immediately be deorganized; that the *true people*, of whom it was believed Christ had a remnant among the sects, would at once, on the presentation of these evidently scriptural views, embrace them, and thus form the union of Christians so long prayed for; and so would be established the Kingdom of Jesus in form, as well as in fact, on its New Testament basis. All the powers in array against this newly established kingdom, whether in the churches of Protestantism or Romanism, would soon surrender at the demand of the King of kings.

The "new discoveries" Givens omitted were the stages of conversion, Scott's "plan of salvation" discussed by Hayden over the preceding ten pages. Hayden's own brother, just to add a personal touch to my own version, was chosen to preach alongside Scott, not because he was a student of the scriptures, but "for his powers of music."[1]

Givens and Grow would also have us believe that Pratt and companions went to Morley's farm, "and began to share their message about angelic visitations to Joseph Smith and the restoration of authority to preach the gospel" (39). There is no evidence of any such "message," except that Lucy Diantha Morley Allen in an undated recollection said some message was originally rejected.[2] She was also

---

[1] Hayden, *Early History*, 174
[2] Reported in Givens and Grow, *Parley Pratt*, 410 n.12; Mark Staker, *Hearken*, 53

the teenager who cleaned the house that Pratt called on, and who directed him to the home of her father, Isaac Morley, doubting her employer would care to idle away the day talking about miracles and the like. It is doubtful that she also heard their message that day, having sent them there herself. The intrepid biographers quickly run us through the Kirtland successes, describing a flood of heart-warmings, roads crowded with Christians eager to hear the news of the true restoration (at last!), and then Rigdon's (reported) counsel to Morley's flock that they "not contend against what they had heard," taken from the mouth of Levi Hancock (41). He does not mention that Rigdon did not convert immediately, but waited a "fortnight," and did not by that night have many sheep left to direct. Morley's family had very nearly all embraced whatever it was Pratt was preaching. By "embraced" I speak vaguely and in metaphor, leaving the burden of describing what changes came about to another chapter. These authors also insist that, "Authority was a crucial issue for both missionaries and converts," using as their source the Painesville Telegraph's dismissive report. The pair summarize the report thus:

> The *Painesville Telegraph* noted the missionaries' claim to be "the only persons on earth who are qualified to administer in his name" and to properly baptize and to confer the gift of the Holy Ghost. Priesthood authority also enabled spiritual gifts (though the *Telegraph* reported that the missionaries had "totally failed thus far in their attempts to heal" and to prophesy) (42).

Here again we find authority being paired with spiritual gifts, close as a couple of fingers. In reality, as we'll see, the authority *was* the gifts conveyed; the sign of their authority to baptize was found in the gifts that followed them that believe. Before I can hope to support that claim—that the authority presented by Pratt was the gift so eagerly sought by Morley, and later disparaged openly by Campbell— we must run against more thorns of tradition, back to the pages of BYU Studies. Their tales are pronounced by authors less shy about marrying tradition to history. Their essays are the seedbed for traditions cultivated into histories by scholars like Givens, Bushman, and Mark Staker.

## TRADITIONS MARKING DESCENT

Like a found-object long before forged, perhaps for war-making or refining sugar, or binding captives, left rusting in an abandoned factory; now found and displayed on the shelf of some vintage "Ye Olde Clothing Shoppe," so Scottish Independent theology landed on the American frontier, and became a fetish for those imagining a return to the New Testament. Rather than dig and sift, excavating layers of culture, Mormon historians have been content, we'll see, to pretend the found-object qua fetish was a mere precursor to the "real" thing. An empty form, a place holder, a ritualistic keeping up: Not unlike a Pacific Islander's cargo cult, fashioning airstrips in the forest, wooden planes, and radio boxes in preparation for the return of wealth- and weapon-laden airships that—from their perspective—seemingly at random landed during the early 1940s. But no anthropologist would imagine these cargo cults—in form derived from World War II U.S. Armed Forces machinery, though as a general practice of far deeper historicity—were sui generis, only coincidentally related to U.S. planes and airstrips; or somehow—allowing dogma to invert chronology—cults really *did* bring about the airplanes and cargo. Yet, Mormon historians treat Rigdon's club of disciples as "waiting" in Kirtland, Ohio, for the "authentic" Restoration, brought to them by Parley Pratt and companions in fall 1830, complete with priesthood authority to baptize and give the Holy Ghost.

Professor of history and religion at Brigham Young University, Richard Lloyd Anderson published in his university's Studies an essay titled, "The Impact of the First Preaching in Ohio."[1] He begins infelicitously: "Specific plans to preach the restored gospel in the west matured during the second conference after Church organization, held September, 1830" (474). In fact, no mention of "restored gospel" is found in any known contemporaneous "Mormon" document, certainly not the command which directed Cowdery and others to "take thy journey among the Lamanites"; nor do meeting minutes support him, the four men only being "appointed to go to the Lamanites" (475). Indeed, Anderson quotes from letters written by Ezra Booth, published in *Ohio Star*. Booth reports Oliver Cowdery recording his calling thusly:

> I, Oliver, being commanded of the Lord God to go forth unto the Lamanites to proclaim glad tidings of great joy unto them by presenting unto them the fulness of the gospel of the only begotten son of God, and also to rear up a pillar as a

---

[1] Richard Lloyd Anderson, "The Impact of the First Preaching in Ohio" BYU Studies (vol.11 no.4)

witness where the temple of God shall be built in the glorious New Jerusalem . . .
I will walk humbly before him and do this business.[1]

The commission was signed by his companions, P.P. Pratt, Ziba Peterson, and
Peter Whitmer, as well as Joseph Smith, Jr. There is no mention of "restored
gospel," although "fulness" is given, without definition, as the sort of gospel he
planned to present. Anderson finally mentions "Restorationism" some pages later;
although as a throw-away line, writing that "Pratt sought out Sidney Rigdon with
a more thorough-going Restorationism than Rigdon had once presented Pratt."
What was his more Restorationist Restorationism? "The Mormon Elders," he
apparently explains the term, "arrived in Rigdon's locality to declare new
revelations, and the recreation of the spiritual power enshrined as a dead letter in
the Bible" (478). Also, one finds buried on this same page in a footnote this cue:
"For Rigdon's pre-Mormon convictions of Restorationism, see A. S. Hayden,
Early History of the Disciples in the Western Reserve (Cincinnati, 1875)." Rather
than, say, Rigdon's *practice*, Anderson curiously speaks of his "convictions," as
though the preacher believed in such, and was waiting. Convictions about what,
exactly? Several pages later Anderson describes Rigdon as relationally more
Restorationist than Campbell—their measure being devoid of definition—even as
Pratt was to Rigdon, "whose vigorous views of the restoration of the primitive gifts
went beyond Campbellite concepts" (481). One is more Restorationist than the
next, and yet what exactly each was more of, this is never explicitly stated. It is
taken for granted, in this and other histories, that what is called Mormonism is
Restorationism matured. Being an abstract ism, the term allows readers to guess at
its meaning, or just assume everyone means precisely what one supposes when
saying or writing it. It is true of historians as it is of their subjects. And just as the
"Elders" were not yet called "Mormon," neither did they present a more
Restorationist Restorationism: this is Anderson's way of circumventing the
inconvenience of chronology. Namely, that Campbell's Restoration—described
in his own Christian Baptist, drawing from Scottish Independents and
Covenanters—and Pratt's conversion to such by the preaching of Rigdon, these all
preceded by several years the publication of the Book of Mormon and the
founding of Smith's Church of Christ. Indeed, the Book of Mormon was mostly
absent from their preaching, being but a sign of something. What converted
Rigdon and so many disciples of Christ was the thing they were converted to:

---

[1] Anderson, "The Impact," 477. Quoting Ezra Booth to Ira Eddy, 24 Nov 1831. In Ohio
Star, 8 Dec 1831

metatext. Anderson quotes from the *History of Edward Partridge, Jr.*, in which Lydia Partridge, wife of the later Mormon leader, reports she,

> [W]as induced to believe for the reason that I saw the gospel in its plainness as it was taught in the New Testament, and I also knew that none of the sects of the day taught those things (490).

Ever willing to obscure the origins of her new "restored" church, Anderson admits Lydia reports "she had joined 'the Campbellite Church,'" yet he follows this by explaining, "but she was in reality a 'Rigdonite,' baptized by him and having faith in some form of modern revelation and spiritual gifts" (490). Lydia Partridge was among those who "doubled the membership of the Church and created a solid nucleus for rapid growth," Anderson concludes (496).

Having "declared the fulness of the gospel," the four men baptize a total, we are given in the recollection of Peter Whitmer (an 1831 "journal"), and in his brother John's history, "130 members." (That figure is more than double the recorded total of members in Smith's Church of Christ at the time.) Rigdon was not initially among them (478). The preacher, as we know, waited "a fortnight" before converting. Anderson writes Rigdon was "finally convinced, he counted the cost (which was considerable) and fearlessly submitted to baptism" (479).

A passage from the Painesville Telegraph is given in Anderson's own essay. The editor is scoffing about "Cowdray," for the preacher "holds forth that the ordinances of the gospel have not been regularly administered since the days of apostles till the said Smith and himself commenced the work . . . " (481). This is no Mormon description, nor does it mention restoration of priestly powers. It is a mocking report, calling Cowdery "one who pretends to have seen angels," and that rather than converting to a church, the initiates "have been immersed into the new order of things" (481). We cannot know whether the author quoted a preacher, or gave their sermons his own gloss. In support of his tale of the conversions in Kirtland to a restored church, however, Anderson quotes from the recollections of John Murdock (himself a minister) compiled into another *Autobiography* (481). Though not present for the meetings, Murdock—according to Anderson—"carefully questioned a half dozen who had been confirmed." He discovered "a manifestation of the spirit attended the ministration of the ordinance of laying on hands . . ." (482). Murdock is described by Anderson as one who "already believed in the literal restoration of primitive Christianity," and so we have reason to doubt his framing of the events is strictly empirical, being darkened by a Restorationist's lens. So we have a problem: Scarcity of non-Restorationist reports. One Restorationist describes the preaching of a Restorationist to a Restorationist club, or another Restorationist scoffs at those he regards as "fanciful," attributing to them beliefs they did not evidence at the time. These chains are shortened by historians inheriting traditions. Yet even in Murdock's report we get a clue to our solution.

The voices of Campbellites, former Restorationers, and Forgot-I-was-Campbellite: these disciples of Christ dominate the histories relied on by Mormon historians. Their conversions ameliorated the epic fail enjoyed by missionaries among "the Lamanites." As Anderson, "The Lamanite Mission achieved its main success among those prepared for the message on the Western Reserve, not among Indian peoples, where," he turns apologist, "political and cultural conditions were not yet ripe" (496). Ripe? As in, pre-existing? Indeed not, although one wonders why revelation would've directed Cowdery to souls unprepared for churching? One also may wonder if Cowdery and Pratt had bypassed Kirtland, and finding the Delaware Indians willing readers, whether Mormonism would've merely taken on Native American notions, its later historians claiming that the Indians were "ripe" and waiting for one with some lost thing, at last arrived to pluck them from the Tree of Life? Perhaps that sounds cynical or snarky, but given the following, not implausible.

One reads a version of the received tradition in an essay by Milton Backman (another aptly named professor of Church history and doctrine at BYU), a summary of a larger work, titled "The Quest for a Restoration: The Birth of Mormonism in Ohio."[1] Published a year after Anderson's essay, it shows even more sleight of hand, and begins like Anderson with four elders who "proclaimed the restored gospel" (347). He notes that "about twice as many people were baptized in the Kirtland area in one month as had been converted in other parts of the new nation during the first half year of the history of the Restored Church" (347). Having set up the chronology backwards—Restorationists now proclaimed the gospel in Kirtland to some other waiting people—he then asks, "Why was the Western Reserve such a fruitful field ready to harvest at the beginning of the 1830s?" (347).

His answer begins by charting four "societies" in Kirtland: "Congregationalists, Methodists, Regular Baptists, and a group sometimes called 'reformers' who were not affiliated with any denomination but were seeking a return to New Testament Christianity" (347-8). Already Backman has blurred

---

[1] Milton V. Backman "The Quest for a Restoration" BYU Studies (vol.12 no.4)

the truth, suggesting some vague collective called "reformers," having no "denomination" were "seeking a return"; rather than, as easily demonstrated, being a readership guided by Alexander Campbell's preaching cohort, gathered around the notion that they *were* that return to New Testament Christianity. Backman instead describes this "religious movement" as calling "themselves 'Reformers,' 'Reformed Baptists,' 'Reforming Baptists,' 'Christians,' and 'Disciples'" (350). "When the missionaries to the Lamanites," he explains, "introduced the restored gospel in the Western Reserve, there were approximately fifty Reformed Baptists living on Isaac Morley's farm in Kirtland. All these reformers joined the Church." Morley's family were not Reformed Baptists, and neither was Campbell after the dissolution of Mahoning Association. Yet he insists that around Kirtland were "Many others seeking a restoration," and they ". . . also joined the Church shortly after the gospel was introduced in Ohio" (351). Rather than seeing the historical sequence—that Restorationists did not "join" any church so much as graft the Book of Mormon onto their own metatext, and were later called Mormonites by those called Campbellites—Backman and other historians insist that the identity of Rigdon's and Campbell's doctrines to later Mormonism merely shows this: how well the Lord had prepared the field for harvest! Astonishing it would be for farmers to return to a field they sowed, and find there the very crops previously planted.

In order to sustain this chronologically dubious revision, he treats recollections as contemporaneous reports, as if something apparently sincerely composed in the 1840s was reliably recounting the living as it unfolded in 1830. He draws from the "History of Joseph Smith" serialized in 1843 to claim that prior to his move to Ohio, "Sidney Rigdon had concluded that the Baptist creeds contained incorrect expressions of faith; that all the popular creeds of Christendom should be replaced by one rule of faith, the Bible." This is tradition building, not history writing. Backman adds to Rigdon's supposed realization, "that there was a need to restore the ancient order of the gospel," without actually referencing until several pages later Campbell's extensive use of that phrase, years before Rigdon's 1830 "conversion." Rather than ignorant of Campbell, Backman instead conceals the man's influence on Rigdon, writing that,

> In 1824 many of Rigdon's beliefs were in harmony with tenets popularized by Alexander Campbell; and Rigdon's temporary withdrawal from the ministry coincided with Campbell's increased popularization of the impropriety of creeds and the need to restore the ancient gospel. Rigdon had become acquainted with

Campbell's beliefs through personal conversations with him and by reading *The Christian Baptist* which Campbell commenced publishing in 1823 in Bethany, West Virginia (then Virginia) (353).

For his source Backman cites the "History of Joseph Smith," and also Richardson's *Memoirs of Alexander Campbell*. The BYU professor of church history and doctrine at last mentions "a series of thirty-two articles appearing in *The Christian Baptist* entitled, 'A Restoration of the Ancient Order of Things'," but only admits such when the title is framed by Backman's claim that the series "clearly emphasized his belief concerning the need for a restoration" (353). The next page has Backman further positioning Campbell as anxiously awaiting restoration—rather than engaging in self-promotion—claiming that the Irishman in an 1825 meeting "expressed an earnest desire to witness 'the ancient order of things restored'" (354). Further obscuring Campbell's influence on Rigdon, Backman writes,

> While serving as a minister in Pittsburg, Rigdon rode to Kentucky to witness a debate between Campbell and a Presbyterian preacher, the Reverend W. L. Maccalla. Rigdon took notes during this debate which aided Campbell in the preparation of a tract published in 1824 (357).

As detailed already, Rigdon travelled with Campbell to the debate, and his seemingly jotted-on-a-whimsy "notes" amounted to the official transcript; rather than a "tract," the publication exceeded 400 pages! The debate mostly concerned baptism, and found Campbell arguing for immersion effecting remission of sins.

The aptly named Backman's creative fracturing of history extends into Rigdon's relationship with Walter Scott, widely credited (in sources Backman cites) with formulating the preaching-to-conversion sequence: faith, repentance, baptism for the remission of sins, and the gift of the Holy Ghost. Given that Mormons claim this sequence is the foundation of their restored gospel, one can imagine that Backman has some back flips to perform, if he is to teach received tradition. The professor says Scott was in 1827 called to preach by the Mahoning Association, "and, shortly after this appointment, he began proclaiming six basic principles: faith, repentance, believer's baptism, remission of sins, reception of the Holy Ghost, and eternal life." Rather than giving Scott's sequence as the preacher stated it, Backman here summarizes, adding his own obscuring verbiage, and a sixth to Scott's five steps. Yet on the next page Backman acknowledges that only "five items" were given by Scott in 1828, as reported by his contemporary, Samuel Robbins (358). Insisting on misdirecting history, Backman includes in a footnote to the above passage the following explanation:

> Scott claimed that he taught the concept of baptism for the remission of sins to Campbell and Rigdon and that Rigdon converted the Mormon missionaries to that belief. Although it appears that this doctrine was not emphasized in the preaching of most reformers before 1827, Campbell and Rigdon understood this concept before that date. The view was clearly enunciated in the Book of Mormon and in the instructions of John the Baptist to the Prophet Joseph Smith and was therefore endorsed by Latter-day Saints before the LDS missionaries arrived in Ohio (357-8 n.36).

Ignoring the obvious chronological problem that accounts of John the Baptist visiting Smith did not circulate until the early 1830s, and that the Book of Mormon was not published until 1830, Backman also anachronistically names "LDS missionaries" as endorsing baptism for remission. Moreover, Scott did not merely teach about "remission of sins," he gave Rigdon the *entire sequence* later adopted by Mormons. Backman adds to this misdirection what is obviously a historian's attempt to perform authority, while preventing a checking of his facts, advising, "For the views of Scott on this subject see Walter Scott to Br. Emmons, Mayslick, 22 October 1851, copy located in Disciples Historical Society, Nashville, Tennessee" (358 n.36).

The professor of history and doctrine then proceeds to suggest that Campbell himself sensed the restoration of the true church in 1830, because his new periodical, Millennial Harbinger, had as its banner a quote from his translation of REVELATION 14:6. The passage reports "another messenger flying through the midst of Heaven, having everlasting good news to proclaim to the inhabitants of the earth." (Disciple-Mormonites would later identify Moroni as that angel, his message the restoration of the gospel, rather than the Book of Mormon itself). Moreover, Campbell, we learn from Backman, "proclaimed early in 1830 that groups had already commenced to restore the ancient gospel." The Irishman obviously meant his own movement, gathered around his publications, was that restoration; not the Church of Christ formed by Joseph Smith's earliest followers in April 1830. A last stitching to this suggestive summary is a quote from Campbell, that the gospel went missing, "since the great apostacy from Christian institutions" (360).

Finally left for Backman's pulling tradition from the jaws of history is the prestige of "priesthood authority." That is a concern which would rightly distinguish them from Campbell, even though the very terms they use would come from his teachings (pulled, admittedly, from the Bible). The preacher espoused, as Backman correctly notes, a "traditional Protestant position regarding authority," namely, "all believers in Christ were bearers of the priesthood" (362). Presumably Pratt and Rigdon believed as much—being ordained to preach and baptize according to Campbell's teachings—so it does take some effort for Backman to make this later concern of a lack of authority (and thus waiting for its restoration) also one thriving on the Morley Farm in 1830. He proceeds to recollections, giving us a quote from the "Journal of John Murdock" without acknowledging as Anderson did, that the "Journal" was begun at least a year later; adding to his post hoc-ery is the 1839 recollection of Edward Partridge, who also reports—in the words of Backman, "further remembered"—his own pre-conversion supposition that God must "again reveal himself to man and confer authority upon some one, or more, before his church could be built up in the last days, or any time after the apostacy" (362; in Edward Partridge Papers, 26 May 1839). Having set the table—transmuting practice and belief into seeking and awaiting, recollections into events—the professor brings in Parley Pratt (relying on his *Autobiography*). Pratt, we learn,

> unfolded to these seekers many truths which they were seeking. Before his conversion to the restored gospel, Pratt had been a reformer and had learned the message of the restoration which Sidney Rigdon was proclaiming, and therefore explained efficaciously the glad tidings of the everlasting gospel to the inhabitants of the Western Reserve (363).

Thus a humble group anxiously seeking restoration of ancient things, and the authority to administer the same, was gathered into the restored church by baptism.

Is the received tradition—that Mormon Elders preached the restored gospel to prepared and convicted, humbly seeking Disciples of Christ Reformed Baptists, administering the ordinances (rites) of said gospel by the authority of the priesthood, and by the resulting spiritual manifestations converted hundreds to the Restored Church and its restored gospel—really found in every report? Thus far, we find that nearly every account relies on Richardson's *Memoirs of Alexander Campbell*, and retrospection from Mormons long since brought into a restored church claiming the authority of priesthood. Can we tell Mormon history from sources not already implicated in Mormon tradition, willing to forget its relationship to Campbell's writings, and revising all along the way? The clue previously mentioned opens a way for us to understand what Rigdon's and Morley's flock meant by "authority" and "power," and what convinced them to listen to Smith, so long as he did not stray from their Bible.

We can turn to histories of the Disciples of Christ. They have no horse in the Mormon's race to priesthood authority, although they certainly desire to set themselves as far apart from Joseph Smith's movement as possible. In their versions we find more details than are provided in LDS tradition. One historian retells—with a jaundiced eye on establishing Rigdon's role in the Book of Mormon—what Parley Pratt aroused among hearers on the Morley Farm in fall of 1830. The details are revealing, and dovetail with early Mormon conversion stories found in recollections written near this time. He writes that Rigdon feigned concern over the baptism of so many of his flock, "re-immersed in one night into this new dispensation." Thus to Pratt and company, Rigdon spoke:

> He told them what they had done was without precedent or authority from the Scriptures, *as they had baptized for the power of miracles*, while the apostles, as he showed, baptized penitential believers for the remission of sins. When pressed, they said what they had done was merely at the solicitation of those persons [i.e., the Family]. Rigdon called on them for proofs of the truth of their book and mission.[1]

At this request, Cowdery and Rigdon debated whether an angel could reveal the truth, or whether one might be deceived merely by seeking for a sign. The report is detailed enough—contradicting Hayden's plan to appoint Rigdon the author of the new book—to suggest considerable accuracy in the telling. The important phrase? Baptized for the power of miracles. Rigdon's club was, according to Hayden's telling, baptized unto the power of miracles, not into a church. What one was baptized *for, into* or *unto* was an explicit concern of Campbell and friends. And so Rigdon presses Pratt and Cowdery for evidence that miracles are joining their Restoration. The dispensation Pratt was heard preaching about concerned the dispensing of gifts of the Spirit: miracles, tongues, healings. Priesthood authority would come later to their awareness and tongues, and rename their

---

[1] Hayden, *Early History*, 211. Italics added.

desire to see the power of godliness resting upon them. The Book of Mormon was a sign of miracles, and not of priesthood. It added the keystone to their hope for restoration.

Perhaps you doubt this report? We need only dig one more level to come to answers. Not explicitly naming his own sources, Hayden apparently derived his account from a letter published in the Painesville Telegraph under the title "Mormonism."[1] It was submitted by "M.S.C.": Matthew S. Clapp, whose brief biography is given by Hayden ten pages before his summary account of Rigdon's rebaptism.[2] Clapp was baptized by Adamson Bentley in 1828, and in the fall of 1830 he married Alicia Campbell, sister of Alexander. In a strange twist, Clapp made his way to New York City in the early 1840s, where "he received instruction in Hebrew under Sexias [sic], a Hebraist of note, the very same son of Abraham who came to Kirtland, Ohio, in 1830 [sic], and instructed the Mormons in the 'unknown tongues."[3] More accurate than Hayden's summary, Clapp's letter to the editor does not credit Rigdon with fabricating the Book of Mormon. Instead, he provides important details—no doubt from his perspective, according "to his language, unto his understanding"—about what was preached, and what brought about so many being rebaptized. After their "book was read and pronounced a silly fabrication," Clapp recounts, the four preachers suggested the audience "pray for a sign from Heaven." A few days later "seventeen persons" were rebaptized. Why? We have two reasons given. First, the book was said to contain "a new covenant, to come under which the disciple must be re-immersed." Clapp writes that when asked how their covenant differed from that mentioned in HEBREWS chapter eight, verses ten through thirteen, "they would equivocate, and would say, (to use their own words) 'on the large scale, the covenant is the same, but in some things it is different." It seems like Pratt and company believed they had something significant to offer, but a thorough explanation was not among those things. Not swayed by vagueness, but by the possibility of inheriting Pratt's spiritual gifts, eventually some requested baptism.

> At this Mr. Rigdon seemed much displeased, and when they [preachers] came next day to his house, he withstood them to the face—showed them that what they had done was entirely without precedent in the holy scriptures—for they had immersed those persons that they might work miracles as well as come under

---

[1] Painseville Telegraph 15 Feb 1831; 2, no.35:1-2
[2] Hayden, *Early History*, 198-203
[3] Hayden, *Early History*, 200.

the said covenant—showed them that the apostles baptized for the remission of sins—but miraculous gifts were conferred by the imposition of hands. But when pressed upon the point, they justified themselves by saying, it was on *their part* merely a compliance with the solicitations of those persons. Mr. Rigdon again called upon them for proof of the truth of their book and mission: they then related the manner in which they obtained faith, which was by praying for a sign, and an angel was shown unto them.

What is not clear in Clapp's account is the manner of "compliance with the solicitations of those persons." Was it the working of miracles, or to come under "the said covenant"? Given Rigdon's reported turn to scripture, and rejoinder that "miraculous gifts were conferred by the imposition of hands," I believe it was miracle working which was requested by the initiates. And yet, it appears that the baptizers brought them by this rite into a new covenant! So, we come to a satisfactory answer. Pratt apparently baptized them with an understanding that the book required it, and likely enough, even believed some power had been given him which was absent in his previous ordinations to baptize. Yet, the initiates were less interested in covenants than they were in the power of miracles. In 1830 it was the power of miracles that he added to their restoration of Christian communism, moving them even further from Campbell's orthodoxy. Rigdon did not seek for it, nor fight with Campbell over gifts. That is Campbell's version, and it seems to have come after Rigdon was made to take up Pratt's new covenant.

To the spectacle of preachers of the Gold Bible, and one of their own shepherds lost among them, came Walter Scott. Whatever secret family Rigdon hoped to maintain while keeping house in Mentor with more mainline Campbell disciples, all was exposed to the light of day, and by editors' pens. Surely Rigdon had some explaining to do in Mentor, where a home was being built so that he could minister to Restorationists there. So Rigdon followed the Family, perhaps convinced in part by his difficult situation as much as by tangible experience that Pratt and his companions were taking the straight and narrow path. Rigdon would continue to press for "the power," as Mark Staker's account makes clear. When we tarry longer in Kirtland in a following chapter, through 1832, we see that Rigdon's desire for an "endowment" of "the power"—eventually called "the priesthood"—remained at the top of his concerns. I trust you can draw your own conclusions about his pressing for it.

What matters is not, of course, who was correct about covenants and miracles. The ritual of baptism requires two persons, and here we see that two perspectives came along to the water's edge. One seeking for miracles to add to communism, the other merely doing what a Restorationist reading the Book of Mormon would do: baptizing just as he read about on its pages. Given that this book is a history of the Book of Mormon, my concern remains: What were the effects of bringing in a tightly knit "family" catechized by Rigdon into the tenets of Christian Restoration, a group which quickly outnumbered in these formative years by two-to-one any other disciples in the Church of Christ? It will take us into next volume if we hope to trace the effects. Here we can see that Clapp's letter is long and detailed, and recounts conversations with Rigdon which apparently occurred only a week before it was published. If accurately reported (and I believe it is, for Clapp seems certain of his cause, and knows he need not deceive his jury of readers), the conversation explains much about early Mormonism, as we'll see.

His account takes our history into 1831. In the face of bizarre behaviors described hereafter, and after many reportedly failed prophecies and attempts to heal, Rigdon apparently denied to Clapp that the Book of Mormon would be confirmed by miracles, for "it was not designed to be thus confirmed." Clapp answered that the book contradicted Rigdon, and indeed proclaimed that miracles are "thus to be established." Clapp then asked "whether it enjoined a single virtue that the Bible did not, or whether it mentioned and prohibited a single additional vice, or whether it exhibited a new attributed of Deity? He said it did not."

> "The Book of Mormon," said he, "is just calculated to form and govern the millennial church; the *old* revelation was never calculated for that, nor could it accomplish that object; and without receiving the Book of Mormon, there is no salvation for any one into whose hands it shall come." He said faith in the Book of Mormon was only to be obtained by asking the Lord concerning it.

Clapp explained that "I have given a simple statement of facts for the purpose that you might not be deceived by the pretensions of these false prophets. They proclaim the ancient gospel, putting their own appendages to it." What seems especially to get Clapp's goat is the apparent non-standardization of their message; that is, "Mormonism" did not yet have a single message, delivered by trained missionaries for whom the speaking of the message was an act making their collective identity. They had taken the words of Campbell and Scott and Stone, and added the Gold Bible as ballast.

When they think it will best suit their purpose, they say nothing about the Book of Mormon, and at other times make it their chief topic.—Mr. R. said to me, since he became a Mormonite, that it was no part of his religion to defend the Book of Mormon, he merely wished the people to give heed to the *old* revelation, to humble themselves, and enter into the privileges which it conferred upon its believing subjects.

He concludes by comparing Mormonites with early Christians, who suffered all manner of evils for the sake of their religion. "They have no sacrifice to make," Clapp figures, "no loss of fortune or reputation to sustain—they are in a land of liberty." Contrasting the easy path surely taken by Mormons, Christians, he explains, "had to forsake their relatives, leave their possessions, and forfeit their repution [*sic*]. Scourging and torture, imprisonment and death, were often staring them in the face . . . ." "So," he concludes unwittingly prophetic, "whether their religion was true or false, they proved their honesty."

## NEWSPAPERS TELLING TALES

We now turn to the few reports contemporary with the times they speak of. They come from sources not affiliated with Morley's family or Rigdon's or Campbell's disciples. The Painesville Telegraph found itself reporting regularly on the questionable doings of a growing body of believers in what decent folks were now calling the Gold Bible. Under that title it published articles beginning in November 1830, only six months after the Book of Mormon was published. The first summarized the now standard origin story of "new revelations from Heaven, having been dug out of the ground," composed in "Egyptian Hieroglyphics," translated "by one Smith, who was enabled to read the characters by instruction from Angels."[1] A fine thing when encountered on the pages of a local weekly, but now inconveniently walking among their readers were actual men involved in the fable, as if Paul Bunyan stopped by for corn dodgers one morning:

> About two weeks since some persons came along here with the book, one of whom pretends to have seen Angels, and assisted in translating the plates. He proclaims destruction upon the world within a few years—holds forth that the ordinances of the gospel, have not been regularly administered since the days of the Apostles, till the said Smith and himself commenced the work—and many other marvellous things too numerous to mention.

---

[1] Painesville (Ohio) Telegraph, 16 Nov 1830

The editor of the Telegraph reports that "twenty or thirty have been immersed into the new order of things; many of whom had been previously baptised," and gives the preacher's name as "Cowdray," "bound for the regions beyond the Mississippi, where he contemplates founding a 'City of Refuge' for his followers, and converting the Indians, under his prophetic authority." Hereafter the book plays second fiddle to the "ordinances of the gospel" being again "regularly administered," and to the ambitions of believers eager to gather the elect before the Day of Judgment. Lamanites would come, surely, but here in Ohio was a convenient harvest. Two days later the Observer and Telegraph published a long letter from an incredulous citizen of its home town of Hudson, Ohio.[1] He mentioned that "four individuals, said to have formerly resided in the State of New-York, have appeared in the northern part of Geauga County, assuming the appellation of Disciples, Prophets, and Angels." As yet unaffiliated, they preached "a species of Religion we are not at all prepared to embrace; for we are convinced it does not accord with our old-fashioned Bible." He then gives the origin story of the "Golden Bible," with a little confusion here and there. Of greater significance, however, is his account of the preachers' presentation and explanation of the book:

> This new Revelation, they say is especially designed for the benefit, or rather for the Christianizing of the Aborigines of America; who, as they affirm, are a part of the tribe of Manasseh, and whose ancestors landed on the coast of Chili 600 years before the coming of Christ, and from them descended all the Indians of America.

A tale hardly worthy of serious notice, yet one which the writer, A.S., cannot understand somehow deludes so many. "But sir," he recounts nearly out of breath,

> could you see the multitude that follow those pretended Disciples, and know the number they have baptized each night, (many of whom 'tis said have now been immersed for the third time;) were you informed, that a certain Elder hesitated in deciding whether to reject or receive the new Revelation, and that the "social Union," or as it is more familiarly called in its vicinity, the "common stock family," have gone into the water again in token of embracing it; and consider that their great object in bending their way to the West is to convert the Indians

---

[1] Observer and Telegraph (Hudson, OH) 18 Nov 1830, "The Golden Bible, or, Campbellism Improved."

to the new faith, among many of whose tribes Christian Missionaries are faithfully, and through the blessing of God, successfully laboring—I say in view of this—in view of the worth of souls, liable to be deluded and lost, will you not as a Herald of the Cross of Christ, raise the note of alarm, in your widely circulating paper?

He appended the twelfth chapter of the Second Book of Nephi to his exasperations, and the editor responded in kind. "Slow to believe" but not surprised by his account of readers "duped" by "so barefaced a deception," the editor explained that the "Elder referred to, is the famous Campbellite leader, who has made so much noise on the Reserve for a few months past."[1] The "common stock family," he correctly added, "is a club of Campbellites," who reportedly "hold their meetings till late at night, and afterwards retire to the river, and baptize by the score." Unlike other Campbellites, "they profess to have the power of working miracles." It was the promise of working miracles which Parley Pratt carried back to them, he having departed as a Restorationist preacher and returned with Cowdery bearing news of ancient powers restored. Considering themselves practicing the "Restoration of Ancient Things," although not in perfect harmony with Campbell's tune, the Family merely added to their list the restoration of miracle working, something long accepted by other Christians, but absolutely rejected by Campbell.

What about the book? As recounted by A.S. in his letter, "It is maintained that this is not a new Gospel, but that it explains the New Testament."[2] Their framing of the book as an extension of the New Testament was frequently reported, as in the Vermont Watchman and State Gazette, under the title, "Fanatics."[3] It says Cowdery, David Whitmer, and Martin Harris "had a new revelation which they call a codicil to the New Testament….They say the world is to come to an end within 15 years." This phrase, "codicil to the New Testament," is used in other reports relaying this warning of the world's ending in fifteen years, as for instance, a letter to the editor of the Hudson Observer and Telegraph.[4] The Jesuit or Catholic Sentinel similarly reprinted a passage from an article titled "Delusion," published by the Geauga Gazette.[5] The Gazette reported

---

[1] Observer and Telegraph (Hudson, OH). 18 Nov 1830 "The Golden Bible"
[2] Observer and Telegraph (Hudson, OH) 18 Nov 1830, "The Golden Bible, or, Campbellism Improved."
[3] Vermont Watchman and State Gazette 14 Dec 1830; Montpelier, 25 no.12
[4] Observer and Telegraph (Hudson, OH) 30 Dec 1830
[5] Jesuit Sentinel (Boston, MA) 18 Dec 1830, p.125

the preachers of the book "claimed [it] to be a condict to the New Testament." The phrase occurs frequently enough to suggest it was promoted by the earliest preachers, and not merely invented by an editor. Rather than some vulgar imposition or blasphemy, now the Book of Mormon was said to be a key to unlock the Bible, a thing of hubris perhaps, bringing about greater faith in its veracity before the coming of the terrors depicted in the Book of Revelation. One wonders how many supposed converts, baptized into something, had actually read the book.

Not the editors of the Cleveland Herald, who admitted that having purchased the book "for the gratification of our curiosity," "We have not read it in course, but have perused it sufficiently to be convinced it is one of the veriest impositions of the day."[1]   The list of books is given correctly by the Herald (no Pukei here), and their explanation of its true origins is offered, following a tart depiction of the peddling of books once practiced by Cowdery:

> Mr. Cowdery and Mr. Smith the reputed author, have taken the old Bible to keep up a train of circumstances, and by altering names and language have produced the string of Jargon called the "Book of Mormon," with the intention of making mony by the sale of their Books; and being aware that they would not sell unless an excitement and curiosity could be raised in the public mind, have therefore sent out twelve Apostles to promulgate its doctrines.

More than mere curiosity was aroused in the public mind by these apostles, as the Painesville Telegraph, under an editorial respectfully titled, "The Book of Mormon," reluctantly realized.[2]  "To record the thousand tales which are in circulation respecting the book and its propagators," they lament without acknowledging the newspaper's role in their spread, "would be an endless task, and probably lead to the promulgation of a hundred times more than was founded in truth."  The editors stated carefully, without the customary smirk, that "100 in this and an adjoining county have embraced the ideas and assertions of Joseph Smith, jr. many of them respectable for intelligence and piety."  Regarding the book itself, they not only reprint the title page and testimony of witnesses, but take pains to circumlocute sufficiently to cloak their personal assessment, explaining, "after having an opportunity to canvass some of its claims to a true revelation from

---

[1] The Cleveland Herald 25 Nov 1830 "The Golden Bible"; the phrase was picked up by the neighboring Republican Advocate of Wooster, OH, 4 Dec 1830, "The Golden Bible."
[2] Painesville Telegraph 30 Nov 1830

God, we have not been able to discover testimony which ought to elicit faith in any prudent or intelligent mind." Thankfully, the preachers had moved on to the "far west,' where they say a Prophet is to be raised up, in whom the tribes will believe."

Rather than take the society-system-faith-new-order-movement head on, the editors of the Telegraph instead reprinted warnings from other papers, such as the Milan Free Press.[1] They declined to state their belief in the Free Press's tale, explaining that "We know the sensitiveness of a great number of individuals in this section, on every thing that may be said touching the new Bible and its propagators, many of whom view it as a sin to say aught against Joseph Smith or his apostles." Notably absent is the Golden Bible and Jo Smith, moneydigger; editors realized that their own readers may have been apparently duped by the same.

The Book of Mormon, whether for good or evil, found safety in popularity, and instead of mockery it now faced warnings. In the Free Press article, the acts of Parley Pratt were recounted, how after receiving a commission to preach as a disciple, he "ran away from a constable, and numerous creditors," and was in New York arrested for debts, having "sold property belonging to one of his neighbors to the amount of several dollars," as though his poor credit counted against the validity of the book. More relevant to this history, however, is the report of a conversation with Pratt, where he justifies his belief in the book, not because the text tells the truth about Indians, but because "he had seen visible effects of the descending of the Holy Ghost, upon persons whom he had baptized." When asked about the effects, Pratt reportedly answered in an appropriately Restorationist way, that effects were manifest "in the same way we read of in the Gospel." The Book of Mormon—as a sign or omen, and not as text—was initially interpreted by convert-devotees of the New Testament as something like the Gospels, their group being understood, at last, as yet another "new religion."[2] The book was now popularly regarded as propounded by a sect, to the New Testament as this "new religion" was to Christianity: a sort of codicil.

Often careless with details, but at times insightful even in error, newspapers described Harris, Cowdery, and Whitmer "as the translators of the Bible (who are looked upon by their followers as prophets)." Only briefly described—after the book earned some respect—as something other than an

---

[1] Milan (Huron County) Free Press. 14 Dec 1830 "Beware of Imposters"
[2] The phrase comes from the Philadelphia Album, 18 Dec 1830, p.405, reprinting from Auburn (New York) Free Press.

ignoramus, Joseph Smith would soon move into the background of what would become a recognizable religious movement. Now just a "Mr. Somebody who could neither read nor write," Smith was regarded as notable mostly for his stupidity.[1] That quality alone made his book all the more miraculous; and it was miracles, and not necessarily Book of Mormons, which Rigdon, Pratt, and many others—first christened by the Rochester paper, "The disciples of Mormon . . . propagating their new light"—miracles they dearly desired. Dismissed by Emerson as not one with the blowing clover, miracles would bring Campbell-Rigdon's Restorationists more fully into the New Testament imaginary. Smith's translation was the Mormonites'—they began 1831 with a name, at last—his book was their donkey to ride to the Bible's New Jerusalem.

Is it so implausible that Restorationist disciples were receptive to Pratt's teaching that miracles were again dispensed to humanity, and that Rigdon, trained in rationalist Campbellism, doubted his authority to baptize unto miracles? First, Mormons many decades later continued to baptize for various reasons: ailments, a new start in Utah, even membership in "the United Order." One was not "baptized a member of the Church," and that was an end to the dipping, as it is spoken of today. Baptism good for one time was not less good a second or third, and for many a reason. Second, it is clear that "authority" to baptize in fall 1830 did not mean "Priesthood authority" as received tradition has it: there is simply no public mention of priesthood ordination from John the Baptist or anyone else, by Joseph Smith, until later in the decade. We are left reading Pratt's *Autobiography* and wondering if he made up all that stuff about realizing Rigdon's lack of authority, or whether his term "authority" changed in meaning as Joseph Smith spoke of new kinds of "authority," gained by ordination at the hand of John the Baptist? Pratt and others likely read a concern over generic power to ordain and baptize, such as he thought belonged to the apostleship, and projected it back onto restoration generally—to him, an essential feature, this power being lost in apostasy. Later it fell like so much else under the aspect of Priesthood.

Here in Hayden's and Clapp's accounts we have a simple resolution to Pratt's seeming prevarications: the concern of Rigdon's was as Pratt recalled: one of authority. The *specific* authority, however, concerned the working of miracles—a new dispensation of powers; that is, a gift—and was not a general dispute over authority itself. By *dispensation* one might mean in 1830 something like an age of the world; but also something dispensed, like a gift. The book was a sign of the

---

[1] Rochester Republican 28 Dec1830 "Book of Mormon"

miracle of tongues. The new covenant he found in the Book of Mormon would've mandated or evidenced a new dispensation, as Campbell himself would say. That authority—to dispense gifts and miracles—was what moved "Rigdonites" into the water, whatever Pratt thought to accomplish concerning a new covenant. Restoration was complete with the return of miracles (again!), yet another gift of the Spirit dispensed to disciples of Christ. Disciples could now compare their experimental religion favorably with one long professed by Methodists. Pratt and Cowdery moved on to Missouri. Rather than establish a church among the Lamanites, however, they would begin their own Zion.

How many Book of Mormons were circulating among these disciples? Staker guesses that two copies were handed out, for the entire community. One need not read the new sacred text. A lax catechism and having no board of examiners to discern the faith of those desiring baptism were absences making for more converts. Converted to what, then, becomes the question. That one might leap into rebaptism because a seeming jolt of power, or warm feeling, or vision, or dream, or whathaveyou occurred? This made for rapid conversions, free of dogma and creeds. Is that a movement? Are they Mormons parading out from the cold Disciples of Christ and into Joseph Smith's restored church? What later historians would call "Rigdonites" actually brought to Joseph Smith was a sort of hybrid machine: retooled by Alexander Campbell, but lacking the fuel to really burn, burn over the frontier. With Smith's translation they found fuel for their Bible Restorationism, and the movement at last did what movements should do: move. The Book of Mormon was not irrelevant. It simply wasn't read all that much (who had the time, or even a copy?); being a sign of miracles, that so ignorant a man could produce what came to be called "a codicil to the New Testament," and that angels apparently vouched for someone's explanation that the restoration of ancient things was at last accomplished, and in full. For the time being.

That it began with baptism unto miracles, and thus miracles are so often mentioned in the diaries of early Mormons—as a sign of the truth of their faith, and of the restoration of ancient things—this makes sense of two trends. First, Pratt and others recall a concern over authority, but apparently also generalized from baptism unto miracles to the power of performing authentic baptism itself. Second, Mormons recorded many miracles in journals and diaries—leading Richard Bushman to suggest they were "composing another Book of Acts"[1]—but not much on priesthood authority to perform ordinances. Nothing, that is, until recalling what all the fuss was about in the early days of the Church, when they

---

[1] Bushman, *Rough Stone Rolling*, 154

were all joined on Morley's farm preaching (Campbell's) restoration of ancient things. Perhaps miracles were regarded as the sign of authority, and so the reconsideration by Pratt and other early historians was that they *really* were waiting for priesthood authority? Indeed, one Mormon recalled, as quoted in that BYU masters thesis, that the Methodists did not lack for authority generally, but were thought to lack "the gift of tongues, of prophecy, and of miracles."[1] What more would demonstrate these gifts than an ignoramus translating a record composed in hieroglyphs, revealing God in the Americas, with a liturgy expressed more clearly than one finds in the New Testament; just as American religion simplified much that the Old World drew into Gothic buttress and Baroque filigree? Recall that "revelation" often meant, "God revealed to man," and not "mysterious sayings or stories," and the Book of Mormon shows, in its day: tongues, revelation, prophecy, and miracles. By "Book of Mormon," I mean in that statement: metatext, the Gold Bible; not the actual text. Seldom read, it was regarded as little more than confirmation of the New Testament (even Campbell's 1827 translation).

So many early Mormon leaders came out of this region—Orson Hyde, Sidney Rigdon, Parley Pratt, Edward Partridge, Lyman Wight, Philo Dibble, Isaac Morley—that we need not quibble over "influence." It was the Gold Bible with which they stitched themselves into a movement, taking from patches and shreds of Campbell, Scott, Stone, and others. Mostly Campbell, though: he carried Scottish Independents' brand of covenant theology into the frontier, and spread it thick in thousands of copies of the Christian Baptist. He delivered to would-be Mormons a cleaned up tradition lifted from a long history of strife and blood, tumultuous and hardly reeking with charity, faith, and hope. They made Mormonism, and made it from Campbell's writings as fragmented across their Bibles, in their voices even while preaching communalism on the farm. Future converts to Mormonism inherited their Restorationism, though without any knowledge of its sources. It had a name, and whatever it named, *that* was Mormonism.

Pratt's own future was not bloodless, nor free from faith; his honesty proven far from home, by powder, ball, and a knife's blade that would cut short his autobiography. Historians inherited traditions from early Mormons like him, as text begat metatext across bodies (dipped in water, as the good book says), and these became biographies. Mormons as restoration metatext were created by the movement of Morley's family into the Bible's new dispensation of miracles.

---

[1] Jones, *"We Latter-day Saints are Methodists,"* 111

When disciples were rebaptized, had they joined Smith's church, they would've found themselves in another Church of Christ, and to it they brought Restorationism seemingly free of Campbell's parentage. Campbell happily sent them away, slapping on their back the label *Mormonites*. If these were Mormons in 1831, who were the disciples inquiring of Smith in New York? Were they seeking restoration? Of what? How?

# Six  The Writing of Oliver Cowdery

WITHOUT OLIVER COWDERY, THERE WOULD BE NO JOSEPH SMITH. Prior to Cowdery's arrival, Smith had progressed very little in his translation of the ancient record. Only a few pages he could show for his first effort, relying on Martin Harris as a scribe and keeper of those pages. By the few Mormon historians who bother to write of his life and contributions to their religion, however, Cowdery is seldom more than a passage to Smith. Cowdery is rarely credited with anything other than being a copyist. Yet, Cowdery was no mere follower. It is said that prior to writing for Smith, while boarding with Smith's parents in Manchester, New York, in early 1829, the young school teacher did "receive divine visitation calling him to assist Joseph Smith."[1] Joseph would say (in his unpublished 1832 history) that the "Lord appeared unto ... Oliver Cowdery and shewed unto him the plates in a vision and also the truth of the work and what the Lord was about to do through me his unworthy servant."[2] Cowdery reported little about this experience, one of the rare times his tongue was not a match for a fire shut up in his bones, that conflagration so often spilling forth what reads today as very purple prose indeed. Full of circumlocution and biblical cliché, it is not altogether charmless; after one acclimates to his ponderous putting on of university airs. For this reason—his inability to take up the Bible as his word—he would find himself supplanted by Sidney Rigdon, that walking Bible who remade Cowdery's movement in the image of Campbell's Restoration.

The remarkable thing is not only was he displaced by the very preacher he converted, and not even a year after the book he transcribed had been published by Grandin; but that Mormon historians today continue to leap at the chance to

---

[1] Welch and Morris, "Introduction" in John Welch and Larry E. Morris, ed., *Oliver Cowdery: Scribe, Elder, Witness* (Maxwell Institute, Brigham Young U, 2006), ix

[2] *The Joseph Smith Papers: Histories*, vol.1 (SLC: Church Historian's Press 2012), 16

diminish his place in Mormon history, relying on post-Rigdon revisions, doing unto Oliver as a historical figure what Sidney and his Bible had done in realtime. Without Oliver Cowdery, however, there is no Book of Mormon; no Joseph Smith; no Corporation of the President of the Church; no temples nor polygamists and that silly musical would not have grossed a billion dollars a few years ago. One statement from Cowdery would have ruined the whole Gold Bible business: something like, "It was all a fake got up to make money, and here is the whole truth . . . ." Although he would likely have said, "As the curtain of years woven into endless tapestries of centuries falls and falls again, across the lives of many millions of men, weaving their sorrows and desires into the warp of the next scene readying to rise, of men content to pass along their wandering existences like vagabonds of Israel, freighting the heavy toll of ignorance upon a next generation made thereby more giddy with the currents of . . . ," and so on, the audience tiring of his exposition, and probably exiting the theatre long before he ever got around to confessing his role in the Gold Bible scheme.

He never did, though: never turned against the book, never said it was a fake, but always insisted it was divine revelation, even when it would've made him a rich man to incinerate Joe Smith on the altar of religious fakes. Cowdery never publicly, nor on record privately, spoke against that book: although before the first decade of Mormonism was used up, he found himself slandered in LDS periodicals, blamed for exploiting for cash money every sin of that often very foolish people, his old friend Joseph Smith standing by, silent in defense. There is something delightful about a man who can see his reputation burned by his former companions in the work of the Lord, and who departed without vengeance after excommunication from a church he founded; who kept his own counsel thereafter, at one time joining a Methodist church for company on Sundays, when he was not lawyering to pay the bills. After Brigham Young's portrait was raised above all others, on the walls of the Mormon's Nauvoo Temple, after Smith was gunned down in nearby Carthage jail, Cowdery returned and asked for rebaptism, but desired no role in leading the Latter-day Saints.

Like Parley Pratt, Cowdery is hardly a name before 1829, his biography mostly bound up with the text he wrote as it flowed from Smith's mouth. A few trivial facts can be said of his early life, and these walk alongside catastrophe. He was born after a summer of terrible drought in the ominously named township of Wells, Vermont, in 1806, the third day of October, to a father whose father was a

Congregational minister seeking to reclaim the covenant of Israel.[1] The century had begun with one of a thousand failed predictions of the End, with what is known as "Woodscrape." Near Oliver's home was Middletown, where a Congregationalist minister named Nathaniel Wood led a few followers, mostly kin, out of the wilderness of apostasy and paraded them under the blessed banner of Israel to his new Jerusalem. In an interesting twist, the term "wood" once designated a sort of madness caused by a daemon, affected like a druid bewitched after drinking from Odin's (Woden's) well of wisdom. They were mad after one swallow of the Bible, but not wise enough to keep drinking. So they awaited the slaughter of millions that the Lord would oversee at his predicted return.[2] Wood's Israelites, however, committed the cardinal sin of assigning a year to the destruction, and sourced it to an earthquake; against which they prepared the lintels of their doorways with psalms painted in lamb's blood. The group dispersed quietly in 1802. Later historians see in their brief congregation and fervor and gathering of rodsmen to discern the shaking of the earth another prelude to Mormonism. The land was made ready, by one force or another, parching and intoxicating madness, for Oliver Cowdery's coming.

Before he had memories of her, his mother would fall like millions of unknowns to "consumption" (on 3 Sep 1809), leaving his father with too many mouths to feed, and only grief to pass out in abundance. Oliver was sent to his aunt Huldah Glass's home for nearly four years, and his arrival again brought death. Huldah was broken by "a plague" in 1813, her husband a few months later. Their deaths are now thought to be the work of typhoid fever, which gave that same season the young Joseph Smith a lasting weakness, having infected the bone in one leg.[3] After its removal by crude tools rooting about his shin bone, Smith was more like the mythical Smith—Vulcan or Weyland—approximating as he hammered out from gold a new thing, limping but always the strongest man in town. Where the plague delivered young Oliver is unknown, but he spent his final youthful years at cousin Arunah's home. Where he passed most of the 1820s is lost to us these centuries later—maybe tending a shop, selling newspapers or books, nothing suitable for biography. In late 1828 he shows up near the home of Joseph Smith, Sr., where he would sometimes board while teaching at the Manchester school. By April of '29 he was writing the words of Mormon.

---

[1] Larry Morris, "Oliver Cowdery's Vermont Years and the Origins of Mormonism" (in Welch and Morris, *Olivery Cowdery*), 14.
[2] Morris, "Oliver Cowdery's Vermont Years," 19
[3] Morris, "Oliver Cowdery's Vermons Years," 16

Nobody drawn that near to Smith in that year would leave uninjured. So Oliver Cowdery, school teacher with a gentle hand and trained pen, and a good ear, ended up second to Joseph Smith in the history of Mormonism. He become its most eagerly dispatched figure, by Mormons and Mormon haters alike. Some peculiar integrity was in the grain of Cowdery, for he alone could have killed Mormonism in its infancy, with a single public confession, or by telling a lucrative fiction.

## THE COWDERY ARTICLES OF THE CHURCH OF CHRIST

It is time again to concern ourselves with traditions, and divide them from what we can call history. Sometime in 1829 Oliver Cowdery wrote the "Articles of the Church of Christ," a copy of which is found among his papers kept by the LDS Church. The text is on a single large page, folded in half to give two sides, making four pages in all.[1] Three of the pages are filled by his Articles, which comes to nearly 1500 words. It is guessed that the copy was made in 1830 or 1831, although the only date on the paper is 1829. That may mark the year the copy was made, just as it might refer to the year of the copied text's reception. No analysis of the page or of the ink has been done, as far as I know, in an effort to date the document. "Written in the year of our Lord and Saviour 1829," the document concludes, "A true Copy of the articles of the Church of Christ." Just as Oliver duplicated the entire Book of Mormon manuscript that year, readying it for Grandin's press, he may have copied his own revelation with a plan for its preservation. 1831 is given as the terminal year for the copy, for summer of that year found Symonds Ryder, a preacher who like so many left Alexander Campbell for Joseph Smith, looking back, reportedly because an early revelation spelled his name "Simonds." I suspect more than misspelling drove a thorn in his flesh, for it was in June that a great "enduement" of power was expected among the Mormon elders. More than a few doubted its delivery, as we'll see in a later chapter.

Ryder was looking over his shoulder, literally, as he apparently filched Cowdery's copy and a stack of other revelations kept in the church's recently established headquarters in Ohio. Ryder's great-great-granddaughter unrolled his theft, discovering it behind a drawer in an old dresser, in the 1950s. The documents landed in the vaults of the LDS Church by 1960, where a prejudiced

---

[1] A copy is published in Scott Faulring, "An Examination of the 1829 'Articles of the Church of Christ' in Relation to Section 20 of the Doctrine and Covenants" (in Welch and Morris, *Oliver Cowdery*)

archivist believed the now separated pages were two distinct writings, the first of which he proceeded to label, as though suddenly finding himself a skeptic in matters of religion, "A supposed revelation to Oliver Cowdery."[1]   Cowdery's reputation had fallen as Smith's had risen to the divine, and there could be, by 1960, only one prophet and revelator.   "It may seem odd that Oliver was the actual compiler of the revelation," Scott Faulring of BYU admits, "when his role as scribe for the Prophet seems so commonplace."   He then points out that Oliver's reception of revelation was not in violation of policy in 1829, for it was not yet revealed that only "Joseph Smith, and Joseph Smith alone, was the Lord's appointed mouthpiece."   Faulring like most LDS historians cannot resist a dig at the Cowdery of 1829, advising the unlearned Mormon reader in a circumlocution befitting Dickens' office of that name, that "it should not be automatically assumed that God's word to Oliver is precisely the same in nature as Joseph's revelations" (164).   To give you yet more sense for how historians employed at a school owned by the Corporation of the President of the LDS Church attend to matters of history, when conflicting received tradition, consider his sequencing of revelations concerning the founding or restoring of "the Church."   What follows is a convoluted textual history, but I will try to make it as simple as possible.

Faulring claims the "earliest revelation that specifically mentions the impending establishment of the Church was given in late summer 1828," and gives us what is now published as Doctrine & Covenants Section 10 as that revelation (159).   That revelation's year of reception was long dated to 1829, however.  It was changed to 1828 by B.H. Roberts in the early 1900s, mostly to fit his sense of how history should've unfolded.  Surely Faulring knows this.  He is wrong, even by his own church's standards.  The later date of April 1829 was given in the recent *Joseph Smith Papers*, the latest word on official things like dates and names and so forth, as decided by editors at the Church Historian's Press. Section 10 is a mess of traditions trotted out for historians to stumble over, but Faulring's dating it to 1829 only adds to the muddle; and not coincidentally conforms to received tradition, being the declared date in the 1981 LDS Church Doctrine & Covenants used at BYU.  Worse still, Section 10 is only partially preserved in what is called the Manuscript Revelation Book 1, begun in 1831 and the first compilation of early Mormon texts.  Pages 3 through 10 have been torn from the book.  The second half of Section 10 begins on page 11, and is the only portion we can say existed in 1831 (let alone 1828).  The missing pages were replaced in 1838 by a few handwritten ones that derived their content from the

---

[1] Faulring, "An Examination," 190 n.70

published, and much revised, 1835 Doctrine & Covenants. The fact is that we have no complete Section 10 from before 1833, when it was first published in the Book of Commandments. When we begin asking for evidence, we find very little of Mormon tradition is confirmed by history.

Faulring's tale is tangled for being weaved with tradition (and perhaps a regular paycheck). He writes that a "few months later, in March 1829, the Lord spoke again on this subject, telling Joseph Smith and Martin Harris that the restored Church would be patterned after the New Testament-era organization" (159). Not in so many words, however. Nor was "the Savior," as Faulring claims, "Expanding the earlier precondition [of Section 10]," saying, "And thus, if the people of this generation harden not their hearts, I will work a reformation among them, . . . and I will establish my church, like unto the church which was taught by my disciples in the days of old" (159). This text came a month *before* Section 10. Faulring ignores changes to this revelation, moreover, telling traditions for histories. In the oldest published version from 1833 Book of Commandments (from which he draws the above quote, removed by 1835), the description of the church is far from promising. Cowdery oversaw the publication of the Book of Commandments, which warns, "O ye unbelieving ye stiffnecked Generation," addressing the readers directly, "Mine anger is kindled against you."[1] By 1835 the target of his anger has been changed to, "This unbelieving and stiffnecked generation," as though the Lord were venting to Joseph Smith about his neighbors, and not giving warning to the Church of Christ. An entire warning has been removed by Faulring's ellipses, and from the 1835 Doctrine & Covenants. The 1833 version reads:

> If the people of this generation harden not their hearts I will work a reformation among them, *and I will put down all lyings, and deceivings, and priestcrafts, and envyings, and strifes, and idolatries, and sorceries, and all manner of iniquities,* and I will establish my church, like unto the church which was taught by my disciples in the days of old.

Rather than absolute assurance that "my church" will be found among what the Book of Mormon calls "Gentiles," we hear that upon conditions, "my church" will be established. Other passages (from later D&C 10:48-53) point to the

---

[1] Verse 8; the most accurate and detailed record of the many changes is found in Robert Woodford, *The Historical Development of the Doctrine and Covenants*, 3 vols. (PhD dissertation, Brigham Young University, 1974), 158.

Remnant of that book's Lamanites as "my people," among whom "I will establish my church"; if it is established at all. In "this generation" there is, at best, "the beginning of the rising up and coming forth of my church out of the wilderness" (D&C 5:14). Its course ambiguous: the voice does not say which church among which disciples "in the days of old" would be their model. Surely Mormons, of any people, ought to be able to imagine more than one set of churchmen called *disciples*, and something other than that church described in the New Testament. Restorationist metatext has imposed not only on the Book of Mormon but also on scripture attributed to Joseph Smith.

Conditional Ifs abound. Although ignored by Faulring, the voice in the Book of Commandments continues,

> And now if this generation do harden their hearts against my word, behold I will deliver them up unto satan, for he reigneth and hath much power at this time, for he hath got great hold upon the hearts of the people of this generation: and not far from the iniquities of Sodom and Gomorrah, do they come at this time: and behold the sword of justice hangeth over their heads, and if they persist in the hardness of their hearts, the time cometh that it must fall upon them.[1]

It may be worth recalling that the Bible was said by the Book of Mormon to have been corrupted by the Great and Abominable Church, of the Kingdom of the Devil, for the purpose of hardening the hearts and blinding the minds of men. As a result, iniquity and abomination thrive among all nations of the Gentiles. Ignoring and insisting on misunderstanding the Book of Mormon's relationship to the Bible, Mormon historians since 1831 have taken pains to remove, revise, rewrite, tear up, and otherwise erase evidence of the Lord's dissatisfaction with their attempt to restore biblical Christianity.

June 1829 is dated the receipt of what is now D&C Section 18, given in answer to queries about how to create a church which should outlast the gates of Hell. The voice mentions Cowdery's baptism "by the hands of my servant Joseph Smith, Jun.," (v.7), indicating that it was received after May 15, when the baptism was said to occur after the scribe had recorded what is now 3 NEPHI. (While Cowdery attributed his baptism to his writing of 3 NEPHI, where Jesus instructs the people on its performance, he never attributed the organization of the Church of Christ to his reading of that book.) Section 18 is an important part of the puzzle pieced together here, and is likewise absent from the earliest record of

---

[1] In Woodford, *Historical Development*, 160

revelations, Manuscript Book 1. "The first part of the revelation that came in answer to their prayer," Faulring explains, "implies that Oliver, in particular, wanted to know how to organize the Church. The Lord told Oliver to 'rely upon the things which are written, for in them are all things written concerning [the foundation of] my church, my gospel, and my rock" (163, brackets original). I give the current rendering from Doctrine & Covenants 18, which does not differ much from the earliest existing version:

> [B]ecause of the thing which you, my servant Oliver Cowdery, have desired to know of me, I give unto you these words:
>
> Behold, I have manifested unto you, by my Spirit in many instances, that the things which you have written are true; wherefore you know that they are true. And if you know that they are true, behold, I give unto you a commandment, that you rely upon the things which are written; For in them are all things written concerning the foundation of my church, my gospel, and my rock (D&C 18:1-4).

The instruction turns to warning in the next line, that "if you shall build up my church, upon the foundation of my gospel and my rock, the gates of hell shall not prevail against you" (v.5). The addressees are told they "have my gospel before you, and my rock, and my salvation," (v.17) and then its description follows: they are to "ask the Father in my name, in faith believing that you shall receive, and you shall have the Holy Ghost" (v.18). Mention is made of ordination of priests and teachers, "to declare my gospel, according to the power of the Holy Ghost which is in you, and according to the callings and gifts of God unto men; And I, Jesus Christ, your lord and your god, have spoken it" (v.32-33), "by the power of my spirit have spoken it" (v.47). Cowdery and Whitmer are commanded to repent, to preach the same, and are "called even with that same calling with which [Paul] was called" (v.9). Without "faith, hope, and charity, you can do nothing," they learn, being warned to "Contend against no church, save it be the church of the Devil" (v.19-20). There is some emphasis on taking upon themselves the name "which is given of the Father" (v.24), and that twelve others "shall take upon them my name" (v.27). The men "are ordained of me to baptize in my name, according to that which is written; and you have that which is written before you; wherefore, you must perform it according to the words which are written" (v.29-30).

What was "that which is written"? According to Faulring (guessing upon no evidence whatsoever), Oliver Cowdery "set about to use the as-yet-unpublished manuscript of the Book of Mormon, along with several early manuscript revelations, to compose the statement on Church procedure and organization that he called the 'Articles of the Church of Christ." Thus Cowdery "literally fulfilled the command given him the previous June when the Lord told him to 'build up my church,' by 'rely[ing] upon the things which are written'" (163-4). In fact, "the Lord" never told Cowdery to build up "my church," but only warned that *if*, "if you shall build up my church, upon the foundation of my gospel and my rock, the gates of hell shall not prevail against you" (18:5). To this end, apparently, the professor of church history sees Cowdery cutting and pasting from existing texts, "the things which are written," taking for his Articles some "selected doctrinal or essential ordinance passages from the unpublished Book of Mormon manuscript, integrated those passages with material from several of the Prophet's 1829 revelations, and added a few lines of his own commentary" (165). Faulring insists that "Oliver incorporated procedures and ordinances gleaned from the Book of Mormon, supplemented by modern revelation or commentary of his own origination, to write his Articles of the Church of Christ" (166). That is how he relied upon the things written, Faulring says, to build a church that might withstand Hell itself.

Faulring is not ignorant of the content of the Cowdery Articles, only ignoring what they say, because they say *Cowdery*. If Joseph Smith were addressed in the document, the writing would be committed to the memory of every Mormon, framed in the halls of every chapel, and revered for restoring sacred biblical truths lost since the Apostasy. Cowdery instead is made into a lazy plagiarist: not once does he cite a source or even refer to the Book of Mormon or "the Prophet's 1829 revelations." The text (rather than Faulring metatext) of the Articles of the Church of Christ (copied in 1829) indeed describe Cowdery doing something rather different than taking here a line, and there a line, copying from existing materials. Cowdery claims to hear it all from the mouth of Jesus Christ himself. Given the dating of all these texts to 1829, it is entirely possible that "the things which are written" actually referred to the Cowdery Articles, as well as the Book of Mormon. This is a possibility with implications; now for the evidence.

Faulring presents a typescript of the 1829 document in an appendix to his essay, from which I have taken the following extracts (I also compared them to Woodford's typescript). The Articles begins by naming itself "A commandment from God unto Oliver how he should build up his church and the manner thereof." We can assume the masculine pronouns refer to God, and not Oliver. "Oliver listen to the voice of Christ your Lord and your God and your Redeemer," and write—not from existing texts added to a few comments—but "write the words which I shall command you concerning my Church my Gospel my Rock and my Salvation." Many of the words of Jesus seem to quote his purportedly "earlier" revelation discussed above (e.g., Section 18), emphasizing a world "ripening in iniquity," in need of repentance. Oliver like "Paul mine apostle" is "called even with that same calling with which he was called," and told how to baptize "whosoever repenteth and humbleth himself before me." The text also seems to quote directly from 3 NEPHI, giving the ritual language and instruction for performing baptism. "And ye are also called to ordain Priests and Teachers according to the gifts and callings of God unto men," just as Section 18 directs, but the Articles again add ritual language. It then explains the duties of priests, and administration of bread and wine, giving prayers used in offering sacraments to the Church. That entity is commanded to "meet together oft for prayer," and among them should be "no pride nor envying nor strifes nor malice no idoletry," nor many common vices listed thereafter.

The final page begins by addressing "the Church," calling on them to repent "and be baptized in my name," for "there is none other name given whereby men can be saved," but "the name which is given of the Father." The Articles concludes, "Behold I am Jesus Christ the Son of the liveing God," explaining that "these words are not of men nor of man but of me Now remember the words of him who is the first and the last the light and the life of the world." Again, perhaps to emphasize that Cowdery did not simply steal from another man's revelation, it reports that "I Jesus Christ your Lord and your God and your Redeemer by the power of my Spirit hath spoken it Amen." For those who require such things, Cowdery adds this coda: "And now if I have not authority to write these things judge ye behold ye shall know that I have authority when you and I shall be brought to stand before the judgment seat of Christ." Addressing some anonymous reader, Cowdery blesses him or her to be saved "Eternally in his Kingdom." Perhaps doubting that the text will be treated as described, Cowdery concludes by giving his credentials in this explanatory passage:

> Behold I am Oliver I am an Apostle of Jesus Christ by the will of God the Father and the Lord Jesus Christ Behold I have written the things which he hath commanded me for behold his word was unto me as a burning fire shut up in my bones and I was weary with forbearing and I could forbear no longer Amen—

Written in the year of our Lord and Saviour 1829—A true Copy of the articles of the Church of Christ &c.

Ignoring everything Cowdery claims for it, Faulring insists—at this point surely too much—that "Oliver's 1829 document should be read and understood simply as a preliminary step taken by the Second Elder to assist in laying the administrative groundwork for the organization of the restored Church" (168). The "preliminary step" was but a "short procedural statement" (175). Faulring thus divines that "even though Oliver's Articles were written in the first person of Christ's voice, it does not rise to the same stature of original and authoritative revelation" (175).

Just as Faulring would remove Cowdery from "his church," the Articles was nearly all ripped from Revelation Book 1.[1] Pages 15 through 22 are missing from the book, leaving the sequence of copied "Commands" jumping from "8th" to "17th." Cowdery's Articles commences on page 23 of Book 1, midway with the liturgy of sacrament. That book's copy of the Articles continues through the prohibition on pride, strife, envy and malice, to the end described above. In Revelation Book 1, however, the blessing from Oliver and his declaration of apostleship have been scribbled over, literally. The following two pages from Book 1 are missing. Instruction later published under D&C Section 5 and Section 10 was also partially removed after inscription in Revelation Book 1, giving us a mystery. The most controversial passages—dealing with the loss of 116 pages by Martin Harris (D&C 5); one explaining Cowdery's failure to translate by his "thing of nature," a magic root later euphemized as "the gift of Aaron," with a promise that he will be given ancient records to translate (D&C 9); another promising him ancient records (D&C 8); one resolving problems about translation of the Book of Mormon, after the loss of 116 pages (D&C 10); and the Articles presenting Cowdery as an apostle; and presumably several others—have all been completely or partially removed from Revelation Book 1.

Both Harris and Cowdery were excommunicated by 1838, and one can suppose, but never prove, of course, that Sidney Rigdon sought to expunge them from the church's history, just as BYU historians who carry on with his Campbellism-as-Mormonism still insist on giving it a college try. They do so, perhaps, because their leaders are not bigger hearted: One official Church

---

[1] Book 1 was "procured sometime during the first year after the church was founded in April 1830," *The Joseph Smith Papers: Revelations* (fascimile edition, 2009), xxv; 4-5. The Papers' editors suppose that it was begun in March 1831 by John Whitmer as copyist.

Historian whose grandfather was Hyrum Smith summarized Oliver Cowdery's attempt to translate ancient Reformed Egyptian, using a magic root, as "a failure." Indeed it was. While D&C 9 has the Lord explaining to Cowdery that he failed because "he took no thought save it was to ask," and did not create something first in his mind to offer up, the Church Historian (having no training in history, but instead being descended from a church president) supposed that, "It seems probable that Oliver Cowdery desired to translate out of curiosity, and the Lord taught him his place by showing him that translating was not the easy thing he thought it to be."[1] Nor is writing history so very easy. What matters most, perhaps, is no church leaders today bear the name *Cowdery*.

## THE ARTICLES AND COVENANTS OF THE CHURCH

Joseph Smith alone must have the ear of Heaven and give it voice, for modern Latter-day Saints. Following tradition they cannot see as in fact very recent, they preach "follow the prophet" today, as though it was more than a metaphor, but substantively instructed one to take a definite path through life. Their leaders, it is said, derive their authority from Joseph Smith. Smith is credited with founding their church, with restoring the Plan of Salvation (Walter Scott's Faith, Repentance, etc.) as part of the True Church; restoring "the priesthood" and its three grand orders (taken from Rigdon, who took from Campbell, who plagiarized Crawford); with ensuring that Mormons alone have all the power and authority necessary for and essential to obtaining Heavenly rewards. Smith's words are read like Evangelicals read their Bibles (that is, under pretense of piety) as though they were written as given precisely from Heaven, when they were not so well recorded nor preserved. Smith's voice has been made into a Mormon analogue of the Christian Bible, a theme explored in the Epilogue.

Recent publications under the series title *The Joseph Smith Papers* only continue the fiction, for the editors publish that which they attribute to Smith, directly or not (hence his name is a modifier for "papers," which are not necessarily "his"); as though he indeed received all things from Heaven, and that everything they attribute to Smith indeed came from his mouth (and not Cowdery's, Rigdon's, nor Campbell's). Yet as one historian concludes, "About half of Cowdery's revelatory manuscript was printed as divine revelation to Joseph Smith

---

[1] Joseph Fielding Smith, *Church History and Modern Revelation*, Series One; 1947:46-47, in Woodford, *Historical Development*, 193.

(D&C 17:8; D&C 18:9, 22-25, 34; D&C 20:37, 60, 73, 75-79)."[1]  Smith has become a funnel, as we'll see, a modern author, and everything tradition finds exemplary of Mormonism can be run through the mouth of the Prophet, a process not unlike that described by Bakhtin's principle of ventriloquism.[2]

That one can demonstrate these claims are false; that nearly everything before 1831 is tradition fashioned in retrospect, and obscuring the movement of Campbellism; that Scott preached the plan of salvation in 1827; that others taught Smith about priesthood orders; that Cowdery organized the Church of Christ; that nearly everyone hoped to restore Primitive Christianity, and only a slightly smaller majority sought to reclaim the "Red Man" to Christian civilization; that the House of Israel had become a euphemism for restored Christianity as early as the sixteenth century; so many facts do little to derail the train of tradition that chugs along, upon the strength of many billions of dollars and no little domination of politics, economics, and culture in the American intermountain west.  Money and power, however, do not change facts, although one may tear pages from books, revise histories and insert false copies and alter dates: the truth is living, and a sly boots, unbarrellable and not for them to buy and hide.

The truth is that Oliver Cowdery is just as likely to have received his Articles before the Book of Mormon was translated, as he is to have copied some passages from it during June 1830.  (So long as we assume divine instruction is possible, of course.)  He was reportedly visited by Jesus while he boarded at the Smith home in Manchester, before meeting their boy Joseph.  Prior to his springtime epiphany, according to Joseph's mother Lucy (recalled many years later), Oliver heard the tale of the Golden Plates and Joseph's struggle to translate them.  After giving it much thought, Cowdery told her, "The subject upon which we were yesterday conversing seems working in my very bones, and I cannot, for a moment, get it out of my mind; finally, I have resolved on what I will do."  The fire in his bones was at last put to paper, and his teaching of school concluded.

---

[1] D. Michael Quinn, *The Mormon Hierarchy: Origins of Power* (SLC: Signature Books, 1998), 275 n.33

[2] Terryl Givens mentions Bakhtin's work on "dialogicality" but does not seem to understand it.  He suggests that "dialogicality" means "a dialogue," and gives a sort of folksy, back-and-forth model of "revelation" he finds in the Book of Mormon as exemplary of "dialogicality." Bakhtin means something like "multiple voiced," however; that rather than "monologicality" such as one finds in traditional first-person narration, writers like Dostoevsky create narratives that take up several "voices," thereby introducing psychological qualities like doubt and irony, complexity absent from monological narration.  This matter is further taken up in the Epilogue.

She says he told her, "If there is a work for me to do in this thing, I am determined to do it," and Cowdery departed, when spring made travel easier.[1] The existing primary materials do not support one tale—mine or tradition's—over another. We have a hole, and ought to leave it open. Tradition and all its fatness and desire for gain and power would have you believe that when Cowdery reports the words of Jesus directly, he means something else; just as historians who recite little white lies here and there have no problem telling them, if it conforms with corporate orthodoxy. These are the foolish ways of what will be called "Gentiles" by the Book of Mormon; and their grasping for power always leaves them with many beams in their eyes, and idols before their faces. Blind spots: born of small town smugness; certitude by having never been challenged; priestly platitudes embraced as truths; these inevitably leave a bland landscape, and lazy eyes; much is not seen by tradition-tellers, and easily picked up and examined by anyone willing to look around. The easiest thing is to say, "Show me," or to show them what they counted on some shadow cast by their bigness to conceal.

So we turn to traditions around D&C Section 20, that text said to be pure Heavenly revelation to Joseph Smith, and not at all related to Cowdery's Articles. As Faulring insists, historians who "imply that Joseph Smith revised and expanded Cowdery's earlier Articles" are "both inaccurate and misleading."[2] Knowing that one can be inaccurate and not misleading, and misleading but entirely accurate, Faulring is perhaps the ideal historian of church history and doctrine. He would have you believe that direct quotes from Cowdery (reportedly from Jesus) are not found in Section 20, which tradition ascribes to Smith. Before we cruise through his house of mirrors, we should note that what historians call "The Articles and Covenants of the Church" (D&C 20) was not recorded in Revelation Book 1 until page 52, dozens of pages after Cowdery's Articles, and long after they supposedly were read in 1830 and accepted as the constitution of the Church of Christ. These now official Articles and Covenants are credited to Joseph Smith alone, and are found in Book 1 between commands dated January 2nd and January 5th 1831. There are no Articles other than Cowdery's we can date to 1830. Yet the published D&C 20 is presented by historians as the Church of Christ's founding document. No evidence supports this claim, except that Cowdery titled his copy "Articles of the Church of Christ," and D&C 20 was (after 1831) labeled "Articles and Covenants of the Church of Christ." The longer title was recorded in the Far West Record (apparently begun around 1831) as

---

[1] Lucy Mack Smith, *History of Joseph Smith by His Mother* (SLC: Bookcraft, 1958), 139
[2] Faulring, "An Examination," 167

naming the text read by Smith at the first conference of the Church of Christ held in June of 1830. It was at this conference that Smith also read from EZEKIEL 14, remember, warning about stumbling blocks and idols set up before their faces. So the published one (20) is said to be the one read at the founding of the Church of Christ, *because its title matches*. That title, of course, was given to it in publications years after the church consented to follow a document similarly titled.

Faulring insists that D&C 20 "bears little or no resemblance to the earlier Cowdery Articles," (168) and reasons that "roughly one-fifth of section 20 relies on the Book of Mormon, while more than half of Cowdery's Articles are either direct quotations or paraphrases with slight deviations from the Book of Mormon," (167). Ignoring the obvious fact that much of D&C 20 gives Smith's biography, Faulring insists (without too much specificity) that "Apparently a large percentage of the Articles and Covenants came by direct revelation to the Prophet" (167). The irony is that while Cowdery reportedly wrote the word of the Lord, D&C 20 makes no such claim. Cowdery is mocked in Faulring's concession that he was "probably involved in writing section 20, this time it was only in the mechanical sense—as the Prophet's scribe" (169). To this he adds pure speculation designed to tarnish the man's character. "Brigham Young described how Joseph had to struggle with Oliver," Faulring says, "as the Prophet dictated a revelation on priesthood—evidently the 1830 Articles and Covenants." He continues by revealing his source, honored with the title of "President Young," who reportedly said,

> "You read that Oliver Cowdery was the Second Elder and you remember the Revelation on the Priesthood [section 20]; . . . Joseph was over two hours laboring with O[liver C[owdery] to get him to write the Revelation in humility." The fact that Oliver Cowdery had compiled an earlier set of Articles could at least partially explain his reluctance or difficulty (169 brackets and ellipses in original).

In an endnote Faulring claims that Brigham Young can only mean the Articles and Covenants (D&C 20), because "In the Latter-day Saint scriptures, there are only two other revelations given to the Prophet Joseph Smith that overwhelmingly focus on priesthood, D&C 84 and 107" (186 n.46). He claims that Section 84 was written when Cowdery was "in Zion," and "there is no evidence to suggest that Cowdery was in conflict with Joseph Smith over the contents of, or involved in the writing (scribal or otherwise) of, D&C 107, parts of which were given in 1831 and 1835." Should we bother showing his reasoning runs on nonsense?

First, Section 20 makes no mention of "the Priesthood." That is pure Faulring supposition. Given that it is and was referred to as "The Articles and Covenants of the Church," it seems implausible that Young would suddenly call it "the Revelation on Priesthood." In fact, in the current Doctrine & Covenants Section 84 is described in its modern introduction thusly: "The Prophet designates it a revelation on priesthood." Second, were this story taken as "evidence," Faulring could dispense with doubts "that Cowdery was in conflict with Joseph Smith." John Whitmer said that Sidney Rigdon invented the notion of priesthood, and that Joseph Smith took it up after his arrival in Kirtland. One can imagine that rumor causing a little friction. Third, Brigham Young was not in the Church of Christ in 1830, but was by the time D&C 84 was written. There is more going on here than Faulring and tradition will say.

To give you something to estimate Faulring's apologetic prowess with, and his desire to impugn Cowdery no matter how weak the evidence, we can turn to his endnote 47 (on his page 187). He gives the source for Young's quote, recorded by a clerk in 1868 at the Provo School of the Prophets, and reasons that Young "was probably relating information he heard from Joseph Smith or someone else present in 1830." Notice Young is hearing "information" and not gossip, and he was telling a story almost thirty-five years old, and no where else recorded. Young and other leaders were no Cowdery fans, and took every pain to speak evil of him, just as Latter-day Saints do now; for reasons apparently not unrelated to the effects of certain stumbling blocks. Rigdon replaced Cowdery, and with Pratt he—the walking Bible—became the voice of Mormonism.

Here I give the current version of D&C 20, said by Latter-day Saints to be the foundation of their restored church, revealed to "The Prophet Joseph Smith" and surely setting forth the same organization found among early Christians. The text is described by Woodford (currently an editor with the problematic *The Joseph Smith Papers*) as suffering from maladies not unlike those afflicting a few other important, and apparently controversial, revelations, commands and prophecies. "The historical background of Section 20," he writes in a classic 1974 dissertation, "is somewhat clouded by the inability of anyone to attach a date to it."[1] His dissertation published for the first time the Cowdery Articles, after it was discovered in that dresser drawer and subsequently buried in LDS Church archives. Woodford describes the Cowdery Articles, contra Faulring's later assessment, as "an early draft of the Articles and Covenants of the Church, in Oliver Cowdery's handwriting." One might wonder why this LDS historian has

---

[1] Woodford, *Historical Development*, 286

no trouble calling the Cowdery document an "early draft" of D&C 20? It is because he misunderstands who wrote it, taking Cowdery as the scribe. In other words, he supposes that Cowdery merely wrote what Smith dictated, because, well, I'll let him explain: "If it was a commandment, how that commandment was received is important. If the procedure was the same then as now, such a commandment would have come through the Prophet" (290). So he believed that Cowdery acted as scribe to Smith's revelation, completely missing the obvious statements setting out who was speaking to whom. This should tell you something about how Mormon historians will misread a text, when tradition, fostering so many idols, has blinded their minds and hardened their hearts.

One more thing, before I give you D&C 20. Look for statements about how the Church of Christ restores Primitive Christianity; or is founded upon the authority of the priesthood; or advocates a plan of salvation beginning with "faith" and ending in some manner like Walter Scott's version; that its members are the House of Israel, and the Bible the word of God. You will not find such things, nor announcement that it is a "revelation" to Joseph Smith or anyone else. It certainly does not read to me as Faulring once described: "textual evidence suggests that the Prophet inquired of the Lord and the Articles and Covenants was given by revelation."[1] What would "textual evidence" that Smith "inquired of the Lord" and received even look like? We are left without an answer from Faulring.

Cowdery's Articles reports Jesus speaking to Oliver, while D&C 20 says nothing of the sort. Nonetheless, Faulring's claim was recited in a recent article titled, "The Articles and Covenants: A handbook for new branches." Its author pleases none, by seeking to please all in claiming that like the U.S. Constitution, the Articles and Covenants was revised several times, and,

> required several written drafts from Oliver Cowdery and the Prophet Joseph Smith as the Spirit of the Lord worked within them to produce the final copy. On the other hand, distinct from the Constitution, there is sufficient evidence that much of the Articles and Covenants came by direct revelation to the Prophet Joseph Smith.[2]

---

[1] Scott Faulring, "The Book of Mormon: A Blueprint for Organizing the Church" Journal of Book of Mormon Studies, 7 (1998) no.1:65

[2] Craig James Ostler, "The Articles and Covenants: A Handbook for new branches" (in Whittaker and Garr, *A Firm Foundation: Church organization and administration* (Brigham Young University Church History Symposium. Religious Studies Center and, 2011), 84

Not wholly opposed to Cowdery, Ostler adds that the text draws from the Book of Mormon "as a primary source" and that "through the Holy Ghost, the voice of the Lord guided Oliver Cowdery and later the Prophet Joseph Smith in writing this revelation" (84-85). The text itself is as contradictory as its metatext summaries. The published text of the Articles and Covenants (as D&C 20) is a patchwork of theologies, administrative procedures, and liturgy taken from other texts. Some parts are also found in the Book of Mormon or the Cowdery Articles, other passages show the hand of the Walking Bible, some from Smith. The text is not really from 1830, pre-Rigdon "Mormonism," but a work in progress stopped by publication, a de facto 1833 canonization peculiar to our age. As I said, a version was inserted into Revelation Book 1, from which the Book of Commandments' version was taken (or the other way around). Then it was altered and became D&C 20. The text patches together notions probably from Smith, Cowdery, Rigdon, Pratt, Whitmer, and everyone else who rose to leadership before it was formalized by publication. It is a textual diagram of the mess that was Mormonism during the early 1830s, as Smith and Cowdery saw their church transformed by Restorationists. It begins by stating that Cowdery and Smith received commands to organize "the Church of Christ," one of a thousand so named churches.

> The rise of the Church of Christ in these last days, being one thousand eight hundred and thirty years since the coming of our Lord and Savior Jesus Christ in the flesh, it being regularly organized and established agreeable to the laws of our country, by the will and commandments of God, in the fourth month, and on the sixth day of the month which is called April—Which commandments were given to Joseph Smith, Jun., who was called of God, and ordained an apostle of Jesus Christ, to be the first elder of this church; And to Oliver Cowdery, who was also called of God, an apostle of Jesus Christ, to be the second elder of this church, and ordained under his hand; And this according to the grace of our Lord and Savior Jesus Christ, to whom be all glory, both now and forever. Amen.

The text gives a brief biography of Joseph Smith (v.5-8), and describes the book he translated as "a record of a fallen people," to which description someone added, "and the fullness of the gospel to the Gentiles and to the Jews also" (v.9). The book is said to be, as Givens puts it, somewhat paradoxically, "Proving to the world that the holy scriptures are true, and that God does inspire men and call them to his holy work in this age and generation, as well as in generations of old" (v.11). "By these things we know that there is a God in Heaven," it continues, "infinite and eternal,"

> from everlasting to everlasting the same unchangeable God, the framer of Heaven and earth, and all things which are in them; And that he created man, male and female, after his own image and in his own likeness, created he them; And gave unto them commandments that they should love and serve him, the only living and true God, and that he should be the only being whom they should worship (v.17-19).

This statement clearly contradicts LDS theology, which has two (or three) gods prescribed for man to worship: God the Father and his Son Jesus Christ, and the Holy Ghost. Just as in days of old, "by the transgression of these holy laws man became sensual and devilish, and became fallen man" (v.20). So we come to a passage that adds to our confusion, or evidence of fallen status, if only one being is to be worshipped:

> Wherefore, the Almighty God gave his Only Begotten Son, as it is written in those scriptures which have been given of him. He suffered temptations but gave no heed unto them. He was crucified, died, and rose again the third day; And ascended into Heaven, to sit down on the right hand of the Father, to reign with almighty power according to the will of the Father; That as many as would believe and be baptized in his holy name, and endure in faith to the end, should be saved—
>
>     Not only those who believed after he came in the meridian of time, in the flesh, but all those from the beginning, even as many as were before he came, who believed in the words of the holy prophets, who spake as they were inspired by the gift of the Holy Ghost, who truly testified of him in all things, should have eternal life, As well as those who should come after, who should believe in the gifts and callings of God by the Holy Ghost, which beareth record of the Father and of the Son (v.21-27).

Heaping confusion upon us, this segment concludes, "Which Father, Son, and Holy Ghost are one God, infinite and eternal, without end. Amen." One can find in the first twenty verses "the only true and living god," the Father, his Only Begotten Son, the Holy Ghost, and these are "one God, infinite and eternal, without end." It is not hard to see how Campbell's theology fit into some (but not all) of this declaration; nor to imagine that had Mormons succeeded in baptizing a hundred Roman Catholics in 1830, they too would find the Trinity in this Church of Christ. If any text evidences the sort of cut-and-paste composition Faulring credits to Cowdery's Articles, it is this Section 20.

The Articles and Covenants gives a series of "We Know" declarations, a sort of concealed creed (not built around the traditional "We Believe") readymade to catechize candidates for baptism. "We know that men must repent and believe on the name of Jesus Christ, and worship the Father in his name," it posits, and that men must "endure in faith on his name to the end" (v.29). Rather than giving us Scott's plan of salvation, this text presents what a later volume will demonstrate is the Book of Mormon's sequence: repent, believe on the name, worship the Father in his name, and endure in faith. That outline is also given in an early letter from Cowdery to Hyrum Smith, where Cowdery tells Hyrum to "Stir up the minds of our friends against the time we come unto you that thus they may be willing to take upon them the name of Christ for that is the name by which they shall be called at the Last day."[1] It then explains the "manner of baptism," and the requirements for those desiring it. Rather than baptism being for the remission of sins, it declares that initiates must "witness before the church that they have truly repented of all their sins, and are willing to take upon the name of Jesus Christ," showing before entering the water they have "received of the Spirit of Christ unto the remission of their sins" (v.37). How one takes on "the name"—not by baptism alone—is shown by a later volume to be a central concern in the Book of Mormon, one lost when so many clichés and biblical phrases were found among various disciples of Christ. Section 20 adds a statement not unfamiliar to Campbell's disciples:

> And we know that justification through the grace of our Lord and Savior Jesus Christ is just and true; And we know also, that sanctification through the grace of our Lord and Savior Jesus Christ is just and true, to all those who love and serve God with all their mights, minds, and strength. But there is a possibility that man may fall from grace and depart from the living God (v.30-32).

So the church is warned, and "even those who are sanctified take heed also" (v.34). Showing itself to be a work of at least one committee, the text adds this patchwork of conditions:

---

[1] 14 June 1829; Joseph Smith letterbooks 1:5-6, Joseph Smith Papers, LDS Church archives. In Vogel, *Early Mormon Documents*, vol.2 (1998), 403

And we know that these things are true and according to the revelations of John, neither adding to, nor diminishing from the prophecy of his book, the holy scriptures, or the revelations of God which shall come hereafter by the gift and power of the Holy Ghost, the voice of God, or the ministering of angels (v.35).

The duties of elders, priests, teachers, deacons "and members of the church of Christ" are listed, and here too we find a jumble of doctrines stitched into social roles, even the clarification that "An apostle is an elder." Elders are to baptize, "to administer bread and wine" "to confirm those who are baptized into the church, by the laying on of hands for the baptism of fire and the Holy Ghost, according to the scriptures," (v.38-41). Other duties are given: "teach, expound, exhort," and so on, generic responsibilities concerned with administrative matters that any other church of Christ might also prescribe for its elders, teachers, and deacons.

"Baptism is to be administered in the following manner unto all those who repent," it continues, and gives the liturgy as written in Cowdery's Articles (and also found in 3 NEPHI), with an important difference in the declaration of the elder: rather than "Having authority from Jesus Christ," as Cowdery and the Book of Mormon state, Section 20 gives the elder's declaration as: "Having been commissioned of Jesus Christ." The sacrament prayer is given in 20 as Cowdery and the Book of Mormon have it, although "wine" has since been changed, as it were, to "water." Procedures for disciplining members found "transgressing" are given, as are administrative matters concerned with church conferences and membership records. These are Faulring's "collection of inspired bylaws."[1] This is the stuff of divine revelation? Mostly chaff found in every run-of-the-mill church churned out by frontier Christianity. Let me suggest another version of history.

## COWDERY'S CHURCH

Perhaps Cowdery received his Articles when he was called "with the same calling as the Apostle Paul," that is by vision rather than because of membership in a lineal priesthood. We can see why he thought of copying in 1829 the original words of Christ set a-burning in his bones. These words would've been later recited by Joseph Smith as he translated the Book of Mormon, with Oliver Cowdery as scribe; being attributed to the same Jesus who had come to Oliver several weeks earlier. The resulting witness that the translation was correct would

---

[1] Faulring, "The Book of Mormon: A Blueprint for Organizing the Church" Journal of Book of Mormon Studies 7 (1998) no.1:62

have resolved doubts for Cowdery. Doubts about Smith the earlier scribe, Martin Harris, could not, apparently, leave behind. In Doctrine & Covenants Section 6 a voice speaks as God, and before 1830 addresses Cowdery, telling him to "treasure up these words in thy heart," apparently meaning to keep them unwritten (v.20). He is told, "that thou mayest know that there is none else save God that Knowest thy thoughts and the intents of thy heart," the voice confirms that "the words or the work which thou hast been writing are true" (v.17). Identifying with "Jesus Christ," the voice (spoken through whom, I know not) says to the apostle Oliver that "if you desire a further witness, cast your mind upon the night that you cried unto me in your heart, that you might know concerning the truth of these things" (v.22). He is reminded that Jesus gave him peace of mind, and asked, "What greater witness can you have than from God?" (v.23). The next verse answers, and asks another question:

> And now, behold, you have received a witness; for if I have told you things which no man knoweth, have you not received a witness? And behold, I grant unto you a gift, if you desire of me, to translate, even as my servant Joseph (v.24-25).

Cowdery would "fail" to translate, but not because the Lord found him uppity, and in need of knowing "his place." His failure in part resulted in him being written out of Mormon history, even though he wrote—indeed as a scribe—the book which Mormons claim is their foundational scripture. Why he was written out? That is a question I cannot answer yet. We cannot understand Cowdery's course unless we suppose a few things about Joseph Smith as a translator, and that must wait. This brief survey of the Cowdery Articles gives a few clues, and also shows how post-Rigdon Mormonism imposed traditions, and then revisions and outright falsehood, on earlier figures involved in the translation of the Book of Mormon. Revelation was not Smith's alone to give or receive, but all the words attributed to Christ should witness they came from the same source. What we see from 1831 to 1833, however, is the infiltration of Primitivist traditions and Christian dogma. Smith did not stop these voices from being written into the ever-changing Articles (expanded to include Covenants), nor even across the Book of Mormon. In the transition from the Cowdery Articles to Section 20, we see Smith take what was written and develop it, letting others do the same, sometimes voicing him as the author of their work. He had warned them about idols and stumbling blocks, what more could he do?

If Cowdery wrote the articles of "his church" before the Book of Mormon was translated—a tale no less supported by existing materials than is the traditional account of his cut-and-paste revelation (so long as one allows for revelation, of course)—then some insight can be gained regarding his relationship to the man known among Mormons as the Prophet. A man who is by them credited incorrectly with revealing so many of Rigdon's and Campbell's Restorationist doctrines, as well as Cowdery's Articles. Some version of the Articles was copied and passed around by elders in the Church of Christ, including, presumably, Hyrum Smith as he spoke with Parley Pratt in fall of 1830. These later Articles place the Book of Mormon on a mission to prove to the world that "the scriptures" (whatever that means) are true, and that "there is a God in Heaven." Rather than text, it is metatext these Articles speak of. Now we examine how the Book of Mormon was a sign, and of what, and to whom. Some say of the Bible's corroboration. Among their voices we hear Sidney Rigdon. Others like Parley Pratt, of the dispensation of miracles. Significantly, Pratt's claims could be comprehended by Rigdon's, whose Bible remained the center of cultural gravity. It was from the Bible that he like Pratt discerned the referent of "miracle" and of "dispensation," words interpreted through centuries of commentary and defintion by bodily extension. What Restorationists considered a miracle wrought by "the power" was often far from what they'd call a miracle after Smith arrived in 1831, and they became Mormonites.

# Seven Signs of Confusing Text and Metatext

THE NOTION THAT THE BOOK OF MORMON IS A SIGN IS FOUND IN THE earliest writings, and in the most recent. Such industry can be expected when we speak of signs: everything is a sign, potentially. A sign is anything which represents anything else to somebody, in the accepted definition among those who practice *semiotics*. The analysis of signs attends to processes they create and are created by: the flow of *semiosis*. A banana, for example, can be a sign of yellow, or even of other bananas ("iconic sign" sharing a quality); it could point to the presence of apes in one's bathroom; or excitement in one's pocket being directed at a particular acquaintance ("indexical sign" which points). Finally, a banana could be arbitrarily made to stand for anything else ("symbolize"): freedom, health, disease; whatever two people agree upon, or have learned through using language to make it conventional. To speak of the Book of Mormon as a sign is to say very little: it is like announcing from the steps of Oxford University that the Book of Mormon is a thing. What sort of thing, we'd like to ask, how did it become such a thing, for such and such a people? Rather than pronounce its semiotic reality, let us show we understand how signs work by attempting to explain why the Book of Mormon was taken as such a sign of something, by such a people. In this case, why its earliest readers thought it represented all they believed about the Bible as authentic and true, despite the Book of Mormon text apparently claiming otherwise. To get there, we will consider the analogous question: why current LDS writers find their administrative structure in the Book of Mormon.

We are dealing with words and with what words create. In this case, a body of readers created by the text they claim to read (metatext), and then, imagined by others outside that circle of readers. As so often is the case, Mormons were first baptized into their name by an outsider, although unlike the newspaper christening, this one apparently did not circulate among those it named. Our earliest known naming (18 June 1830) actually comes from a Lutheran pastor of a church in Fayette. Diedrich Willers addressed some reverend brethren in Bearytown, New York, declaring in German that Joseph Smith is "The greatest fraud of our time in the field of religion."[1] After complaining or gossiping about his success among Baptists and Presbyterians—not because of the Book of Mormon, but because of their baptism by immersion—he reports how "this new sect calls itself." In Dan Vogel's translation, Willers reports they refer to themeselves as "the True Followers of Christ," but Willers calls them "Mormonites," "because they believe in the Book of Mormon." Another translator of the letter (D. Michael Quinn) has Willers calling them "True Disciples of Christ" when he writes "Die Wahre Nachfolger Christi." Vogel apparently prefers *True Followers* because that phrase is also used in a letter from John Sherer to Absalom Peters.[2]

Sherer was minister of the Colesville Presbyterian Church, and was involved in some drama with the sister-in-law of Newel Knight. Apparently the minister attempted to abduct the young girl in order to, it was said, prevent her baptism. He writes that after baptism the gullibles "subscribed themselves to be the followers [of] Christ; for they call themselves a church of Christ, and the only church of Christ." Like every other sect, they regarded all others as "having the form of Godliness, but denying the power thereof." Rather than being founded on some notion of "priesthood authority," however, the claims about being favored of Heaven came from their working of miracles: "They have pretended to work miracles, such as casting out devils, and many other things, too blasphemous to write." The casting out concerned Newell Knight, whose body was relieved of its usurping demon in an exorcism conducted by Joseph Smith (for which wonder-working he was arrested). Let us add to this church's claims to work miracles as their sign of power the revelation of Articles reviewed last chapter: somewhere between the Cowdery Articles and the published 1833 version. That

---

[1] Deidrich Willers to Reverend Brethren, 18 June 1830. In Dan Vogel, *Early Mormon Documents*, vol.5 (SLC: Signature Books 2003), 270-78; also, Quinn, *Mormon Hierarchy*, 616

[2] John Sherer to Absalom Peters, 18 Nov 1830. In Dan Vogel, *Early Mormon Documents*, vol.4 (SLC: Signature Books 2002), 93

is what we can say we know about this Church of Christ, said to have grown into a "new world religion."

Many have attempted to outline its history. "The basic nature of the new 'church' changed three times between 1828 and April 1830," writes D. Michael Quinn, a historian anathematized by former colleagues at BYU.

> First, from 1828 to May 1829 "my church" was an unorganized body of "my people" who had no priestly "authority" and which required no religious ordinances. Second, from mid-1829, dozens of new converts were baptized into a community of believers, "the Church of Christ." Although the church had no formal organizations, Cowdery wrote an 1829 document titled, "A commandment from God unto Oliver how he should build up his church & the manner thereof," which referred to "authority," various ordinances, and church offices. . . . Then Smith published the Book of Mormon at Palmyra in March 1830. As the third major change, Smith formally organized "the Church of Christ" on 6 April 1830.[1]

The Church of Latter-day Saints came in 1834, being expanded to the Church of Jesus Christ of Latter-day Saints in 1838. That name is now a trademark owned by the Corporation of the President of the Church of Jesus Christ of Latter-day Saints, a corporation sole formed in 1923. What was changed from what is not clearly described, however, in Quinn's three-church outline. Names? Offices? Purposes? Words? In fact, there is no way, now, to describe what pre-1830 believers or readers of the Book of Mormon were grouped into, and how. Too little remains. Nearly everything else was rewritten after 1831, and revised over that decade for varying purposes, none of which could be said to be the preservation of primary materials. David Whitmer recalled decades later that not only Joseph Smith "gave many prophecies," but also Ziba Peterson, Hiram Page, Oliver Cowdery, Parley P. Pratt, Orson Pratt, Peter Whitmer, "and many others had the gift of prophecy."[2] These same men were called apostles and disciples in documents bearing passages dated to 1829,[3] and it is likely that those terms did not name "offices" so much as honors bestowed without reservation to any believer who worked something like a miracle. "And it came to pass that in the fall of the year 1832," David Whitmer records in a suitably biblical style, "the disciples at Ohio received the gift of tongues and in June 1833 we received the gift

---

[1] Quinn, *Mormon Hierarchy*, 6-7
[2] David Whimer, "An Adress to All Believers in Christ," 32; in Quinn, *Mormon Hierarchy*, 8
[3] Quinn, *Mormon Hierarchy*, 10

of tongues in Zion."[1]  Called the official church historian (a difficult job, for sure), John Whitmer begins his history recording events from the year earlier than his time of writing, which seems to have begun in late 1830 or 1831.  He does not discriminate one disciple from the next, consistently calling what are now said to be Mormons, "the disciples" or "disciples of Christ."  Sometimes these disciples are said to persecute "the saints," suggesting that not only geography divided the disciples from more pure saints, the distinction being formalized with the new name in 1834.  It seems likely that both New York members (mostly migrating to Missouri) and Ohio members were called *disciples* or *followers* when speaking of their own, and *brother* or *sister* when addressing one another.  *Saint* was apparently used to speak of "real" disciples, after 1834.  Terms like *elder* or *teacher* were likely not used for address, but reserved for introductions and other formalities.  Smith alone is called "Joseph the Seer," suggesting a distinct epithet among pre-Rigdon believers, apparently not used by converts arriving after the early 1830s, when he became "the Prophet" or simply "Brother Joseph," after his leadership was no longer in doubt.

Little else can be known about these early days of what some would call Mormonism.  What we read is mostly retrospection, recollection, revision, tradition, outright fabrication, guesswork.  Gaps there for the filling in.  Texts have been retroactively dated after being altered and the originals misplaced.  We have little to compare post-Rigdon documents against.  "Significant changes have been made in the published texts of LDS scriptures and in church documents published by official histories," Quinn complains, "These changes retroactively introduced concepts, people, names, and structures which did not exist in the original revelations and historical documents."[2]  Changes are difficult to discern, and often cannot be checked against earlier text.  It is a mess.  The more difficult changes to track, however, come not from an inserted phrase or a title or office.  When the words seem the same—disciple, apostle, authority, dispensation, restoration—but the meaning has changed: that is when we risk retroactively reading inherited traditions covertly back onto the past.  More dangerous than formal changes, these changes in meaning have regrounded post-Rigdon Restorationism into the imagination of Mormons, and seemingly into the Book of Mormon itself.

---

[1] John Whitmer, *From Historian to Dissident: The Book of John Whitmer*.  Bruce Westergren, ed. (SLC: Signature Books, 1995), 103
[2] Quinn, *Mormon Hierarchy*, 5

So we return to tradition-tellers. This time our goat is John W. Welch, a law professor at BYU who spends his spare time discovering ancient Hebrew poetics in the English Book of Mormon, sending computers on author-discovering jaunts, and deliberating with anyone doubting his genius. He also responded to historians like Givens and Underwood who said that few Mormons read or knew their new scripture by writing an article (published by his university's press) insisting the Book of Mormon was the basis of the entire administrative apparatus that governed the early Church of Christ (presumably he would mean both the 1830 and the 30 AD organizations).[1] Under a section titled, "PEOPLE READ AND KNEW THE BOOK OF MORMON," he sets out to prove his clients innocent of the charge of ignorance and lack of use. He does indeed find "people" of which it could be predicated, "read and knew the Book of Mormon." As proof that at least one people he trots out summaries of the journals of William McLellin, the earliest known personal records kept by a Mormon, dating from 1831. Here is the summary he provides, a quote from the editors of the McLellin journals:

> By far the most frequent topic in his sermons was the Book of Mormon, evidences in its behalf, prophecies about its coming forth, testimonies of its divinity, and validations of its worth in opening the glories of the latter days (26).

The editors describe metatext: evidences (from the Bible); prophecies (from the Bible); testimonies of its divinity (from McLellin). What is meant by "validations of its worth" I cannot say, but that phrase does not come from the Book of Mormon. Although his essay does not admit it, Welch was actually editor of the BYU Studies 1994 publication of this very diary; the summary is his own. Cleverly he quotes as though it was merely an assessment made by objective readers of the McLellin documents.

These McLellin journals and notebooks tell us more about modern Latter-day Saint historiography than about how "people" knew and read the Book of Mormon. Now notorious forger and murderer Mark Hoffman in the 1980s fooled the leaders and professional historians in the LDS Church into buying his faked collection attributed to McLellin. Their reason was, apparently, not because

---

[1] John Welch, "The Book of Mormon as the Keystone of Church Administration" (in Whittaker and Garr, *A Firm Foundation*)

they were blinded by a desire to see their histories told from his perspective, but because (fake) McLellin reported rather delicate and embarrassing details about life in the early church. The irony is that after Hoffman injured himself with a bomb (having killed two others previously), LDS Church archivists actually looked into their own vaults and removed the beam, discovering they had since the early 1900s owned the real McLellin diaries. Neither Hoffman nor Church historians and inspired leadership came away without injury. One was exposed as a forger with a life to live in prison; historians looked like toadies to hierarchy; the last were foolish consumers of anything damaging to the church's sterling reputation, willing to hide it and forget it. Keep in mind this is a religion that for nearly a century publicly declared that not only is Heaven populated by many gods; they marry goddesses, and live a sort of communism, being former mortals on another world. Polygamy was its sacrament, theocracy boasted of and actually implemented in the United States. Aside from a theology now too un-Christian to be mentioned, early Mormons also made deception into religious virtue, took oaths of vengeance, killed "Lamanite" Indians regularly, bribed and then cursed the leaders of the United States, and reportedly practiced "blood atonement" (vengeance killing) on wayward Saints (and passing wagons of Missourians). I think of all these deeds and doctrines as favors done for modern Mormons: what could we now be ashamed of, really, given this history? Is there any rule our pioneer Mormons did not break and exalt in the flouting? Any tradition, moral, or virtue rejected as an insult to Heaven? Our "pioneer forebears" have left us little to worry about, when it comes to public relations disasters resulting from exposure by discovery of some early Mormon diary. Short of eating babies, they pretty much did everything; and then wrote it down, and printed it in newspapers. In Welch we find a re-imagining the past when it cannot be bought and concealed; the latest in a long century of follies, with men like McLellin made into pious moderns.

Their religion was strictly biblical, of course, and right out of the Book of Mormon. Welch adds that "In his journals, Wilford Woodruff reports that he preached about the authenticity of the Book of Mormon six times in the 1830s."[1] That total averages out to fewer than one sermon a year, even "about" that book, by an apostle of the LDS Church. What was said—whether it came from the Book of Mormon, or was derived from the Bible and connected to it—is not explained in Welch's essay. Perhaps such distinctions do not matter to some in their search for proof to make a case. He finds that Joseph Smith likewise is

---

[1] Welch, "Book of Mormon as Keystone," 29

among those "people" who knew and read. "Scouring the pages of the Teachings of the Prophet Joseph Smith," (a compilation edited nearly a century later, badly, but never worthy of being scoured, as it were), "one finds numerous ideas and phrases that most likely originated with distinctive passages in the Book of Mormon." He gives as examples, and I am not making this up, the following:

> October 25, 1831: Joseph admonished the Saints to do their duty patiently and in perfect love: "Until we have perfect love we are liable to fall." This comports with Moroni 8:26, "which Comforter filleth with hope and perfect love, which love endureth by diligence unto prayer, until the end shall come" (31).

Sixteen more bullet points follow this, and he started with his best evidence. Of course, even these "ideas and phrases" are not really from Joseph Smith: they come from diaries and letters, sometimes from sermons reported by men like Wilford Woodruff, more recently cleaned up, compiled and made ready for publication to the members of the LDS Church. His conclusion is grand, that "it was not only the Book of Mormon, it was indeed the only Mormon book; and throughout Joseph Smith's life it remained the quintessential Mormon book" (33). I'll leave you to divine the meaning and import of that conclusion, merely noting that whenever Mormons talked about the Book of Mormon in public, they always (as the next volume will demonstrate) brought up the Bible as well, taking pains to show that it does not replace the Holy Word, but merely corroborates it. Whether that defines Welch's quintessence of a book, I cannot say. His analyses are the sort of foldorol that result from not distinguishing between use and mention, text and metatext, topic and quote, year of copying from year of the thing copied; from not seeing that what one understands when reading an 1831 document may not be what was meant in that year; not seeing that most words don't project one single meaning.

Welch presses his data to speak today, concluding that the Book of Mormon advocates the model of administration thought to characterize the LDS Church, where a "prophet, seer, and revelator" directs the course of Zion. "Turning the pages of the Book of Mormon, any reader is hard-pressed to miss the will of the Lord regarding such things as following a single prophet-leader," Welch claims, adding that by contrast with other churches, there is not found in its pages "a council of elders or a sea of bishops or a congregational priesthood of all believers" (35). This clear model of authority was found by "people who knew and read," our early Mormons. The book thus "encouraged the Latter-day Saints to look primarily to the Lord's true prophet for guidance in all ecclesiastical matters" (35). Turning some pages past Welch's essay (in a volume titled *A Firm Foundation*), one finds another essay that concludes,

> . . . an appraisal of the minutes of the quarterly meetings held during the first years of the Church's existence as an institution reveals not a narrow hierarchical leadership but a shared, even symbiotic, collaboration. This relationship remained the essence of the genius of Church organization and structure throughout the lifetime of Joseph Smith.[1]

This contrarian essay is unwittingly titled, "Seeking after the Ancient Order," and finds that perhaps symbiotic collaboration probably was how early Christians also held counsel. Not himself as hard-pressed as Welch to find a "single prophet-leader," Darowski sees rightly from his review that Joseph Smith "was not always as prominent a participant as might be expected" (98). Instead, Sidney Rigdon is often the more prominent voice in church meetings.

When dealing with topics, themes, ideas and notions—abstract nouns and the like—it is easy to find exactly what one is looking for, like some wizard, precisely where he intends to find it. What is true of BYU professors of law searching for ancient-modern orders of things in an 1830 text is also true of disciples in that year, who found in the Bible their order of things. Since then we've found and find in the Book of Mormon: priesthood authority, and also polygamy and then monogamy, capitalism and communism, theocracy and democracy, blood atonement and St. Anselm's atonement. That is the sort of thing Restoration allows: it is a term rooted in a sort of power to remake a text to reflect contemporary practices and processes of hierarchy making.

It is difficult enough to reconstruct Mormon history when Mormons have been "restoring" historical documents in a manner to make Mark Hoffman pause in admiration. It is more difficult when abstract nouns like *authority* or *priesthood* are redefined in ways that push traditions deeper into history, beyond the days of their infancy and into a pre-existence. That the actual history—as disciples lived in 1830—resulted in traditions which make understanding them nearly impossible is, I suppose, a fate we are condemned to; so long as we fail to see how terms can mean one thing today, and another tomorrow, and not think this blindness of

---

[1] Joseph F. Darowski, "Seeking After the Ancient Order: Conferences and Councils in Early Church Governance, 1830-34," (in Whittaker and Garr, *Firm Foundation*), 97

mind a problem.  In fact, even historians attempting to challenge the current LDS claim to follow a single prophet-leader in a manner that has always marked the Lord's Church often end up validating that tradition.

Another Mormon historian attempting a more nuanced reading of history in relation to the Book of Mormon, ends up projecting back the same structure Welch and Faulring happily paste onto it.  His concern is "authority," an abstraction which is easily divined wherever one's rod bends the mind.  He outlines first how the Book of Mormon depicts authority differently from the current LDS Church.  Authority comes from angels to men, or "directly from God."  Then,

> Second, authorization came in the form of "the spirit of the Lord" being upon him, with no mention either of angelic appearance or of the laying on of hands. Third, Alma baptized himself and Helam simultaneously.  Finally, although Alma acted under divine authorization, no ordained office was mentioned.[1]

Greg Prince finds the early Church of Christ using terms from the Book of Mormon, like elder and disciple, in a manner derived from that record (as though no one else used them).  Then he compares these offices with those in his metatext Bible and Book of Mormon, finding in them a definition suggesting a "higher authority equivalent to that given by Christ to his apostles in Palestine" (20). Thus, the early Church of Christ defined their terms—elder, disciple—in the same way.  Already we should see the problems in his tale.  Prince is using the word *authority* in an expansive sense which fits with current LDS norms, but which may not have been used in the first century before Christ, in the Americas, among speakers of an unknown Egyptian-Hebrew hybrid; nor among whoever tagged along with Jesus so long ago.  To use purported ancient records to understand the meaning of 1830 terms is probably a more restorationist restorationism than the most zealous of Saints ought to suffer from.  His purpose, let's be clear, is to chart how "charismatic authority" as described in the Book of Mormon (and the early Mormons) was channeled into bureaucratic authority evident today in LDS chapels.  Moving from that book into more imagined history, he says of early Mormons like Cowdery and Whitmer, that their

---

[1] Gregory A. Prince, *Having Authority: The origins and development of priesthood during the ministry of Joseph Smith* (John Whitmer Historical Association Monograph, Independence MO: Herald Publishing House, 1993), 18

higher authority was the same described in the Book of Mormon, as it stated of the twelve disciples Cowdery and Whitmer were to choose, "You are they which are ordained of me to ordain priests and teachers," the same duty given twelve disciples/elders in the Book of Moroni (20-21).

The author has carried into his text a hierarchy and structure of social relations packed into terms like *elder* and *disciple* (which he freely interchanges, because, of course, they once meant the same thing). Prince is attempting to reconcile existing early Church of Christ records with later recollection, also with his own traditions and reading of Book of Mormon metatext. When we pick up the matter of "authority" in a later chapter, his concerns will be more carefully explained. I want to emphasize here that readers may find any organizational structure in a few offices or titles. On the Book of Mormon metatext, like the Bible, one can play any tune. So it is a sign of the continuity of priestly authority from the ancient Americas into the corporate LDS Church; or not. The book will let you please yourself, while it waits for readers willing to listen to what it says about its characters, and about its readers.

The tune playing is easier when we begin with abstract nouns, topics, themes, ideas, names and other ill defined and regularly redefined words. Prince asks the wrong questions, like Welch and Faulring—what does the Book of Mormon tell us about authority—because his questions come from a tradition which started in 1831. When we realize that the "authority" spoken of by Parley Pratt and early leaders concerned the "gifts of the spirit," like exorcism and healing the sick, euphemized as the power of godliness, then many contradictions born of tradition do fade away. Their tradition of restoration has made nearly everything before it match the doctrines that came along with Rigdon and other disciples on Morley's farm. Restoration today is no better at giving accurate history from text than it was in 1830 or 1630.

Rather than finding in scripture their single-prophet leader model, or symbiotic counsels, or charismatic authority, writers outside LDS tradition find particulars which seem to invalidate the text's claims. Dan Vogel edited a volume of essays collected under the titled *The Word of God*.[1] Some are prescriptive in orientation (e.g., "Beyond Literalism"), advocating the metadiscursive term "inspiration" over "revelation" when speaking of the Book of Mormon. Others take as their subject

---

[1] Dan Vogel, ed. *The Word of God: Essays on Mormon Scripture* (SLC: Signature Books, 1990)

a vague "Christianizing [of] the Old Testament," or similarly discuss cultural influences on the text of the Book of Mormon. Altogether, the collection is overwhelmingly conceited and not carefully considered. A follow up collection edited by Vogel (and Brent Lee Metcalfe) was published in 2002.[1] It begins with the insistence that, "Had the Book of Mormon been what Joseph Smith said—not an allegory with spiritual import but a literal history of Hebrew immigrants to America—this should have been verified by now,"[2] as though it was on a game show and the buzzer of truth had sounded. They continue convinced by their own conclusions, that "To acknowledge the obvious fictional quality of the Book of Mormon is not," patting believers on the head, "is not to detract from the beauty and brilliance of the sermons, visions, and other imagery" (ix). The collection includes essays on "Automaticity"; others on problems of native American DNA studies (always third-hand research) not validating their own reading of the Book of Mormon; revisiting "influence," this time of Anti-masonry; and trotting out "biblical studies" to show how the Book of Mormon does not give us an authentic ISAIAH translation. This collection deserves all the accolades of the first, and more for having a decade to mature its virtues. The problem with so much writing on the Book of Mormon is that it is approached not as it purports—to be a translation done in 1829 of a text not currently available, said to draw on non-biblical sources because the Bible was corrupted by the Devil—but as LDS tradition has created it. Metatext, then, is not only found among Latter-day Saints, but often ex-Mormons acquire that prefix because they discover that their metatext does not conform with what someone (an "expert"?) says about Indian-Jewish genetics; ancient steel or husbandry; or what the Bible (metatext) says about this or that. Perhaps the most instructive of all the attempts to show the Book of Mormon is not divine revelation—that it is a sign of its own invalidation—came from David Persuitte in 2000.[3]

His argument retreads an old one, that Joseph Smith drew from, was inspired by, or got something from a book called *View of the Hebrews*. This concern over authorship marks non-LDS writings, just as showing continuity of authority and form, passing from book to body of people (as metatext) is the mark

---

[1] Dan Vogel and Brent Lee Metcalfe, ed., *American Apocrypha: Essays on the Book of Mormon* (SLC: Signature Books, 2002)

[2] Vogel and Metcalfe, "Editor's Introduction" (Vogel and Metcalfe, *American Apocrypha*), vii.

[3] David Persuitte, *Joseph Smith and the Origins of the Book of Mormon*. 2nd ed. (Jefferson NC: McFarland & Co., 2000)

of an orthodox LDS writer. So long as he like Welch cannot see any difference between theme and text, word and meaning, idea and narrative, having an idea for a book and actually writing one, the argument from influence—concluding in proof and disproof of the book's authenticity—makes perfect sense. I include Persuitte's argument here not because it is laughable, and also presented with the confidence of a Welch or a Faulring. It shows how metatext inform readings of text. Persuitte's search for origins illustrates that the same hunt for influence or abstractions is pursued by LDS writers, as by those rejecting their claims. The latter depends on the former's approach to the text, circulation of metatext, and overlay of tradition and social structure across the Book of Mormon.

The argument about *View* was first publicized by B.H. Roberts in the early 1900s, and he could not ignore or refute the possibility of some vague connection between the two. Vague is the key word. "Only an extensive in-depth comparative analysis of the two books," of *View of the Hebrews* and the Book of Mormon, that is, "would settle the matter, and in this book, I present such an analysis." Persuitte announces in wholly opaque, but dazzlingly legalistic terms that "The resultant preponderance of evidence demonstrates conclusively that the BOM had its conceptual origins in the View of the Hebrews" (3). Among his supposed origins of the origins are books identifying the Lost Tribes of Israel as the Indians, and one by Sir Hamon l'Estrange published in 1652 which identifies the aboriginal people as coming from the Tower of Babel. "Like the lost tribes school of thought, the tower of Babel school had advocates well into the early nineteenth century" (103). Indeed, a pope declared the indigenous Americans descendents of the Tower of Babel even before l'Estrange, but the Book of Mormon does not say anything about the Tower of Babel. Nor does it name the Indians the Lost Tribes. These are metatextual readings.

Rather than stick to particulars, Persuitte flounders amid the General, finding that Ethan Smith's "views are echoed throughout the Book of Mormon, despite the obvious fact that Joseph would have been perfectly free to modify them for his own needs" (107). Among these echoing views is one concerned with Native Americans and the books of the Bible: "By Ethan Smith's argument, if the American Indians are proved to be descended from the tribes of Israel, then the Old Testament is proved to be true, and there the New Testament is also proved to be true" (115). Again, the problem is that the Book of Mormon does not say anything about Native Americans, unless one wants to call them Lamanites or whatnot; the book does not. Moreover, what it says about the Bible has been clearly presented: rather than corroboration or proving it, the Book of Mormon I read is designed to undo its work of captivating men, blinding their minds and hardening their hearts. Persuitte even finds proof of borrowing in the absence of such. Concerning one absence, "Pastor [Ethan] Smith was particularly taken with Isaiah 18, and he devoted much of his book to his ideas about that chapter; yet, curiously, there is no mention of Isaiah 18 at all in Joseph Smith's latter-day 'revelation.'" His solution? "But it is perhaps precisely because Ethan Smith made so much of Isaiah 18 that Joseph warily refrained from quoting it directly" (116).

With similar insight he explains why *View of the Hebrews* was extracted in the Mormon newspaper Times and Seasons in the 1840s, an apparent oversight of Joseph Smith's, if indeed he relied on it to give his readers their scripture. "In response, we could perhaps consider that Joseph felt he had sufficiently disguised his use of View of Hebrews in composing his book," and so confident of his ruse was Joseph, that he figured "no one would notice that it had its source in Ethan Smith's book." Having run into the mind of a trickster seer, Persuitte realizes "there is another possibility. It is possible that Joseph did not compose The Book of Mormon himself, but went through the motions of pretending to translate what was actually someone else's work" (125). Given that Joseph Smith said approximately that—he was translating someone else's work—we can see yet again Smith outwitting so many Sherlocks sleuthing after him, hot on the trail of his crime.

I give Persuitte space in this chapter because he has reduced the search for origins to an absurdity. There is no origin to find. How different, though, is his search from those taken up by John Welch, or disciples claiming to find in the Bible the origins of their churches? The only difference is found where the reader self-identifies, with respect to the tradition of the writer: inside or outside? The Book of Mormon is a sign to everyone—of a fraud, of a corporate church's ancient presence, of one kind of authority or another being authenticated on its pages, or of the power of blunt literary criticism and not-yet discarded Bible studies methods to give us confirmation of what we already believed about metatext. Metatext is a sign of the text, like a picture of a banana is a sign of bananas. Some are nourishing, but if you eat a child's scrawl said to be a banana, you will be dissatisfied with the result, and probably complain about it. Bonobos and chimps recognize these truths; and will use the hand sign for "banana" to ask for an actual banana. They do not eat the hand sign. Children will show a banana in order to request that an adult peel it for them. The Book of Mormon as an actual text generated metatext, and these stand in for it. They are the subject of criticism and searches for this or that; and seem to confirm one's beliefs about authority or administrative procedures, or Hebrew genetics and the Tower of Babel. It is the semiotic nature of the book, in fact, which will require us to jettison our notion of authorship, inherited traditions of authority, and instead offer a reading that makes sense of Joseph Smith as a translator. Our Epilogue takes up that responsibility. Now we meet the popularizer of the "book is a sign" phrase, professor Terryl Givens, whose history of the Book of Mormon is a most subtle and sly swapper of tradition for history.

The spectacular manner of the book's coming forth, he supposes, "seem[s] to suggest what it signifies as event may be more important than what it actually says."[1] Here Givens begins in a manner that reveals he is dealing with the Gold Bible as viewed by Restorationists, and not the Book of Mormon: with metatext tradition, rather than text itself. At certain key points he will leave his posture of documenting how so-and-so interpreted the book, and himself advocate covertly for traditions developed from the very history he claims to tell. That is to say, Givens and his book and theory of book-as-sign are products of the actual history he attempts to represent in his own book. I imagine that is a difficult statement to parse, but obvious when understood.

He is one fruit of the hemlock I am whacking at in this volume, a slippery banana among the bunch. Givens agrees with Jan Shipps and Grant Underwood that the scripture's "earliest uses were primarily eschatological and reflected as well as reinforced a millenarian world view." Strictly attending to metatext Gold Bible, he stresses that "the book was more important, even in this regard, as a sign than as a theological document" (70). A review of "2000 articles and publications on the Book of Mormon going back to 1830," is cited by Givens,[2] and the reviewers concluded that mention of the Book of Mormon clearly overrides "meaningful discussion" taken from its pages. Here again we are dealing with metatext: mention rather than speaking from its pages, from actual use. So far, Givens stays on task, giving us a history of how Mormons have ignored or interpreted the book as a whole.

Posturing as objective academic, he explains in quasi-technical terms that "the history of the Book of Mormon's place in Mormonism and American religion generally has always been more connected to its status as signifier than signified," citing Saussure's *Course in General Linguistics*, "or its role as sacred sign

---

[1] Givens, *By the Hand of Mormon*, 63
[2] Givens, *By the Hand*, 70; 568; cites Amos N. Merrill and Alton D. Merrill, "Changing Thought on the Book of Mormon," Improvement Era 45 (Sep 1945)

rather than its function as persuasive theology" (64). What Givens is actually telling you is that something said about the book was said about the book; and, *is* the book's message. The notion promoted by Givens to historical fact—book as message—merely repeats an old mantra of Media Studies made popular by 1960s guru of the global village, Marshal McLuhan, that "the media is the message." Itself not bothering to say what the "media" as "message" was, the phrase was recited around academia even into the 1980s. That it described *nothing* was quite important in making it say something about its reciter; and like a koan, it put the hearer on her heels, wondering if the speaker knew something no one else knows. Givens apparently caught McLuhan's meaning at this time, for he too utters his own koan: "the 'message' of the Book of Mormon was the manner of its origin" (84). He imagines his reading is *the meaning*, and not just an interpretation by someone, say, inheriting a tradition from Restorationists looking for miracles. His loose treatment of signs and message is reminiscent of early 1970s "symbolic" anthropology; and before that, 1960s structuralism. Both projects failed because they forgot to ask: to whom is it such and such a sign, for whom does it mean that, to what person does it carry that message, when, for how long? Givens answers thus, summoning the the author-translator in support of his tale about the metatext: "Joseph apparently also believed the message was the manner of its coming forth or he would have spent some time writing or preaching about the Book of Mormon's content, instead of repeatedly talking about how he produced it" (85). That is, because Smith talked metatext, that was the message of the text: it had a strange history. But what had that history? Text, obviously.

He is speaking of metatext, confused into thinking he is telling you about text itself: that because some persons thought the book indicated ("indexical sign") a return of miracles, then that was the message of the book. So certain is Terryl Givens of his claim about the "sign" that he says, "Even those disaffected members who came to repudiate the prophet could not escape the logic of his connection to the Book of Mormon—which they generally refused to renounce." His summary provided below frames the quoted passage, given after:

> The three witnesses, all of whom broke with him sooner or later, were unwavering in their belief that the record he produced was unimpeachable proof that, at the time of its translating, he held the keys of the kingdom as God's holy prophet.

He then quotes for support from the journal of William McLellin (not one of the "three witnesses"), who states, as Givens quotes him, that he has "no faith in Mormonism," and "no confidence that the church organized by J. Smith and O. Cowdery was set up or established as it ought to have been. . . . But when a man goes at the Book of M[ormon] he touches the apple of my eye."[1]  As I read McLellin, he seems plainly to contradict what Givens asserts about "the logic" of Smith's power being bound to the book, having no faith in Mormonism nor interest in what he thought was Smith's church.

Givens's work illustrates just how desperately historians must distinguish between text and metatext, particularly historians of religion.  At various points Givens swaps out his historian's coat for the theologian-preacher's robes; whenever he tells you what the Book of Mormon really says.  Failure to keep them distinct can result in a scholarly history of scripture which merely selects and preserves certain traditions, honoring them with historical laurels by collapsing metatext into text.  In the beginning this was done by churchmen like Rigdon or Whitmer or Pratt; now their words are recited and made into histories, and the Book of Mormon seems to second them.

Sometimes Givens does quote from the Book of Mormon, and the careful reader can see that its message is not the metatext.  One thing Givens says it describes is that Jesus told "the Nephites shortly after his resurrection" how his teachings would be preserved by them, and "shall come forth from the Gentiles, unto your seed" (65).  Some teachings mentioned in a quote Givens (on p.66) takes from 3 NEPHI 29:1-4, moreover, make it clear that "these sayings shall come unto the Gentiles according to his word."  Clearly the Book of Mormon says that to whomever it comes, they probably should regard themselves as Gentiles. Rather than confront the problem that early disciples of Christ in New York and in Ohio apparently thought of themselves as the restored House of Israel because they had the book-as-sign, the professor retreats to the robes of the historian.  "The Book of Mormon has had a tremendous role to play in the establishment of the Latter-day Saint church," he concludes, "a role grounded largely in its obtrusiveness as miraculous artifact, portent of the last days, and sign of prophetic power."  Admitting that for Mormons, "This role appears to have little or nothing to do with particular doctrines that are explicitly taught in the revealed record" (196), Givens acts as if he is not himself participating in that very tradition as he writes his tale of the history of the book.  Posturing as an objective historian

---

[1] Givens, *By the Hand of Mormon*, 87; quoting letter of William McLellin to James T. Cobb, published in Larry C. Porter, BYU Studies, 10 no.4 (summer 1970), 486

merely surveying Mormon thinking, he is unwittingly giving you his version of Mormonism.

Givens claims that the book indicated "that the great work of gathering—a literal gathering—has commenced, and that the American Indians ('the remnant of the seed of Joseph') along with the Latter-day Saints adopted into the house of Israel together share in the promises made to Abraham" (68). Whether he is explaining the Book of Mormon, or someone's understanding of that book, this is not made clear. It is clear that the Book of Mormon says nothing about "the Latter-day Saints adopted into the house of Israel," being joined to "the American Indians," his parenthetical "remnant of the seed of Joseph." He has decoded the text with a magic ring of LDS tradition, and yet does not explain to the reader that his metatext may not be what the text actually says. Because he is a Mormon, and reading uncritically his own tradition as history, he is able to take his own as "someone's understanding of that book," and map it onto those of earlier Mormons. The professor slips from the posture of describing what early Mormons believed, into voicing what the book actually says, as though there was no difference between them—because it says that to *him*. Coming from a tradition he describes as ignorant of the book's content, it is no surprise that our professor cannot diagnose this blindspot.

As an inheritor of Restoration, Givens cannot seem to not read the text as LDS tradition has rendered it: corroborative of the Bible. Trading in his historian's coat for the preacher's robe, he suggests that the book gives us "those first principles from the New Testament" (196); that is, the plan of salvation taught by Walter Scott. We see in this shift from "so-and-so thought the book means X," to "the book really means X," a play for the reader's imagination, to tell him or her that the book means X, Y, or Z. Really means it, as text. And not merely to some misinformed, barely literate reader drunk on apocalyptic Bible nonsense. The confusion comes from writing uncritically a history of a scripture, of a relationship of text and metatext. One may let metatext stand in for text when thinking of scripture and actually confuse one for the other. It is essential to see the difference.

The book was a sign of miracles to someone, for some time; surely the content is not unrelated to that interpretation. Were the pages blank, I doubt the book-object would be considered a sign of miracles, no matter the stories about its origins. The same confusion of metatext for text leads Richard Bushman into saying that, "Altogether, the Book of Mormon can be thought of as an extension of the Old and New Testaments to the Western Hemisphere,"[1] without bothering to explain for whom it can be thought of as such an extension. A chapter later we find Bushman playing surveyor, or maybe theologian: "In the Book of Mormon, Gentile Christianity has apostatized" (103). His reading becomes somewhat problematic when we realize that "Gentile Christianity" (never mentioned in the book, nor is "apostasy") gave him the tradition of restoration which has him thinking the Book of Mormon is "an extension" of the books of the Bible. History, tradition; tradition, history: movement between the genres is made possible by swapping of metatext for text, which can be cited after being framed by traditions. The slippage is particularly easy to let happen when writing a history of scripture. It is even more difficult to discern the swap when one has inherited Restoration reading practices: those making it too easy to take terms from text and built them into metatext, generating living scripture by building that relationship outward into society, bodies, biographies and the landscape.

Would that the problem were as simple as one of bias or deceit! Instead, convoluted metadiscursive practices have generated Mormon culture and history, and also ways of being "Mormon" connected to reading and telling that history. We saw in an earlier chapter how Givens excised from Amos Hayden's history of Scott's preaching (copying from Hyrum Andrus's BYU Studies article), effectively leading readers into believing that Scott "prepared" the people, all waiting for a "new Bible, a new religion." I doubt Givens intentionally misleads us ever; but one's eyes may be blinded by Restoration practices, confusing metatext for text no matter how poor fit. For the most obvious example of Givens telling traditions for history, I conclude with this passage. Not only does his chapter titled "The Search for a Mesoamerican Troy" skip over the problems pointed out by archaeologists investigating Mormon speculation that the Nephites lived in the Yucatan, but he gives this, in tacit support of the most general supposition among the broadest segment of (mostly BYU housed) Book of Mormon geographers:

> The mental map that Joseph must have been forming for Book of Mormon history apparently encompassed both north and south American continents. Two virtually identical maps exist, allegedly produced by Joseph himself, entitled "A chart, and description of Moroni's travels throughout this country." . . . In the right-hand margin are the words, "Moroni's Travels starting from Sentral America to the Sand hills Arizona then to Salt Lake U[tah] T[erritory], then to

---

[1] Bushman, *Rough Stone*, 86

Adam on Diammon Mo, then to Nauvoo, Ill, then to Independence Mo, then to Kirtland Ohio then to Cumorah NY" (99).

Rather than comment on the obvious problems of such a map being attributed to Joseph Smith, he seems to use it in support of the tradition that (someone believed?) Nephites had lived in Central America, because "Joseph himself" "must have been forming" some sort of map; here is a map attributed (by an unnamed someone) to him. Again Givens has voiced Joseph Smith delivering some message. I'll not point out the obvious problems, which Givens should've noted. Why note it? So that readers could be sure he was not merely interested in passing off traditions, but was serious about one of two responsibilities. One: telling readers the story of metatext (like maps) generated by readers of the book; in which case his own book would've been five volumes, minimum. Trust me, five volumes. He picked one (absurd) map over another, however. Mormons have also identified East Africa, Italy, New York, and Baja California as the setting for the Book of Mormon. Why not give these equal pagetime? Two: he could realize that he's giving traditions he believes in and pretends at times to speak of as an objective historian. Neither self-accounting can be found in his text.

What is explained is that he, like Bushman, pretends to tell "faithful history," or gives a "cultural biography," a history of what someone believes (and not merely themselves). Of what someone believes, without arguing whether their beliefs were rational or well considered, and so on: something like what anthropologists do in ethnography, under the guise of cultural relativism. Merely documenting a culture, let's say. The pitfalls surrounding such paths, when undertaken by "natives," should be obvious, at least after reading this chapter. Their voices tend to speak inherited metatext, where the non-native historian would voice a reading outside the tradition; as well as take on at times, in quotation, for instance, a "native" voice. But Terryl Givens does not like being troubled to write, "alleged revelation" or to put "revelation" in quotes. His "Author's Note" to *By the Hand of Mormon* invites him to take every escape:

> . . . the disputability of the facts is too obvious to bear repeating on every page. I have therefore avoided constructions like "Joseph Smith's *alleged* vision," or "the *purported* visit of Moroni," as they would become tiresome and pedantic if repeated on every page. My focus in any case has not been on whether the Book of Mormon or the account of it given by Joseph Smith is true. Rather, I have tried to examine why the Book of Mormon has been taken seriously—for very

different reasons—by generations of devoted believers and confirmed skeptics (n.p).

The result is self-deception, a posture: like he isn't actually telling you what he believes, selecting traditions concealed by the guise of doing something more like, "to examine why"; that is, surveying the record of some quaint, historical culture. All because it would be inconvenient or pedantic to identify who claims what about what? What sort of historian cannot be troubled to attribute a claim to a source, an interpretation to a voice, to distinguish her own beliefs from those she writes about? Givens's own book indeed serves a sign, warning all who unwittingly tell traditions for histories. Rather than attribute bad faith to Givens, however, we can see that he like Parley Pratt has been a victim of scripture, restoration readings, and their institutionalization. Caught in the text-metatext relationship—scripture—that encourages traditions to develop into histories, their voices say more than they mean to, revealing to critical readers how difficult it is to escape the whirlwind of the scripturalizing process.

WARNING SIGNS

Semiotics is an ancient practice, developed among Greeks ("gentiles") as they studied augury, bird omens, liver spots, diagnosed illness, and divined the future. They understood representation, one thing standing for another: imitation; substitution; pointing; propaganda; art. Although entirely secular today, semiotics remains the only reliable way to talk about signs, and of books as signs. It means little to say, "the book is a sign of X." What matters is why it is X to some people. In this chapter, we've seen the book (metatext) is a sign of the LDS Church's ancientness, or Joseph's wily use of the *View of the Hebrews*, of symbiotic collaboration being approved of the Lord, of it being a sign of its history. Every study I've surveyed here collapses metatext into text, just as Restorationists have done for four centuries, pretending their imitations of an imagined New Testament church were qualitatively the same thing. It is important we see this, and do not simply replicate the structure, merely inserting some new thing for another. What matters to me, and this history I'm telling, is that whatever X, Y, or Z the book represented to Mormons by 1832, that thing apparently was not pleasing to the voice speaking through Joseph Smith. Why not? We return to our chapter's sourest of the bunch, John Welch. Recall his client desired proof that "people knew and read the Book of Mormon," and that it taught the Saints to follow a "single prophet-leader"?  Even he is forced to concede that "By 1832, however, the Saints were forgetting to follow the Book of Mormon in certain ways.  Significantly, a revelation mainly 'on priesthood' placed the Church under condemnation until they remembered the Book of Mormon 'not only to say, but to do according to that which I have written' (D&C 84:57)."  How does Welch explain this condemnation?  Only as a modern Latter-day Saint could:

> This mandate would seem to reinstate and reinforce a clear direction that the Church was to use and follow the Book of Mormon as an administrative guide, for just as Jesus had said at the end of his first day among the righteous survivors at Bountiful, serious condemnation would come upon the Church if the directives given on that occasion should be ignored.  Jesus said, "Keep these sayings which I have commanded you [this day] that ye come not under condemnation" (3 Nephi 18:33).[1]

Turn back two more years.  In fall of 1830 we see for Joseph Smith aglow, before being shadowed by Sidney Rigdon.  The minutes of the second conference of the Church of Christ record that he was "appointed by the voice of the Conference to receive and write Revelations & Commandments for this Church," an appointment which led Mormons to attribute everything they call Mormonism to the voice of the Prophet.  Perhaps in response, he rose and read from the fifth chapter of ISAIAH:

> Now will I sing to my wellbeloved a song of my beloved touching his vineyard. My wellbeloved hath a vineyard in a very fruitful hill: And he fenced it, and gathered out the stones thereof, and planted it with the choicest vine, and built a tower in the midst of it, and also made a winepress therein: and he looked that it should bring forth grapes, and it brought forth wild grapes.

> And now, O inhabitants of Jerusalem, and men of Judah, judge, I pray you, betwixt me and my vineyard.  What could have been done more to my vineyard, that I have not done in it?  Wherefore, when I looked that it should bring forth grapes, brought it forth wild grapes?  And now go to; I will tell you what I will do to my vineyard: I will take away the hedge thereof, and it shall be eaten up; and break down the wall thereof, and it shall be trodden down: And I will lay it waste: it shall not be pruned, nor digged; but there shall come up briers and thorns: I will also command the clouds that they rain no rain upon it.  For the vineyard of

---

[1] Welch, "Book of Mormon as Keystone" (in Whittaker and Garr, *Firm Foundation*)

the LORD of hosts is the house of Israel, and the men of Judah his pleasant plant: and he looked for judgment, but behold oppression; for righteousness, but behold a cry.

After this bleak and ironic use of ancient prophecy, Smith continued to warn by proxy, applying text to their own biographies and bodies:

Therefore my people are gone into captivity, because they have no knowledge: and their honourable men are famished, and their multitude dried up with thirst. Therefore hell hath enlarged herself, and opened her mouth without measure: and their glory, and their multitude, and their pomp, and he that rejoiceth, shall descend into it. And the mean man shall be brought down, and the mighty man shall be humbled, and the eyes of the lofty shall be humbled: But the LORD of hosts shall be exalted in judgment, and God that is holy shall be sanctified in righteousness.

He read of woes upon the wicked, using their idol's voice to explain their captivity:

Therefore as the fire devoureth the stubble, and the flame consumeth the chaff, so their root shall be as rottenness, and their blossom shall go up as dust: because they have cast away the law of the LORD of hosts, and despised the word of the Holy One of Israel.

Therefore is the anger of the LORD kindled against his people, and he hath stretched forth his hand against them, and hath smitten them: and the hills did tremble, and their carcasses were torn in the midst of the streets. For all this his anger is not turned away, but his hand is stretched out still.

The prophecy turns apocalyptic near the end. What matters, of course, is where the readers locates themselves: from nations far off, or among His people awaiting them:

And he will lift up an ensign to the nations from far, and will hiss unto them from the end of the earth: and, behold, they shall come with speed swiftly: None shall be weary nor stumble among them; none shall slumber nor sleep; neither shall the girdle of their loins be loosed, nor the latchet of their shoes be broken:

Whose arrows are sharp, and all their bows bent, their horses' hoofs shall be counted like flint, and their wheels like a whirlwind: Their roaring shall be like a lion, they shall roar like young lions: yea, they shall roar, and lay hold of the prey, and shall carry it away safe, and none shall deliver it. And in that day they shall roar against them like the roaring of the sea: and if one look unto the land, behold darkness and sorrow, and the light is darkened in the Heavens thereof.

Oliver Cowdery followed with a reading of the Articles and Covenants. Which version, we are not told. "Singing and prayer in behalf of Br. Oliver Cowdery & Peter Whitmer jr.," concluded the conference, blessings upon the men "who were previously appointed to go to the Lamanites."

What they found were no Lamanites, but a gaggle of Restorationists. The difference is subtle, but I hope by this point no longer meaningless. It can be summarized in a single change: John Whitmer's first preaching license identified him as "an apostle of Jesus Christ, and elder of the Church."[1] Men were called apostles or elders or disciples, some of Jesus Christ and others of the Church. In December 1830 some letters of introduction were written by Rigdon "in behalf of John Whitmer." Now he was called "an Apostle of his church." "By the end of 1830," Gregory Prince explains, "a change in policy appears to have been made, and new elders were no longer also called apostles." Prince adds that "use of the term declined quickly. By 1835, when the Quorum of the Twelve Apostles was organized, no mention was made of the earlier apostles." It is time to follow Pratt to Kirtland, to see the Book of Mormon being framed for Restorationers as a sign of the dispensation of miracles, and thus, of the correctness of their Bible metatext, and of the scripting of their bodies and biographies inside its imaginary realm.

[1] Prince, *Having Authority*, 29-32

# Eight  At Last Landed in
# Doleful Kirtland

WHAT MOVES HIS HEART TO REJOICING, AND HIS PEN TO FILL MANY PAGES, is the Book of Mormon's report that glad tidings of great joy are to all people. Here is not set the yoke of tradition on Parley Pratt, for unlike his mind or his tongue, his heart is not burdened by, is not beating to *Primitive Restoration*. Kirtland's Restoration club was likewise full of joy from something—they thought miracles. With them came a witch's brew of covenant theology, having passed through Scottish Independents, bent by Campbell into suitably vague and mysterious biblical language of Restoration. With Pratt they gathered round that Book of Mormon and cast a spell that begot and beguiled Mormons for nearly two centuries. In this chapter we see how a group was formed in reaction to Campbell, and then imagined it had no connection whatsoever. As their traditions were discovered in the Bible, their metatext spread into the Book of Mormon, and outward across social relations they became a movement, and by 1831, a real, publicly recognized church.

Campbell's new 1830 monthly was the Millennial Harbinger. In that title, he remained, as ever, only alluding to events popularly sought for, the rallying point of the decade. He never seriously proclaimed its onset in his sermons. Campbell was confident in the church, that it was enough for now. His followers would eventually become the capital *D* Disciples of Christ after Stone and Campbell merged movements in 1832. Like their pre-formation offshoot Mormons, no few books were quickly published exposing the absurdity of their doctrines, "foolish vagaries and semi-infidel theories."[1] Having begot Mormonism

---

[1] Rev. William Phillips, *Campbellism Exposed* (Cincinnati: J.F. Wright & Swormstedt, 1837), 181

was proof enough, for some writers, that Campbellism was not so much restoring as "taking a retrograde direction."[1]  One writer merely extracted passages on baptism from the Book of Mormon, and compared them to the teachings found in the Christian Baptist, as if that was sufficient to condemn Campbell (the book being beyond refutation).[2]  Restoration remained their watchword, and remains the Disciples web address: *Restoration.net*

"The restoration of the ancient gospel," not anticipated but believed to be realized by 1830, "was looked upon as the initiatory movement, which, it was thought, would spread so rapidly that existing denominations would almost immediately be disorganized."[3]  Mormons too look to that year as the one favored with the restoration of the Church, but in that sentence the writer describes Campbell's movement.  Stories of millennial glory, restoration, and this or that harbinger were simply carried into the other Church of Christ, by other disciples of Christ; dressing it with vocabulary, erudition, theology, and their spiritual father's near-sighted searching for the Kingdom of God.  There was at least one denomination, then, over which the movement of Restoration indeed spread, set roots, and, surprisingly grew into Joseph Smith's hemlock knots.  That group was ostensibly led by Rigdon, although he seems more on their leash than they at his command.  Due to their insistence on communism, Campbell publicly chastened Rigdon just months before Pratt showed up with a codicil to the New Testament. Their Mahoning Association formally dissolved, Rigdon perhaps foresaw that better preachers and brighter thinkers would replace him in Campbell's inner circle.  1830 was the date when they were Campbellites, or disciples, or Restorationists, some of them the Family; and by 1831, looking back, they became, or better said, were called *Mormonites*. They insisted they were *disciples*.

One need not wonder that a more devoted following of the Restored Order of Things, willing to practice community of goods in preparation for the End, would never discard the Restoration: its justification, and specific features; nor the practices of worship, reading and administration which attended their pre-Mormonite meetings.  Whether Smith was consulted about the shaping of a movement formed around him with coarse materials lifted almost wholly from Campbell and friends: that question remains unanswered.  He seems bemused by the whole thing, busy translating the Bible with Rigdon at his side.  Although

---

[1] Phillips, *Campbellism Exposed*, 19

[2] Summerbell, J.J. *Campbellism is Rebellion: A Handbook on Campbellism* (Dayton OH: The Christian Association, 1913), 50-51

[3] Hayden, *Early History*, 183

most Rigdonites, as they came to be called anachronistically, would minimize their involvement in Restorationism before joining another Church of Christ said to be led by the young Joseph Smith, they did not abandon—nor acknowledge the sources of—very many doctrines espoused over the previous decade by Campbell and company.  Neither did Campbell show much interest in pointing this out, at least not for a few years afterward.  His attention was on the book.  That silly book.

THE POWER IN THE NAME

Under the heading, "Mormonism," Painesville Telegraph editors updated readers on the comings and goings of this now named sect.  After reporting that "a new batch of revelations" have come from Joseph Smith, they explain that Whitmer came to "inform the brethren that the boundaries of the promised land, or the New Jerusalem," extending from Kirtland on "the eastern line and the Pacific Ocean the western line."[1]  A similar report was published by the Republican Advocate of Wooster, Ohio, only days later.[2]  Within a year of its publication, then, the Book of Mormon had not only been mapped into social relations—giving us Mormons at least in name, if Restorationists in spirit—but also projected its tale across the very map of America.  Here was metatext regrounded by readers as they moved across the land, making the way strait, as it were, for future readers.  Givens gave us one version of that map, a silly one, instructional in more ways than one.  Indeed, one needed not even read the actual text to become a Mormon, after 1830; nor to know where its New Jerusalem would stretch forth the stakes of her tent.  Mormons inherited traditions upon conversion, and by walking or riding to Kirtland, and then, Missouri, Illinois, and Utah, they moved through lands made sacred by the book's interpreters.  See there Adam's altar, and a Nephite bulwark, and there the Lamanite Zelph killed by a Nephite spear, his skeleton unfolding a story beyond even the book's bounded narrative.  Their migrations would, a century or so later, become part of a tradition of sacred "pioneer" tourism—visiting Mormon sites restored by Mark Staker and others—doing unto these earliest Saints what they had done to the imagined figures and realms of their neglected scripture.

One can imagine that the name *Mormonite* was not merely mocking a belief in the book, but also their predilection to follow, seemingly, after names

---

[1] Painesville Telegraph 18 Jan 1831
[2] Republican Advocate 29 Jan 1831 "the Golden Bible, or The Book of Mormon"

(Rigdonite, Campbellite, etc.). The names *Mormonism* and *Mormonites*, not coincidentally, occur first in Ohio papers, not in New York ones. Palmyra's *Reflector* printed a letter in February 1831 calling them "'Gold Bible' converts," among whom was "Elder S. Rigdon," who proclaimed "dreadful vengeance on the whole state of New-York" before leading Smith's followers, and then the Smith family, to Ohio, "just within the east bounds of this new land of promise, which extends from thence to the Pacific Ocean."[1] Indeed, all reports of what Ohio papers would call "Mormons" came in Palmyra papers under the heading, "Gold Bible." The exception comes from that German letter, a private correspondence suggesting a term of derision, and one seldom spoken. In New York their public presence was tied to the Gold Bible, and they were its believers. Such a pattern of use of *Mormon* and its variants is not unexpected, given the argument made over previous chapters: Restorationists became the referent of *Mormon,* not because they became "Mormon," but because they became what the word *Mormon* meant.

After 1831, a would-be Mormon would come to Kirtland, and learn Mormonism from Restorationists. Even Joseph Smith made his way to their stronghold, and what he found may surprise modern Mormons, given the sanitized Methodism now said to "influence" the earliest Saints. The *Republican Advocate* report, for instance, expanded on the *Telegraph's* account, describing how "a young man" with his friends gathered in the woods, and as predicted,

> a letter descended from the skies and fell into the hands of the young man. The purport was to strengthen his faith and inform him that he would soon be called to the ministry. They declare their solemn belief that his letter was written in Heaven by the finger of God."[2]

Thus we find the first hints of "authority" generating discussion among Mormonites: and a very literal reading it was. No priesthood ordination, nor chains of authority here. "The style of writing," we learn, "was the round Italian, and the letters of gold." In addition to letters (which quickly vanished), the news explains,

> It is alleged that some of them have received white stone . . . . Such of them as have 'the spirit' will declare that they see a white stone moving about the upper part of the room, and will jump and spring for it, until one more fortunate than

[1] Palmyra Reflector 1 Feb 1831; 2, No.12:95
[2] Republican Advocate 29 Jan 1831

the other catches it, but he alone can see it. Others however profess to hear it roll across the floor.

Adding to these scandalizing tales, we hear in this report about "a man of color, a chief man, who is sometimes seized with strange vagaries and odd concerns. The other day he is said to have jumped twenty-five feet down a wash band into a tree top without injury. He sometimes fancies he can fly." This is notorious Black Pete, to whom "the newly founded religious movement quickly looked to . . . for direction; and as this small Church of Christ spread, it seemed to take on a life of its own."[1] Pete was a freed slave, Mark Staker supposes he had been initiated into "the shout tradition" brought by African slaves to these shores. Something of an enterprising charismatic on the Morley Farm, Black Pete received revelations to marry a white girl, and apparently asked Joseph Smith to approve, validate, or otherwise sanction his proposal.[2]

The Advocate's 29 January 1831 report concludes with a description of what, by *Mormonites*, they mean: they live together, sharing food, and "As to matters of apparel, and indeed other things, where any one wants what he has not, he takes it any where in the family where he can find it unoccupied. All things are common." The Family is here described, and identified as the referent of *Mormonism* itself. That is, *Mormon* was first a term used in public by out-group speakers, and its "correctness of reference" was merely a matter of agreement among that audience. In this case, readers of the Wooster paper, or of the Painesville Telegraph, referred to those gathered on Morley's farm with this term. They constructed the term, and picked out what that term meant. Any gaggle of fanatics, the crazier the better, could be lumped into Mormonism. It was not like there was a Press Guide, legal department, and a trademark to enforce (as one now encounters in the LDS Church). Moreover, converts who began to identify as "Mormons" (in print, often in scare quotes) relied on these initial constructions to find and follow, and indeed, become Mormons themselves. So what was Mormonism?

The winter of 1830-31 was among the worst in a century, and plenty of crazy piled up around Morley's farm. "Members seemed to have accepted Isaac Morley as their temporary leader, but no one, including Morley, had been 'instructed in relation to their duties," Mark Staker explains, "including what role leadership would play in the community and who should or could receive

---

[1] Staker, *Hearken O Ye People*, 65
[2] Staker, *Hearken O Ye People*, 105

revelation for the group" (64). Staker's history is quite thorough, although it suffers from several anachronisms. One is using capital *D* when speaking of "Disciples of Christ," as though they were members of the organization formed in 1832. Titles like *disciple of Christ, apostle,* and *elder* were tossed around by Restorationists everywhere, without capitalization. Another anachronism is the existence of "new converts," who Staker seems to find were, "Members [who] retained a strong sense of the importance of the Holy Ghost in their lives and a desire to follow the influence of the Spirit in their worship," although the "group" had "little clear direction on how they should do that" (64). Staker supposes these disciples "apparently understood they were to rely on the Spirit after their baptism as they were given the gift of the Holy Ghost" (64). What was going on, really? "Believers called themselves 'disciples' in the 'Church of Christ," he admits, "but outsiders call the movement 'Mormonism' and its believers 'Mormonites" (74). Staker notes that among this supposedly new movement, "retention was poor, and membership fluctuated" (72), as though they actually thought of themselves as members of some unique church, and not just disciples in the (generic) church of Christ. "As a new congregation of believers," Staker continues insisting they were Mormons before they would be named Mormons by their detractors,

> they also called themselves the Family. Members still used language appropriate to the Family context including calling themselves "the disciples," a continuation of the terminology they had used as Disciples of Christ but also a practice reinforced by the Book of Mormon use of the term for faithful members (73).

If we realize that no caps were present in the spoken name *disciple*, and re-read that passage, we get closer to historical reality, evident in Staker's own next sentence, "When Joseph Smith arrived in Ohio, he also called believers 'disciples' and a revelation to believers identified them as 'my disciples" (73). Little if anything had changed for these disciples, after their rebaptism by Pratt and Cowdery. Even Staker admits that "Believers continued to call themselves disciples and organize communal structures that characterized the Family, with little doctrinal change from the religious communities," he adds, "they were leaving" (76). What were they leaving, then? Not their names, nor their leadership, nor their use of the Bible, nor the doctrines, or the land. "Leave" is perhaps not the right verb to use here.

Let me outline it for you: regularly rebaptized disciples belonging to some vague church of Christ (informally organized) accepted rebaptism "unto miracles" at the hands of one near to (but not of) their Family, Parley Pratt. They then took up no new name, still being disciples in the church of Christ, on the Morley Farm. Having no direction from Pratt or Cowdery, who quickly departed, and only a few copies of the new scripture, they did what many Christians had done for many decades: experienced the "power of godliness" (in contrast to the "forms thereof"), euphemized under the name *Holy Spirit*. These miraculous deeds of power included "the exercises": the barking exercise, the laughing one, the bends, the jerks, the falling exercise, the dancing one, the shout, the muting, the lay on the ground and not move for three hours exercise, the dance with serpents, the falling on each other's laps exercise, the take off all your clothes and dance the night away exercise, and probably a few others not suitable for public naming.[1] This spiritual epidemic, we now may suppose, was instigated by Pratt baptizing them "unto miracles." It was because of these experiences they proclaimed they did not have merely the forms of godliness, but indeed possessed the power thereof. Because such displays would quickly be regarded as very poor form indeed, the term eventually was thought to refer to "the power of the priesthood," a rather more buttoned-up force.

Today found mostly at rock concerts, or the Prom, the exercises were a sign of the Spirit, of the Powers of Godliness, and first spread like fire among Christians at Cane Ridge, Kentucky; where a young Barton Stone whipped up the crowd, like he was some Rolling Stone. It is not surprising then, that Staker notices gossip about "free love," which he is nonetheless quick to dismiss, assuring faithful Mormon readers it only "reflected misunderstandings about the relationship between the Family and Owenite communities that sought to reform marriage." Staker does add, "perhaps isolated incidents fostered the claims" (105). Right. By January 1831 there was still no change in leadership, nor name; no direction from Joseph Smith nor any other disciples in the other (New York) church of Christ. What, exactly, was different for the Ohio crowd, after baptism, except now they freely, publicly, called their deeds inspired of the Holy Spirit? "Those who had had 'the power' and converted were called 'saints,'" Staker

---

[1] Staker, *Hearken O Ye People,* 75-79. The Holiness Churches that Warren Stone influenced continue many of these exercises, and "speaking in tongues" provides matter for interesting studies. See, for examples, J.T. Triton's *Powerhouse for God: Speech, Chant, and Song in an Appalachian Baptist Church* (Austin: U Texas Press, 1988); William Samarin's *Tongues of Men and Angels* (NY: Macmillan Co., 1972) remains the most detailed study; and F.D. Goodman's *Speaking in Tongues: A cross-cultural study of glossalalia* (U Chicago Press, 1972) compares many practices now classified under the academic term.

suggests (16), and he does not merely refer to Mormons. The usage was common among Christians on the frontier.

Joseph Smith arrived in February, and very little changed. Space was made for the young prophet, and he was given a scribe and a store to sweep. By June of 1831 Joseph Smith told another batch of missionaries to the Lamanites to take Indians as plural wives, a rather surprising colonization scheme if indeed the Family had strictly adhered to Puritan sexual mores until that very month. Wherever "the Power" had descended, you can bet the old morality was quickly pushed out.

News did not travel so fast, back then. Only by Mid-February do we finally read in the Palmyra Reflector that "Rigdon, with about 20 of his flock, were dipt immediately" during the November visits of Cowdery and Pratt. "Many were converted before they saw the book," the editor explains with a smirk. Converted to *what*, however, is not made explicit, although presumably "this new religion"—whatever that was—is the "what."

> They then proclaimed that there had been no religion in world for 1500 years,-- that no one had been authorized to preach &c. for that period—that Jo Smith had now received a commission from God for that purpose, and that all such as did not submit to his authority, would speedily be destroyed.[1]

In New York papers, then, Smith remains the center, if only to diminish his followers. But notice that this claim only comes after Rigdon's club (e.g., Pratt) had decided to narrate what the Gold Bible was for, and what Joseph Smith had received. Smith's revelatory powers were apparently his authority, being miraculous indeed when found in one publicly said to exhibit no trait more prominently than a profound ignorance. Some thought him feebleminded, even, and so his book all the more miraculous, Smith's charisma all the greater. Other disciples apparently required more explicit credentials.

The Palmyra, New York paper reprints the story about letters falling from Heaven, "commissions and paper were exhibited, said to be signed by CHRIST himself!!! Cowdery authorized three persons to preach, &c. and descended the Ohio River." Quickly the new Mormonites overwhelm every public discussion of the Book of Mormon. One could be that social person, and not even have read the book; just as the Gold Bible generated social positions, and yet was not even a

---

[1] Palmyra Reflector 14 Feb 1831, series 2, no.13:102

real book. Converts (it remains unclear to what one converted, at this point) had quite a menu to select from, then, if Mormonism was their desired course. Take, for example, a letter published in the Painesville Telegraph. The writer, "A friend in Chagrin, Ohio," speaks of "fanatics," so called because they "call themselves apostles, prophets, &c.—perform miracles—call down fire from Heaven—impart the Holy Ghost by the laying on of hands." Prophecies mostly concerned their own blessedness, as they "say they shall be renovated and live a thousand years. The old women say that they shall again become young, and become fruitful and replenish the earth. They have all things in common," we learn again, and foreshadowing a contentious future, the group is said to "dispense with the marriage covenant. They assume the general name of Mormonites. They have a new Bible which they call the Book of Mormon."[1] In that same letter from Matthew S. Clapp, we read of the "wildest enthusiasm," men rolling upon the floor, "even females were seen in a cold winder day, lying under the bare canopy of Heaven, with no couch or pillow but the fleecy snow." They grimaced, crept like beasts, even "going through all the Indian manoeuvers of knocking down, scalping, ripping open, and taking out the bowels." Others would "preach to imagined congregations, baptize ghosts," jabber while "running over the hills in pursuit, they say, of balls of fire." Finally, "They say much about working miracles, and pretend to have that power."

These stories and more are told by Ezra Booth—once a Campbell companion, then a Mormonite, and then finally something else—in a series of humorous, not easily dismissed, letters published in the Ohio Star. In one letter to Edward Partridge, his question shows, I believe, an eye for detail:

> Have you not frequently observed in Joseph [Smith], a want of that sobriety, prudence, and stability, which are some of the most prominent traits in the Christian character? Have you not often discovered in him, a spirit of lightness and levity, a temper of mind easily irritated, and an habitual proneness to jesting and joking?[2]

Joseph Smith shows up in reports about the Mormonites or their Bible as an ignoramus par excellence, a sort of king's fool. While Rigdon engaged in public spats with former friends, and others went about hollering curses and warning of the near-end of the World, Smith hardly appears in print; scarcely himself saying

---

[1] Painesville Telegraph 15 Feb 1831, series 2, no.35:1-2
[2] Ohio Star 24 Nov 1831, "Mormonism—No.VII" 2, no.47

anything about the Book of Mormon (which silence Givens takes a sign of his mantra's truth). Those who reportedly encountered him rarely have a bad word to say, for unlike his "followers" he did not catechize or debate theology, nor identify every doubter as the seed of Satan. One English woman, jaunting through the American country-side, found "many men, of both influence and wealth" among Smith's dupes. Amid the insults and taunts thrown at her skepticism by William W. Phelps, Martin Harris, and Sidney Rigdon, the "seer" Joseph Smith answers her condemnation of his course thusly:

> "The gift, has returned back again, as in former times, to illiterate fisherman." So he got off, as quick as he could. He recollected himself, wherefore, and returned to pass the compliment of "Good-by." A good-natured, low-bred, sort of chap: and that seemed to have force enough, to do no one, any harm.[1]

I give Ms. Towle's report not only because it portrays how little Smith held his followers in his grasp—he rarely seemed to direct or follow their lead in sermonizing on this doctrine or that text—but also because she relates Smith speaking of a gift, and not of priesthood authority. Moreover, she reports their catechism, what the Book of Mormon according to the Ohio Mormonites, apparently "enjoins":

> 1ST, "Baptism by emersion, as a condition of acceptance with God:"— (which they consider, an acknowledgement of faith, in His Inspired Word: and a "*being born again of water, and of the Spirit.*") . . . .

> It inculcates, 2dly, "That every such member, shall come out from the world: forsake father, mother, wife and children; nor call aught of his possessions, his own." Hence they are to embody themselves together, at some particular place; "*have all things in common;*" . . . .

> It enjoins, 3dly, "That every distinct member, be found at the Lord's Table every Sabbathday, to commemorate His death and sufferings *until He come*;--and, moreover, that such, "exercise faith in God, of working miracles;" according to the attainment of the primitive disciples: viz. of healing the sick, raising the dead, casting out devils, and of imparting the Holy Ghost, by the laying on of hands, &c. . . . They believe, according to the Book: "That a day of great wrath, is

---

[1] Nancy Towle, *Vicissitudes Illustrated in the Experience of Nancy Towle in Europe and America*, 1832, 137-47

bursting upon all the kindreds of the earth; and that in *Mount Zion, and in Jerusalem*, alone, *shall be deliverance in that day* . . . (ellipses added; italics original).

Not a single passage is quoted from the Book of Mormon in these principles, which instead appear to be direct quotes from Restorationist-Mormonites. Most of the points would be acceptable to Alexander Campbell and company (if one merely substitutes the Bible for the Book of Mormon, of course).

Now, I suppose you are thinking, "Why bother reading badly informed anti-Mormon writers?" Just as Mormonites were social things, named by anyone refering almost to anything, so the Gold Bible did not necessarily have much to do with the Book of Mormon. In 1831 each term was more a name than a named thing: in the beginning, was the word, let us say, but not the thing. The referents of these terms were still being created in what one might call the social imaginary. The Gold Bible I've called metatext; and *Mormonite* is merely a social identifier not yet claimed, and not used by those who would call and gather themselves to it. Nothing fixed these terms to any particular object or person or movement. When words came together, however, often quite literally when papers circulated across markets, new stories came to fill in the meaning of these words. So Mormons were born in the public sphere, and all the traditions of Restoration brought into their new movement; integrated into new scripture which hardy anyone actually read.

By the end of March 1831 the Painesville Telegraph discovered a more derisive descriptor for the power of Mormonites. Under the title, "The Gold Bible fever" they breathe easy that the madness "seems to be somewhat abating," and then publish a piece originally printed in the Palmyra Reflector.[1] At last these two pillars of journalism joined into an arch, sharing thereafter the names *Gold Bible* and *Mormonites* between them, these two inventions—metatext and movement—linked forever after. Newspapers around the region learned the name, and with it came more efficient story-telling. Rather than wade through a long story of some book's origins, a spindle shanked ignoramus, hieroglyphs and such, one's gossip now had a handle. "I could sit and write about the mormonites all day," one man admitted in a letter to a friend, subsequently published in a Vermont paper.[2] They appeared in the Warren, Ohio weekly under this name; in Baltimore's Niles' Weekly Register, and were said to "profess the doctrine of

---

[1] Painesville Telegraph, 29 March 1831
[2] Universalist Watchman, Repository and Chronicle (Woodstock, Vermont); 13 Aug 1831, n.s. 3, no.16:127

Mormonism" in the exasperated Republican Advocate.[1]   Some papers explicitly introduced them, because "Many of our readers, we suspect, are scarcely aware that a new religion has sprung up in the west"[2] This article mocked editors found "trembling in their shoes," who seemed "really alarmed for the safety of their own faith."   They then pointed out that, concerning the Book of Mormon, "it is not more ridiculous than the stories of the origin of some other books which are now referenced as holy by large portions of this earth's inhabitants."   The social group—a religion, movement, or sect—fixed the genre of their book into one previously occupied by the Bible.   As a result, what one found deplorable about the group could project back onto its text, and vice-versa.   Criticisms levied against the Mormons' book—the Gold Bible—also could be turned back onto the Bible by knowing wags.

This is not a history of Campbellism, I know.   It is a history of the Book of Mormon.   What we've arrived at, however, is a framework for understanding how that book was translated by what would become Mormons; people who simultaneously generated metatext as they created a group to embody that text in their practices, social structure, traditions, and so on.   Mormons, that is, who were not born Mormon, but who were called that after being called Methodists, Campbellites, Baptists, disciples, and so on.   In 1830 these Restorationists called themselves disciples of Christ; in 1831 they called themselves disciples of Christ. All that was really added in fall and winter 1830 to a "common stock family" in Ohio was the Book of Mormon— a sign of miracles.   The new appellation coined by outsiders, soon taken up themselves (first by post-1831 converts), seems to mark with greater freight what was often a very minor addition to belief: the Indians were not only Hebrews, they once were Christians.   Indians could now be added to the Restoration, if not really to the church.   The linkage between Mormonite and Mormon was sure, and the book was burdened with histories, biographies, stories, theories, doctrines and antics not of its making.

The book was knit into Bible society.   Thus its readers very early on diminished just how new it was and just how much it really added to their movement.   They had a space for miracles in their restoration, although its coming in a book was, no doubt, altogether unexpected.   When opened it generated—like some holodeck in the hand—an imaginary; a metatextual realm where New

---

[1] Warren (Ohio) Reserve Chronicle, 30 June 1831, p.3; Niles (Baltimore) Weekly Register, 16 July 1831, 4:853; Republican Advocate, 16 July 1831
[2] Working Man's Advocate (New York), 14 May 1831, 2 no.39

Testament and Old combined, miracles graced the faithful, and the End was very near.

Alexander Campbell weighed in on this new quasi-biblical scripture, delivering a two hour "eloquent discourse" to "a large and respectable audience." Drawing on his extensive review and critique of the book (treated hereafter), Campbell insisted that God would not "ever make a new revelation of his will to men," and that all previous revelations "were communicated by men of good repute and credibility." "It was impossible," the preacher concluded, "that he should make known his will by a *moneydigger*" (italics original).[1] Following the sermon, Campbell conversed but not amiably with Rigdon, and these two branches of a single tree would seem thereafter wholly distinct plantings. Apparently Rigdon had answered Campbell's refusal to accept the book—as anything other than a deception—with more than the usual threat of damnation. He called his former mentor a liar, a "child of the Devil, you are an enemy to all righteousness, the spirit of the Devil is in you."[2]  The first breaches in their relationship concerned the "common-stock" practice, and not the Book of Mormon, as we know.  The book clearly divided the men forever, and both seemed pleased to separate.  Campbell would caricature Rigdon as a frenzied miracle-seeker, when he was really interested in communism, a Christian practice more difficult to dismiss.  Rigdon would pretend Campbell was just another false preacher among the world's priestcraft.  Their friendship never mended, although Rigdon continued to read the Millennial Harbinger and to draw inspiration from Campbell's pen.

In February 1831 Alexander Campbell would review the Book of Mormon, and his father would respond to Rigdon's "public challenge" to answer its claims, setting himself the task of refuting its "divine pretensions."  I consider the father's letter first, before taking up Campbell's construction of a metatext Book of Mormon on the pages of his Millennial Harbinger.  Thomas Campbell prefaces his letter, copied from one sent to Rigdon, with its justification.[3]  Rigdon refused to "make good his empty, boastful challenge," and so elder Campbell has taken his argument before another court of opinion, sure of a verdict upon the "feigned pretensions of Mormonism," "the dupes of a shameless combination of unprincipled religious swindlers—whose unhallowed design is to rob the simple both of their salvation and their property."  In the letter he addresses Rigdon as

---

[1] Painesville Telegraph, 21 June 1831 "Mr. Alexander Campbell . . ."
[2] Ezra Booth, Ohio Star, 24 Nov 1831 "Mormonism—No.VII." 2, no.47
[3] Painesville Telegraph, 15 Feb 1831 "The Mormon Challenge," 2, no.35:2

one considered, once, "not only a courteous and benevolent friend, but as a beloved brother and fellow laborer in the gospel—but alas, how changed, how fallen!" The majority of the letter consists of Campbell chastening Rigdon. For proof that the reverend had read the Book of Mormon, one must look elsewhere. He concludes with six points which he believes "illustrate and confirm" his claim that "the all-sufficiency and the alone-sufficiency of the hole [sic] scriptures of the Old and New Testaments" do render Mormonism, "or any other ism," unnecessary. His first three points establish for what purpose he thinks the Bible was given: to invite "the obedient believer" to enjoy "the greatest possible privileges," gained from virtues "most clearly commanded," and by avoiding vices "that can abase or dishappify"; and, so, "there are no greater motives," but what "the scriptures most clearly and unequivocally exhibit." His Bible was a guide book for proper living, for rendering one's body and biography as bible metatext. Its theology in Campbell's reckoning merely fades into "toleration."

"These propositions being proved," by what he says not, Campbell proceeds to contrast them with "Mormonism." Rather than the book, of course, itself being refuted, it was to be implicated in the "character of its author and his accomplices," "Their feigned pretensions to miraculous gifts, the gift of tongues, &c." Mormons held its translation the first return of Pentecostal tongues, and their own miracles and inner burnings but a first conflagration of Spirit. Campbell thought otherwise, for the days of miracles were long since past. He aims at the "common-stock family," stating a plan to "show that the pretended duty of common property among Christians is anti-scriptural," and that "re-baptizing believers is making void the ordinance of Christ." Finally he comes to the matter of authority and apostasy: "the anti-scriptural assertion, that there has been none duly authorized to administer baptism for the space of four hundred years up to the present time." He outlines a scheme to show "that the pretensions of Mormonism, as far as it has yet been developed, are in no wise superior to the pretensions of the first Quakers, of the French prophets, of the Shakers, of Jemima Wilkinson, &c." The letter concludes with the final point to be addressed in the challenge, "the internal evidences of the Book of Mormon itself." It never materialized.

That work would flow from his son's pen. The younger Campbell, a week before Thomas Campbell answered Rigdon, had finally taken on the Book of Mormon in his Millennial Harbinger, drawing and quartering the text over many pages, for it did not comport with his Bible.[1] Under the title "Delusions" he

---

[1] Millennial Harbinger, 7 Feb 1831, vol.2, no.2:85-96

makes clear his position, if not what exactly is the delusion: the text, or the movement? "Every age of the world," he begins in proper Bible style, "has produced its imposters and delusions. Jannes and Jambres withstood Moses, and were followed by Pharaoh, his court, and clergy." This is not Moses in the Bible, but Moses the cultural figure, imagined and sustained in the Christian metatext Bible, a historical personage, from whose biography one can learn much about righteousness today. Thus invoking metatext, Campbell continues down through history, listing various "false prophets of the Jewish age, the diviners, soothsayers, magicians, and all the ministry of idols among the Gentiles." He gives a history of "Sabati Levi" (Sabbatai Zevi), a Jewish messianic figure of the 1660s, who advocated the return of Israel to England. When pressed to it, this messiah converted to Islam rather than be impaled, and fled Europe. Campbell predicts the same outcome for the cowardly scoundrel Joseph Smith: accused, tried and convicted by Campbell, alongside Zevi, "because of some remarkable analogies between him and the present New York imposter." He mentions Anabaptist leaders (eventually tortured and killed in Munster in the 1600s), the Shakers, "The Barkers, Jumpers, and Mutterers of the present age," and a few lesser known figures from Scotland: for there is again a "most recent and the most impudent delusion which has appeared in our time. The people that have received this imposture are called THE MORMONITES." Now the text, its revelator, and the movement have been linked not only in a single paragraph, but also to Campbell's roster of imposters, impudent knaves and charlatans. It is said to come all from old Jo Smith, and maybe Cowdery, or that farmer Harris.

He reviews "the (Gold) Bible," and of all the early reviews, his alone shows careful reading and considerable understanding of its narrative. He starts with Lehi's exodus from Jerusalem, and takes the reader through the entire history of the Lamanites and Nephites, with only minor missteps in a detailed summary. Where he strays from the text and provides commentary, however, is not insignificant. It treads on metatext. Campbell stitches together the doctrines of the Nephites, finding them "believers in the doctrines of the Calvinists and Methodists, and preaching baptism and other Christian usages hundreds of years before Jesus Christ was born!" Zoramites, he hits perhaps closer to the mark, are "a sort of Episcopalians." No specific doctrines, however, are listed or discussed. His principal contention—never clearly justified—is that such things could not have been, before the life of Christ. Describing the later reign of Nephite judges, Campbell explains that "Masonry was invented about this time; for men began to bind themselves in secret oaths to aid one another in all things, good and evil."

Later he would claim of Moroni, "He laments the prevalency of free masonry." By using contemporary names to describe groups and doctrines in the text, the Book of Mormon does indeed seem absurd. Yet, what does he mean by masonry, Episcopalian, Methodist and Calvinist? These terms describe socially-dependent entities, isms; abstract in their ontology, encountered in word and in deed, but never as a unified thing; and so re-imagined by every reader, based on personal experience, stereotypes, traditions. For readers taking his Millennial Harbinger, such names cannot be compliments.

Such generalizations—lo here Methodism, lo there Calvinism—have been used by Mormon apologists, however, to support the authenticity of the text. Welch, Faulring, Givens and others find various "Hebraisms" and "ancient patterns" distributed throughout the text, their own religion of Restoration embraced by its writers, or maybe some bland Christianity is painted across its pages. Historians who do not want to enact outright apologetics rely on metaphors of "influence" to handle what seem like anachronistic Christian teachings so swiftly put to the cane by Campbell. In all three cases—apologist, historian, anti—there is a move away from the actual text, and a turn to metatext. This they compare with some other vaguely summoned metatext: the Bible, Methodist doctrine, Hebrew poetics, charts of corporate hierarchy, or Calvinism as presented by some historian's pen. Such generalizations do not convince anyone, in my experience, except the already converted, for the logic is one of analogy, forced into false duty as deduction.

Deduction is not the same as analogy, either in form or in conclusiveness. Charles Sanders Peirce clearly distinguished these distinct arguments by the 1890s, showing that conclusions based on analogies are "abductions," a sort of hypothetical, but hardly determined by its premises into truth (his term comes from Aristotle). Deductions, on the other hand (inductions being a third kind of argument), draw a straight line from premises to conclusions. In the arguments of Campbell and Mormon apologists, we see abductions: such a thing is like another thing. What we do not have is any follow through on the guess, testing its conclusiveness. Everything, in some way, is like everything else we might describe, is it not? The Book of Mormon is like a chair (both being objects with flat surfaces); Nephites like modern Arabs, or Gypsies; King Benjamin's teachings like, say, those on Fox News, or *DemocracyNow!* For these same reasons, I rejected the historian's refuge of "cultural influence," their claiming that Calvinism (as an – ism, and thus, abstract and dependent on culture itself for definition, varying from person to person), or Methodism, or any other ism possibly shaped Mormonism (itself not unlike other isms in ontology and function). These are guesses, suppositions, and in every case there is *no* experiment, nor data which could prove or disprove them. It is dangerous to reconstruct histories with them, for obvious reasons.

Though perhaps better read than most historians, one may forgive Campbell his confusion. Mormons and anti-Mormons thereafter, however, have not the comfort of claiming to come before Peirce and philosophy of science, or modern logic. Analogies are not very useful for understanding text or metatext, and less so the more abstract or general one's analogy becomes. Thus to isms. One can find any sort of ism in long texts—the presence of so many "Philosophy and X," where X stands for some pop culture fad (e.g., The Simpsons, Harry Potter, Twilight) has done us all a favor and carried the analogy to absurdity. *The Critique of Pure Reason* (Or Whitehead's philosophy, or Anselm) could be found in the Book of Mormon, as easily as in *Good Mormon America*, or *Good Morning Vietnam*. They both have "ideas," for example. Call the commonality one born of "cultural influence" and one has something sounding both academically legitimate, and yet vague enough to discourage disproof. What shows us we are dealing with social phenomena, and not The Truth, is that the burden of proof is assessed by readers of the Critique, and viewers of GMA. They decide whether it really is analogous, or simply fortuitous similarity. One might appear smart by talking about Kant and Bart Simpson, but only at certain tables in the university cafeteria. Others familiar with these authors will call your discourse another name. Comparison of metatext, then, shows nothing about the represented texts; except that movements and ways of positioning social relations have been generated.

The long history of Scottish conflict, of the Dutch, and Alexander Campbell I have given in previous chapters does not—does not—attempt to tell you where the Book of Mormon, its doctrines, and metaphysics came from. That history tells you whence metatext eventually magnetized to the Book of Mormon drew upon tradition, language, morality, and metaphysics. The cultural history of the Book of Mormon is not the same thing as the textual history of the book (for which I give, as it must be, a hypothesis in *The Abridging Works*). Neither is its history to be confused with a history of metatext, something Terryl Givens has probably figured out by now. Campbell does not seem to find his own teachings in the Book of Mormon, although his detractors thought their presence as easily discerned as the gatherings of Methodists and Calvinists and Masons were to Campbell. Indeed, Ms. Nancy Towle's report, given above, would have one believe the book taught only Campbell's Restoration of the Ancient Order. Again we find that being all things to all people is not an accomplishment unique to the Bible, or Bible (metatext).

Campbell did not seem to precipitate or endorse the rumor that Sidney Rigdon was involved in the book's production, for he was quite aware that Rigdon was very much dedicated to his own Restoration until late 1830. This is an important silence from Campbell, one ignored by critics of the book who rely on all sorts of reasonings and third-hand recollections to place Rigdon by the side of Joseph Smith. Let me take another detour from Campbell's review. Though no evidence supports the guess, when Kirtland Restorationists were rebaptized by Parley Pratt, Rigdon's affiliation provided a shovel-ready explanation accounting for the existence of the Book of Mormon. How else could that ignoramus, an "indolent, careless, shiftless fellow," "and vendor of gingerbread" write that book? One article (from which those quotes are taken) in the Dayton Journal and Advertiser, reprinting from the Cincinnati Gazette, offered this explanation: "The book is supposed to have been written by an ex-preacher, whose name is giving [sic] as Henry Rangdon, or Ringdon."[1] The Ringdon name would show up in many articles giving cursory reports on the Mormonites, alongside "Joe Smith," that book, its devoted followers "tearing themselves from their wives . . . and wives deserting their husbands," and, of course, allowing Joe to retire from the manufacture and peddling of gingerbread. "Rangdon" offered a simple solution to the book's origin, given the alternatives; and even today its doubters link him to its creation.

Never mind that Rigdon was clearly attending Mahoning and to Campbell before the summer of 1830, and that when read carefully, that book teaches much that Rigdon and friends would find contrary to their beliefs about the Bible, and perhaps antagonistic to religion in general. Rigdon was well-known, intelligent if somewhat burdened by the pride of learning without having gained comparable wisdom; and popularly regarded as extravagant in his passions, fanciful upon the rostrum, and not lacking for widely publishing enemies after 1830. Campbellite historians later invented whole, many-years long conspiracies in order to tie Rigdon to Smith, and the mission to the Lamanites as, in fact, their dark plan's culmination. (Campbell did not claim as much.) For evidence, we find them doing much the same thing as BYU professors do in their essays analyzed above. We have hearsay, recollections, never contemporary reports: one prints a letter written in 1873, the writer of which heard her father apparently identify Rigdon as curiously anxious about antiquities, "or of a wonderful book,"

---

[1] Dayton Journal and Advertiser, 4 Oct 1831, vol.5, no.45:1

prior to the Book of Mormon being published.[1]  So many involved in such a scheme, and yet no one exposing it, despite lucrative enticements to do so, and absolutely no historical evidence?  This makes the Rigdon-Smith theory of origins beyond implausible, more in the line of a bad hope than even approaching the blunt edge of a crude hypothesis.

But, perhaps you are wondering: I thought you were saying the Book of Mormon contains so much that was taught by Campbell and others, that it must've been written in 1827, and not from ancient plates?  Well, it depends on which Book of Mormon you mean: the 1830 text? the supposed ancient record? or the metatext fashioned over the years by variously committed students of Campbell?  You may suppose that the latter is, indeed, a thing not unrelated to the Christian Baptist, or the sermons of Walter Scott.  But the former, the actual 1830 text, is far from explained with respect to its origins, if one posits Campbell et. al., as literary and doctrinal resources for its author/translator; or as actual composers of the book itself.  Certain phrases are no doubt similar, and much of the King James is likewise reprinted in whole chapters in the Book of Mormon.  And no one, I hope, seriously says the Bible—or a desire to corroborate it—inspired the Book of Mormon's author(s), after having read essays included in Volume Five of this history.

The Book of Mormon's origins remain something unaccounted for in this history.  My concern here is with metatext: their construction from text, and subsequent generation of groups.  Of groups dependent on the obscuring of text, text subtly effaced by their floating and circulating metatext.  Over the next two volumes I track the Mormon creation of metatext, and the use of metatext to create structures for educating children, teaching missionaries, and excavating Yucatan holes.  For now, we tune in again to Campbell's review.  The "drama" has been taken to the bitter end by Campbell, who describes Mormon as "no Quaker!" although, "He must have heard of the Arian controversy by some angel!!"  After the great battle of their age, "The Lamanites took South America for themselves, and gave North America to the Nephites."  Before setting forth his analysis of "INTERNAL EVIDENCES," of what he calls "the Bible of the Mormonites," Campbell apologizes for so long a discussion, "of which I would have asked forgiveness from all my readers, had not several hundred persons of different denominations believed in it."  Thus we have Campbell and Mormons agreeing that no Campbell readers became Mormons, and surely not Mormonism itself as a thing emerging in the public sphere.  After they had the name

---

[1] Hayden, *Early History*, 240

Mormonites, pity and scorn were found waiting at the offices of the Harbinger, where once their cash money was collected for annual subscriptions. Both Campbell and Rigdon pretend the "delusion" pre-existed any actual person, and no real Campbellite could possibly believe in that book.

Campbell's review did much to make the illusion of autochthony endure. He asserts that either the Bible came from God, or the Book of Mormon did (and he agrees with the Book of Mormon, as I read it). His reasons scarcely determine that conclusion, however. First, he invokes a metatextual reading of the covenant between the Jews and God at Mount Sinai, which required "a priesthood, and a high priesthood." The tribe of Levi was given the first, and the sons of Aaron the second, citing passages from NUMBERS and DEUTERONOMY for proof. The restriction on priesthood to the tribe of Levi, Campbell concludes, forbade Lehi from making burnt offerings, and from Nephi being a priest (as told in 1 NEPHI). This is like saying a reporter lies who describes a story told to her from a criminal, for we have laws against such things as the criminal confesses to. He also presupposes, of course, that the Bible is not telling fibs about history.

Campbell continues to compare one metatext to another, finding that the Book of Mormon "Makes the God of Abraham, Isaac, and Jacob violate his covenants with Israel and Judah concerning the land of Canaan, by promising a new land to a pious Jew." Having admitted that Lehi was said to be from Joseph, and not Judah, Campbell stumbles through this and three other dependent arguments concerning temple worship, families separating from Judah, and the scepter departing. The preacher then turns to its violation of New Testament piety (and having the benefit of translating his own version, he is sure of that text's meaning). "The Twelve Apostles of the Lamb," he begins again, "are said by Paul to have developed certain secrets which were hid from the ages and generations, which Paul says were ordained before the world to their glory—that they should have the honor of announcing them."[1] Campbell assumes he knows their secret, finding that the Book of Mormon reveals it: "600 years before the Messiah began to preach, disclos[ing] these secrets concerning the calling of the Gentiles, and the blessings flowing through the Messiah to the Jews and Gentiles, which Paul says were hid from ages and generations." Yet Campbell seems to forget that the Book of Mormon did not come to Gentiles (so called) until 1830; not 600 years before Christ. So even if some great secret was the pleasure of Paul to reveal, it remained his: the Book of Mormon kept this secret well enough, for some eighteen

---

[1] For more on this secret of the apostles, see forthcoming essay, "On The Book of the Lamb"

centuries. Finally, and most commonly quoted in his review is the claim directing us to Campbell's verdict of anachronistic deceit because its translator, Smith,

> Decides all the great controversies—infant baptism, ordination, the trinity, regeneration, repentance, justification, the fall of man, the atonement, transubstantiation, fasting, penance, church government, religious experience, the call to the ministry, the general resurrection, eternal punishment, who may baptize, and even the question of free masonry, republican government, and the rights of man.

Of course, rather than directly address that list of "truths" said to be taken up by the Book of Mormon, he finds, "All of these topics are repeatedly alluded to," as though the text really does engage in dialogue with modern ministers, theologians, and believers alike. The truth is that the book does not decide such matters, or else why should Smith and others produce subsequent revelations on church government, baptism, and so on? And then so often alter these with new declarations? In fact, the book can be read as teaching that Jesus is the Son of God, and also the Son and the Father; two different baptisms are described, with very different covenants associated; baptism of "little children" it condemns, yet the practice is taken up by Mormons; sermons attributed to figures like Amulek and Alma do not comport with teachings attributed to Abinadi, Helaman, and several Nephis. Its chronologies and plotting of space is internally consistent, strictly so, if not clearly mapped on our charts. Yet doctrines and sermons attributed to various figures are not so consistently phrased. It reads like a long history of a changing society. Rather than deciding Campbell's list, and possibly putting his paper out of that lucrative business, the Book of Mormon does not explain very much with respect to the nature of God, the problem of evil, grace and works, the reason for baptism, how one obtains authority and power, what it is to be baptized "in my name," or a hundred other puzzles long breaking Christianity into so many sects. In fact, it suggests that some other books, yet to come forth, "decide" those subjects. (One of those books, the Book of the Lamb, is said to contain the testimony of the twelve apostles of the Lamb, whose secret may still be kept.) What can be read as solving such and such a problem is metatext, a tradition of interpreting passages in some way conclusive for one's argument. Lo here LDS Church administrative practices, Lo there Calvinism. Campbell can do it as efficiently as Mormon apologists, historians, and preachers.

He concludes a ten-point argument against the Book of Mormon with yet another unwittingly ironic claim. Though the book purports to be "written at intervals and by different persons during the long period of 1020 years," he finds, "for uniformity of style, there never was a book more evidently written by one set of fingers." Given that the text is expressly presented as a translation by Smith, as Campbell well knows, such an impressionistic conclusion is in perfect accord with the published book. Yet Campbell proceeds to list pages of "Smithisms" which apparently compare unfavorably with the actual style of ancient Nephite writers. He can be forgiven the confusion, for even Mormon apologists, some of them professors of law, claim to find in it ancient Hebraic "poetic forms," (although the original was said to be written, not in Hebrew, but in "Egyptian" and "Reformed Egyptian"). Others submit the text to computerized "wordprint" studies (the metaphor pretends to link writing style to identifying features of finger prints), finding that indeed as many authors as they like to count are found to have left their fingerprints in words across the various books! I would guess that most Christians reading the King James, or other versions of the Bible, have no trouble finding a single voice and style throughout these texts, though different authors are said to give us its many books (and many more translators of them; as many as 450 for the King James Version). Ironically, Campbell often claimed that the Bible was the Word of God, in this very review; that "the Oracles of the living God" were written by God. Why, look at the singularity of style and voice! Just as the Workingman's Advocate chuckled, what is said against the Book of Mormon is easily returned upon the Bible, whoever's version it may be. Almost like the Mormon book was a pick to unravel the other's binding, if one only looks for loose threads.

The Painesville Telegraph the week after Campbell ran his review advertised "a pamphlet of 12 pages, containing a review of the '*Book of Mormon*,' from the able pen of Alexander Campbell, of Va."[1] His criticism was free to circulate and generate further discussion and commentary on the Book of Mormon. The pamphlet, "unequivocally and triumphantly sets the question of the divine authenticity of the 'Book' forever at rest," at least, "to every *rational* mind." Campbell's writings about the Book of Mormon flooded long established channels carved out by his publications and preaching. Within a week a Dayton, Ohio paper ran the article "Something New.—The Golden Bible."[2] They reportedly received a letter extracting from Thomas Campbell's published letter, and from his son's review, alongside commentary from the letter writer. So often

---

[1] Painesville Telegraph, 1 March 1831
[2] Evangelical Inquirer, 7 March 1831, vol.1, no.10:217-19

was he linked to the book, that rumors soon circulated that Campbell himself was involved in its coming forth. The Inquirer "Let all those who would identify Mr. Campbell and those associated with him with this Mormonitish absurdity, know that this new project makes no approach towards the reformation in its character or object." Given that Campbell's readership formed the majority of the absurdity, it was perhaps not unexpected that he would be supposed to have fathered it. Like Mormons following received tradition, this paper fails to acknowledge his role in their begetting: "that among the Mormonitish converts are found persons from among the all denominations, Presbyterians, Methodists, and that they are as liable to the charge of having originated the scheme as are the reformers." Two weeks later the Palmyra Reflector took notice of Campbell's plans, reporting he "is going to examine in [sic] *divine* pretensions." The article is number six in their long running "Gold Bible" series.[1]

The matter of its relation to the Bible takes us to a review written by William Owen.[2] This review is important in the history of the Book of Mormon, being the first non-Mormon to treat the book as something other than a gross and vulgar swindle. In fact, he outlines a later course taken by Mormon preachers as they used their book's similarities to the Bible as evidence of the authenticity of both texts. (Mormons plagiarized their enemies as well as their supporters.) Owens finds, after setting aside the matter of origins, "the Golden Bible will bear a very good comparison with the Holy Bible." Indeed, "one seems to corroborate the other," he'd note, and it echoes still today among "believers in the book of Morman," which he reckons "amount already to about 1600." Owen surpasses in sophistication and shrewdness anything on the book written by Mormons in the 1830s:

> I can discover no good reason why the generality of Christians should scoff, as I have generally found them do, and hoot at the idea of believing in such a monstrously absurd book, unless it be that they consider the endeavor to pass off a new Bible, very similar to their own, as a divine book, as likely to induce many persons, who cannot swallow the miracles and pretension of the Golden Bible, to question the veracity of the historians who relate similar miracles and put forth similar doctrines, in the Holy Bible, which they have been accustomed to venerate as a divine production. . . . Christians can hardly read the book of Mormon without remarking a striking similarity to their own scriptures, and the

---

[1] Palmyra Reflector, 19 March 1831, vol.2, no.16:126-7
[2] Free Enquirer (NY), 10 SEP 1831, "A Comparison…"

believers in the Old and New Testaments cannot consistently deny the *possibility* of a single circumstance related in the Mormonite scriptures.

His summary of the book's narrative lacks the critical attention given it by Campbell, and concludes, "I should consider satisfactory proofs of the genuineness of the Golden Bible as strong evidence of the divine origin of the Holy Bible, so consistent are they with, and corroborative of, each other." As noted above, the book and its new "followers" were drawn into analogy with the Bible and its believers.

Mormons, ironically, could be put into play for the purpose of scoffing at Christians and their silly book. Indeed, it is as if the Book of Mormon was written to make so much the easier one's doubting of the Bible; of the metatext Bible, that is. (The actual Bible, at least versions I've read, does not say so much about being, and it alone, authored by God.) Several years after it was published, the Temple of Reason found in the Book of Mormon, "as if specially ordained for the purpose," a corollary between "the rapid spread of the Mormon *delusion*, as it, in common with all new systems, is called, till age and success have dignified them with the name of religion." Here was Campbell's restoration turned on its head, I suppose, to be paddled at its other end. The editorial continues to note the irony of Christians mocking Mormonism, for "The rise and progress of these two delusions, present many coincidences, if not a perfect parallel. An obscure individual pretends to have found a golden Bible, the contents of which rival in silliness the pages of its *holy* predecessor."[1] Atheists, Deists, Rationalists seemed to understand what the text had set as one its many tasks. Their understanding was uncanny: "Persecution," they note somewhat prophetically, "is alone wanting to place Mormonism on a footing with Christianity." The Western Examiner under the title "ANCIENT AND MODERN MORMONISM" likewise found in Mormonism a finger to shake at Christians: "You are to understand then, that we have other Mormon books, or revelations of more ancient origin; and there is one to which I would particularly allude, which was got up about eighteen hundred years ago. The real history of this ancient Mormon book, so far as it is known, bears a close analogy to my anticipations of the modern one."[2] This absurd translation from Gypsy-Hebrew hieroglyphs, recounting flying prophets, language to command trees and shake down prisons, lighted rocks, Christians preaching redemption "a great many thousand years" before Christ, and so much detail far

---

[1] Temple of Reason (Philadelphia), 25 July 1831, vol.1 no.12:90-91
[2] Western Examiner (St. Louis), 10 Dec 1835, vol.2, no.46:366-67

beyond even the Bible's tales, had been said, already by 1832, to: corroborate the Bible; satirize it; confound it. Such a book must be worth reading, just as a resurrection is worth considering, as one theologian said, because it is absurd.

As the New York disciples of the Church of Christ moved to Kirtland during the long winter and wet spring of 1831, the separation of former Campbell disciples (unaffiliated, mostly), and what would become Campbell's Disciples of Christ, was a fracture gladly pressed and preserved by both sides. The New York elders, disciples, apostles and so on had been received by Sidney Rigdon, who found himself in a tradition not entirely different from the Restorationist movement of Campbell. It was different, he surely believed, after visiting Smith in New York, and persuading him to prophecy that the elders would be "endowed with power from on high," if they moved to Kirtland. This power was, in the words of one historian, "something Rigdon had concluded to be lacking in the missionaries who had converted him, but who had failed in their attempts to work miracles."[1] The power of godliness was not yet upon Rigdon, even after his rebaptism in Kirtland. Emboldened by the word of God delivered to Joseph Smith, Rigdon prepared for a great work of restoration of the ancient order of things. As the prophecy now reads:

> Behold, verily, verily I say unto my servant Sidney, I have looked upon thee and thy works. I have heard thy prayers, and prepared thee for a greater work. Thou art blessed, for thou shalt do great things (D&C 35:3).

Rigdon learned that he was "sent forth, even as John, to prepare the way before me, and before Elijah which should come, and thou knewest it not." His efforts are praised, his baptisms before joining Smith's church of Christ apparently accepted:

> Thou didst baptize unto repentance, but they received not the Holy Ghost. But now I give unto thee a commandment, that thou shalt baptize by water, and they shall receive the Holy Ghost by the laying on of hands, even as the apostles of old (v.5-6).

The prophecy seems to validate everything Rigdon does thereafter, although it may be that the Lord is not malicious, he is subtle. "And it shall come to pass,"

---

[1] Prince, *Having Authority*, 33

Rigdon is told, "that there shall be a great work in the land, even among the Gentiles, for their folly and their abominations shall be made manifest in the eyes of all people" (v.7). The prophecy turns into a promise of miracles, signs, and wonders, "unto all those who believe on my name"; eschewing any association with "priesthood authority," the voice explains that "whoso shall ask it in my name in faith, they shall cast out devils; they shall heal the sick," resight the blind and give the deaf hearing, make the dumb speak and walk with the lame. "But without faith," it adds, "shall not anything be shown forth except desolations upon Babylon, the same which has made all nations drink of the wine of the wrath of her fornication" (v.11). A difficult prophecy and warning to parse, to be sure. It is not clear that Joseph Smith even "revealed" this prophecy, or if Rigdon himself received and wrote it. Although said in the earliest copy of the prophecy to be a "Commandment unto Joseph & Sidney," Smith is never addressed. Unlike Rigdon, he is spoken of, but never to. As common as prophecy was among the disciples, it seems likely that the minister was its mouthpiece. If we forget tradition, we have no reason to say Smith spoke the prophecy, and Rigdon simply recorded it. Textual evidence indicates that Rigdon received it: he is addressed by the voice.

Rigdon would replace Cowdery as Smith's scribe in the Great Work. Rigdon saddled up by Smith, just as he had once hitched his wagon to Campbell's star and scribbled notes during so many debates. This odd couple set about to write a more plain translation of the Holy Bible, picking up in Kirtland in 1831 where Smith and Cowdery had left off translating before the failed mission to the Lamanites. They started with that obscure figure, Melchizedek. His was a power that Rigdon desired to look upon and to hold for himself.

# Nine  Malvolio's Great Work

B Y GROUNDING THEIR DISCOURSE IN THE FAMILIAR TERMS OF THE BIBLE, Restorationists made it possible to forget that such ideas transmitted from preacher to preacher. Doctrine fragmented into general metatext, becoming a "religion" and its social origins disappeared, a process we'll examine more fully next volume. It seemed as though the religion was all found in the Bible, and not in metatext transmitted by newspaper, preacher and commentary. By the mid-1830s the LDS Messenger & Advocate, a paper edited by Oliver Cowdery, could publish a series of articles on "the gospel," "the millennium," and the "faith of the church" which may well have been reprinted in or plagiarized from Alexander Campbell's Millennial Harbinger. This Mormon newspaper was among the few widely circulating resources creating what would become the doctrinal fraction of the referent of the term *Mormonism*. It often reprinted (and silently revised) content from the first Mormon paper, the Evening & Morning Star, which ran from June 1832 until a Missouri mob destroyed the press in July 1833. Publisher W.W. Phelps was preparing a run of the Book of Mormon bound to the New Testament when, like Assyrians upon Israel, a gang burned down his building. The Bible and the Book of Mormon would not be bound together for another 150 years, although that union merely formalized a common law marriage, long years of (often forced) living in sin. After the Missouri destruction, Cowdery took the press to Ohio, and published the Messenger & Advocate from October 1834 to September 1837. In these papers, Campbell and his teachings would be represented as entirely opposed to these other disciples of Christ.

Campbell's pamphlet was well travelled, and Mormon preachers often responded to its charges regarding the terrible unbiblicalness of their scripture, denying first of all, that it supplanted or replaced the Holy Word. One Mormon wrote to Cowdery from Illinois, describing a local paper's criticism that the Book of Mormon was not only authored by Solomon Spaulding, but worse still, seemed "Romish."[1] Page 25 of the 1830 edition the Mormon book, it noted, has an angel describing Mary as "the mother of God." The letter and Cowdery's reply came under the title, "Trouble in the West," and by 1837 the trouble was remedied, in part. The angel was made in that year's Kirtland edition to rephrase his description, instead calling Mary the "Mother of the Son of God." "Son of" was inserted before "God" throughout the vision of Nephi, whenever it was describing the mortal character of Jesus. Problem solved.

By the time Cowdery responded to Campbell, a pile of objections needed answering. Cowdery finally responded to Campbell's pamphlet that showed how unbiblical was the Book of Mormon, naming his response in mockery, "Delusion."[2] His reply (circulated only in Mormon papers) excerpts passages from the Campbell pamphlet and gives his rejoinders, having no doubts about their validity. Ignoring Campbell's misreading of the Book of Mormon, Cowdery instead responds to his biblical notions of priesthood, and Lehi's lack thereof. "How did it *happen* that Moses had authority to consecrate Aaron a priest?" Cowdery asks, and "Who had laid hands upon him?" (91). "Should Mr. C. finally learn," he adds in triumph, "that Moses received the holy priesthood, after the order of Melchesedek, under the hand of Jethro, his father-in-law . . . and that Lehi was a priest after this same order, perhaps he will not raise so flimsey an assertion, as he does when he says the validity of the Book of Mormon is destroyed because Lehi offered sacrifice." Rather than cite Smith in the passage, Cowdery gives some obscure prophecies from GENESIS 49, and DEUTERONOMY 33. These he presents as promising the seed of Joseph "the everlasting hills," should they do the work "of his bullock, and his horns are like the horns of unicorns: with them he shall push the people together to the ends of the earth." How could Joseph's seed, he asks, "push the *people together to [from] the ends of the earth*," if they were not spread throughout that earth? These verses—along with a smattering of ISAIAH, JEREMIAH, EZEKIEL, and PSALMS—would become pillars of the Mormon preacher's sermon on the Book of Mormon, finding it prophesied plainly in the Holy Bible, if you'd only read its most obscure passages.

Cowdery, it was said by Mormons (in 1877), learned his Bible doctrines from Parley Pratt, who months after meeting Smith "brought forth from the prophecies of Isaiah, Jeremiah, Ezekiel, and other prophets, abundant proofs

---

[1] LDS Messenger & Advocate vol.1, no.7:105
[2] LDS Messenger & Advocate vol.1, no.6:89

concerning the work which the Lord had established through his servant Joseph." After Pratt's lectures, "a great many of the Latter-day Saints were surprised that there were so many evidences existing in the Bible concerning this work." Pratt reportedly boasted that even Cowdery and Smith "were surprised at the great amount of evidence there was in the Bible concerning these things."[1] The sermon attributing to Pratt so many insights is found in Volume 19 of the Journal of Discourses, a British monthly begun in the 1850s that reprinted Salt Lake City sermons from Mormon leaders.

George Cannon, the speaker quoted above, was himself a British convert, well read, witty, gregarious with a lovely accent to his English; probably mesmerizing to converse with, and at the time (1877) a member of the U.S. House of Representatives, although only a territorial delegate. While the earliest apostles like Parley Pratt, whose vast biblical understanding he would report, claimed that the revelation of God was indeed "the rock upon which this Church is built," they often meant by that phrase, "God revealing himself," and not "knowledge given from Heaven," nor something like "inspiration." By Cannon's time the latter understanding of revelation had taken over. As a speech genre it was anchored in signs of power that became dominant under Brigham Young's reign in Utah.

> The rock upon which this Church is built, and the foundation stone thereof, is new revelation from God to men, and that revelation being of divine origin it must of necessity agree with the revelations which have already been given; hence, as [Wilford Woodruff] has said, the doctrines taught by the Prophet Joseph Smith, and the organization of the Church as he was directed to accomplish it, was all in perfect harmony with the truths contained in this book (the Bible). It can not be otherwise and be what it professes to be.

Cannon boasted that by "revelation" (a term now describing a manner of receiving knowledge), Smith learned and taught the same material as the ancients, although the Seer was perhaps ignorant of their writings found in the published scriptures:

> It made no difference to Joseph Smith whether he read and was familiar with every doctrine taught by the Apostles; he was under no necessity of framing his teachings therewith that there should be no difference between that which he taught, and that which had been taught, because the same spirit that revealed to

---

[1] Givens and Grow, *Parley Pratt,* 33; quoting George Q. Cannon, 16 Sept 1877, Journal of Discourses 19:105-7

the ancient Apostles and Prophets, and inspired them to teach the people, and leave on record their predictions and doctrines, taught him also and enabled him to teach exactly the same truths.

What exactly matched is not specified. The tale is given about Pratt bringing forth ancient truths from the Bible which validated the Book of Mormon and the restoration of the Church of Christ. Cannon concludes that not only the "Prophet Joseph was inspired of God to teach the doctrines of life and salvation," but also:

> I have heard President Young make the same remarks. He said that he never consulted the Book of Covenants, he never consulted the Bible or Book of Mormon to see whether the doctrines and counsels which he was inspired to give, corresponded with these books or not. It was a matter that gave him no particular concern, from the fact that he endeavored always to be led by the Spirit of the Lord, to speak in accordance therewith; hence these men have had very little care resting upon their minds as to whether their doctrines and counsels were in harmony with the doctrines and counsels of those who preceded them. It was for them to seek to know the mind and will of the Lord and comprehend his Spirit as it rested upon them, to speak in accordance therewith; and the doctrine that has been taught under the inspiration of that spirit will be found to be in perfect harmony with the doctrines which have been taught by men inspired of God in ancient days.

By locating "revelation" as a kind of knowledge gained by inspiration, rather than a specific thing revealed (i.e., Jesus), the ignorance of post-1831 Mormon converts was translated into assurance of the divinity of their inheritances, of their prolonged ignorance as well. Ignorant of the source of their claims of restoration, of the plan of salvation, about being the House of Israel, and so on; of claims made for three centuries previous, and circulated in scripture metatext for decades; this ignorance becomes by the second generation of Mormons reframed as signaling their own unique access to and dispersal of inspiration from the Holy Spirit! Having not read sacred text, they find agreement in metatext, and call that divine, directly from the mouth of the Prophet. Apologists do likewise, as did Alexander Campbell and David Persuitte, although they arrived at different conclusions. As we'll see in the next volume, Mormons in Utah had upon metatext readings built a towering power structure.

The following week Cannon finished his sermon, eulogizing Brigham

Young who'd passed away a few months earlier. His emphasis on the Priesthood shows plainly how it repositioned Mormons at the center, even the pillar, of the restoration of the House of Israel:

> We have been bereft of our President. We have been bereft of the man who has stood at our head and guided us for thirty-three years, and we have learned to look upon him as the mouth-piece of our Father to us, but we ought, also, to have learned, as I have no doubt the majority of this people have learned, that he was but an instrument in the hands of God to accomplish the work entrusted to him, and that he being gone, the Lord will raise up and strengthen those who remain, and give them the power necessary to accomplish his work and carry it forward in the earth; and if they fall too, as they likely will, the column of humanity, the column of the Priesthood will still press forward, until all that the Lord has appointed to his people, he will accomplish on the earth, and Zion will be established and fully redeemed according to all the words of the Prophets.[1]

Near the end of the sermon Cannon lists exactly what is unique about Mormonism, what will be found among the Church of Christ irrespective of time or place, continents, oceans, words or epochs. We can see he enunciates an earlier Mormon teaching, one dispensed by missionaries to England when he was a boy, and which he might have heard from some others in the United Kingdom. Why is Mormonism attractive to him?

> It is because it is a system of power; it is because there are gifts connected with it; it is because I was told when a child that if I would be baptized for the remissions of my sins and repent of them, I should receive the gift of the Holy Ghost. It is because there are in this Church Prophets and Apostles, the gifts of revelation, of healing, and discerning of spirits, and all the other gifts, that were ever enjoyed by the ancient people of God.

Here is the foundation upon which his later hope sets up the pillar of men called the Priesthood (bearing the "power" given the same name). This foundation came from Parley Pratt, Sidney Rigdon, and Oliver Cowdery, as they cobbled together a crowd of Restorationists, communalists, free-love types, seekers for "the power," Black Pete, not a few we'd currently diagnose as having doubtful mental clarity, and God knows what else into the disciples, then the Saints of the Latter Days. One thing seemed to hold it all together, and it wasn't the Book of Mormon.

---

[1] Cannon, 23 Sept 1877. Journal of Discourses 19:108

Priesthood and its restoration became the explanation of what Joseph Smith was really up to.

"The Priesthood" served to obscure the origins of Mormonism in Campbell's teachings, and Walter Scott's, and so many other Restorationists— many who would become Mormons themselves, or debate them regularly, demanding justification for their new-restored movement. That Parley Pratt was said to find the same things they taught in the Bible, of course, merely shows that he taught Mormons Restorationism, and the Book of Mormon was thought to confirm the Bible's newly uncovered message. Rather than removing idols and stumbling blocks, the Mormon book was used to secure these inherited things to its translator. They waved over his head their banner of Israel, only recently laid down by Puritans busy with witch burnings. That every LDS president who came after Joseph Smith also arrived after Rigdon and Pratt only adds to the irony. They knew nothing of Campbell, Scott, and Stone; Rigdon and Cowdery would be soon discarded as apostates, and so only Joseph Smith was left to voice so many traditions. Few records survived to contradict what became oral traditions, and then retrospectives by the 1840s, church histories by the 1900s. Campbell was quietly forgotten, although not by all.

## CAMPBELLISM REMOVED

With one important exception, the earliest Mormon writers who mention Campbell are among the New York "followers of Christ," and not from the Ohio crowd. Even as they answered Campbell and others, they seemed to move far from his doctrines, however; and eventually would appear entirely distinct from his Disciples of Christ as the Irishman returned to respectable Reformation principles. In responding to Campbell and other critics, however, early disciples made Mormonism as much an answer to their critics' questions as anything wholly original. It was at times almost like a filling in of gaps pointed out by Campbell. When one debates the king, of course, one must use the King's tongue; but to speak so fluently is perhaps not necessary. To plagiarize him is probably excessive.

Mormonism would by appearances seem so distinct, but be a religion very much in dialogue, emerging with him as a silent interlocutor. Later Mormon leaders like Brigham Young, Wilford Woodruff, and John Taylor who arrived after 1831 would inherit the New York saints' ignorance of the paternity of Campbell, and regard all that they knew of Mormonism as Heaven-delivered in

April 1830. Campbell happily consented to this fiction of separation for many years. He later called them plagiarists and poachers, but that was long after both movements had advanced beyond his 1820s Restoration teachings, a thousand miles separating their headquarters. By then both sides were either content to forget their union, or really knew nothing of it. How they left their father and cleaved to another is itself worth reviewing, and so we return to the early 1830s.

One disciple took up a debate "in the midst of a society commonly called Campbellites," with "a Mr. J. M. Tracy," for "some of the Campbellites in Huntsburgh have hired him to preach for them."[1] As expected, the debate was an epic two-day affair. Only two accepted rebaptism from elder M'Lelin (William McLellin). After Joseph Smith delivered a three hour sermon the following day, four more "came forward and, 'were buried with Christ by baptism;' and were confirmed by the laying on of hands, in order that 'they might put off the old man with his deeds and arise and walk in newness of life." What was meant by that phrase, I cannot divine, but rebaptism was frequent, and often prescribed for our modern ills. Sin was widely held to cause illness, and by purging one of sin, one's health might return. In fact, in 1842 Joseph Smith and Sidney Rigdon were rebaptized in the Mississippi, among others seeking better health. One unlucky soul was carried away, not by the Spirit, but by the water, and drowned amid the enthusiasm.[2] The gift of healing could follow directly from baptism, then, assuming the baptizer conveyed this gift (healed) by the laying on of hands. Like doctrines, many of these ritual practices would be fragmented in Mormonism over its first decades, being regarded as distinct and under the supervision of one authority or another. In the early years one might be baptized for miracles (to experience them), and healing could be one of many miracles evidencing "the power." This basic outline existed before Mormonism, and was by 1834 the material upon which a new priesthood (holding the power) was erected.

Like Cowdery, William M'Lelin was not an Ohio disciple, and as with so many non-Ohio Mormons, he too would be ex-communicated by preachers that soon took to calling themselves Saints, making sure their position on what exactly was restored. As early as 1834 they became Latter Day Saints (akin with Former Day Saints). The name change isn't that important, for what concealed their long love affair with Campbell's Restoration was "the priesthood"; a term bearing doctrines recalled by more than one early Mormon (decades later) to have been

---

[1] LDS Messenger & Advocate vol.1, no.7:102
[2] Quinn, *Mormon Hierarchy*, 640

taught to Joseph Smith by Sidney Rigdon, while they read from the Bible during 1831. The truth is not so simple.

In the LDS Messenger & Advocate, after enduring Cowdery's circuitous attempt to tell with pseudo-Romanticist poetic embellishment the history of Joseph Smith and his translation of the Book of Mormon (only arriving at fall of 1823 by his tenth letter), one might read an essay on "The Ancient Order of Things."[1] This order "has engrossed the attention of the religious public to some extent in modern times," the author "R.," begins with no mention of Alexander Campbell, merely noting that it "has given rise to many parties and sects in the so called christian world." Without irony, he laments, "each one in their turn supposing that they had the ancient order of things among them, and had come to the standard of righteousness set up in the scriptures," and asserted that "other religious denominations" have "come short of the glory of God . . . ." Some take one part of the order, "and add to it their own invention; others take another part of it and add to that," he objects to their cafeteria-approach to the Bible. So far, we might as well identify R. as Alexander Campbell, or a million other Restorationists. Like a thousand other writers, the author is sure that if those seeking the Ancient Order simply read their books, all would be revealed. That order, he clarifies, is "revealed in the Bible, and taught to mankind by the holy prophets and apostles," and so one must "have recourse to the book, and let it speak for itself, and set forth the ancient order of things . . . ." What R. reads in his Bible is his own experience with what was then called Mormonism, or the Church of the Latter Day Saints. There is, however, very little about priesthood— in fact, nothing at all—in his description of the ancient order realized among them as Mormon history.

First, "our Heavenly Father" "inspired a man, or some men, and called them from among the rest of the world, to be his messengers to the world." These men received revelation and commandments, visions and knowledge of "his will concerning the generation among whom they lived." Promises "which should be fulfilled upon their own heads" were delivered, "and the fulfillment of these promises was to be a testimony that the Lord had sent the men who had administered them." What was the promise which should be a sign of their embassy? R. turns to Paul's letters found in CORINTHIANS and EPHESIANS, that God gave apostles and prophets to the church, "and after that miracles; then gifts of healings, helps, governments, diversities of tongues" (1 Cor. 12:28). First come

---

[1] LDS Messenger & Advocate vol.1, no.12:182. Sidney Rigdon is identified as the author on page 192.

titles and honors, "the office of apostles or witnesses, became prophets, and after they were prophets, they became evangelists," he sequences these. Then came gifts and miracles, and "Such then was the ancient order of things, and in this manner did the Son of God build his church on earth . . . ." This order was created "for the salvation of men," he explains. No better summary of Mormon Restorationism can be found—certainly not Oliver Cowdery's tedious Full-of-O!-and-Woe-exclamatory history, nor Joseph Smith's brief narrative—than in Rigdon's reading of "the ancient order of things" restored in his own biography. The phrase he learned from Campbell, depicted in full upon his Bible, had oriented his experience as a disciple. In that light it is instructive to read Rigdon's definition of an apostle:

> In order then to be an apostle a man must in the first instance believe on the Lord Jesus Christ, and in the next place must repent of all his sins, and then must be baptized for the remission of sins, and must receive the gift of the Holy Ghost; after that he must continue in faith and obedience until he has obtained a manifestation of the Savior; for it was not sufficient to make apostles, that they saw Jesus Christ while he was in the flesh; but it was necessary that they should have a manifestation of him after he rose from the dead, that they might testify to the world, that he lives, and that he is on the right hand of the Majesty in the Heavens; this made men apostles, or witnesses for Jesus Christ (184).

Beatific Vision was said to come after receiving the Holy Ghost "by the laying on of hands," after which one would "see visions, and to dream dreams, and by these means grow up to be witnesses of Jesus Christ also, and become apostles," and then prophets, and so on gaining honors and biblical offices. The offices, in other words, and contrary to Mormon claims today, and to their historians' tradition-telling, followed after, were gifts of the Spirit. Such a sequence, we can assume—and given the history thus far, more than assume but hardly doubt—was advocated by Parley Pratt and Oliver Cowdery, apostles who rebaptized so many Ohio Restorationists "for miracles," promising reception of the power of godliness: visions, healings, apostleship, discipleship. They had the power and not merely the forms, it was boasted. This power was the authority, as demonstrated by the existence of the Book of Mormon: it being given by translation of tongues, the first gift dispensed in our age.

Apostles of some definition (unlikely Rigdon's) were common in the churches of Christ, no less than disciples, saints, prophets, elders, and so on: these were names taken on, or given away, with varying criteria and definition. Mormons scarcely differed from other Restorationists in these things, likewise they found their doctrines in the Bible, and some forgot that it was from Campbell, Scott, and Stone that they had learned so much about the ancient order. In this essay, however, Rigdon moves away from Campbell, promoting the Beatific Vision as the principle feature of an apostle: for Rigdon claimed to have seen the Son of God in an 1832 vision.

A letter to the editor of LDS Messenger & Advocate published in 1834 makes it clear that Rigdon not only wrote about the ancient order being established by gifts and visions, but also preached it.[1] Ambrose Palmer said that Rigdon among other "mormon preachers" arrived in his town in April 1833, and "opened the scriptures to our understanding," "showing us the fruits which the gospel produced in former ages, as also the gifts that were in the church—such as visions, revelation, the ministration of angels, the gift of the holy spirit, and prophecy." These were, it was preached, "again restored to the world and were found in the 'mormon church.'" Within a year over sixty souls were added to the church.

The year 1835 saw Mormons designating a Quorum of Twelve Apostles, formally identifying men formerly called apostles; thereby restricting the term to those called and consented to by vote at church conference. Or, to say it more accurately, they instituted internal sanctions for those taking up the title in the presence of those called to the official Quorum. Excluded from that quorum were Sidney Rigdon, Oliver Cowdery, and John Whitmer, a church historian (i.e., copyist, recorder, and revisionist) who had taken over the editing of the LDS Messenger & Advocate. *Apostle* became an office in the church, and so revisions were undertaken to "restore" that term's new definition in usage prior to 1835. It seems that thereafter, the result of receiving baptism and the gifts of the spirit made one a Saint, and that was it to the pursuit of honors. No longer were apostles made by revelation of God (i.e., Beatific Vision), but only by the revelation of God (as a speech genre) to a church authority who "called" him to that office. What defined "real" apostles for some saints, however, would not be settled for another decade, after schisms followed the death of Joseph Smith.

The same significance attributed to a revelation of God is pointed to by Rigdon in an essay on the "Order of the New Testament Church," written as he says, to expound upon a "subject I conclude which is not very well understood, if I may have the privilege of judging from what passes before my eyes, and what is

---

[1] LDS Messenger & Advocate vol.1, no.4:62

sounded in my ears."[1]  He perhaps did not refer to non-Latter Day Saints, but to those reading his words.  To apostles alone, real apostles, he insists, "God had given the power to act on a commission," and that power came in "but one thing . . . and that was a revelation from God" (214).

His phrase does not mean, "information conveyed by God," but again refers to the vision wherein God reveals himself to men and women.  Just as his mentor had done before him—denying that miracles proved anything, and instead insisting on his own understanding given by biblical inspiration—Rigdon defines the power as being bound to something he could claim as his own, and not simply part of the order of things easily redefined.  Miracles could be claimed; sometimes folks did get better after baptism; honors and offices bestowed at will; but few would say like Rigdon that they saw the Lord Jesus in vision.  This vision occurred in 1832, and set him apart not only from other Mormons, but also from his former Mahoning associates.  Half a decade removed from their movement, and Mormons spoke of Campbell's Restoration and his Disciples of Christ as just another false tradition, entirely unrelated to their own.  Ignorance could be expected; but it was not without some nurturing by those who knew better.  Consider this essay, setting off the year that Mormons would finally experience their "endowment of power" in their newly built temple, only to abandon it before the decade was concluded, Rigdon and Smith escaping as cargo in a midnight wagon bound for Missouri.

# LATTER DAY SAINTS'
## MESSENGER AND ADVOCATE.

VOL. II. No. 4.]        KIRTLAND, OHIO, JANUARY, 1836.        [Whole No. 16.

| For the Messenger and Advocate. | Mr. Stone has done any thing more |
| BROTHER WHITMER:— | or less, than to profess belief in the |
| A short time since | things which are written in the New |
| I got the 12th No. of the 4th volume | Testament.  Now if he had quoted |

The fourth number of volume two began with a letter to the editor, John Whitmer.  It describes with plenty of vinegar the writer's reception of the latest volume of "the Evangelist (as the editor calls it)," which reported an ongoing debate between "somebody whom the editor calls 'our respected brother Stone;'" and the editor, a "Mr. Scott."  Stone apparently thought the "promise of the gift of

---

[1] LDS Messenger & Advocate vol.2, no.2:212

the Holy Spirit" was still on offer to the faithfully baptized, while Scott demurred, in the letter's telling, "that he did not believe in the ancient gospel," and this, "after preaching it with the most untiring perseverance." Stone had joined with Campbell in forming the official Disciples of Christ in 1832. Walter Scott became an independent preacher, though surely not an enemy to his former co-laborers in the gospel. The letter compares Scott's denial to one enunciated by "Mr. Campbell, one of the same brotherhood," who debated a Mr. Bosworth on the subject, and whose "Campbellites . . . has to be hid under a refuge of misrepresentation to conceal it from the shafts of truth" (242). Indeed. The letter then mentions "Mr. Bentley's bombast in Wethersfield," "where he cursed the author of this piece, as the Indian did the king on the other side of the hill, and declared that he dare not meet *him* [Mr. Bentley] and investigate the subject of religion." When the said author bravely accepted the challenge, daring Bentley "to show as much boldness in my presence as he had done when he was fifty miles off," he "indulged himself in slandering my character" (243). Simonds Rider comes next on the list of bad men showing their yellow, so many "Campbellites, and they have proven themselves to be destitute of candor and honesty in their pretensions," not one of whom is "possessing the common intelligence which belongs to men, who dare hazard an investigation before the public, on the subject of the Holy Spirit as set forth in the new testament" (243). The dispute, we learn after all this name-calling and score-settling, concerned not whether the Holy Ghost was received after baptism, but whether its reception necessarily brings about the working of miracles.

The letter writer, signing at the end, of course, under the name Sidney Rigdon, was sure that miracles must follow the Holy Ghost's bestowal. They were diagnostic of one's authority: "it will try every man's authority whether it is of God or not; for that gift was never enjoyed, only as it was administered by those authorized to do so by direct communication from God and by his calling to themselves" (245). Like Parley Pratt, Rigdon had got religion, as they say. He would now conclude that it is "the gift of the Holy Ghost as administered by the apostles, by the laying on of hands, which makes the difference . . . and the society which has this power are the people of God and those who have not are not" (245). This matter of authority divided real apostles from those merely taking the title, and according to Rigdon the rights to give the Holy Ghost came by direct revelation from God. Man could not give what he had not received. Despite later Mormons' attempts to blame him for introducing "the priesthood" to Joseph Smith, conniving their young leader into a hierarchies upon hierarchies, it seems that Rigdon was not the sole voice speaking about authority. The word seldom meant the same thing when spoken by different Saints, being non-referential and found as an explanation for why one felt the effects of the Holy Spirit. Its complex structure is outlined here.

As used by disciples of Christ, saints, and so on, *authority* minimally referred to an intangible essence that was credited to preachers, by those feeling physical effects attributed to the intangible essence called the Holy Spirit. Like I said, complex. It had a peculiar staying power inside Mormonism because so many converts were made precisely by finding "authority" evident in their bodies' sensations. Those failing to feel "the power" or "the Spirit" simply did not convert, presumably; or did so with an expectation to get it later; or out of bad intention or mere curiosity; or just to give it a try. Those who stayed, and endured conflict and poverty for their church were surely those who had felt "the power" at some time, in a place it could be attributed to divine authority being given to particular men. But more than a logic of practice (and population sifting) is at work in the term *authority*. Like the word *restoration*, it describes a way of speaking, of revising and reordering traditions into something seemingly uniquely powerful; of embodying metatext.

When Parley Pratt and Oliver Cowdery discussed their authority to baptize unto miracles, and to give other gifts of the spirit by the laying on of hands, to the Family on Morley's farm in fall of 1830, they created a discursive possibility. When a preacher was found to "have authority," by some other convert, the term generalized into an essence not bound to a particular experience or event. Authority was not given only present on the evening of October 30, 1830, and removed. It was held to subsist, and to provide general coverage of the preacher's other acts, declarations, and commands. Alexander Campbell held that authority was given by the congregation, and so it was. Mormons took authority as a social construct (related to contracts)—and turned the term into an organizing principle for a movement. As that movement embraced a mythology of restoration, it increasingly forgot where its words, doctrines, and metatext came from. It was found in the Bible, and the Book of Mormon. It was revealed by Joseph Smith. He was the author, and the authority, and his authority was soon said to pass from person to person.

What *authority* did, then, was reverse the actual order of things. As Mormons converted to a tradition that forgot its relationship to Campbell's Restoration, that term retroactively projected upon Joseph Smith all that came after the failed mission to the Lamanites, including the growing amnesia about

Campbell and friends. Once sourced to Smith, his translated text could be looked over, overlooked, and found to confirm all that he was said to reveal. The "powers of Godliness" became the "priesthood," elders called *apostles* became apostles of a church, and bearers as well as members of that priesthood. The terminology shows all the footprints of revision, recollection, retrospection, and confusion. That was "authority" in the Restoration: to remake religion backwards and to grant those now positioned at the entelechy of its reconstructed arc the privilege of having received their knowledge from God. It is the secret of its success and enduring power today. Thus as early as 1834 Mormonism was built, invented its own history, and given serious horsepower for moving into the future. Terms like authority, restoration, and biblical offices made the process appear seamless, fooling more than a few good (and faithful) historians in our day.

Pratt apparently declared his authority to baptize unto miracles, and to this Rigdon submitted, being perhaps far back in the line of Restorationists awaiting this gift. Cowdery spoke of being an apostle, of founding "his church" by direct communication with Jesus. Rigdon later claimed one must witness Jesus on the right hand of God before being authorized to give the Holy Ghost. Others claimed to receive apostleship from the hands of Cowdery, or Smith, or Martin Harris. Some simply called themselves apostles, disciples, followers, and saints. The Book of Mormon was said to be a sign of miracles, of the authority of apostleship returned, and now the miracle factory known as the Holy Spirit could be passed out in abundance. It cannot be too often stated, I suppose: the resource pointed to for all these claims was the Bible (metatext); that same text seemingly made unity out of so much diversity, and created the appearance of Adamic originality among so many family relations. If you wonder why I spend so much time discussing "the priesthood" and how it obscured Campbellism, and came of many divergent theories of authority; it is because Mormon readers assumed that power, and moved into a very different part of the map of history sketched by the Book of Mormon. The next volume follows them beyond its map, bearing their power into a new Zion, far over the mountains in the distant west.

## HOUSE OF ISRAELISM

Many threads of various traditions would come together by 1836, weaved by Joseph Smith like a boy in a field playing with strands of grass, patches further acervated, sometimes cleverly embroidered upon by many Mormons since: "the priesthood" was proclaimed the authority restored, and it justified the "restoration of the Church" in April 1830, and it was this priesthood which gave the Holy Ghost after performing authorized baptism. Such has become tradition, although it can be shown to be without the support of historical materials. It persists. The tradition binds Mormon imaginations into reading themselves not as Gentiles when they read their Book of Mormons, but as restored bearers chosen to hold the ancient priesthood of Israel. As we saw with so many Restorationists, being a restored church was hardly sufficient for the ambitions of Europeans. Bible metatext stretched across bodies and biographies and over entire populations. By being the new chosen of Heaven, they claimed to occupy the House of Israel.

Unlike anything seen in other Restoration groups, we encounter something of a puzzle which remains in Mormonism to this day. Not only were the Latter-day Saints said be the exclusive people of God, but also, somewhat inconveniently, as an article in the Messenger & Advocate explained, "the book of Mormon has made known who Israel is, upon this continent": so many Indians looked upon by "Our venerable President of these United States," soon be "gathered by the gospel" (245). No other Restorationists had this problem: Mormon scriptures inconveniently identified another people as Israel. Whatever. Maybe the Indians were also Israel. Every other Christian organization had long been Christianizing these nations; and if Mormons were anything, they were Jonny-come-latelies, seldom interested in thinking a new thought. It was fortunate that so few Indians received their gospel, or perhaps the early Saints would have had a real conundrum on their hands. What if indeed Indians converted, and New Jerusalem was not built and the Millennium was delayed? So long as Indians were avoided, neglected, or just refused to go along with Mormons, they could be pointed to, as we'll see next volume, as the cause of the delay in the Lord's Coming. It is, let's say, always wise to select the most unlikeliest of people as the House of Israel; if one also hopes to claim to be its doorkeeper in their absence. Let them stay away, and maybe the place will be all yours, someday.

The writer of this particular report waffles somewhat about the Indians' preferred status: "In speaking of the gathering, we mean to be understood, according to scripture, the gathering of the elect of the Lord, out of every nation on earth," Indians *and others*, eventually to join the saints in their city of Zion. Eventually. For now, let the government gather "the Lamanites," those "Red men" protected in its paternal embrace:

The joy that we shall feel, in common with every *honest* American; and the joy that will eventually fill their bosoms, on account of *nationalizing* them—will be glory enough, when it comes, to show, that gathering them to themselves, and *for themselves*, to be associated with themselves, is a wise measure, and reflects the highest honor upon our Government. May they all be gathered in peace, and form a happy union among themselves. To which thousands may shout, *Esto Perpetua* (248).

Finding rather more success among Restorationists (who happened to attend the missionaries' congregations), the mission to restore the House of Israel was left to the U.S. government. Mormons seemingly forgot that once four of their men started out from New York to preach the gospel to what they thought were the Lamanites, among whom "my church" would be established (and not simply colonizing them). Mormons set about making themselves more full of the Restoration than even the Campbellites would attempt. They claimed the gifts of the Spirit, miracles, healings, diverse tongues and discernment of its operations. Soon they would realize they had the priesthood; were of the Order of Melchizedek and some of Aaron, not knowing, of course, that the very framework they developed in response to Campbell's criticism of the Book of Mormon came from his own writings. And he plagiarized another Alexander, Mr. Crawford of Maine:

> One non-Mormon observer captured the state of the Church up to then [1831-33]: 'Even after Rigdon became known as a Mormon, his sermons were filled with as sound Disciple doctrines as they had been before he joined up with Joseph Smith.' He was not the only one who brought his old beliefs along with him. . . . Parley P. Pratt, Orson Hyde, John Murdock, Isaac Morley, and Lyman Wight. Numerous converts to Mormonism were former Disciples of Christ who brought most of their old beliefs with them.[1]

Let us return to Kirtland, June 1831, and see how "the power" manifest in the gifts of the Holy Ghost was redefined as "the priesthood," again restored as in the days of Abraham to these Gentiles, wonderfully confounded into believing they were God's own Israel.

By summer of 1831 Joseph Smith had worked through much of GENESIS in his rewrite of the Bible, with Sidney Rigdon by his side, ostensibly serving as scribe. After tradition made him voice and author of all things Mormon, and all others

---

[1] Staker, *Hearken O Ye People,* 320

his scribes and copyists, their translation-rewrite of the Bible was added to things established upon his good authority. Who is the author of such things? Smith had once discussed with Oliver Cowdery the matter of baptism while translating the Book of Mormon, so it seems he was not merely dictating to, but engaging his scribes as an equal, they having no qualms about challenging his readings. Cowdery even doubted traditions about John the Beloved having never died, so Smith was left using interpreters (seeing stones) to scry a parchment that concluded that indeed John was still walking the earth. Cowdery's question came as a result of translating the Book of Mormon, where "three disciples" (mistakenly called by Mormons, "the Three Nephites") are added to the number of immortals, requesting the same privileges given John the Beloved, to witness all the "doings of the Father."

Smith and Rigdon no doubt conversed about the Bible, and the resulting "Joseph Smith Translation" cannot conclusively be said to come from Smith's mouth any more than the Articles and Covenants of the Church of Christ can be said to emanate from him alone. Sidney was blamed by ex-Latter-day Saints for teaching Smith about priesthood during these sessions. As David Whitmer guessed,

> Rigdon finally persuaded Brother Joseph to believe that the high priests which had such great power in ancient times, should be in the Church of Christ today. He had Brother Joseph inquire of the Lord about it, and they received an answer according to their erring desires.[1]

Rigdon cannot be blamed entirely for knotting priesthood into Smith's head, however. He was concerned with high priests. In Campbell tradition, they were not necessarily implicated in priesthood. Adam or Jesus might be of that order. Priests had power, and that was Rigdon's concern. *Priesthood* was a body of priests, not a power for these early Mormons. It was others arriving later who named *priesthood* a power, apparently. So we come to the Mormon (Smith-Cowdery-Rigdon) translation of GENESIS. It expands upon stories of Enoch, Cain, and others like Melchizedek who had long fascinated Christians, in part because so little was said about them in their Bibles. What it told of Melchizedek is now thought to frame what would happen in June 1831, when "the power of

---

[1] David Whitmer, An Address To All Believers in Christ (1887), 64; in David John Buerger, *The Mysteries of Godliness: A history of Mormon temple worship* (San Francisco: Smith Research Associates, 1994), 2

godliness," as some said, or the "order of Melchidezek" as others recalled, was returned to Man. The important passage, cleverly inserted by Smith into the great idol of the Bible, reads:

> Now Melchizedek was a man of faith, who wrought righteousness; and when a child he feared God, and stopped the mouths of lions, and quenched the violence of fire. And thus, having been approved of God, he was ordained an high priest after the order of the covenant which God made with Enoch; It being after the order of the son of God; which order came, not by man, nor the will of man; neither by father nor mother; neither by beginning of days nor end of years; but of God; And it was delivered unto men by the calling of his own voice, according to his own will, unto as many as believed on his name.
>
> For God having sworn unto Enoch and unto his seed with an oath by himself; that every one being ordained after this order and calling should have power, by faith, to break mountains, to divide the seas, to dry up waters, to turn them out of their course; to put at defiance the armies of nations, to divide the earth, to break every band, to stand in the presence of God; to do all things according to his will, according to his command, subdue principalities and powers; and this by the will of the Son of God which was from before the foundation of the world. And men having this faith, coming up unto this order of God, were translated and taken up into Heaven. And now, Melchizedek was a priest of this order; therefore he obtained peace in Salem, and was called the Prince of peace. And his people wrought righteousness, and obtained Heaven, and sought for the city of Enoch which God had before taken, separating it from the earth, having reserved it unto the latter days, or the end of the world. And hath said, and sworn with an oath, that the Heavens and the earth should come together; and the sons of God should be tried so as by fire. And this Melchizedek, having thus established righteousness, was called the King of Heaven by his people, or, in other words, the King of peace (JST Genesis 14:26-36).

This passage was said to open the matter of priesthood for public dispensation in the June 1831 conference of the church of Christ. Nothing here is said of "priesthood," although we have "a priest of this order" working wonders, having "power, by faith, to break mountains, to divide the seas," and so on. The same things can be found in the Book of Mormon—faith being the power to break mountains, command trees, and so on, with priests like Melchizedek and Alma being mentioned as men of this order. Nothing is said of priesthood, however; so how can we get from one high priest with faith, to a priesthood being authority restored to administer the rituals of New-Old Testament Christianity? Talk of priesthood was apparently not uncommon then, as we've seen. Alexander Campbell spoke of three orders of priesthood, drawing on his Bible for inspiration.[1] In fact, it was not uncommon to hear Bible readers talk of the priesthood of Aaron, of Moses, of Abraham, of Melchizedek, of Messiah, of John, and even of Adam. Not many thought these various "orders" needed restoration, however; Jesus was thought to put an end to the old covenants, and to offer a dispensation of mercy, or a new covenant of grace.

Joseph Smith seems to have misunderstood Christian covenant theology, or ignored it, having his eye on something perhaps not explicable to Restorationists. A decade later, Mark Staker explains, Smith continued to preach, to order, as it were, and refine priesthood: "In Nauvoo, Joseph Smith defined three orders of priesthood, somewhat as the Campbellites had earlier taught, but he understood those orders in sharply different terms." In the prophet's commentary on HEBREWS, he explained that Paul was "treating of three different priesthoods, namely the priesthood of Aaron, Abraham, and Melchizedek," but that of the "three grand principles or orders of Priesthood portrayed in this chapter," Melchizedek's "was not the power of a Prophet nor apostle nor Patriarch only but of a King & Priest."[2] What Joseph did in Nauvoo was bring Latter Day Saints back to where he started, in that rewrite of GENESIS, reducing all orders under a single power, merely graded or parted out to others. As Mark Staker paraphrased, "'All priesthood is Melchizedek, but there are different portions or degrees of it,' Joseph taught."[3] Mormons had travelled far from the faith of Melchizedek during a decade of unceasing hardship.

Two priests make a priesthood, apparently, and so the Order of Melchizedek was thought to be entered by faithful men—called priests, of course—attending the upcoming conference. How exactly Smith described the conference is no longer known. It was held near Kirtland, over a few days in early June. The stories around it do not interest this history, except that it was here that "the power," "the power of godliness," the "authority" held to be manifest after the giving of the Holy Ghost by the laying on of hands was first thought to be formalized into an office in the Church of Christ. This story is only half accurate, though. Later Mormons would revise their records accordingly, inserting

---

[1] Staker, *Hearken O Ye People,* 149-50
[2] James Burgess notebook, 1843; Franklin D. Richards "Scriptural Items"; in Ehat and Cook, *The Words of Joseph Smith,* 245-6
[3] Staker, *Hearken O Ye People,* 164

priesthood, or Melchizedek priesthood, wherever it was thought to belong in earlier writings. Richard Bushman writing about priesthood notes that the term is applied "retroactively, but the June 1831 conference marked its first appearance in contemporary records. The term 'authority' frequently appeared, but not 'priesthood.'"[1] Parley Pratt said it was the first time priesthood had been given "in this dispensation," causing considerable problems for readers who want to have him bringing exactly that priesthood to Kirtland and Sidney Rigdon. It has caused Mormon historians grief for nearly two centuries, with various explanations how a priesthood said be necessary for giving the gift of the Holy Ghost was not yet given to Mormon elders until June 1831.

Did Pratt mean "office" when he said "priesthood"? Did "high priesthood" really mean "high priest"? Was he confused? What about the problem that no one was talking about priesthood before that conference? In modern LDS practice, a boy or man is ordained and given the priesthood (of Aaron or of Melchizedek, as a power of some kind), and set apart to an office in that priesthood (as a collective body). It happens once for Aaronic priesthood, and once for Melchizedek priesthood ordination; the wording has changed, but is supposed to be recited verbatim as found in official manuals. Not surprisingly, modern historians strain to see in Kirtland their current practices, and end up projecting their own confusion onto participants' recollections: "Subsequent attempts by participants in the meeting to explain what happened that morning, suggest that the high priesthood given there may not have been a new priesthood conferred for the first time," Mark Staker guesses, repeating what is now received tradition, "but a distinctive office in the priesthood they already held that had not been recognized before." He adds, always careful to show that Campbell's version differed, that this was an "office that countered Disciple of Christ understandings of ancient high priesthood and the presumed obsolete figure Melchizedek" (158). In this Church of Christ, however, there is no simple sequence as the modern LDS Church imposes on ordinants.

My interest is not in solving this puzzle. In fact, I doubt it can be solved. There seems to have been several different understandings of "authority" and "power" at the time, and of what exactly was passed around by putting hands on another man's head. In other words, the solution I offer is: there was no single notion of "priesthood" or "authority" in 1831, or even by 1835, nor apparently by 1845. We merely impose one reading across others to insist on a single solution. This many-strands reconstruction is supported by accounts of the conference.

---

[1] Bushman, *Rough Stone,* 157

Many times Joseph Smith and others laid hands on other men, pronouncing blessings and offices and ordinations and gifts, and then were themselves similarly handled by other men. There were rounds and rounds of ordinations and blessings. Staker attempts to reconcile the ordinations of power, squaring circles upon circles:

> After Joseph gave Wight, who was already an elder, the high priesthood, he directed Wight to give others including him (Joseph Smith) that same high priesthood. This may have been done, not because Wight was giving Joseph authority but because he was conferring priesthood office within a defined category of authority already held. In other words, Wight set Joseph Smith apart in the office of high priest, but Joseph already held the authority needed for that office (158).

The modern distinction between "office" and "power" (reviving the old Roman Catholic one) is projected onto the conference in hopes of explaining its enigmatic cycles and descriptions of a new priesthood being dispensed or joined. The earliest accounts, however, do not give us any reason to hope for an explanation grounded in modern LDS practices. As Ezra Booth later reported, he "felt the weight of hands thrice, before the work was rightly done," which repetition, Staker takes as resulting, believe it or not, from Wight having "trouble getting the wording of this new ordinance correct" (159).

In fact, Staker has the answer before him: they were giving out "the power," in various currencies and figures, and there were many different ideas about what "the power" was: the Holy Ghost; the order of Melchizedek; godliness; authority. Indeed, Staker notes that Booth reports men were "set apart," "ordained to 'gifts,' ordained to 'office,' or ordained to 'high priesthood' as though all of these terms were equivalents." Rather than accept the obvious—that Joseph Smith did not govern the proceedings and ordain men to an office in the Melchizedek priesthood, but instead it was a sort of revival meeting with everyone passing around the powers they believed they could pass around—he opts for this insightfully vapid supposition: Booth's description of many blessings, and their "survival in his written record possibly signaled an inadequate understanding of distinctive activities performed on behalf of different individuals or the lack of an established vocabulary to explain what occurred" (159).

It was said that Rigdon also ordained Smith: to what is not recorded. After Rigdon failed to follow Brigham Young to Utah, however, this story too would be anathema. Young's version is as convoluted as any historian's: "I have been told since I came here that Sidney Rigdon ordained Joseph a high priest. I would ask who ordained Sidney Rigdon? What priesthood he had he got from Joseph; and then he turned around and ordained Joseph to an office, the authority to hold which he had received from Joseph."[1] Staker attempts to solve the riddle thus: "Brigham Young, who was not at the conference, mistakenly understood that Sidney Rigdon had played this role rather than Lyman Wight. However, he may be been correct in understanding the nature of what occurred." What is clear is that some kind of crazy happened at the conference, including men leaping backwards out windows, hopping from rooftops, crawling like snakes, and Lyman Wight (from Morley's farm) apparently being possessed by demons, after receiving the power from Joseph Smith. When the "man of sin" was thus revealed in the body of Wight, Smith proceeded to exorcise the beings. The power to drive out demons too was passed around.

What emerges from reports of the conference is not a gathering of staid, buttoned-up religious professionals. It looks very much like what happened on Morley's farm through the winter of 1830 into 1831, the reports of which spectacularities circulated in regional papers, presumably to the delight and horror of a rubbernecking Campbell. If Rigdon wanted gifts (and there's no evidence he did, before Pratt starting baptizing unto miracles, and some reported actual miracles starting to happen), he could have them. Hence Campbell gave it out that his dispute with Rigdon was over charismatic gifts, a sort of knowing wink at readers to look what the disloyal fool has got himself into. Very little had changed for disciples by June '31, although some were now satisfied that Pratt's claims to baptize unto miracles was finally made good in the showing forth of power. But not everyone. The proof of the powers of godliness, rather than the enunciation of the mere forms, was in the experience.

As stated, Pratt himself said he was ordained into the high priesthood at this conference, emphasizing that upon his head were laid the hands of Joseph Smith; not Rigdon, nor Cowdery (who'd previously given him a commission in the same manner, and authority to preach, baptize, and give the Holy Ghost). Not everyone was convinced about "the power" or "priesthood" or whathaveyou. It was said later that "some doubting took place among the elders, and considerable conversation was held on the subject. The elders not fairly understanding the nature of the endowment, it took sometime to reconcile all

---

[1] Deseret News, 6 June 1877, vol.26, no.18:274, in Staker, *Hearken O Ye People,* 170 n.50

their feelings."[1]  Corrill's version reported many "visionary and marvellous spirits," and that in order to chase them out, the power was "introduced, and conferred on several of the elders.  In this chiefly consisted the endowment—it being a new order—and bestowed authority."[2]  No single version of the conference has yet been accepted by historians, and so the skepticism and confusion continues today. It is likely that no single version happened, just as no single baptism happened when Pratt dipped Restorationists because his new scripture said he should, and they submitted because that book was a sign of miracles being dispensed.  Given his reluctance to preach about priesthood, and his emphasis on Beatific Vision, it is probable that Rigdon was among the skeptics left cold by the conference.  He and many other Saints, disciples, elders, apostles and priests began to build a temple, where a real endowment of power could be received.

## DOLEFULL KIRTLAND

Rigdon spent the latter part his first year by Smith's side shoring up his position, making accusations against leaders like Edward Partridge in a letter addressed to Isaac Morley and John Corrill.  The charges were minor, in our reading today more than a little petty.  The fifth charge he laid against the new bishop was "having insulted the Lord's prophet in particular & assumed authority over him in open violation of the Laws of God."[3]  Partridge's impudence seemed to bother Rigdon far more than it did Smith, or the elders in Ohio, who wrote to Rigdon,

> that whereas the duty of a disciple of Christ is to promote peace union harmony & brotherly love & not at any time imprudently prefer charges & demand confession & settlement of the same in the absence of a br[other]. after having had a privilege of doing the same face to face, and more expecially after sitting in Conference in the name of the Lord & communing together at sacrament.
>
> We do therefore after deliberately weighing the subject before us earnestly entreat our b[rothe]r. Sidney for the good of the cause in which we labor & for which we suffer persecutions, to candidly reflect upon the subject of the aforementioned letter and ask himself whether he was not actuated by his own hasty feelings rather than the Spirit of Christ when indicting the same.

[1] John Corrill, 1839 History, in Staker, *Hearken O Ye People,* 164
[2] In Prince, *Having Authority*, 36
[3] *Far West Record* (Cannon and Cook, ed. SLC: Deseret Book, 1983), 10 March 1831, 41-42

> After having conversed with b[rothe]r. Edward freely upon the subject we can say with assurance that he is willing to make every confession which b[rothe]r. Sidney as a disciple of Christ could require & forever bury the matter.

Having hitched his wagon to a new movement, disciple Rigdon rode shotgun with Smith in late 1831 to refute the letters of Ezra Booth, and their tales of extravagant spiritual operations, and many failed prophecies and unfulfilled commands. Booth's experience as a Mormon was brief, and comprehended Zion's Camp. Here Smith had gathered what men he could to march to Zion (Missouri), and its re-enactment would make for a marvelous Monty Python film. Booth's letters describing the experience were published in newspapers. Then more trouble came. By early spring 1832 Smith had returned to Kirtland, and was rumored to be involved more than spiritually with some local girls. A gang stirred up by ex-Mormonite Simonds Rider (also with Booth on the failed adventure to Zion) used the rumors as pretense to assault Rigdon and Smith, dragging them from their beds and across a frosty field. Rigdon was presumed dead by Smith, seen prostrate on a scattering of hay. The Mormon prophet was stripped, held down, and threatened with emasculation. When faced with the task, however, the doctor roped into doing the duty cowered, and instead the gang tarred and feathered the prophet, taking pillows from Rigdon's home to make a cock of the man. Overcome by a spirit of some kind, Rider apparently leaped on the naked Smith, and as Joseph tells it, he "scratched my body with his nails like a mad cat," yelling, "God dam ye, that's the way the Holy Ghost falls on folks."[1] Some later said that Joseph actually died in the attack, and floated above his body, observing the scene with the sort of bemusement only Smith could muster.[2] Finding Rigdon not dead the following morning, and himself cleaned of tar and feathers but plenty bruised and suffering a chipped tooth, Smith was threatened by his co-religionist. "The trauma of the mobbing," Bushman concludes generously, "may have deepened Sidney's tendency to manic-depression" (180). Rigdon asked his wife for a razor to kill Joseph. When Mrs. Rigdon refused, he asked Joseph for a razor to slice her neck with. She and Joseph must have been equally surprised and frightened by his behavior. "What a freak had got into Sidney's head," that was the way Hyrum Smith told it.

Mormon tradition blames the "exposure to cold" that came of the midnight raid for causing the death of Smith's infant son, Joseph Murdock Smith,

---

[1] In Bushman, *Rough Stone*, 179-80
[2] Heber C. Kimball, quoted in Staker, *Hearken O Ye People,* 352

a twin adopted by Smith after his own pair had died at birth only weeks earlier. The Murdock twins had no mother to nurse, for Julia Clapp Murdock had died in childbirth. Emma Smith would raise the twins in place of her own. Here is a little truth in tragedy, almost something out of Isaiah: Campbell's own kin were thus adopted by Smith, and his own preacher (Rider) apparently brought on the death of baby Joseph Murdock, then suffering from measles. Rider eventually left the region, having burned too many bridges. He was replaced as minister of the Hiram congregation by Amos S. Hayden, president of their college and composer of many histories of the Disciples of Christ. Hayden too would've known little Joseph Murdock, had the twin survived, for many Clapps continued to preach for Campbell's restoration of ancient things. His twin Julia survived the cold, and was raised by Emma and Joseph. Spiritual sons and daughters of Campbell, these Mormons would be carried into his adventures. He their nursing father, at times distracted by their idols; all the while seeking to restore the House of Israel by bringing forth long lost knowledge; stories everyone else was convinced they already carried around in their Bibles, telling them they were that house and Joseph was their keeper. Maybe hostage is closer to the truth, I don't know.

A few weeks after the raids, his head free of its freak, Rigdon sat near Smith gazing into eternity, reciting a vision of Heaven, Jesus, Lucifer's fall, and more. One version was canonized as D&C 76. It came from Rigdon, and bears a striking resemblance to some of Campbell's theories about three kingdoms, in terminology not so different from that used by Walter Scott to describe supernal realms.[1]   Mormon historian Mark Staker explains the coincidence in a manner almost arousing admiration, such is his cross to bear under these traditions of the LDS Church: "Until February 1832 much of the doctrine believed by the growing Mormon membership came with them from their congregations—principally from the Disciples of Christ," adding that Rigdon was blessed by his exposure to Scott and Campbell, who "prepared his mind to search out the insightful questions" (331). Other than showing the continuity of doctrines from Campbell (whose newspaper was still read by Rigdon), the vision itself does not shape our history here.

By July 1832 Rigdon was again frenzied, bursting into a prayer meeting and shouting that the "keys of the kingdom are rent from the church," forbidding anyone to pray any further "until you build me a new house."[2]  Smith with his wife Emma, passing strangers, new converts, hired girls, and the various infants he

---

[1] Staker, *Hearken O Ye People*, 321-24
[2] Bushman, *Rough Stone*, 186

took in all shared a room above a store in Kirtland, which Rigdon well knew, for the Bible translating was conducted here. But like his god, Sidney desired a more commodious place to rest his weary head.

The clock was ticking, for the voice had told Joseph Smith that Kirtland would be a "stronghold" for only five more years, and then it would be time to move on. The temple was started to meet this deadline, and a foundation stone for another laid in Missouri by the party Booth thought so foolishly directed. When commanded to write a description of the lands surrounding the proposed temple in Zion (the lands of Missouri), Rigdon produced something to appall both Oliver Cowdery and Rick Steves, being full, his biographer recounts, of "tortuous prose and interminably long sentences."[1]  Always patient but never accepting self-aggrandizing, pseudo-classical nonsense in commissioned writings, the voice told Joseph, "his writing is not acceptable unto the Lord, and he shall make another" (D&C 63). His embellishments at times wearied even Heaven.

The saints eventually finished their temple in Kirtland, and the promised endowment of power again came to some, but not to all. Gods clothed in flame and many angels were reported strolling the halls, lingering on the roof; and even the apostle Paul was seen upon the stand, seated among the leaders of the church. By spring 1836 the Saints could not ask for more proof that they were the chosen, favored of Heaven, their sacrifices accepted. Kirtland and its glorious temple would be theirs as a pillar in Zion, forever. So they started a bank. Actually, their application for a bank was denied, although they had already begun printing currency. Rather than waste all those useless bank notes for the Kirtland Safety Bank, instead they stamped "Anti-" before bank, to which they added "-ing Co." Once before, I suppose, a simple change in names had considerably altered their fortunes; why not again? Thus the notorious, daring, ridiculously conceived, gloriously named Kirtland Safety Society Anti-Banking Company began only months after the miracles of the modern LDS Pentecost. It was an early sort of investment bank, and that meant high risk with high returns. Rigdon was the first to purchase its stock in October '36. He paid $12 toward 2,000 shares, starting the firm with a push onto a conveyor belt of a foundation driven entirely by wheels of land speculation.[2] Anti-Mormons gossiped that the investment bank's vault was stacked with boxes marked $1,000, but aside from the top layer of the uppermost boxes, they were surely filled with sand.[3] Like other apostles, Parley

---

[1] Van Wagoner, *Sidney Rigdon*, 103
[2] Staker, *Hearken O Ye People*, 463
[3] McKiernan, *Voice in the Wilderness*, 77

Pratt was part of the Society, which boasted Smith and other barely enumerate Mormons on its board of directors. On a mission to build Zion in some god-forsaken land, Pratt was unable to meet his obligations to a note taken out from the bank on lots in Kirtland, lots that everyone was sure would develop, now that God had come to his temple. Imagine the value of acreage in the Celestial kingdom, and wouldn't you wish you got in before the prices went sky high? Smith had sold the lots to Pratt for $2,000, as the apostle later tells it, because "it was the will of God that Lands Should Bear such a price."[1] For Joseph, however, the Lord thought less than $100 in cash was about fair-market value, only a few months earlier.

Something weird was going on, and it was not, as stories then and now tell it, that Joseph was converted to the worship of Mammon; nor thought by land speculation to make a buck off converts arriving in Kirtland. After Pratt's payments, as his biographers tell it, "lagged, Smith turned the debt over to the Kirtland bank for collection." Rigdon not only demanded the lots, but withdrew money from the missionary's accounts, telling Pratt he also "wanted my house and homes also." Pratt returned to find Kirtland in total nuclear meltdown, and added to the disaster by denouncing Smith in the temple, where only a year before they had all shared the bread of revelation. Eventually the Cowdery brothers (Oliver and Warren), three Whitmers, Martin Harris, Pratt and many other leaders would either leave the Mormons to their mess, and Joseph to his inscrutable games; or be driven from their midst by those who stayed seemingly loyal to the Prophet: Sidney Rigdon, Brigham Young, and a few others who'd lead the church after Young's death in 1877.

The irony is that Smith and his voice had warned them five years before, under command from God, that they had exactly five years to build a temple and move on. It was almost as if Smith conceived the absurd Safety Society as a way to ensure that every Mormon would be driven from the region, and he from their good graces. Anyone surprised by his antics had not been paying very close attention. Joseph consistently bankrupted businesses he operated, often within a few months. If Rigdon had no talent for poverty, Smith had a gift for it, being unable to demand a fair exchange for goods he offered at sale. Wealthy farmers shared in his gift, when they sought advice on matters that the Lord gladly leaves to Mammon. If you continued to demand his participation in land speculation, then Joseph might inflate the value 200%, and bring down the entire scheme within six months.

---

[1] Givens and Grow, *Parley Pratt*, 97-98

He was  man of many talents.  So it was that Rigdon and Smith escaped, riding under a blanket in January 1838, off to the blessed lands of Zion; lands Rigdon perhaps still thought deserved embellishment, for the Lord had not graced them with an abundance of virtues.  Not yet.  When they arrived, they found Zion not quite so ruined as Joseph's Kirtland.  Rigdon replaced as postmaster the long-established W.W. Phelps, and quickly found accusations to press against Phelps, Cowdery, and anyone else doubting his authority over the church.  He had seen Jesus, after all, and had a great work, to show the foolishness and abominations of the Gentiles.  He would lead the redemption of Zion, crusading for God.  The voice told Smith that the Saints were again to build a temple, this time in Far West, Missouri.  They never, and this seems important, got beyond setting the foundation stone in place.

Zion had been overrun by usurpers, even though Joseph had marched a scabby, lice-ridden, dysenteried, barely armed Zion's Camp from Kirtland some years before, promising to claim Missouri for their own, once and for all.  After refugees of the failed bank scheme dragged into Missouri through 1838, and rumors and evidence of Mormon-operated political machines spread, the rubes, slave masters, and exiled troglodytes inhabiting areas around Jackson County gathered up the pitchforks and torches and marched on Mormon homes.  Rigdon responded as he so often did, by doing exactly opposite what wisdom dictates.  He delivered what is now called the Salt Sermon in June 1838, declaring an early independence from mobocracy.  He commanded those Gentiles occupying the saints' land of Zion to be exterminated, cast as salt that hath lost its savor.  If non-Mormons and apostates like Cowdery were not willing to be driven out peacefully, they would be led as from Eden before the angry fist of God.  Nothing seemed to convince non-Mormons that this land is our land; it is not your land.  So Missourians responded by signing a petition warning Cowdery (without a friend), the Whitmers, and other Mormons to leave or be expelled by force.  And they had guns and few reservations about committing murder.  Mormons went around setting stones for temples, scuffling with pukes, and preaching extermination.  Smith and Rigdon, who increasingly seem like co-stars juxtaposed in a silly movie, set a cornerstone for the new temple on the Fourth of July.

They departed for Adam-ondi-Ahman, the land where Smith said Adam was driven after his own exile from Eden.  On their way to Adam's refuge, they spied a "deer or two on the way.  Pres[iden]t Smith set his dogs after them one of which was a gray hound which caught the deer," the scribe adds, "but could not hold him, although he threw him down."  An omen for those who hunt for that which might be caught, but not possessed, the deer "injoured the dog so badly that he let him go, and we lost him, The race was quite amusing indeed." Two days later his remaining allies in Kirtland wrote Joseph, that "Kirtland is not our home, it looks dolefull here."[1] Eventually Rigdon and Smith and Pratt and others were locked in chains in an unfinished courthouse near Jackson County, justice being delayed for various reasons. One can truly sympathize with Smith, chained to Rigdon for months thereafter at the bitterly named Liberty Jail, listening to Rigdon recite a tale of woe that would, when played before judge and jury, leave no eye without a tear. Pratt was again by their side, in Liberty, and would compose one of the finest sketches of Joseph Smith, most noble when in chains, barking orders at his own keepers to silence their infernal conversation.

It was in Liberty where Joseph came back to earth, and regained the form that saw him translate the Book of Mormon and expand the Bible's accounts of Enoch and Melchizedek into material used to build a priesthood. That eventually came crashing down on him, as he fell from another prison's window to escape yet another mob. That last leap was in Illinois, where Joseph and the Mormons were driven in the winter of '39, crossing rivers frozen in a sort of uncanny mockery of the Bible's version of blessed exoduses. They had fled Zion, not inherited the promised land; driven into the cold and dreary world, as Joseph would later tell them in a drama now called "the Endowment." Still the saints insisted they were the House of Israel, and definitely not like those Gentiles who raped their women, shot their men, and burned their homes and stole their farms. They were foolish and full of abominations. New York. Ohio. Missouri. With each new land, the Book of Mormon was mentioned less frequently, the saints' own vanity and ambitions increasingly obscuring the view of a once clear landscape: Lamanites lived there, Zion would be here, and this is our duty. As we'll see next volume, during the 1830s the Book of Mormon is notable mostly by its absence in Mormon discourse; if mentioned at all, it is to explain that the book in no way replaces, supplants, or runs contrary to the Holy Bible.

Fleeing their promised land, and landing in the cursed muck and miasmic swampland of Commerce, Illinois, Smith and his regrouped Saints "gave to the brethren and friends of the Neighborhood a brief history or account of the coming forth of the Book of Mormon."[2] Another elder was recorded giving a "very interesting discourse on the subject of the Book of Mormon . . . and afterwards proceeded to read portions from the Bible and the Book of Mormon concerning

---

[1] *The Joseph Smith Papers: Journals*: vol.1 (SLC: Church Historian's Press 2008), 276-80
[2] *The Joseph Smith Papers: Journals*: vol.1:342

the best criterion whereby to judge of its authenticity." The criterion was a promise found in the Book of Mormon concerning "land which is choice above all other lands," and the book which would spring forth from the soil. While a city called Nauvoo was raised from the swamps to rival the size and influence of Chicago, and this after only four years of effort, no more books leaped from the earth. Smith's own hopes in the Saints seem to have risen not quite so high as the city. He implemented secret societies, never trusting one without advising the other to keep track of the first. Smith created mazes of connubial relations, of which we will never, ever make our way to their end. He ran for president. Of the United States. He said god was once a man, and he did not mean only Jesus. He said humans would become gods, and created a ceremony now totally obscure in its meaning and purpose. He sent a letter to Sidney's teenage daughter Nancy, proposing she marry him and obtain the promise of salvation for her entire family, her father included. Here the man who'd claimed to see Jesus, with Joseph Smith seated nearby, was promised *salvation*, for his daughter's hand! Rigdon must've exploded: *O impudent rogue!* Even though he publicly castigated Rigdon, Smith was never free of the proud but pathetic gentleman, now often ill, increasingly stooped and rumored to suffer another addition to his house of madness. The letter to Nancy is pure Joseph Smith, teaching that our Father does not withhold what is good for our appetite, if we only ask before partaking of the apple otherwise forbidden. There were serpents aplenty in Nauvoo, too. Nancy refused Smith's offer of marriage, exposing him to public shame, giving fuel to men coveting his power, and spreading doubt about his continuing status as the favored seer of Heaven. After Nancy refused, she was reportedly visited by a dead sister, who warned her not to forsake Joseph and follow after her own pride. She was cautioned to not make of this refusal a balm for her father's wounds, those stripes that came too often now by Smith's harsh words: this desire for vengeance must depart, this hope that for once Smith would get his come-uppance. He did get it; in a series of events not unrelated to her exposure, and to Sidney's weakening, and to Joseph's indiscretion. Joseph was Sidney's shepherd, and the great work of the weak man was well begun. So it could finally end.

   The life of Joseph Smith was in his own hands, although he stated that if it was of no worth to his friends, it was of none to him. He had known good and evil, becoming like the gods. How else could he exit the stage? Had Joseph not ordered the destruction of a Nauvoo paper that exposed his amorous spirituality while calling on him to step down to the level he had fallen to in their spying eyes; had he refrained from bashing in the door, and glorying in this one act of dumb, human retribution and refused this domination by force of will and great strength, then all the conspiracies and warrants and powers of Hell and Earth combined would not have driven him to that window sill on the second floor of Carthage Jail, whence he was pushed to the earth like an angel.

He fell, but not like innocent Enjolras; although hit by the same shot and iron balls that come from the lesser angels of our natures. That ground was cursed for his sake, a dirge by Phelps would declare. Thorns also and thistle shall it bring forth to thee, other voices would say, for dust thou art, and unto dust shalt thou return. Before departing to Carthage on that last summer day, Hyrum Smith read aloud from the Book of Mormon, turning to what is now ETHER chapter twelve. It reads in part:

> Thou hast also made our words powerful and great, even that we cannot write them; wherefore, when we write we behold our weakness, and stumble because of the placing of our words; and I fear lest the Gentiles shall mock at our words. And when I had said this, the Lord spake unto me, saying: Fools mock, but they shall mourn; and my grace is sufficient for the meek, that they shall take no advantage of your weakness. And if men come unto me I will show unto them their weakness. I give unto men weakness that they may be humble; and my grace is sufficient for all men that humble themselves before me; for if they humble themselves before me, and have faith in me, then will I make weak things become strong unto them. Behold, I will show unto the Gentiles their weakness and I will show unto them that faith, hope and charity bringeth unto me--the fountain of all righteousness (v.25-28).

Joseph would say he was as calm as a summer's morn, although like a lamb going to slaughter. His brother's final reading from the Book of Mormon would draw from Moroni's parting words to a portion of his readers:

> And again, I remember that thou hast said that thou hast loved the world, even unto the laying down of thy life for the world, that thou mightest take it again to prepare a place for the children of men. And now I know that this love which thou hast had for the children of men is charity; wherefore, except men shall have charity they cannot inherit that place which thou hast prepared in the mansions of thy Father. Wherefore, I know by this thing which thou hast said, that if the Gentiles have not charity, because of our weakness, that thou wilt prove them, and take away their talent, yea, even that which they have received, and give unto them who shall have more abundantly.

And it came to pass that I prayed unto the Lord that he would give unto the Gentiles grace, that they might have charity. And it came to pass that the Lord said unto me: If they have not charity it mattereth not unto thee, thou hast been faithful; wherefore, thy garments shall be made clean. And because thou hast seen thy weakness thou shalt be made strong, even unto the sitting down in the place which I have prepared in the mansions of my Father.

And now I, Moroni, bid farewell unto the Gentiles, yea, and also unto my brethren whom I love, until we shall meet before the judgment-seat of Christ, where all men shall know that my garments are not spotted with your blood. And then shall ye know that I have seen Jesus, and that he hath talked with me face to face, and that he told me in plain humility, even as a man telleth another in mine own language, concerning these things (v.33-39).

Eight years earlier, before the brothers' corpses were wheeled back to Nauvoo, back when the glories of Kirtland's Pentecost were still near the saints, Rigdon went a-preaching in the countryside, as he once had with Adamson Bentley, Alexander Campbell, Scott and Stone. His experience was recalled forty years later. Honoring the notorious Mormon's 1876 passing, a letter to the editor of the Pittsburgh Telegraph published an account of his sermon that summer day, as recalled by "Rural," who found himself seated just as "Mr. Rigdon was upon his feet and speaking."[1] The Mormon preacher, famed for being widely respected, and then for accepting Mormonism sincerely, was back in his native element. "The audience was large," Rural continues, "and he was telling a wonderful rigmarole of an eagle arising in the East and flying to the West, and of the rod of Ephraim breaking the staff of Jacob, &c., when the audience broke in with, 'Mr. Rigdon, we want to hear all about the Mormon Bible, and where Joe Smith got it." The Mormon visionary obliged. Rural recounts that he told about the "spectacles of Samuel the prophet," and described the "sword of Gideon," and that after hearing the tale, a lawyer named Potter flung a handful of shelled corn at the preacher. He continues smiling, avoiding a stone cast before him as a stumbling block. The rostrum is scattered with kernels reflecting gold, some sticking to drops of sweat and to Sidney's tattered jacket, clinging yellow to his stained breeches. Here is a great work, showing forth the folly and abominations of the Gentiles.

---

[1] Letter to Editor, 24 Aug 1876, in Vogel, *Early Mormon Documents*, vol.1:48-50.

# Epilogue   Author and Translator

THIS VOLUME HAS SURVEYED THE SCRIPTURALIZING PROCESS: HOW metatext determined the reading of text, and in so doing, generated scripture taken up by a religious movement that was itself grounded and given shape by biblical metatext. If the history seems convoluted and somewhat inside the spiral, it is because the process for making scripture is convoluted: revisions are made, metatext predate text, traditions are told often enough to become history strung along citation chains, and more revisions are made to fit the movement to contemporary notions of what it surely must've been like back then. So I have told the tale of early Mormonism in several voices: one a narrative history shot through by a critical voice scrutinizing traditions that have grown like weeds from gaps in the historical record. Rather than a tight spiral, we find a lot of play in this scripturalizing engine, room for telling other versions, creating other traditions. Here I also speak as a native Mormon, as one dissatisfied by how that identity feels, and hoping for something more pleasingly cultivated, for and by others seeking another way. Not a middle way, some false compromise between fact and falsehood; nor the lesser of two bad choices, continuing this blindness of mind and hardness of heart. Another way, following the truth as far as we have it and refusing falsehood as far as we discern it.

The Mormon religion has been proclaimed a new world religion, and this pleases both academics and native Mormons, they imagining a global church set to remake the world in its image; scholars getting on board early, setting their tracks for others to follow. Neither party has explained why Mormonism—alongside similar new religions of the book, in fact, religions like evangelical Christianity, Jehovah's Witnesses, not coincidentally built on metatext—has thrived in an age of mass (but not classical) education and cheap printing, using text-fracturing media like television and radio. Mormons see population growth as a sign of being favored of Heaven, like some corporation trumpeting another expansion into another market signaling its organizational genius and the undeniable virtues of its goods. Scholars like Rodney Stark have given supporting game-theory-like explanations, predicated on market logic, calculations of cost-benefit, and without any seeming concern about the particularities of the movement said to be the next world religion. I believe the secret of its success can be found in Restoration being attached to a new book. Rather than the more loudly proclaimed notion of Revelation, it is the discursive logic of Restoration—running on the platform of the Book of Mormon—which blew an ordinary Christian Restoration into a potential world religion. Restoration makes possible the recycling of effects of terms like *revelation*, one of which is the accumulation of power to generate metatext.

There are no simple answers to questions like, "What did they mean by *revelation?*" in part because these words worked by concealing any suggestion of defining them, doing so in a way that made their speaker seem not different from some other speaker. That is, Mormons did not begin with the notion that they were Mormons, and different; and so set about making a dictionary of uniquely Mormon terms, or interpretations of common terms. They spoke in terms common to other Christians, because before they were called Mormons, they were Christians. These terms came from the Bible, but their meanings did not. It is easy to underestimate the saturation of the Bible, as an imagined, interpreted, and often fetishized metatext, sopped upon early Mormons. It is easier even to believe that such saturation constrained them, and that they had to be *converted* to notions like continuing revelation, God the Father being separate from God the Son, Indians being the House of Israel, dispensations dividing the Bible as they divided history; the church being restored, the priesthood being given for the working of miracles. But ease of belief, unfortunately, is no sign of truth. One could speak of miracles and not mean what others meant when they said *miracles*, and the same is true of every word useful in Christianity. What has religion become, if not a registry of abstract nouns worn like brand names and logos, but not often bearing Logos? Thus many called by their enemies "Mormons" perhaps shared only a few notions among themselves, though their words sounded very much alike. And because some of them carried around a different book, and used it to summon a metatext that to non-Mormons seemed different from the Bible . . . this difference alone, it seems, earned them the derision of being "Mormons." Not surprisingly, Campbell did not intervene and clarify they were, in fact, very much still orthodox

Restorationists.

Words themselves display no preference for monogamous referentiality; neither anciently, nor today. So there's work for historians with an eye on how words are used, with what effects, and not merely content with matching up similarly looking things, or checking a dictionary for "the meaning." Once we listen a bit more carefully, we find that early Mormons were not so "Mormon" as Mormons now imagine: they spoke with terms used for centuries—restoration, covenant, dispensation—but were not always clear that they knew they meant what we think they meant. Nor that they understood one another, or thought of themselves as anything other than the Church of Christ enjoying powers not given to others. These words brought disparate readers into a group, a sect into religion, and they proceeded to construct a scripture out of so much metatext, like a lens used for bringing into focus their new text.

How does Restoration work: explaining that is the concern of this first volume. It would seem like an utterly unrelated problem to the cultural history of the Book of Mormon. Let me explain why I think otherwise, if already I have not. Restoration for four centuries has described a metatextual project: fracturing a text-metatext relationship that sustains a social fiction called scripture, obscuring its social origins. Discovering the authority of the Bible yet again, enjoying its mass circulation after the invention of moveable type printing press, the movement became an engine for metatext. Not only printed ones. In Restoration one's voice becomes scripted by text, one's thoughts very often were stitched with passages from text; names and social roles; identities broken from the text and carried about in society; disciples and apostles and church and baptism, repentance, deities, signs and miracles take on flesh and we embody metatext, where once they were but stories and words. That is the aim and effect of Restoration: it is the realization of metatext in bodies and across human relationships, over many biographies. The Word really is made real, and once real, we can look at it, and decide if we'd like to keep it around.

There is stability to the movement as a result of metatext, but also insistence, dogmatic (if implicit) creeds, often narrow ranges for interpretation of text, and reverence for scripture, though perhaps seldom read. If opened by adherents of the Restoration, they generally read to find themselves reflected back, they being first generated by the text-metatext relation itself. In a very real way, our bodies and relationships become scriptural: to that extent the scriptures themselves take on fetish qualities, not unlike desirable commodities that seem magical in the store, filling our imaginations with false idols, revealed as more junk if carted home. When Restoration is put into the modern economic and technological environment, it will fly. Give it a book to reposition itself as modern restoration distinct from others ones and you've strapped a rocket to the car.

The text fracturing dynamic that sustains a movement upon the fiction of scripture is empowered by media. What is mass media but a factory for fracturing text and recirculating its parts in the bodies of actors, to be taken up by viewers and uttered or mentioned around the office, the dinner table, pew and the classroom? When Mormon leaders distribute their sermons, faces, and voices over television, internet, and print, and then ask Mormons to recite and reread these sermons, take notes, contemplate their meaning in personal diaries, and otherwise promote the fracturing of text across genres of metatext, their words take on quasi-scriptural qualities: being reverenced, printed in vinyl and pasted onto hallways, used as book titles, and otherwise given the deference of godliness, if not the power thereof. The meaning of their words can be reduced to zero, it seems, and still some audience will regard them as scripture. For what is scripture, but the use of text to create widely circulating metatext that fracture into consumable parts? Mormon scripture is whatever text is displaced and fragmented through its culture, carried in metatext. Every scripture is this. Restoration, however, is an efficient machine for organizing otherwise exploding metatext and for exploiting the effects of their fracturing in social space. All can be said to be grounded in scripture, and indeed in a very real, if distant way there is truth in that proclamation of source. So long as we remember what we mean by *scripture*.

The history told in this volume unravels the scripturalizing process so that you might understand how it worked over a few years, from 1829 to 1832. The histories before those years extend back to Rome and forward to the death of Sidney Rigdon. They are told in narrative exposition, not critical explication. They merely frame—for native Mormons and scholars needing an introduction to "background" matters of theology and such—the chapters purposed with splitting the hemlock knots of tradition. My aim is not to replant the cleared ground with other traditions, but merely to show that many weeds, plants, and maybe a tree of life hides in the undergrowth, or may need replanting by some caring gardener in a field less crowded. Thus I have taken metatext—newspaper reports, satires, commentary; Mormon historians' versions; recollections by Mormons and Disciples involved in the events they described—and arranged them in a way that shows their interdependence. Not on historical fact, but on each other. Where they are most knitted, there we find great silences in historical materials, absences for us to fill in. By our filling in, we show what we really believe, and what we desire for our world.

Metatext create enduring structures to interpret text, and so require wide spread unraveling if we are to be rid of them. Were I to present, say, a deconstruction of Parley Pratt's *Autobiography*, many readers would point to other histories, recollections, and metatext to counter my effort. These all hang together, you see, and they surely cannot be hanged separately. They hang from each other, in a spiraling, sticky web of a non-linear process that generates and sustains scripture, like standing waves being made durable by the constant fluctuation of sound: the word made flesh, as it were. One of the striking holes in this web shows the absence of Joseph Smith in the daily life of Book of Mormon metatext.

Rather than a sign that metatext is approved by the translator, as proposed by Givens and presumed by many others, I think his absence is a space we can expand into a portrait of the Prophet and see what made him so unique, perhaps even favored by Heaven. Joseph Smith is credited with anything one desires to call Mormonism, or the Restoration, or maybe admirable charlatanry or committed self-delusion. The author of this or that, presumed to have authored scripture, or religion, or simply to have authorized the church's rituals, being a vessel of authority dispensed from on high. As a name he functions very much like the Bible. He called himself the translator of the Book of Mormon, though. Translators are very different from authors.

Who is the author of the Book of Mormon? Which one? If we, for a brief minute, pretend that the Book of Mormon is what Joseph said: a translation of an ancient record kept by Christians who fell and were destroyed by their own evil, given in warning to the inhabitants of this land so that they might show forth greater faith in the promises and wonders of a merciful god who became human, and was crucified and resurrected. Let's say it is this: who is the author? Not Joseph Smith. Not Mormon, nor Moroni. They abridged the writings of others, wrote the visions of ancients, adding commentary where appropriate. What about the source writings on the Plates of Nephi, or of Ether, or the Plates of Brass? These recorded the sermons, arguments, wars, conspiracies, wonder-working and stories told by others. Who are their authors? Back we climb, realizing that words have fragmented, being taken up as a cause or title or honor, something to fight for or about, record and preserve, summarize, mention and build another society upon. We cannot escape the text-metatext process, but we can slow it down, observe it. Maybe matured in our understanding, we might harness it and ride the spiral up, or down, or all around. First we must jettison our notion of author, authority, authorization, for these tighten the spiral and give it demonic energy.

My problem with authority remains, even if we think the Book of Mormon a pious fraud or a money-getting scheme. Who is its author, then? Not Joseph Smith, for we must speak of "influence," and skeptics look to Ethan Smith and his *View of the Hebrews*, or Solomon Spaulding's romance. Maybe Alexander Campbell or Alexander Crawford, or their words, or their ideas, or notions, or vague somethings generally described? Or notions from preachers, or rodsmen in Vermont, or magical talismans, or cunning men and hermeticists in medieval Europe. Where is the source of the fountain: the clouds, sweat pores, the riverbed, the toilet? Just so, Mormons seeking to establish the authenticity of their scripture will look to ancient Hebrew texts, or Maya sculpture, or Aztec ceremony. Who is the author of the Book of Mormon? The question makes no sense, and only gives us bad solutions: Joseph Smith, Ethan Smith, Ethan Allen; an arc of culture, a gene, meme, or a cosmic rhythm? Let us look to translators, for here we might find a stepping stone, rather than a stumbling block, to lead us out of this world authored by the Bible. They have a voice which is not monological, a single narration from nowhere, to anyone; but instead preserve another voice, speaking its meaning in a manner fashioned intentionally to reach some well considered readership.

*What is an Author*: the title of an essay by philosopher-historian Michel Foucault.[1] For those concerned with such things, this man died in the 1980s from AIDS, apparently acquired from some anonymous sexual encounter, perhaps in an underground S&M parlor, or bath house. He was a man who submitted his notions to the tests of the flesh: if he doubted the validity of sexuality to liberate us from repressed society, he proved the truth of his doubts. He also is to be regarded as something of a prophet, a seer of the recent past and of the near future, whatever you think of his sexuality, his non-politics, or his personal life. Joseph Smith is hardly a model American male, you might recall. He seems to have flouted every rule known then to be "happifying" and found in Holy Writ, and Foucault did as much in his own day.

His essay seems very nearly written for Joseph Smith and for those churchmen who'd make him the author of their religion. It begins with a brief discussion of two themes of literary criticism: writing as self-referring, and writing

---

[1] Michel Foucault, "What is an Author?" in Paul Rabinow, ed., *The Foucault Reader* (NY: Pantheon Books, 1984)

as death. The first makes critics possible and is the process that generates metatext and all the cycles and dimensions diagrammed in Figure 1. By being self-referring, a text can be opened to questions of "influence," what brought it about, and what it brings out later. The second theme, writing as death, is an old one that Foucault himself exemplified in a tragic way: the author seeks to live by dying in the writing, thus securing immortality in word. Like an ancient Greek hero whose deeds are preserved in epics, he wanders among the shades in a sort of half-living. Literary types have spoken of the "death of the author" for at least a century, and find in James Joyce's *Ulysses* the epic anti-hero and the dying author. The author as narrator disappears in his epic and readers are left with a "stream of consciousness," but not of the author's mind; of the characters he has made to live and let run in Dublin for a day. Joyce lives through that book and in metatext created by critics, popular cultural references and allusions, and inside the minds of readers, and at times in their flesh. It was said that Samuel Beckett wore Joyce's shoe size, but not merely to honor the blind seer; nor were his feet fitted to so small a shoe.

When we speak of the "death of the author" we do not mean machines will be making text and stories and such; only that the "narrator" aspect of the author, telling a tale from one perspective—that this way of telling tales has been overcome. Think of it like the literary version of lopping off the king's head and giving power to the people; or cutting up the Bible into source texts, each more doubtful for being sourced to imaginary authors and ages, fragments of Sumerian hymns mistranslated by Babylonian scribes, and badly rendered into Hebrew but beautifully into English. Or God turning over his Kingdom to creations given inalienable agency to make or destroy. Read *Ulysses* and you'll understand how creative the technique of telling a tale without an author can be; or think of a "movement" that emerges without a leader; or imagine, silly spontaneous dancing in the street making its own music as the dancers' feet strike the pavement. Such things are seldom found, but more readily created in words on a page.

So, the author is dead, critics have said. We have not realized the benefits or implications of this death, however. Foucault names two causes for our failure to see what we have killed; to collect, as it were, our plates of brass from his treasury. First, the "idea of work," that is, of the author's body of work. "Even when an individual has been accepted as an author," Foucault writes, "we must still ask whether everything he wrote, said, or left behind is part of his work" (103). What of shopping lists, personal jottings, preliminary drafts, correspondence, childhood scrawls? Are these of the "work"? "How can we define a work amid the millions of traces left by someone after his death?" Foucault asks, and concludes that "A theory of the work does not exist, and the empirical task of those who naively undertake the editing of works often suffers in the absence of such a theory" (104). For an example we need only look to *The Joseph Smith Papers*. The volumes thus far published include previously published texts, diaries (written in another hand), and Revelation Books containing texts not certainly attributed to Joseph Smith. What about diaries recording his sermons? Rumors about him? Words attributed to him, but saying things we doubt he said? Retrospectively constructed as the Mormon Author, all others have become his scribes. When we read of a revelation or prophecy to Oliver Cowdery, said to record the words of Jesus Christ, in the *Papers* volume, it is because Oliver is regarded by Mormons as a scribe, writing the words of the author Joseph Smith. It is not difficult to see that we are assured of overestimating the number of works credited to Smith and to misattribute texts created by others regarded as scribes.

Even though Smith was a translator and his revelations record the words of gods or angels, and he is dead; he is treated in a manner that literary critics and historians have treated the author. A creator of a body of work: and so long as we have no theory of "work," we rely on folk notions to find authorship in this or that text, but not in that one, nor that other one. In Mormonism it has resulted in a religion supposedly authored by Joseph Smith, every text regarded as authoritative being sourced to his mind, or mouth, or genius. The truth is we often work in reverse, locating in Smith what we'd like to call our religion. We find ourselves with a "prophet puzzle," created mostly by our own myth-making confusions, and traditions of an author's work.

The second notion blinding us from realizing the benefits of the death of the author is "writing," which "seems to transpose the empirical characteristics of the author into a transcendental anonymity" (104). In the case of Joseph Smith, that anonymity has been converted into a corporate religion, which acts from his supposed claims to have seen gods, and to have received authority from them to perform the rites and make the promises offered by the LDS Church. What Foucault means is something like this, I suppose, but not exactly the same. The character of the author disappears in the "writing," and is thought to be hidden behind his or her words; latent, and brought forward by knowing critics, priests, or scholars. Thus the author becomes the writing itself, and this is a problem. Rather than securing its death, writing so conceived "runs the risk of maintaining the author's privileges under the protection of writing's *a priori* status: it keeps alive, in the gray light of neutralization, the interplay of those representations that formed a particular image of the author" (105). Rather than lament or proclaim the author's death, and preserve artifacts made when the author was very much thought to dominate his world (a "Work" and its "Writing"), Foucault suggests we "must locate the space left empty by the author's disappearance, follow the distribution of gaps and breaches, and watch for the openings that this disappearance uncovers" (105). The "watch for openings" is my concern, for reasons Foucault suggests: there are traditions which can be expanded with a slender wedge inserted into the slightest gap, like Joseph's use of a corndodger for a wedge and a pumpkin for a beadle, to their breaking. There is no other way to split hemlock, and although no saint, Foucault gives us a very sharp wedge to use on the author. It may take a few tries, but we will split it.

Rather than concerning myself with authors like a literary critic might, I have instead taken on the Work and Writing of a religion, one said to be authorized by Joseph Smith, his book and his god. A new scripture generated these forces of authorship under the cover of Restoration. As with Joseph Smith, the author's name functions in ways that other names do not, "it is the equivalent of a description" (105), Foucault writes, something which organizes (like metatext) genres, histories, markets, priesthoods, schools of study, even education regimes. The name does this by establishing "a relationship of homogeneity, filiation, authentication of some texts by the use of others, reciprocal explication, or concomitant utilization," further providing cues for addresses as readers, to receive authored texts in a manner that bestows and spreads cultural status or "capital" (107). Restoration invokes the Bible as Author, unifying readings of metatext under a single voice. Once christened into a movement—say, Mormonism—that voice can be delivered by messengers, debated in its claims, and converted to. Voicing of a non-human agent, a religion restored, is traced in the next volume.

Further specificity of the ways a name works also leads Foucault into speaking of the "author function," of the things that an author accomplishes which other mere writers do not. He takes a brief tour through the history of authorship, of rights of authors and publisher relations. These legal realities began in earnest when copyright was instituted, primarily to punish authors who transgressed political and religious boundaries, and to reward those who did not. Yet not all texts require authors. Foucault notes that the "author function" indeed varies in time. Some centuries require authors of scientific text, but by the 17th century authors are more relevant as an organizing function in the genres of poetry or the novel (109). The Reformation did much to make this function, in these genres, secured for centuries. Authors also allow for cultures to project their notions onto the imagined soul, psyche, or biography of the author, as when

Joseph Smith is psychobiographed by Fawn Brodie and others, in effect writing him into "the operations that we force texts to undergo" (110). Finally, the author is fragmented, as any scripture is, into many selves. These voices are gathered and collected into the author by those who psychologize it, edit and compile collected writings or works, and establish metatextual economies (such as literary schools, dictionaries, guides, curriculum, adaptations of work, and so on). *The Joseph Smith Papers* should be sufficiently descriptive to tell us that the author function applies to more than literary works.

This attempt to create and sustain the author in the face of its death, Foucault traces to the Catholic arguments over canonicity of texts, a process "trying to prove the value of a text by its author's saintliness" (110). Saint Jerome developed four criteria for deciding authentic texts from pseudepigraphal ones, and his methods define the author as "a constant level of value," (meaning inferior texts are considered doubtful); "a field of conceptual or theoretical coherence" (thus contradictory texts are eliminated); stylistic unity is imposed by excluding those which seem extraordinary, and texts with passages quoting statements or mentioning events after the death of the author are regarded as spurious, basically giving us an author "as a historical figure" crisscrossed by contemporaneous texts, but incapable of foresight or prophecy (111). Entire institutions and juridical systems develop as they create authors in circular ways, and a church is just one of many institutions that control, disseminate, and make possible the creation and circulation of metatext. It is also a thing one can voice, a sort of author of you.

One of the more potent practices that come of institutions ostensibly built on founders like Marx, Freud, Calvin and Joseph Smith is "the inevitable necessity, within these fields of discursivity, for a 'return to the origin.' This return, which is part of the discursive field itself, never stops modifying it" (116). Rather than adding to the metatextual domain, such returns end up "transforming the discursive practice itself" (116). What we've seen in this volume, and will track over the next two volumes, is this seeking a return to the origin: first to Christian origins, and then, as we'll see, a desire to get back to the early days of Mormonism before it became supposedly polluted by movements and philosophies "outside" the culture. The reality, then, is quite different from the myth of Restoration: Mormonism is the effect of a seeking to return to the origins of the Christian Church, but that was no historicizing effort. It refashioned and aggregated metatext Bibles, and reconfigured them to run like a dynamo, possessing readers as it fueled a movement using the Book of Mormon's potency.

What Foucault advocates as a possible strategy for dealing with our inheritances of Catholic canonization of texts, and the author functions that resulted in and were generated by the New Testament, are of considerable interest, but this page is not the place to explore them. He closes with great insight, and we should listen in: the author (think of Joseph Smith as we imagine him; or the Bible as Restorationists speak of and use it) is sustained, culturally, historically, and institutionally as our solution to the question: "How can one reduce the great peril, the great danger with which fiction threatens our world?" (118). By fiction he does not mean what that term has come to mean: he means, I suppose, something like that which we create, but not as authors; as channels or fountains for the flow of a rushing water. Here we approach the fountain, these translators acting as channels.

> We are used to thinking that the author is so different from all other men, and so transcendent with regard to all languages that, as soon as he speaks, meaning beings to proliferate, to proliferate indefinitely. The truth is quite the contrary: the author is not an indefinite source of significations which fill a work; the author does not precede the works; he is a certain functional principle by which, in our culture, one limits, excludes, and chooses; in short, by which one impedes the free circulation, the free manipulation, the free composition, decomposition, and recomposition of fiction (118-119).

Were we really cognizant of the implications of the death of the author, we would, Foucault concludes, no longer hear bad questions like, "Who really spoke? Is it really he and not someone else? With what authenticity or originality? And what part of his deepest self did he express in his discourse?" (119). Instead we would create our own tales, but not any for owning by individuals, nor for institutions to build upon. Tales to tie to other tales, like lives spread across time and space, encouraging a proliferation of meaning. What would Mormonism be without the function of Joseph Smith (the name), without making him or the Bible the authority for all that is said be Restored and Mormon? Rather than build a machine fabricating his name and punching it helter-skelter like a brand to proclaim some quality of a text (its revelatory nature, its veracity, genealogy), we might come to occupy in our tales the positions his creation has made possible. That is, we might come to be like Enoch the scribe, sitting in Heaven, writing a story; and Enoch who returns to the story he once told to Noah before the fountains of the deep were unlocked; entering the tale of a translated being and begin proliferating meaning across many worlds.

What is a scribe? What is a translator? These are the sorts of questions we must answer—with an eye on social effects—if we hope to understand Joseph Smith, as a person creating something, and not as an author or authority of some work or movement. The movement created him in the image of the Restorationist's Bible, a single narrator directing all things, it would have us believe; attributing to him all that is regarded as essentially powerful or divine, whatever the facts say about these attributions. The Book of Mormon as they saw it merely secured this possession of theirs. Joseph Smith the person was a translator, though. How does that differ from an author? One cannot seek for the origins of the Book of Mormon in the mind of Joseph Smith, nor hope to recover the "real" meaning of some passage by a return to the origin. These are quests undertaken with an author, not a translator. Translators move a text from here to there, from a cave to a printing press. One might seek the cave, and you'll find another translator-translation, and so on, forever. Translators give us their voices while preserving something from the voice of another.

Look not merely back but also to the future to understand a translator. Joseph as translator (or Mormon, or Moroni) takes no dominant position over the narrative, but instead seeks to move its meaning from one domain into another, in some way accomplishing two ends: preservation of meaning across domains; and making intelligible to readers the difference in meaning between the matrix domain and the receiving domain. His is a work of dialogical revelation, as Bakhtin might say. We know we cannot read the Book of Mormon as written by God, because it says it is not, and is a weak thing with many errors. He does not ventriloquate God, but Joseph does claim to translate the words of many men, turtles on the backs of turtles, so the old saying put it. We cannot hope to recover the original, because there is no such thing, only more descriptions of ideas and words of others, themselves never without error. There is no pure Mormon scripture: they are human writings; which realization ought to make us very different from Fundamentalists reading The Scriptures.

Why is this translator's difficult task more dangerous and honest—but more highly regarded—than the author's? By translating he conveys to the receiving domain (1830s America) a sign of their difference from some other way, preserved in the matrix domain (Book of Mormon world). That is, both worlds are shown to require translation, and are shown to be somewhat arbitrarily constructed. Humility and hope should follow from this realization. Consciousness may even grow inside us, as the narrator gives way to the readers, leaving it to them to make of scripture what they will. They are invited into the spiral, rather than taken up like a Dorothy in Kansas. What is the meaning of the poem by Robert Frost I've included in this volume's introduction? Would not it seem absurd to look for that font in order to understand the poem? Or to find what influenced Frost or to get at his psychological state when it was written? Poetry is the most honest of the genres, for it demands the reader to take of its matter and organize it into a world. If they let the matter sit, sit it will. The author tells us, by contrast, that *this* is the meaning, and that it is wrong to say otherwise. Embodied in names, the author as a social function organizes metatext and obviously never hears us, that we say he or she created all these proliferating texts. Sometimes wondering why they did so. The author sits accursed; overlooking a world created on his behalf, in his name, but not really by him. Joseph Smith is the author for Mormons, as much as the Bible is for Restorationists who take of it and give to their congregations.

Translators are more like poets: they show us one thing, and then another we claim as our own: language, culture, religion, etc. They bridge the poetry composed by a poet and interpreted by a reader. Continuity of meaning can be by the translator's hand, then, made to cross these borders; so we may discern that borders do indeed mark real differences between domains. But the borders of a good translation do not block our movements. These differences between domains cannot be recovered nor erased by further searching the fields, minds, mountains, or influences conceived in these domains. They simply are, and so can be understood.

Once realized—this gap between a foreign world and their own— recipients may seek to create, rather than merely receive, a world; if it was this way then, and differs now, why couldn't it be different in the future? This happened for early disciples when they were translated into Mormons, and the bible world they delivered remains with us today. Another world can be created, and it is one that I believe Joseph Smith had hoped might come to be. In this world, power is not a domination of one being over another, but the source of the creation of fiction: of the translation from one domain to another without end. Mormons are well prepared, I think. There are no books written by God that the Book of Mormon promises us. Instead, we have prophecies about translations: the Plates of Brass, the Book of the Lamb, the Plates of Nephi. That means translators, texts no longer readable but reshaped for our minds. These are the means of restoration of the House of Israel. We do not have these texts, apparently. I doubt any translations will be done until there are readers capable of treating them as translations, and refusing to make of them catapults for restoring ancient Jaredite religion or waging Enochian politics. We must read texts like the Book of Mormon in the same way we read poetry: to inspire imagination, and that is not necessarily different from discovering truth. Over the next volumes I will show that we always have read it that way, but our notion of Restoration has blinded our minds into searching for some past perfection to remake, as though in the past these souls sought for a past perfection to remake. If they did, they failed, for we are not it.

The Bible obtained its power over imagination and then the flesh, I suppose, by virtue of the god whose story it partially tells. J.R.R. Tolkien's essay, "On Fairy Stories" describes how this process works: how a story becomes real and not just hoped-for, nor pretending-to-be; but really, actually, real. I do not mean by this statement the dressing up of men like they imagine Hobbits, Elves, Hamlet, Apostles and Disciples. Not mere costuming, staging, and reciting; but the fragmenting of their potency, of their qualities through culture and over history. When created carefully—often through a sort of death of the writer-as-translator—such fictions can be fractured and taken up, inhabited by actual humans, maybe even the gods. Are they to be regarded as fictions, then? Such true creations are seldom seen, obviously. The last world was generated by the Bible. Other candidates for world-making have been pointed to: Shakespeare's effort has endured and continues to unfold in our lives. Even Tolkien's world may yet unfold new vistas for our own, as we find in his tale "Leaf by Niggle." It can be done again, I suppose, this opening of faery. Real changes are necessary, though. Authors are one problem. Our notion of fiction is another. Both Bakhtin and Peirce recognized that fiction cannot be distinguished from non-fiction, except by arbitrarily imposed assumptions and the prejudices of personal experience. The Book of Mormon is fiction? Depends on what you mean by fiction. It is not a genre, I think; but a translation of a historical record that someone actually composed from other writings. It has expanded in the world of the Bible, though. It has reached the limits of that framework, and so remains bound in our categories of fiction and fact. Rather than explode that world, the Book of Mormon now appears to support it from collapsing under the weight of historical criticism, and from falling into a vacuum, suffering the fate of many gods, namely, being ignored.

After W.W. Phelps demanded Joseph Smith's rewrite of the Bible, which he hoped to include with the volume bound to the Book of Mormon, Smith wrote to Phelps and explained his reluctance.[1]  The letter is full of discontent.  Smith seems troubled by the reports of the "deciples," that "the Devel had been to work with all his inventive immagination to reward us for our toils in travling from this country [Kirtland] to Zion [Missouri]," leaving their families to be tended by "brethren who you know sometimes are found to be unstable, unbelieving, unmerciful & unkind" (271).  Discord again strained the Ohio disciples' bonds of love toward the New York saints who'd landed in Zion, accusations of every vice flying eastward and westward.  The poor inspired to leave Ohio were gathering to Zion, but Phelps complained that "there have already too many deciples arived there for the means," to which Joseph responded, "your own wickedness hedge up your own ways, you suffer your children; your ignorant & unstable Sisters & weak members who are acquainted with your evil hearts of unbelief," for many have written "wicked and discouraging letters to there reletives who have a zeal but [not] according to knowledge and prophecy falsely" (273).  He answers Phelps's request, "concerning the translation" of the Bible, thus: "I inform you that they will not go from my hand during my natural life for correction, revisal or printing and the will of the Lord be done" (273).  Despite this explicit warning, later LDS historians would write, "it is clear that as early as 1832 Smith already had a keen eye toward the eventual publication of the manuscripts," a desire they discern from, and I'm not making this up, the nature and color of pencil markings on the various pages of Smith's Cooperstown Bible.[2]  Smith has been translated into the Bible, even though he refused to hand over his translation of it.  Phelps proceeded to plan for the translation's publication, regardless of the translator's warning; and for its binding to the Book of Mormon.  His project finally ended in fire as a gang destroyed the building only days before the planned printing was to commence.

What is an author?  An old question once asked, "What is Torah?  It is: the interpretation of Torah," plainly telling that scripture—like law—is a relation between text and metatext.[3]  What is an author?  It is the translation of authority, the taking of a name to make an institution that secures an enduring production of metatext.  Authors imagine they can give monologues, inject their own voices straight into readers' brains.  Having read enough from students and heard from the few who read my work, I no longer subscribe to this foolish vision.  Indeed,

---

[1] Smith to Phelps, 31 July 1831.  In Dean Jessee, ed., *The Personal Writings of Joseph Smith* (SLC: Deseret Book, 1994), 269-276
[2] Paul Lambert and Thomas Wayment, "The Nature of the Pen and Pencil Markings in the New Testament of Joseph Smith's New Translation of the Bible," BYU Studies 47, no.2
[3] Wilfred C. Smith, *What is Scripture? A Comparative Approach* (Fortress Press, 1993), 116

some of the writings of Joseph Smith would suggest that the sin of unrighteous dominion could be charged to authors who would feign control a text and impose a single voice upon it. Dialogical voicing is less sure and more like the work of a translator.[1]    Admitting to what Peirce called "fallibilism"—the principle that our declarations are provisional—translations are judged by what they do with matrix text, for some other readers. A translation is only to be accepted in some always-future judgment. Smith took up the voices of others, but did not speak over them, nor simply let a "thousand flowers bloom," abdicating his stewardship for the reign of whatever, anomie, chaos, nonsense. *What is a translator?* It is the death of the author at the threshold between two worlds. That death makes possible the proliferation of meaning across worlds and the intercourse of those who inhabit them. This history now turns to hear the many voices Smith's translation has begotten in a newly opened world. It follows their unceasing translation—from text into metatext, word into flesh, biography into institution—of the Bible into the world of the Book of Mormon; a misunderstanding of authorship Restorationists have insisted on cultivating for nearly two centuries, while waving from Mount Zion the standard of Mormon.

---

[1] Although given more detailed review in later volumes, Bakhtin's theories should be mentioned here. For a summary of them, see Michael Holquist, *Dialogism: Bakhtin and His World* (2d ed., NY: Routledge, 2002). Bakhtin developed his theories of "polyphonism" and voicing, chronotopes and more over many essays, including those found in his *Problems of Dostoevsky's Poetics* (edited and translated by Caryl Emerson, Minneapolois: U Minnesota Press, 1984); *The Dialogic Imagination: Four Essays* (Michael Holquist, ed., Caryl Emerson and Holquist, trans., U Texas Press, 1981); *Speech Genres and Other Late Essays* (Emerson and Holquist, ed., Vern W. McGee, trans. U Texas Press, 1986). His theories are derived from the study of literature and philosophy (Marxism and Kant), and though suffering from being developed before the refinements in the study of language were made after the 1960s, their originality has not dulled, if in need of a little polish.

SCRIPTURALIZING PROCESS

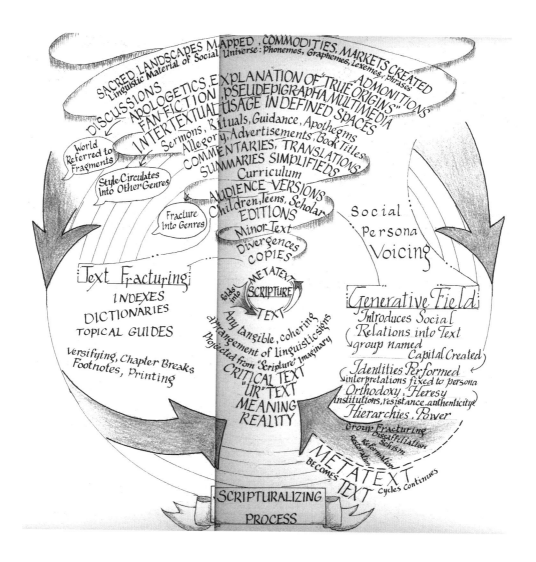

READERS should begin at the hole in the center of the word SCRIP ¤ TURE. (They may also turn to the two-page illustration at the beginning of this book.) What is scripture is a matter now being given serious thought outside the traditions that scripture itself has generated. That is, rather than explain scripture from some tradition that builds metatext into its answer—something like explanations based on speech genres, as in, "scripture is the Word of God given to Man," or, "scriptures are folktales used by Man to control people"—we ought to see that scripture is a folk notion. It is not an analytical one. What is scripture? It is a relationship between text and metatext, and a very unique one: between them some power is corralled and generates all that is diagrammed in the upward expanding spiral given above METATEXT. The downward spiral is also blown from its engine. That spiraling up and down describes the SCRIPTURALIZING PROCESS, which to think of properly should be envisioned as stabilizing TEXT-METATEXT as much as it is generated by that relationship. Underneath TEXT you will find what scripture-readers seek for, in their reading of so much METATEXT: the original meaning, the ur-text, the critical edition, what the author or God really meant, even some magic powers to be gained by having the true, original, or authentic reading at last. Restorationists seek here for "original" forms, and to use them to map various landscapes—biographical, somatic, social, geographical—of readers. It is important we don't limit our notion of TEXT and METATEXT to things composed in words and letters. If one's congregation takes up the titles, phrases, social roles and speech styles found in some TEXT, then that congregation *is* METATEXT. They may generate written commentary, but that does not make them more METATEXT than before.

This first volume is mostly concerned with Restoration efforts to find in the Bible the Old Time Religion, and the next volume watches them map that religion onto the pages of the Book of Mormon and onto the bodies and biographies of readers of that SCRIPTURE. This brings up the question: What is the Book of Mormon? Do you mean the 1830 edition, the 1837 edition, the 1981 version, or the oral text spoken by Joseph Smith so long ago, or the pile of plates "having the appearance of gold" said to be buried in the Americas somewhere? Or is it the meaning of these things, what someone interprets them to say about life, liberty, and the pursuit of salvation? The TEXT- METATEXT relationship unfolds the folk term SCRIPTURE, making it suitable for analysis; freeing us from folk questions. When realized, we see we are really dealing with tornados when we hear believers speak of The Scriptures.

Maybe you want to get at "what it really means" by seeking some more original text? You merely follow projections from a "scripture imaginary" to a false foundation, deceived into thinking you might no longer be dealing with signs needing interpretation, but actually are at reality that interprets itself. Your endless search underwrites the upward spiral of METATEXT, telling us what TEXT means, and what sorts of people know such things. The Book of Mormon is SCRIPTURE, then, and neither exclusively TEXT nor METATEXT. That is, the phrase-title names a relationship, stabilizing it for some readership between these two levels of text.

The stream of sound is, in a most basic way, broken into characters printed in ink on a page. Without this basic fracturing by transcription and, in the modern era, in publication, TEXT cannot generate social movements. This *Text Fracturing* creates stable METATEXT which are, as we move "upward," linked to communities of interpretation and circulation. Copies of a text are the most stabilizing of METATEXT, giving the appearance of a single work carrying some single meaning to be interpreted correctly by readers of dispersed copies of TEXT. Their interpretations are not copies, however. Upward from that disjuncture of form and interpretation, we find minor errors in copies, and then named editions: the 1830, the Nauvoo, etc. *Text Fracturing* also occurs in the creation of dictionaries and encyclopedia which cut up phrases and re-arrange them according to alphabetized nouns; by indexes to break some word or phrase from sentence context and mark it as important enough to be listed and given a page reference; in topical guides that label parts of the text and refer to it. These and other subtle fracturing can be seen in Book of Mormon editions, as verse numbers were introduced in 1879, allowing TEXT to be referred to in fragmentary patches; in chapter introductions brought inside TEXT; as footnotes divide up narrative and tie it to other TEXT. Thus the KJV Bible became METATEXT for the Book of Mormon, and vice versa. Volume Two traces how "Mormonism" was built from this relationship.

Moving upward, after editions and copies circulate, the groundwork for a social imaginary has formed. Here we find *Audience Versions*, explicit editions for teens, children, missionaries, parents, scholars, students, and so forth. Assumptions about the respective reader's psychology, purposes for use, and market presence filter into METATEXT at this point. Volume Three mostly takes up the history of these editions and the social realities they create, and explains the ways that markets shape METATEXT. With these *Versions* we have ventured into social space. The spiral thus generates another dimension, labelled "Social Persona, Voicing" and marked with an arrow to the box identified as "Generative Field."

Social relations are here introduced into readings of text, proliferating METATEXT and linking them to roles and identities. Thus, priests to interpret the TEXT by creating METATEXT arise, or preachers and teachers to find believers in it. Here again we see METATEXT describing more than "words on a page," but also one's "state of mind" as a "believer" in something about TEXT (it being "true," for example). A group may congregate under a name (perhaps taken from TEXT), and membership in it encourages the creation of cultural capital (carried in one's body, voice or biography). Really the focus of Volume Three, cultural capital is distributed in notions of "worthiness" or "power" and so on. It is used to rank members according to a hierarchy loosely anchored in TEXT. While this first volume traces the initial movement from Restorationists to Mormons, the second volume treats the Generative Field in greater detail, reconstructing how LDS apostles first circulated METATEXT pamphlets that were later voiced by dlders delivering a "message" enunciating "Mormonism." Those at the "top" of the field, like apostles, are typically also those who create METATEXT circulated in the voices of lower ranked members; or, when you find yourself voicing another's words, consider yourself their possession. At some point, to return to generalities, they and their followers tend to collapse METATEXT into TEXT, just as authoritative voices find their way into mouths of adherents. Very often some schism will attend this substitution or collapse. Priestly or apostolic METATEXT may become new SCRIPTURE for some new movement or rising generation, and the SCRIPTURALIZING PROCESS continues to spiral upward and downward. Volume Three further explores how capital is created in this Field, and identities are performed, with hierarchies expanding; heresy becoming possible, and movements speaking of Reformation, Correlation and Restoration abound. These social relations are created by and creative of METATEXT, but are bound to TEXT in such ways as to give us SCRIPTURE.

It is important to keep in mind that METATEXT exist only in as much as TEXT exist to speak about, to comment upon, or otherwise report, explain, or expand. Thus, much of the reverence granted SCRIPTURE may bleed into other METATEXT, and these may take on almost a quasi-scriptural quality, being regarded as worth preserving, studying, and commenting upon, perhaps even starting a new movement for these purposes. For example, a sermon by Joseph Smith or Brigham Young or Orson Pratt expounding upon the Book of Mormon (and thus its METATEXT) may take on almost canonical reverence, being bound in leather, published in critical editions, enjoying scholarly commentary and priestly advocacy. The process is not one way, but is a spiral, generative of social imaginaries or "faith communities," (i.e., cultures). At any point some METATEXT can become the TEXT that becomes SCRIPTURE for some new group.

If we follow METATEXT upward, past the spin-off Generative Field, we find fragmentation of various kinds. METATEXT fragment into speech genres: first with *Audience Versions*, and then into sermons, prayers, liturgy, translations, simplifications, commentary, curriculum, and other genres bound to speech events where a specific audience hears and recirculates METATEXT. Listeners may return home and record in diaries and journals what they learned from a sermon, or experienced in a ritual, or doubted about a lesson. METATEXT further fragments into reported speech, as "Intertextual Usage In Defined Spaces" begins to link phrases, terms, and styles with audience identities. For example, LDS teenagers are asked to memorize passages from the Book of Mormon, and to "apply" these stripped-out sayings "to their daily lives," in effect using the TEXT as a prospective map for one's biography or body. Rankings of good and bad sorts of persons are re-introduced into TEXT by such METATEXT, allowing reader identification with textual characters, and textual characterizations to form into social stereotypes. One may call another group "Lamanite" or "Zoramite," or a person "Korihor," presupposing one's interlocutor is familiar enough with TEXT to link the name to circulationg stereotypes and apply them to living persons. (The Generative Field should not be viewed as distinct from rising spiral, so much as another dimension of it; a sort of fractal image of ongoing processes). TEXT is further fractured into quotes stripped from and recited in sermons, for instance. Phrases may be used for book titles or for advertising commodities, or memorized and given as apothegms of wisdom or to "inspire" people. This level fractures words, phrases, styles and "forms" from TEXT and locates them inside other institutions, like schools, churches, shops, hospitals, and government facilities.

Stylistic features most prominent in TEXT—and distinct from common, "unmarked" speech—may also give rise to METATEXT and social roles. For instance, sermons that take on "thee" and "thou" or grammatical endings like say–eth and did-st; or familiar phrases like "It came to pass" are used to sell BYU Football tickets; sometimes for ironic effect by juxtaposition, or for poking fun at

TEXT ("And it came to pass that I, Daymon, being of goodly parents, beseech thee to partake of this donut"). This is the sort of thing that gave us the early satires on the Gold Bible. As stylistic fracturing occurs, then, TEXT can be exposed to oblique criticism by ironic tropes, or mocking use of its phrases, style, or perhaps "archaic" language. Here undercurrents of discontent are stirred by TEXT itself, as it fractures throughout society, and is taken up by figures who appear to use TEXT for purposes other than those it is read, by someone, as God originally intended. One might write a salesman's manual using the Book of Mormon as a guide text, or management potboiler, or some diet plan. Such METATEXT opens TEXT up for alternative readings, challenges, criticism. Others may write fan fiction using markers of style, building plot outward from proper names, and start a movement, becoming its authoritative leader. While Volume Two watches Mormons build maps that link the Book of Mormon to the Bible narrative, Volume Three tracks how the Book of Mormon was employed to generate social landscapes. These further intergrate TEXT with dependent but socially implicated METATEXT, as bodies, biographies, markets and books increasingly mingle.

As we move upward into METATEXT we find further fracturing, as the world referred to by TEXT has been sufficiently distributed through a culture by virtue of METATEXT. Thus, the world of the Nephites can be re-imagined in fan fiction, its authors writing "pseudepigrapha"; computer games created that explore the world of Zarahemla; lucrative sentimental or scoffing musicals created, plays adapted, and television shows piloted. Even amusement parks may be constructed, and tours of sacred sites conducted as landscape takes on things referred to in TEXT. Obviously, a market has been created in these imaginings, and the market is not without effects on TEXT. Where tourists can be taken, safely, comfortably and profitably, for example, may also provide us tours of places said to be found in the pages of the Book of Mormon. Thus, there are no tours of "Book of Mormon Lands" conducted in San Francisco, California, nor in the Atacama desert of Chile, or the jungles of Panama. One can find tours of various Mexican locales already prepared with an infrastructure for American tourists and profitably conducted. Not surprisingly, further TEXT fracturing occurs as markets gather to organize TEXT by METATEXT that conform to the logic of capitalism.

After the world referred to by the text has fragmented into commodities, tours, computer games, musicals, jewelry, teddy bears, and so much religious kitsch, then we find emerging scholars of varying intellect who find a niche in a division of labor, spending their minds on the world imagined in the text. Thus, Mormon archaeologists show up with funding sufficient to conduct extended digs, organize conferences and publish journals. Critics of TEXT also emerge to challenge the claims (METATEXT) made by scholars and apologists. More METATEXT results, as do more ways of "being" involved with the scripture: as a believer, skeptic, reader of it as "literature," literalist, fundamentalist, aphorist, and so forth. Historians may come along and explain the "origins" or "influences" of some thing or another on the SCRIPTURE. These are identities (social roles) tied to the way TEXT-METATEXT can be recalibrated by a Generative Field and to the capital to be claimed, created, and destroyed by those inhabiting some field. For example, one may be an instructor of history at Brigham Young University and write books about how LDS Church structure is found in the pages of the Book of Mormon, or is not. Or that Maya DNA matches Jewish DNA, or does not. Or that some stele shows a scene depicted in TEXT. Critics and doubters may respond, and in their responses they also create hierarchies, orthodoxies, heretics and so forth, in a "secular" posture.

Finally, at the top of the page, we reach the utter limit of fragmentation of TEXT, as it becomes so general as to be knit into the world itself: our phrases, our notions of good and evil, jurisprudence, economy, politics, diets, fashions, sexual habits, growth and maturation rates, language, celebrity, sport, and on and on. Here METATEXT has simply become common, daily life, as Christians or Muslims or Jews gather to this or that land, and make calendars and governments and so much from TEXT that becomes "normal" and taken for granted. The scripture called "The Bible" has faded into and become just such a reality, although, obviously there is some book we insist really is the Bible. Where does it stop, though? Surely not at the page's end. Thus, many imagine foolishly that if they reject the Bible and become atheists, they are no longer bound into that bible world. But in their reaction they continue the cycle marked by the Generative Field, and more often than not simply replace one scripture for another; say, Darwin's *Origin of Species*, or something by Richard Dawkins, or Stephen Hawking. Copies circulate, priests emerge, METATEXT circulate, and heresies and orthodoxies established and re-established, spiraling upward and downward through culture-history. If one imagines stepping out from the scripture of the Bible, one is deceived: it cannot be done, for even your notions of freedom, liberation, and "breaking away" were constructed by that scripture. Bodies, biographies, social relations, landscapes, and much else is METATEXT to it, and these are less easily doubted than TEXT. No addition of METATEXT or TEXT is sufficient to stop the spiral, so that you can get off. What must be thought out, however, is how to use the process of scripture-making to create a world we'd prefer, rather than one merely inherited from ancestors, fallible humans, often foolish and wicked on bad days, cat scratch crazy for weeks at a time.

The process that generates SCRIPTURE is given extra oomph under the practices of Restoration. As we see in this volume, that term translates METATEXT into social realities, making, as it were, the Word flesh. Restoration can be understood as collapsing METATEXT into some imagined text (e.g., what the Bible originally meant). It then advocates the uptake of fragments broken from METATEXT into one's own life: becoming a disciple, practicing biblical baptism, dietary laws, and so forth. It is an implicit theory of scripture, but rather than write a book about it, its practioners embody it.

Rather than Reformation, or its slyer sister Restoration, we need a new book to behold, and to reorient ourselves upon: where rather than spinning so many yarns to bind others with, our yarns weave tapestries and carpets, tapa cloth, harps, and many happy evenings where truth, lands, ourselves, and a good story are at-one. The history I give in these volumes, starting with this one before you, is what I believe can provide greater consciousness of the scriptural spiral. With keener consciousness one might work more carefully inside that whirlwind, rather than simply spin with it. Just as a theory of gravity does not immediately provide for one's escape, however, neither does the diagram, history, and raised consciousness—together a waking up to the mesmerizing spiral, or a turning away from some ancient column of fire—these do not immediately provide escape from its dizzying spin. Having a theory of gravity, however, leads to its testing by practical means. After a few centuries, we learn how to escape earth's gravity, and not merely temporarily as when we leap in the air and fall again to the ground. Rather than leap and find ourselves falling on others attempting a leap, often from swampy ground, shifting sands, and criss-crossing conveyor belts, we might someday escape from the gravity of the Bible. It will still be there, of course, but distant and observed. I suspect, however, this will only occur when we've done the math, built the parts, trained some astronauts and aimed ourselves at a glowing orb in the Heavens. We need, in other words, something to aim at; where we can set our minds on ground not spinning around so many scriptures, priesthoods, orthodoxies, pain, sacrifice, violence, money, kitsch and meaningless identity politics. It can be done: for it was done long ago when scholars and priests made the stuff that became our bibles. A thousand years after they worked, other scholars and priests made SCRIPTURE central to their political and economic

Reformation, thence to our modern world where the bible has fractured into all of us. When we read the Book of Mormon, it is with its long fingers pointing the way through, and sometimes obscuring, its TEXT.

- 307 -

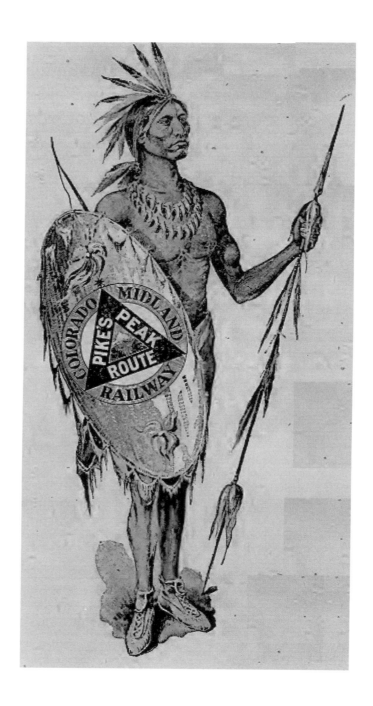

- 309 -

# As If You Care . . .

THE AUTHOR somehow got a PhD from the University of Pennsylvania by writing a (longish) dissertation on the history of language use in Mormonism. It begins in the 1880s anti-polygamy raids of the Mormon Underground, surveys the fractures of the modern church, ending in a history and analysis of the Priesthood Correlation program. This work, *The Last shall be First and the First shall be Last: Discourse and Mormon History* (2007) is further explored in an award-winning series on the LDS blog, ByCommonConsent.org. Copies of the dissertation can be downloaded there. Yes, for free. He has since published *The Book of Mammon: A book about a book about the corporation that owns the Mormons* (2010). The basis of award-winning podcasts for MormonStories.org, the "cross-genre" book has been called "awesome" and "awful" (by the same reader). It draws on his (brief) employment in the bizarre cubicle world that is LDS Church corporate headquarters.

Daymon's strange *The Abridging Works* (2012) presents the Book of Mormon in a reader-friendly sequence he supposes it was composed in long ago, by ancient authors giving us a kind of epic and personal history. Essays in that volume sketch out theories of translation, an argument against the tradition of Large and Small Plates, and pose other—to him, anyway—interesting puzzles, and even a few possible solutions. Shamelessly, he self-publishes his books and even designs covers for them. More essays and funny stuff like the 1950s Beehive Girls Manual can be found on his blog, www.daymonsmith.wordpress.com. You cannot follow him on Twitter.

The awesome illustration/diagram/whirlwind of the Scripturalizing Process was created by the hand of Amber J. Smith. You'll have to figure out the cover illustration on your own.